Cognition and Symbolic Structures:
The Psychology of Metaphoric Transformation

edited by

Robert E. Haskell, Ph.D.
University of New England

Ablex Publishing Corporation
Norwood, New Jersey 07648

Library of Congress Cataloging-in-Publication Data

Cognition and symbolic structures.

Bibliography: p.
Includes index.
1. Symbolism (Psychology) 2. Metaphor – Psychological aspects. 3. Analogy – Psychological aspects. 4. Cognition. I. Haskell, Robert E.
BF458.C58   1987   153   87-11486
ISBN 0-89391-368-5

Ablex Publishing Corporation
355 Chestnut Street
Norwood, New Jersey 07648

Contents

This volume is dedicated to Joseph J. Kockelmans who saw potential in an unsocialized mind – so profoundly different from his own – and saved it from ever wandering in the intellectual margins of academia and life.

I would also like to thank Richard B. Gregg who, with his gentle and learned Being, helped to shepard me through a critical turning point in my life.

Preface

Prefaces are rather odd sections of a book. I was made sensitive to them by my closest friend and colleague Dr. Aaron Gresson. I became aware that different authors use them for various kinds of comments which do not seem to fit elsewhere in a volume. Occasionally prefaces are used by authors to say something personal to the reader, and about the subject matter. I always found that refreshing. Often I find myself wondering how an author became involved in a particular subject, reflecting a minor interest of mine in the history of ideas. Certainly the subject of metaphor has had a long, interesting, and controversial past. And so in this preface I would like to briefly describe my own personal journey into metaphor. No doubt many readers of this volume have had their own journey into metaphor.

I recall many years ago being made aware of an article that described analogic reasoning using the mathematical and geometric form of the spiral of sea shells. The author of that article wrote it, I was told, in a mudd floor hut in the mountains of Italy. This was not by choice, but due to the author's finances. Such dedication. My journey is certainly neither as colorful as the one just described, nor quite as dedicated. Nevertheless, this volume on cognition and metaphor has come about as consequence of a long standing fascination with what is called metaphor.

As an undergraduate in 1965, some twenty years ago now, I became intrigued with metaphor and analogy. Even then, however, my interest never leaned toward their literary aspects but rather with their cognitive significance, a view that was not held in psychology at that time. How my involvement with metaphor began I am not quite sure, but it had something to do with Freud's *Interpretation of Dreams* which I had read years earlier.

While I am not at all a Freudian – whatever that means these days – nor even primarily a clinician, the metaphoric and analogic reasoning processes in that volume fascinated me. Not only those processes found in the dreamwork, but Freud's analogic reasoning itself was masterful. Very early in my academic career, I read General Systems Theory, which was largely analogical in its initial stage of development. Perhaps, too, an early interest I had in writing poetry influenced my fascination with metaphor, as possibly did my job in Army Intelligence of decyphering codes play a part. The behavioral psychologist in me knows very well what at least initially reinforced my continued research into metaphor and analogy: as an undergraduate I had two papers on the subject accepted for publication, and as any academic, or writer, knows the reinforcement value of ones first publication is of such a magnitude as to strongly resist extinction.

In any case, my thesis in those two rather clumsy first articles was that metaphor and analogy were not simply literary devices; they were a manifestation of a deeper cognitive process. They contained most of the ideas developed in my later work. In 1965, however, metaphor and analogy were hardly what were considered "hot" research topics, except in departments of Literature, English, and Rhetoric. Just about everyone else still considered them to be linguistic embellishments. This was especially true in psychology, with a few exceptions like Charles Osgoods work, and Robert Oppenheimer in physics. Metaphoric and analogic reasoning were considered dangerous and misleading, especially in science and philosophy. But analogic reasoning was considered somewhat more respectable than was metaphor.

I chose the term "analogic" to be the generic label of which metaphor was the subset. There was then and is now historical precedent for this view. In any event I believed then and still do that what is called analogic reasoning is the basis of what is called metaphor, of which allegory, proverbs, transfer, transposition, perceptual constancy phenomena, and stimulus generalization are also subsets. Underlying them all is an abstract set of cognitive operations generating transformations of invariance. Since my conception of metaphor and analogy were quite different from how they were commonly understood, perhaps I should have selected another term. I did not do that largely because I wanted to retain what I considered to be the end product of a developmental process. Because metaphor and analogy were considered to be two different creatures, which in fact they are from a traditional point of view, the two bodies of research literature were then and now remain quite separate. As it turned out the term "metaphor" has retained its dominance.

After completing my masters thesis in 1968 on a general theory of analogy, life's little personal detours sidetracked me for a few years as far as active research was concerned. Then in teaching small group processes and studying the language use in those groups, I once again, but with an entirely new perspective, began to see the cognitive structure of metaphoric/analogic reasoning and its relation to spontaneous language production. I noticed that the ostensibly literal language used in those groups was simultaneously metaphoric/analogic; that the literal language and topics of the groups were metaphorical, describing what was occurring in the group. The linguistic distinction between literal and figurative did not exist.

In 1978, I completed my doctoral work with a dissertation utilizing those data from small group language use. In about 1976, I read the seventeenth century philosopher Giambattista Vico's *New Science,* where he laid out his theory of metaphor. For the first time in my experience here was a truely cognitive theory of the development of what was called metaphor, a theory that was not just poetic speculation. I first "met" Vico, in passing, in a freshmen sociology course. He was briefly mentioned in the text for his ideas on social theory. It was but a short paragraph. I met Vico more formally some fourteen years later while in graduate school. J. J. Kockelmans, the reknowned phenomenologist and Heideggerian scholar at the Pennsylvania State University had "adopted" me even though I was not a philosophy major and despite the fact that we saw the world quite differently epistemologically. He had mentioned to me that a young philosopher there, Phillip Verene, had just co-edited a volume with Giorgio Tagliacozzo (1976) who was head of the Institute for Vico studies. I had read the *New Science* and then the above volume and was amazed that Vico held, in fundamental outline, the same cognitive view of metaphor I had been developing for some years. I was as bewildered then as I am now that Vico had not been discovered and was not more well known by metaphor researchers. If Vico had been discovered and understood by mainstream metaphor researchers years ago, the literature on metaphor so hopelessly locked into the Aristotelian figure-of-speech framework would not have been so ponderous and confused.

In 1977, I heard of a conference on "metaphor and mind." I went and was disappointed. Most of the participants were still quibbling over what I considered to be an antiquated aristotelian definition of metaphor. When they were not doing this they were endlessly arguing about the interaction view of metaphor. The conference itself, as indicated by its title, was symbolic of an organized shift in focus within metaphor research, and its organizer Anthony Ortony was obviously on the vanguard of this incipient paradigm shift. I went home mumbling to myself in self-righteous indignation, "Well nothing is going to be happening in metaphor research." As it turned out I was wrong.

In 1978, I presented a paper, at the International Vico conference in Venice, Italy, on Vico's theory of metaphor and using my own work as further confirmation of Vico. Most of the scholars there, however, did not seem overly concerned with Vico's revolutionary theory of metaphor, as such, let alone my own rather strange findings. With some exceptions, the Vico scholars seemed more interested in his social theory and philosophy. Even within metaphor research proper, so to speak, Vico's work was virtually unknown, and remains so today. Despite the ostensible interdisciplinary character of metaphor research, each field concerned with it seems to largely stay within its own confines.

Being caught up in life's survival activities, I remained unaware of a surge of interest in metaphor by a small group within psychology doing hard research during the 70's. I was aware of Ortony's work, and of Howard Gardner's. Then in 1978, a very good acquaintance and colleague Bob DiPietro, now chair of the Department of Language at the University of Delaware, with whom I became acquainted through the Vico conference, and who had been working on metaphor himself, sent me a notice of the *Metaphor Research Newsletter*, edited by Bob

Hoffman at Adelphi University, Psychology Department. I contacted Hoffman who I learned was an experimental psychologist. I thought to myself "what is an experimental psychologist doing in metaphor research?" I soon found out. There was and had been for some time experimental work on metaphor being done. Bob Hoffman revitalized my demoralized interest in metaphor.

As a result of my correspondence with Bob Hoffman, I was later contacted by Howard Pollio of the University of Tennessee, department of psychology, who was developing a journal called *Metaphor and Symbolic Activity* which grew out of the *Metaphor Research Newsletter*. Howard asked me to write a piece for the new journal. At the end of the summer of 1983, I sent him a manuscript putting together what I had intended to put together for years, but because of my demoralization with the subject, and because of health problems I had not done it. It was a cognitive developmental theory of metaphor based in part on the work of Vico, Ernst Cassirer, and my own empirical data on language use.

The manuscript laid out what I considered to be the fundamental cognitive basis generating all forms of what has come to be called metaphor. I also incorporated many of the authors work that appear in this volume. I had been familiar with Laurence Mark's work on cross-modal transfer. Brenda Becks work however I had in my file but had not read, until Bob Hoffman suggested it was a "must." By this time, I had become familiar with Honeck, Reichman and Hoffman's conceptual Base Hypothesis that was similar to my concept of deep cognition. So I incorporated it as well. My thesis is that all that goes by the name of metaphor is based in deeper neurological substrate operations generating multiple transformations of invariance.

And so I find myself putting together this volume on cognition and metaphor, a kind of cathartic culminating labor of love that has spanned many years. I say "culminating" as I think, for me at least, there is no where else to go with the traditional notion of metaphor per se. Metaphor has led me into another place where metaphor as commonly understood becomes excess baggage. In this new place there are only abstract "metaphorical" transformations of invariance – into the world of cognition and dream research.

R. E. Haskell
Great Island, Maine
1985

Foreword

During the period between 400 B.C. and 1900 A.D., it was commonly accepted, with Plato and Aristotle, that metaphor basically was a figure of speech. The term "figure of speech" refers to a large variety of uses of words, phrases, sayings, clauses, and even sentences to achieve desired effects in meaning. Traditionally, the term was defined as a derivation in the use of words from the literal sense, or at least from common practice. Metaphor was said to be the most basic of all figures of speech; it states an analogy, a similarity, or some other relation between two things. Usually metaphor was defined as that figure of speech which consists in the transferrence to one object of an attribute or name that literally is not applicable to it, but which can be applied to it figuratively or by analogy. This conception of metaphor has been largely maintained until the present, and is the conception which most people have in mind when hearing the term.

Yet, in the contemporary literature on metaphor, some very drastic changes have taken place over the past 70 years or so. Whereas, traditionally the concern with metaphor was concentrated mainly within the domain of rhetoric, in contemporary discussions, concern has shifted from rhetoric to semantics, and still later from semantics to hermeneutics and literary criticism. Greisch has suggested dividing the *philosophical* literature on metaphor into three major sections: (a) there is the analysis of the function of metaphor in the Anglo-Saxon philosophy of language (I. A. Richards, Max Black, Menroe Beardsley, etc.); (b) then there is the study concerning metaphor's link with interpretation (Ricoeur); and, finally (c) there is the ontological or metaphysical question concerning the meaning of metaphor in philosophical discourse itself (Heidegger, Derrida). The most important contribution in analytic philosophy consists in the realization that, in addition to the classical, rhetorical theory of metaphor as unfolded by Aristotle, which sees in metaphor a substitute of one word for another, there is also a semantic theory of metaphor in which metaphor is taken to be the effect of meaning which comes to the word but has its origin in a contextual activity which brings the semantic fields of several words into interaction with each other. Ricoeur has tried to show that the true place of metaphor is neither the name, nor the sentence, nor even discourse itself, but rather the copula of the verb *to be*. The metaphysical "is" namely signifies both "is like" and "is not." Finally, Heidegger and Derrida are mainly interested in the question (first raised by Nietzsche) of whether or not the use of metaphor is constitutive for metaphysical discourse as such.

If we now turn from philosophy to the sciences, we shall see that there, too, important changes have taken place and intriguing discoveries have been made. Some of these discoveries were made in he sciences that concern themselves with language and literature. Yet another large area in which some very stimulating and novel ideas about metaphor have been proposed is that of the human sciences and of cognitive psychology in particular. Where, formerly, it as universally accepted that metaphor is inherently a linguistic phenomenon, many social scientists today have come to the view that what one usually calls metaphor is really the linguistic manifestation of a very fundamental *cognitive* operation. In other words, metaphor does not primarily refer to a figure of speech, but rather to a fundamental form of man's knowing. This cognitive theory of metaphor was anticipated in the work of Vico, and it has been influenced also by the work of Richards.

The essays on metaphor contained in this anthology focus mainly on metaphor taken as a cognitive operation. The editor and the contributors to this important volume are to be congratulated for their efforts to inform the contemporary reader about the "use" of metaphor in the domain of the human sciences today.

Joseph J. Kockelmans
The Pennsylvania State University

Contributors Page

Brenda E. Beck: Ph.D., Oxford University. Dr. Beck is Professor of Anthropology at the University of British Columbia. She has published papers in *Current Anthropology, Researches Semiotiques Semiotic Inquiry, Canadian Ethnic Studies,* and other journals. She is the author of *Peasant Society in Konku, Perspectives on a Regional Culture, The Three Twins: The Telling of a South Indian Folk Epic.*

Richard M. Billow: Ph.D., Adelphi University. Dr. Billow is Associate Professor of Psychology, Institute of Advanced Psychological Studies, Adelphi University. He has published papers in *Journal of Experimental and Child Psychology, Bulletin of the Menninger Clinic, Psychological Bulletin, Developmental Psychology,* and other journals, including chapters in various volumes.

Susan Boxerman-Kramer: Ph.D., Adelphi University, is currently Senior Psychologist at Woodhull Medical and Mental Health Center, Brooklyn, NY.

Richard H. Brown: Ph.D., University of California at San Diego. Dr. Brown is Director of the Washington Institute for Social Research, and Associate Professor of Sociology at the University of Maryland. He has published papers in *Qualitative Sociology, The American Sociologist, Human Studies, Developing Economics, European Journal of Social Psychology, Theory and Society, British Journal of Sociology, Review of Social Economics,* and others. He is the author of *A Poetic for Sociology: Toward A Logic of Discovery for the Human Sciences, Structure, Consciousness, and History* (with M. Lyman et al.), *American Society,* and *The Presence of the Symbol,* and is on the Editorial Board of numerous journals.

Michael Firment: B.S., Xavier University. Mr. Firment had been a systems analyst and is currently a graduate in psychology at the University of Cincinnati, where he focuses on cognition and human factors engineering.

Raymond W. Gibbs, Jr.: Ph.D., University of California, San Diego. Dr. Gibbs is Assistant Professor of Psychology at the University of California at Santa Cruz. He has published papers in *Memory and Cognition, Journal of Verbal Learning and Verbal Behavior, Cognition Journal of Psycholinguistic Research, Journal of Experimental Psychology, Learning, Memory and Cognition, Discourse Processes,* and others, as well as chapters in edited books on language, and presentation on metaphor at American Psychological Association Symposia.

Deborah Goldman: Ph.D., Adelphi University. Dr. Goldman is currently research associate, Department of Psychiatry, St. Vincent's Hospital, NY.

Aaron D. Gresson: Ph.D., The Pennsylvania State University; Ph.D., Boston College. Dr. Gresson is currently on the faculty at the University of New York at Albany. He has served on the faculty of Hersey Medical School, Boston University, and Brandies University. He has published papers in *The Encyclopedia of Bio-Ethics, Philosophy and Rhetoric, Communication Quarterly, The Black Sociologist,* and other journals. He is presently completing a second doctorate in clinical psychology at Boston College, and is on the Editorial Board of *Interfaces: Linguistics, Psychology and Health Therapeutics.* He is the author of *The Dialectics of Betrayal.*

Irene E. Harvey: Ph.D., York University. Dr. Harvey is Assistant Professor of Philosophy at The Pennsylvania State University. She has published papers in *Research in Phenomenology, Telos, Man and World, The Journal for the British Society for Phenomenology, Philosophy and Rhetoric, Philosophy's Social Criticism,* and other journals. She is the author of *Derrida and the Economy of Difference.*

Robert E. Haskell: Ph.D., The Pennsylvania State University. Dr. Haskell is Associate Professor of Psychology at the University of New England. He has published research in *The Journal of Mind and Behavior, Journal of Humanistic Psychology, Small Group Behavior, The International Journal of Group Psychotherapy, Metaphor and Symbolic Activity, The Journal of Medical Humanities and Bio-Ethics, Semiotica,* and other journals. He is co-editor of *Interfaces: Linguistic Psychology and Health Therapeutics,* is completing a volume on *The Cognitive-Structure of Talk,* and is editing a volume on *Cognition and Dream Research.*

Robert R. Hoffman: Ph.D., and **Richard Honeck:** University of Cincinnati. Robert Hoffman Ph.D. is Assistant Professor of Psychology at Adelphi University. He has published papers in *The Psychological Record, Bulletin of the Psychonomic Society, Memory and Cognition, The Journal of Mind and Behavior,* and other journals. He has co-edited *Cognition Psychology and Figurative Language,* along with chapters in other volumes. He is co-founder and Associate Editor of the new journal of *Metaphor and Symbolic Activity: An Interdisciplinary Journal of Empirical Research,* and is co-founder and member of the Board of Directors of "The International Society for Ecological Psychology."

Richard P. Honeck: Ph.D., University of Wisconsin-Madison. Dr. Honeck is Professor of Psychology at the University of Cincinnati. He has published papers in *Memory and Cognition, Bulletin of the Psychosomatic Society, Child Development, The Psychological Record, Poetics,* and other journals. He is co-author of *Cognition and Figurative Language, Experimental Design and Analysis.*

Clair T. Kibler: Ph.D., University of Cincinnati. Dr. Kibler is Senior Research Associate at the IBM Corporation in Endicott. She is co-author of a book on experimental design and analysis, and of several articles on figurative language and categorization.

Joseph J. Kockelmans: Ph.D., Angelico Rome. Dr. Kockelmans is professor of Philosophy and Director of the Interdisciplinary Graduate Program at the Pennsylvania State University. In addition to numerous journal articles, he is the author of *Martin Heidegger, Phenomenology and Physical Science, The World in Science and Philosophy, On Truth and Being*, and other books, including *Space and Time: A Study on the Special Theory of Relativity*, which was awarded a Gold Medal.

Nona Lewis: Ph.D., Adelphi University, is currrently in private practice.

Lawrence E. Marks: Ph.D., Harvard University, and Marc H. Bornstein: Ph.D., Yale University. Lawrence Marks is Fellow of the Pierce Foundation Laboratory and Professor of Epidemiology and Psychology at Yale University. He has published papers in *Journal of Experimental Psychology, Psychological Review, Psychological Bulletin, Perception and Psychophysics, Proceedings of the National Academy of Sciences, Journal of the Acoustical Society of America*, and others. He is the author of *Sensory Processes: The New Psychophysics*, and *The Unity of Senses.*

Marc Bornstein: Professor of Psychology and Human Development at New York University. He has published studies on methodological, comparative, developmental, and cross cultural psychology. He is the Editor of *The Cross Currents in Contemporary Psychology Series, Comparative Methods in Psychology*, and *Psychological Development From Infancy* (edited by W. Kessen). He is on the editorial boards of numerous journals in psychology, and is a member of scholarly societies in anthropology, child development, and visual science.

Howard R. Pollio: Ph.D., University of Michigan. He is currently distinguished Service Professor of Psychology. He has published in numerous journals, and is the author of *Psychology and Symbolic Activity, Psychology and the Poetics of Analysis*, and *Behavior and Existence*. He is editor of a new journal, *Metaphor.*

Patrick Ross: Ph.D., is a Professor of Psychology at the Institute for Advanced Psychological Studies, Adelphi University.

Jeffery Rossman: Ph.D., is a recent graduate of the Institute of Advanced Psychological Studies, Adelphi University.

John E. Shell: Ph.D., Rice University, is currently a doctorial candidate in Clinical Psychology at the University of Tennessee, Knoxville.

Michael K. Smith: Ph.D., University of Tennessee. Dr. Smith is currently instructor in both psychology and linguistics. He has published numerous papers concerned with psycholinguistic analysis of metaphor, *Activity: Interdisciplinary Journal of Empirical Research*, and co-author of *Psychology and Symbolic Activity: and Behavior and Existence.*

Introduction

This volume has come about as a consequence of a long-standing fascination with what is called metaphor. As an undergraduate in 1965, some 20 years ago now, I became intrigued with metaphor and analogy. Even then, however, my interest never leaned toward their literary aspects, but rather with their cognitive significance, a view that was not held in psychology at that time. In any event, I believed then and still do that what is called analogic reasoning is the basis of what is called metaphor, of which allegory, proverbs, transfer, transposition, perceptual constancy phenomena, and stimulus generalization are subsets. Underlying them all is an abstract set of cognitive operations generating transformations of invariance.

Metaphor has had a long and controversial past. Since the time of Aristotle, the subject of metaphor has been the object of analysis. It still is. It will probably remain so for some time to come. On the one hand, the useful characteristics of metaphor have been examined by rhetoricians, and its insightful virtues extolled by poets. On the other hand, its character has been assassinated by most logicians and scientists. Metaphor was originally defined by Aristotle as a linguistic figure of speech. More recently, the term "metaphor" has become polysemically stretched to mean multiple things to its users and researchers.

A scientific model is said to be a metaphor, as is a piece of art. A dancer is often said to be making a metaphorical statement: that the dance is an external expression of inner feelings. The more traditionally inclined gatekeepers of linguistic meaning often object to metaphor being used in this way. Everyone knows, they say, that metaphor is a linguistic device. I am reminded here of the response of Freud's colleagues – or so the story goes – to the application of his concept of hysteria to male patients: That men can have hysteria, they said, is not possible; after all, as everyone knows, the term "hysteria" comes from the Greek term meaning "floating or suffering womb."

This volume is organized around the view that what is termed "metaphor" is an important cognitive process. This conception is not essentially a new one. It has been suggested by others to various degrees. As will be seen later in this volume, it is my judgment that the original cognitive theory of metaphor was the discovery of the 17th century philosopher Giambattista Vico, whose discovery has not been widely recognized in metaphor research. Other poets and philosophers have from time to time suggested the cognitive significance of metaphoric thought, but in a globally intuitive way.

In more contemporary times, the "Interaction Theory" of metaphor put forth by I. A. Richards can be said to be the modern progenitor of a cognitive theory of metaphor. In contrast to metaphor being a simple linguistic comparison, a substitution of terms, it was Richards who maintained that the vehicle and tenor of a metaphor come together to create a new conception; that a metaphor can force a cognitive reorganization.

With the increasing publication of volumes on metaphor in recent years, along with the organizing of metaphor conferences, this volume, among a small list of others, marks the beginning of a new *era* and the end of an old one. The historical *error* has been that metaphor belongs to the domain of language. The new era is that metaphor is an important cognitive operation. Metaphor can no longer be considered the sole domain of language and rhetoric, though this is one important research domain, as some of the chapters in this volume demonstrate. I strongly suspect, and have in fact suggested elsewhere, that what is called metaphor is simply a linguistic manifestation of a more fundamental cognitive operation. Until this is widely recognized, a great deal of research into what is called metaphor will be led astray, as indeed it has been historically. The chapters in this volume reflect the modern history of metaphor in the sense that they cover many of the ways metaphor is conceptualized and applied. No attempt is made to cover in depth old, well-trodden ground. Previous volumes have accomplished that task quite well.

The chapters in this volume suggest and explore a number of functions characteristics and implications of the metaphoric process, including that metaphoric processes originate in a sensory–motor–affective matrix; that it may be based in a neurological substrate; that it manifests itself developmentally in various forms; that, cognitively, the comprehension of metaphor may depend on an abstract, featureless conceptual base; that it is central to concept formation and categorization; that it figures significantly in some pathological syndromes and in therapeutic discourse; that it often functions nonconsciously, both individually and socio-historically; that it may influence communication subliminally; that it is significant epistemologically; and, finally, that the traditional distinction between literal and figurative language is not as distinct as is commonly thought.

The opening chapter by Beck, on "Metaphors, Cognition, and Artificial Intelligence," is broad in scope, yet it is sufficiently detailed to give the reader a feel for the wide range of functioning and application in various fields of what has come to be called metaphor. In doing so, the chapter foretells many of the concerns and issues of the chapters that follow. Perhaps congruent with the very concept of metaphor, Beck does not abstractly define the concept but structures its meaning by her illustrations of its use. Beck, like others before her, points out the role of metaphor in such areas as creativity, scientific discovery, dream processes, and imagery production, and in advertising. More importantly, however, Beck points out that what is called metaphor is a key cognitive function directly involved in the categorization process. Drawing on her earlier work, Beck suggests that, at its developmental origin, metaphor is based in a sensory-motor matrix and is thus not simply a verbal phenomenon.

In Chapter 2, by Gibbs, on "What Does It Mean To Say That a Metaphor Has Been Understood?," the author analyzes some of the core cognitive issues involved in the comprehension of metaphor as it is more commonly defined. Gibbs outlines three linguistic theories of metaphor. In analyzing the works of Max Black, Donald Davidson, and John Searles, he suggests that earlier language-based theories are inadequate to explain metaphor comprehension. Gibbs maintains that contextual analysis is needed to understand a metaphoric statement. Further, but as a part of context, he suggests that the comprehension of metaphor requires understanding the intention of the person generating the metaphor. Gibbs thus clearly explicates the significance of cognitive processes in metaphoric communication. Once the psychological process of intention is recognized, there is no limit, he says, to the possibilities of meaning that a given metaphor may be construed to have. Gibbs thus begins with critiquing traditional linguistic views and ends with a cognitive perspective.

In Chapter 3, by Marks and Bornstein, on "Sensory Similarity: Classes, Characteristics, and Cognitive Consequences," the authors begin from the concept of sensory similarity and the phenomenon of synesthesia, where one sense mode crosses over into another, resulting in some people "seeing sound" and "feeling colors." The authors present findings from neurological data that they suggest as a model for the origins of sensory metaphor and as a model of the early developmental stage of linguistic metaphor. The authors further suggest similar cross-neural coding processing giving rise to the experience of equivalence and therefore to certain classes of metaphor. Their model suggests a neurological substrate for metaphoric thought which is innate or "wired-in" to the nervous system. The authors distinguish two types of metaphor, the first based on cross-modal sensory processes, the second based on learned associations. The former they equate to metaphor, the latter to metonymy. Their view suggest a developmental perspective.

Concluding the first section of this volume, Chapter 4, by Haskell, on "Giambattista Vico: The Discoverer of Metaphoric Cognition," outlines the work of the 17th century philosopher and rhetorician. It is suggested that Vico was the original discoverer of the origin, the cognitive significance, and the development of metaphoric thought. It is pointed out that, with the exception of a small group of Vichian scholars, his work on metaphor has been overlooked. The significance of Vico's work is discussed, and is related to the author's empirical research on symbolic/metaphoric language which can be seen as confirming and extending Vico's work.

Opening Part II of the volume, Chapter 5, by Haskell, on "Cognitive Psychology and the Problem of Symbolic Cognition," is a general critique of mainstream cognitive psychology and its failure to study nonconscious symbolic structure, of which some classes of metaphoric thought are included. Three relatively separate approaches to cognitive research are conceptualized; the last of which is considered to constitute a "Third Force" in cognitive psychology. The third force is composed of work carried out, in large measure, outside of mainstream cognitive psychology. It is suggested that this approach may be precipitating a paradigm shift in cognitive psychology. The concepts of "symbolism" and "unconscious" are explored and related to metaphoric cognition and figurative language. It is suggested that cognitive research needs to be directed at these neglected areas.

In Chapter 6, by Honeck, Kibler, and Firment, on "Figurative Language and Psychological Views of Categorization: Two Ships in the Night," the authors review cognitive theories of categorization and show how traditional psychological theories of categorization cannot adequately explain figurative language studies of categorization. Traditional theories are in one way or another based on the perception of concrete features of similarity. The authors present data and discuss the Conceptual Base Theory of figurative language. Their view is that the cognition of similarity is not stimulus-driven; rather, it is abstract cognitive structures which create the perception of similarity. Concrete features of similarity cannot always explain the transfer of meaning in figurative language use. The Conceptual Base Theory suggests that the abstract conceptual base contains information not contained in "instances" used to create a category. The authors conclude by suggesting how the study of figurative language and cognition has important implications for epistemology and for cognitive research.

In Chapter 7, by Hoffman and Honeck, on "Proverbs, Pragmatics, and the Ecology of Abstract Categories," the authors present controlled studies of proverb comprehension. In particular, the authors investigate the cognitive process by which people come to understand differently phrased proverbs as having similar or identical meaning. Their research suggests a nonliteralist theory. Literalist theory holds that subjects match the literal meaning of compared proverbs and locate the common features of each. Hoffman and Honeck's research suggests that the comprehension of parallel figures is accomplished through nonlinguistic, nonimagistic means, though both may be present. Their study supports their earlier work of the Conceptual Base Hypothesis, which involves featureless family resemblances. Hoffman and Honeck maintain that the comprehension of figurative language involves abstract categories, independent of a storage and retrieval of literal and concrete items.

In Chapter 8, by Billow, Rossman, Lewis, Goldman, Kraemer, and Ross, on "Metaphoric Communication and Miscommunication in Schizophrenic and Borderline States," the authors present findings from their controlled research with hospitalized patients, using both adult and child subject populations. Simple, affective, and abstract proportional metaphors, along with proverbs, are presented to subjects. High affect seems to negatively influence cognitive comprehension of the more abstract figurations. They also find distinct differences for metaphor as opposed to proverb comprehension under varying levels of affect, and cognitive development. The authors suggest that some common assumptions about the metaphoric capacity of schizophrenics may have to be revised. The chapter shows the significance of figurative language for both cognitive and therapeutic research.

In Chapter 9, by Gresson, on "Transitional Metaphors and the Political Psychology of Identity Maintenance," the author outlines and delineates the psychological and social functions of what he terms transitional metaphors. This class of metaphor is seen as emerging from a society in transition. Transitional metaphors serve the individual function of reducing anxiety created by social change, and as a social rhetorical device. In specific, Gresson, analyzes the 1984 political campaign metaphor of the Rainbow Coalition and the response of the mass media to it. In so doing, he also shows the social cognitive importance of such metaphors in the maintenance of individual and group identity. In defining the class of "transitional metaphor," Gresson illustrates a generally undeveloped aspect of metaphor: that the act of creating a metaphor is often a political act and has political consequences.

Opening Part III of this volume, Chapter 10, by Harvey, on "Foucault and Language: Unthought Metaphors," the author delineates and analyzes the use of metaphor by the French philosopher and psychologist Michael Foucault. While, as Harvey points out, Foucault does not have an explicit theory of metaphor, he uses and assigns metaphors to the historical epochs he examines. Foucault maintains that each age is marked by a predominant or root metaphor. The metaphor of the 16th century was the Book of Nature, concerned with resemblance and similarity. For the 17th and first half of the 18th centuries, the metaphor was that of the Taxonomic Table, concerned with exactness. For the 18th and 19th centuries, it was the metaphor of Roots, concerned with history and origins phenomena. The dominant metaphor of the 20th century is that of the Unthought, concerned with the hidden or nonconscious character of phenomena. While Harvey points out the necessity of metaphor in philosophical inquiry, she also points out the dangers of an overemphasis on unity and coherence dominated by metaphoric analysis. She also points out the nonneutrality of metaphor, that it is not a-epistemological.

In Chapter 11, by Schell, Pollio, and Smith, on "Metaphor As Mitsein: Therapeutic Possibilities In Figurative Language," the authors explore the function and use of metaphor in therapeutic discourse. In so doing, they examine the role of metaphor in psychoanalytic discourse, the work of Ricoeur's Hermeneutics, and of the existential phenomenology of Heidegger which they bring to bear on the understanding of a class of metaphor independent of simple linguistic structures. What the authors refer to as "radical metaphor" is the patient's intimate expressions of self as they are manifested in the total therapeutic situation. Such discourse is a metaphoric expression of the patient's Being as such. The metaphors cannot be reduced to a literal, one-to-one paraphrase.

In Chapter 12, by Brown, on "Metaphor and Historical Consciousness: Organicism and Mechanism in the Study of Social Change," he develops the thesis that historical and scientific discourse is symbolic and metaphorical. In particular, building on the works of Vico, Burke, Pepper, and others, Brown analyzes two root metaphors, those of society as organicism, and of society as mechanism, and contrasts the respective implications of each metaphor in terms of explaining social change and in terms of the philosophy of science and epistemology. Based on his earlier work, he maintains that underlying all scientific activity is a metaphorical cognition giving rise to a creative logic of discovery and to what he terms a "cognitive aesthetic." Brown concludes the chapter by pointing out that the choice is not of using or not using metaphor, but rather of being aware or not being aware of the metaphors we use.

Chapter 13, by Haskell, on "Structural Metaphor and Cognition," uses two essays to illustrate what he terms structural metaphor. In analyzing the writing of the French psychoanalyst and structuralist Jacques Lacan, and the reknowned poet and critic Archibald MacLeish, Haskell shows how structural metaphor is achieved. While the achievement is a deliberate stylistic device related to what has generally been called Memesis in the literary field, it is suggested that such metaphoric operations have their origin in cognitive operations. The significance of Lacan's and MacLeish's writing is discussed, and empirical cognitive data is presented suggesting its cognitive origin and implications as a communcation device.

The concluding chapter by Haskell, on "A Phenomenology of Metaphor: a Praxis Study Into Metaphor and Its Cognitive Movement Through Semantic Space," is a "study" of metaphor by using metaphor in its multiple forms to demonstrate the various movements of metaphor in the cognitive processes, as manifested semantically, phonetically, and syntactically.

R.E. Haskell
Great Island, Maine
1985

PART I

Overview and Origin

CHAPTER ONE

Metaphors, Cognition, and Artificial Intelligence

Brenda E. F. Beck,
Department of Anthropology,
University of Toronto

The human mind has a striking ability to advance its mental grasp on an interesting problem by the use of metaphoric reasoning processes. Indeed, this is one of the most exciting and important overall attributes of human thought. In experimental research, metaphors have been strongly associated with innovation, with enhanced recall, and with key social abilities such as leadership. The use of compelling metaphors is also an important dimension of what is normally called creativity. Metaphoric reasoning, furthermore, is a mental skill largely independent of what normally is measured as "intelligence." Unfortunately, despite its central importance, this type of thought process is grossly undervalued by our educational system, and by North American culture generally.

This paper aims to survey the varied types of evidence that suggest metaphoric reasoning is a key human skill. Secondly, using this evidence as a kind of "window on the mind," it will link these research outcomes to current issues facing developers of artificial intelligence: efforts to model the human mind using nonbiological systems, processes, and programs. We will attempt to outline the potential importance of collaborative work between persons working in the area of metaphor and those on the fast-advancing research frontiers of robotics and computer technology. An interface between these seemingly distant research fields holds special promise. Persons working in areas such as storytelling, elementary school science teaching, and on the nature of creative problem solving, have a first-hand knowledge of how the mind operates that is beginning to overlap with the latest design developments in electronic mind modeling.

Persons working on artificial forms of intelligence, by the same token, now hold an interesting mirror to those exploring the mind from a behavioral perspective. What kind of reasoning does the woodsman use, for example, when he whimsically decides to carve up a tree stump left in the woods, making it come to resemble an office "chair"? What lies behind the child's ability to understand what an adult is saying when he or she points to "a big dipper" in the nighttime sky? Electronically, or chemically, how does the mind come to combine concepts as separate as a "forest tree" and an item of "office furniture"? How does it merge "some stars" with the idea of "a kitchen pot"? What kind of search program encourages these unexpected cross-overs? Electronic and mathematical models may eventually have much to tell us about such artist and symbolic types of reasoning. When we can design computer-robots that can "think" in this kind of "creative" way, we will have made a genuine advance, both in understanding the limits of electro-mechanical systems and in our ability to specify what is truly human about our own minds.

THE DEFINITION OF METAPHOR

Some critics would say the first thing one must do in a paper like this is to define what "a metaphor" and "metaphoric reasoning" are. Second, they would want that definition drawn as firmly and as narrowly as possible. This straw person, as I picture him or her in my mind, would demand that I distinguish metaphor from analogy, as well as from metonym, from trope, and so-on. He or she would no doubt want to separate verbal metaphors from sensory-motor ones, and to distinguish signs from symbols. Which specific kind of mental process are we going to focus on? Can't I hone this concept down to something easily identified?

The reason I resist such definitional demands is that experience with my own mind tells me there is no laundry list of discrete, individually separable reasoning processes when it comes to thought. My own stream of thoughts, and my own behaviors, slip around between verbal and nonverbal, part and whole, process and structure, feeling and logic, so fast that often I cannot hold any single perspective responsible for a specific outcome. Ask me where an apple comes from, and I will instantly picture a supermarket, my apple tree, a seed, a Linaenian diagram, plus Adam and Eve. Give me another second or two, and I'll start thinking about an apple's color and shape, its physical core, its several tastes, and the day I had to peel two dozen for my mother's pie. A critic could dismiss this example as a set of "free associations" on my part, not rigorous thought. But it is precisely that kind of reasoning, and its often uncontrolled qualities, that are the hallmark of human intelligence and creativity.

My imaginary critic would continue to insist that "a list of associations is not a metaphor." But I counter that I am ready to make a metaphoric use of my stream of thoughts at any time. What about my association of apples with the "Apple" computer company, and its recent product, the MacIntosh? How did a computer firm come to call itself "Apple"? And how about its popular logo, a rainbow-colored apple with one bite missing? My mind now starts to search for possible parallels between these two domains. Is a computer a kind of fruit? What about differences between apples and computers? I can hardly stop playing with this puzzle, even when I'm asked about something else. Indeed, the more surprising the juxtaposition of domains, the more readily my mind leaps to the challenge. Metaphoric thought, at least for us humans, is not just "turned on" at isolated moments and then put back in storage. It is a propensity that is always with us, providing a playful, contemplative substratum to all we do.

In an earlier article (Beck, 1978), I argued that sensory and verbal reasoning are intimately connected and that our metaphoric abilities are "a window" through which we can study "wiring" diagrams in the mind. The evidence from personal experience is all around us. In speaking, reading, or writing, we constantly conjure up fleeting sensations and images of various kinds. More importantly, when we are straining to express an idea, certain images and feelings tend to well up inside. For example, I often get a sense that an important idea is trying to exit from my finger tips, causing a kind of tingling sensation. When writing, I sometimes sit at a typing keyboard and wave my arms around. Others might think I was trying to talk to my writing machine with the gestures I use for human speech. Some of my colleagues have more visual ways of thinking, using their "mind's eye," rather than old motor habits like me. Either way, these nonverbal efforts often help one to find words, even concepts, needed to clarify a developing chain of thought.

Metaphors, then, are like bridges. They are also mental detours that sometimes help one to sneak around obstacles. Take, for example, the popular technique for remembering people's names, the strategy where one is advised to associate each new face with a particular object in a well-known (mental) drawing room. When one is stuck for a name, one searches that drawing room until the missing information rushes forward by its associative link to a particular item of furniture. There is even a recognizable intermediate phase in such a recall procedure. A particular chair in the room first feels like it has a kind of magnetic charge. It tugs at me while others do not. I then mentally hover around that one chair. This narrowing occurs first, and there is a final step, when the right name and the right object suddenly "click," as if two pieces of a jigsaw puzzle had just been put together. The result is a sensory-verbal union, one which solves the "problem" that had failed to find an answer when my verbal memory bank was first searched in isolation.

Metaphors used for more complex reasoning tasks work in essentially the same way. They force the mind to do an end run around one's mental dictionary, so that motor-sensory information is brought to bear on a given thinking task. If forced to delimit the concept of metaphor, therefore, I would insist on the experiential, body-linked, physical core of metaphoric reasoning abilities. Metaphors often can operate entirely without the overt use of words, as the work of many artists and cartoonists will illustrate. Even if a mathematician used one kind of formula metaphorically, as a kind of inspiration for solving a problem in another mathematical domain, it would have to be a "feeling trace" that linked the two.

By a "feeling trace" I mean a sense of what the body did as it descended through the logic of the first problem. It would be like an experienced logger on a spring river run. For years the man has seen log-jams and has had to go and poke or roll the one key tree that will break the whole mess loose. Eventually he develops a "feel" for the problem. Like the mathematician, the logger has seen "jams" solved before. He knows where to go, which log to single out. The more experience one has at a task, the more of this expert "feel" one acquires. The expert comes to recognize the problem quickly, and hardly needs words. He or she can "leap" straight to the solution, where others must first plod through a long logical list of alternatives. It has recently been shown, furthermore, that Air Force pilots unconsciously change their instrument-scanning procedures with experience. With more flying hours, they begin to look for information appearing on their panels in more flexible and situationally appropriate ways (McLeod, 1984). This is what we mean by the experience called "intuition." Learning leaves nonverbal, sensory-motor traces on the mind.

A third element, however, is perhaps an even more essential key to the development of metaphoric thought. This is the ability to learn separately about different domains and then to "bridge" or link them, as in the example of a tree stump carved to resemble an "office" chair. Such thinking breaks the normal rules of language and experience: one does not find offices in a forest, nor tree stumps in one's study. Furthermore, there is also the matter of creative evolution, the artist's testing of an idea through action. Human intelligence is at its best in interactive situations. A woodsman doing such a carving would see his design change and grow as he worked. At all stages, too, one must appreciate the "joke" driving the carver to attempt such a task. Can we build this sense of humor into computer robots? And if we do, how do we then draw the fine line between brilliance and madness? Creativity, metaphor and a sense of the comic, if built into machines, will later pose serious problems concerning assessment and control.

RESEARCH ON METAPHOR

Let me now detail, briefly, some of the domains where metaphor has been found to be extremely significant. As several others have already observed, metaphors are ubiquitous in human language (Pavio, 1979, p. 475; Hoffman, 1983). They are equally significant, perhaps more so, for thought in general. For one thing, figurative language and idiomatic speech take no longer to comprehend than literal speech. The general perception is that metaphors must be flowery and decorative, and hence the stuff of poets. Research evidence, however, suggests that meanings couched in metaphor can often be grasped faster than when only nonfigurative speech is used (Ortony, Schellert, Reynolds, & Antus, 1978). In strict tests of memory, it has also been shown that metaphoric information can be retained and recalled at least as easily as nonmetaphoric input (Harris, Lahey, & Marsalek, 1980).

There is considerable speculation developing about why figurative language should have this positive relationship to memory. The answer appears to be that metaphors force the mind to construct a high-order linkage between the entities referred to. And it is precisely such higher level abstractions (in contrast to detail) that seem to constitute the most fundamental units of mental recall (Verbrugge, 1977). The concept is similar to one developing now in linguistic circles about basic information categories. For example, the term "piano" defines a basic level category, while "grand" and "upright" pianos constitute subordinate items. "Musical instrument" is a superordinate, less salient term (Rosch, Mervis, Gray, Johnson, & Boyes-Braem, 1976). In using a piano as a metaphor for the heartbeat when called in to see a teacher, it would not matter much whether upright or grand piano was the reference point. Yet the concept of a piano, an instrument that is struck from a keyboard, would make a significant contrast with a metaphor using (say) a wind instrument. In the one case, the teacher would be "touching the keys" in a gentle or a harsh way to create different rhythms or tunes; in the other, the image would be one of wave-like expansion, or contraction, due to forced air. The new concept of "basic categories" in linguistics, therefore, may help us to pinpoint the precise level at which most metaphoric reasoning takes place.

It has also been found, experimentally, that metaphor "invites pretending, imagining . . . (and) in its more powerful forms . . . requests a perception of resemblance by means of an unconventional reshaping of identities" (Verbrugge, 1977). This is a kind of thought that requires active participation on the part of the message recipient. An idea is first encoded or made into a puzzle which the receiver then has to "uncode." The involvement needed to decode that message seems to enhance recall. The phenomenon is similar to the motor-sensory traces left on the mind of a logger (above) or of someone driving a car. If one was driving oneself, the route is usually remembered better than if one was simply carried along in a passenger seat.

Experiments with story-telling have yielded a similar set of findings. When the macro-structure of a story (the setting, basic theme, and resolution) are held constant, but details of action and characterization varied, the whole is remembered best. When the basic structure is varied but most of the details held constant, retention drops off (Pratt, Luszcz, Mackenzie-Keating, Manning 1982). Simply structured material is also easier to recall than are complex texts. These experiments with story telling reinforce other findings regarding image use. For example, material with a high image rating is easier to recall than material with a low rating (Thorndyke, 1977). These many research results, when merged, point to one simple but more general conclusion: the use of imagery and of simple frame structures is very important for achieving impact in human communication. Images, and framing material, are often combined in metaphoric speech.

In one interesting experiment of my own, questionnaires were distributed to a group of 70 persons studying for a Master's degree in Business Administration. Each was asked to identify all of Canada's major banks (there are only five), first by its visual logo and then by its major advertising motto. More students were able to identify the Royal Bank logo, a lion, from memory, than any other bank's equivalent design. Of all five major banks, the Royal is the only one to use an animate image. Even though its lion logo is drawn in a complex and highly stylized manner, one not easy to sketch, students could outline it on paper. Clearly, it was memorable. Furthermore, students were more often able to remember the Royal's frequent reference to itself as the "can do" bank, and less often able to recall the motto of any competitor. The high rate of recall for these Royal Bank materials was unrelated to bank usage patterns for this particular population. It was the fact of an animate image that made the logo stand out (other banks had alphabet initials, or abstract designs) as did the motto that had the strongest use of verbs (Beck & Moore, 1982). Even within the visual domain, therefore, levels of memorability can be assertained. While animate images are high on the visual list, active verbs seem to have the same quality within the language domain.

We also know that good metaphor use is linked to charismatic leadership in some way. One need only to look at the success of certain politicians like President Reagan in the U.S., or Prime Minister Trudeau in Canada, to know this at a "gut" level. Corporations are also discovering the effectiveness of metaphor in management training. The Gandalf Corporation, for example, has a "carrot" theory to describe its R & D efforts. A carrot seed represents the initial product idea, because it doesn't take up much space. That seed needs to be planted in plenty of soil in order to grow. As it gets bigger, it needs more space and lots of nourishment (engineering resources, bright people, money). As mature plants, short and fat carrots are said to give the best return. Long, thin carrots are thought wasteful. Therefore, one needs to pinch off carrot shoots that do not grow well. There is even a carrot award at Gandolf, which is a 3-inch, bright orange model worn on the lapel, on the first day of every month, by winners (Morantz, 1984).

Other research on leadership and managerial effectiveness also points to the importance of using imagery well. For example, a study of branch bankers in Canada asked them to speak largely in metaphor. Results showed those managers who had been promoted fastest were also those who, in interviews, used metaphor most effectively (Beck & Moore, 1984). Other studies concerned with organizational culture, organizational commitment, and productivity point in the same direction (Peters & Waterman, 1982).

Metaphor is also a significant issue in medicine. It has been shown both to create some illnesses and to help cure others. There are many reports, both anthropological and of other kinds, on the phenomena called "voodoo death." These studies demonstrate that people sometimes die suddenly merely by believing the statements of others which warn they will soon be struck by some supernatural force. Metaphor is similarly important to old-fashion witchcraft, of course, and to more modern possession, trance, and vision quests of many kinds. Most significant, for the case at hand, is the link between metaphor and curing. Exorcists often get spirits to leave a patient's body (hereby effecting real cures) by using vivid metaphor techniques. The key is that the patient internalize and believe in the imagery being used. A similar approach is apparently helpful in assisting a cure for patients suffering from some kinds of cancer. And we all know of the "placebo" effect of sugar pills given along with the right suggestive overtones.

Other kinds of curing that use metaphor effectively include hypnosis and Gestalt psychology. One interesting application has been developed, for example, at the Center For Creative Leadership in Greensboro, North Carolina. There, an instructor uses picture drawing and guided fantasy as a way of encouraging creative solutions for otherwise difficult thought problems (Rice, 1984). The author of a recent book on dreaming similarly recounts the story of "curing" a memory failure. One day, he had his watch stolen and had to report it to the police. In front of the constable, he was most embarrassed to discover that he had no idea what brand of watch he had owned. That night, he had a dream in which the watch face appeared before his eyes, far bigger than in life, and he was soon able to read off the name on its face very clearly (Evans, 1984).

Still more striking are the many stories told about individual inventors or scientists who have used dream imagery of a metaphoric kind. Friedrich August von Kekule solved the structure of trimethyl benzene, for example, by dreaming of a ring and then linking that idea to his chemistry formulas. Hermann Hilprecht, an archeologist, took two bits of Babylonian writing that were housed in museums in different countries and merged them in a dream. That bringing together of very separate experiences gave him a clue that enabled him to decipher the language used (Evans, 1984). Even more stunning, from a metaphorical point of view, is the story of Elias Howe, inventor of the sewing machine. He had a dream about a hostile tribe that attacked him with spears that had holes at their very tips. This inspired him to design the needle for his stitching machines. A hole at the sewing tip of a needle was something that had not been tried before (Evans, 1984).

More general stories about inventors working by analogy are too commonplace to even mention. Taking an idea from one place and putting it unexpectedly in another lies at the very base of the art of creativity. Experiments of this kind do not always work, but when they do they can have great success. The brilliance here comes in seeing an unexpected application, a new juxtapositioning. This is the essence of the metaphor, the strategy that must be imitated if artificial intelligence work is to advance significantly beyond the much more confined logic of today's machines.

Before continuing, I want to provide a vivid example. I remember well a

4-year-old who visited my house one day. In his explorations, he opened a drawer in the dining area where he found a wooden hot plate for setting cooking pots on the table. This hot plate was unusual in that it was made of crisscrossed pieces of wood, a kind of lattice of slats. The boy soon shoved this hot plate back in the drawer and went to explore my kitchen. Some 10 minutes later, he was struck by a set of wooden pegs near the sink, which I had meant to be used for dish towels. Looking at these pegs in fascination, the boy then rushed back to the drawer in the next room. He now pulled out the hot plate and carried it to the kitchen. There he carefully, experimentally, placed the wooden lattice over my towel pegs. It fit! His new invention had worked. The hot plate could be stored on the pegs, and not in the drawer!

This kind of experimental manipulation of the environment by the mind may not be recognized immediately as metaphoric thought. But I am hard pressed to see a real difference between such reasoning and a more obvious metaphorical approach. The boy found something in one domain that was puzzling, interesting, and in need of further interpretation. Then, at some later point, when operating in quite a different context, the first experience again leapt to his mind. How and why does the mind allow these cross-overs? Clearly, they happen in the search for comparisons, for similarities, and for differences that may help develop one or both bits of knowledge further. Can two separate experiences, two thought domains, be combined in some way? What do they share? And, so often, this comparing and searching has a pragmatic quality. The mind continues to ask: what could I achieve that would be new if I combined these two ideas, or if I took a little something from each?

Bridging, and the experimental combining of things from disparate domains that goes with it, are keys to metaphoric reasoning. Inventing mechanical search procedures that will adequately imitate this creative human skill is one of the real challenges for artificial intelligence developers today. Perhaps the key lies in the level of structure involved. Like "basic categories" in linguistics, by contrast to superordinate and subordinate ones, an important middle ground is put into operation when metaphor is used. We are not thinking in too much detail, nor with great generality. When we say a man has a "hard heart," for example, our comment is not meant to be taken literally. Yet we also do not mean to talk about a profound worldview where the whole of human psychology is defined by a hard/soft paradigm. Instead, by using a "hard heart" image we move on a middle ground. Crossover insights are productive precisely because they belong to this in between world, neither too high nor too low in the overall scheme of cognition.

CATEGORIES AND SCHEMATA

New developments in language study and in neurophysiology are beginning to break down the earlier assumption, drawn largely from studies in phonetics, that an either/or logic of perceived contrasts provided the foundation stone on which all human knowledge must rest. Although the organization of information by discrete categories is still important, the crucial fuzzy edges of our linguistic domains and their frequent overlap are now becoming clear. Furthermore, while most theorists previously gave all members of a category equal status, they now realize that most domains have a center with key elements playing a stronger role in their definition than others. "Apple," for example, would more likely constitute a basic category, and at the same time serve as a more central member of the superordinate "fruit", category than would the exotic "guava" (Dunbar, 1984).

The concept of a prototype, plus the graded centrality of various items within given categories, also holds for very abstract domains. For example, three underlying elements are now known to combine to create the English verb "to lie." The three are: (a) falsity of belief, (b) intended deception, and (c) factual falsity. In experiments it has been shown that these three become "weighted" in judgments about lying, falsity of belief on the part of a teller is regularly given more importance than is intended deception or actual factual falsity (Coleman & Kay, 1981).

Another related area in linguistic research concerns perceptual salience. We do not classify everything in our experience with equal finesse and energy. Indeed, it is now becoming apparent that we shall never have a complete catalogue of (say) the world's plant species. The number of botanical varieties is nearly infinite. Researchers, therefore, select to focus their work on specific areas. Much of this narrowing and delimiting is motivated by practical concerns, yet human interest is nowhere easy to predict. A nice example is provided by the butterfly. Some persons in our culture are enormously attracted to butterfly classification. Even though such information has little "practical" significance, it seems expressive (to us) of ideas about freedom and beauty. The Tzetal Indians, by contrast, have almost no interest in butterflies, yet they use at least 16 different categories for the classification of butterfly larvae. This is because larvae have practical significance for the Tzetal. They can be eaten, they sometimes attack crops, and a few are painful to touch (Hunn, 1982).

In order to relate language categories to life experience, some linguists are now trying to define them with "activity signatures" (Hunn, 1982). Such activity must be defined broadly, of course, so as to include symbolic concerns, ritual uses, and even mental states like thinking or dreaming. This new pragmatic mood in linguistics also suggests that sheer perceptual salience may be important. Though we see a gnu or a penguin on very rare occasions, the startling visual experience is enough to create a separate mental category for each such animal. Mythical beings not seen in real life, yet depicted in myths or rituals (like the dragon), are also the cause of very special human interest.

In addition to this new work on category formation, language researchers have recently been developing ideas about schemata, the formal structures that encompass and can sometimes override the grammatical patterning of individual word strings. A schemata can have almost any kind of structure, but must be "easily and naturally apprehended by the mind" (Kay, 1978). A schemata for fruit would be roughly the totality of "more or less succulent items, containing flesh and seed(s) that ripen above ground on perennial or woody plants." A temperature schemata would have underlying it a perceptual scale of "hotness and coldness," and would involve notions both of quantity and of statistical distribution.

In the domain of story telling, schemata have a somewhat different meaning. There, one finds sets of assumed characters, issues, and settings. Good readers use a parsimony principle to decide between variant schemata. They equate particular participants with particular settings or scenarios whenever possible (Kay, 1983). Listeners or readers pick up cues to these structuring background principles from the story text, its intonation, its rhythms, etc., and organize their understanding around the frames selected. Good story tellers keep their background assumptions clear and also know how to cue their audience when a significant transition point between schemata is introduced (Beck, 1982b).

Researchers working on artificial intelligence have been quick to pick up on this linguistic idea of schemata, and have now made attempts to enter these same background considerations into program writing. The intent is to design a computer process that also works on a cueing system, such that given contexts or scenarios can be referenced when interpreting particular inputs. A simple example would be a dinner party where someone asks, "Can you pass the salt?" Here, the dinner guest does not want to know whether his or her neighbor is capable of passing the salt. Rather, he or she is asking him or her (politely) to take a certain action (Waldrop 1984d). The appropriate schemata in this case would be communal eating. Far more subtle innuendoes and schemata can be envisioned. Consider the man whose words invite a girl to dinner, but who is really saying, "I love you." Roger Shrank, an artificial intelligence researcher at Yale, is now trying to find ways to program such general purpose schmata (Waldrop, 1984d).

Artificial intelligence experts are also working on problems of category definition in the field of computer vision. A good example is the everyday ability we have to allocate visual imput to a mental category we label "cat." We can easily spot a cat sitting on a window sill, lying on a couch, or creeping in the grass. Despite vast outline changes, we know it to be only that one kind of animal. Color variations do not fool us, nor (within a certain range) would size. More stunning still, we can recognize a "cat" in a painting, in a cartoon, or in a porcelain miniature. It is clear that there is some core set of attributes for the "cat" category, then, which can be subjected to very substantial typological shifts (Waldrop, 1984e).

Work on computer vision has lead to the realization, now emerging from neurophysiological research as well, that we actually store information about cats in many different ways (shape, size, texture, type of movement, color, etc.). An enormous amount of cross over, expectation checking, plus standard deviation calculations must go on, even in such simple cases, to confirm that we have indeed spotted a member of an established category type. If we can solve these complex, cross-over problems for object recognition in the area of computer vision, it will help substantially in solving them for metaphor types of reasoning too.

New speculation about dreams also provides interesting material for the problem of how the brain categorizes things. A recent and intriguing suggestion is that sleep allows a computer-like brain to go "off line," in order to check and update its internal programs. The mind essentially shuts down its sensory intake, similar to a computer that is "down" and will not take directions from normal sources. It is at this point that technicians run checks on the system to make sure all the electronic hardware is functioning properly. While the computer is in this semi-operational state, technicians also "update" their programming instructions so as to remove "bugs" and improve the efficiency of system processes generally. Perhaps the mind also needs a kind of daily updating and "file cleaning," so that new information can be efficiently stored and old programs modified to take into account any new input that could have special significance (Evans, 1984).

Dreams seem to have thematic threads, a finding that relates to questions about how the mind classifies things overall. Evans gives the example of his own recent "fish" dream, which incorporated all sorts of surprising variations on that one basic concept. Though many aspects of his dream made no sense in pragmatic terms, Evans speculates that the mind may choose to run such programs occasionally, just in order to update and check them. He had eaten fish the day preceding his own dream on this topic, perhaps creating a need to "up-date" that particular program. Thematic threads in dreams, writes Evans (1984), "however foolish, illogical, embarrassing or surreal a narrative line they take" can help us to examine how the mind's category structures work.

It is possible that dreams may also give us some insight into how the mind's censors work. In conscious, waking life, many possible thoughts get shut out. Much of this is beneficial, helping us to focus on issues that are immediately at hand. Too much information and too many ideas distract one, as when a person loses a train of thought or day-dreams at an inappropriate moment. External input can also distract. Sometimes I shut my eyes, for example, when trying to express difficult thoughts in conversation. Reducing visual input helps me focus on the more pressing question, the words I am looking for inside. At night, when one sleeps, censored programs and subroutines can be put on line. Now the mind can experiment with cross-overs between categories that could cause serious problems if run during the daytime. Many scientists and inventors get ideas in their sleep, as do artists and writers. When a radical experiment does work in a dream, perhaps it can then be allowed to run "on line" when the dreamer awakes.

IDEA PROCESSING

One of the interesting things about metaphor is that it allows for the productive use of paradox. Metaphors provoke, and are, in essence, paradoxical. This is because they juxtapose things that are not normally compared or combined. Advertising provides many illustrations of this, since paradoxical visual metaphors are often used there to considerable (profitable) effect. Take the British bank whose popular advertising campaign showed a tree with little buildings at the ends of its many (visible) roots. The slogan that went with this sketch read "our roots are our branches." Paradox was obviously a part of this surprising idea, both visually and linguistically. Bank buildings and tree roots draw on entirely different domains in our normal classification system. Within a botanical system, roots and branches are also quite separate subcategories. Yet an interesting (metaphorical) cross-over is possible, an idea that clearly attracts the mind.

Another example comes from a recent illustration on the cover of *Executive* magazine. In the sketch provided, a well-dressed corporate executive holds a large watering can in his hand. Under this, covering all but the manager's tie and face, is a garden of large green leaves. In among the leaves, and on a scale much smaller than that depicting the executive's body, one finds three human researchers in lab coats doing various "scientific" things like measuring chemicals in vials. The caption is "The Nurturing of R & D: Four Companies That Got The Formula Right." The metaphor rests on the comparison of a garden and its need for water, with scientific research and its need for financial support. The magazine cover enhances this paradox by distorting the relative size of peronnel types involved, and by the fact that the research group conducts its technical studies, with lots of hardware, in the middle of the forest of leaves. Looking carefully, one sees that the research team actually stands in flower pots ten times larger in scale than its own lab facilities. Did *Executive* editors make a mistake with this whimsical cover sketch? Of course not. The illustration is memorable and effectively conveys the idea to be developed: "Watering one's R & D effort properly."

One further domain where metaphor and paradox are used extensively to enhance communication is in proverbs. If one thinks about how these sayings are employed in daily life, it is quickly clear that proverbs serve as metaphorical comments on everyday events. If someone is debating buying a tape recorder (say), a friend might volunteer the comment, "A bird in hand is worth two in the bush." If someone whom you think is vulnerable starts attacking you verbally, however, the comment might be, "People who live in glass houses should not throw stones." Using proverbs to comment on an immediate situation is not an obscure art. A listener will easily make the mental leap needed to understand the speaker's intent.

One can even understand (translations) of many proverbs from other languages, provided one is given an appropriate context or setting to link them to. For example, the Tamil proverb "Licking the back of one's hand when there is food in the palm" might sound a little odd in isolation, but if a poor man were buying a new car when his old one would do, and you overheard that comment, the speaker's words would make sense. Like cartoons, using a proverb often carries much more punch than a direct statement of fact. The juxtaposing of two separate domains of knowledge can be energizing. Such surprising analogies often excite the mind and make a comment memorable.

If we move to the realm of poetry, especially of a religious or philosophical kind, these same patterns reappear in yet another form. Take the example of a South Indian mystic who once wrote at some length about baked and unbaked pots. A reader instantly knows that the image is intended as a metaphor, yet just which abstract idea the author wishes to discuss is not easy to say. Sometimes he seems to refer to male and female, while at others it is the soul and the body. In still other contexts, this poet evokes emotional themes like "cruel" and "kind," or brings to mind the ritual difference between the initiate and a novice. Perhaps the poet did not intend that his listeners know, with certitude, which analogy was foremost in his mind. The stimulus and the inspiration derived from such religious poetry lies largely in the search itself. Meaning is process for the mystic, the posing of a continual puzzle or paradox, key words that help lead a devotee deeper and deeper into meditation.

NEUROLOGICAL RESEARCH

Evidence from neurological work also is helpful in advancing our understanding of how metaphorical thinking could actually happen at an electrochemical level. New research suggests that each afferent system in the animal body (those nervous networks that carry impulses toward a nerve center) uses discrete pathways. The anatomical distinctiveness of nerve systems is maintained at least through the mid-brain level, while classes, orders, and even families of animals differ in the degree to which particular kinds of sensory input receive emphasis. As one moves up from rather primitive taxa towards the mammals, a selective enlargement of certain areas occurs. With more complex abilities, there is more subdivision, and the connectivity in each sub-system of neural pathways becomes more particularistic (Bullock, 1984). At a still more minute level, furthermore, it is now known that nerve cells are not all alike. Instead, most human nerve cells appear to occur in sets of several thousand, with detectable differences between clusters, for a total of some 50 million neural sub-sets.

Additional research has found that somatosensory information (in monkeys) is stored in physical regions subdivided according to the source of input. Input for one hand, for example, goes to an area of the brain which is then subdivided to record input from each finger separately. Information for each finger, however, seems to be registered by several thousand cells simultaneously. Over time, this group of neurons seems to develop a cooperative common response to incoming stimuli such that no one cell is particularly significant to that whole (Fox, 1984). It is almost as if each neural group developed its own "cultural" traditions through repeated, and largely shared, experience. Such findings fit well with new developments in learning theory. There, the theme that gets repeatedly mentioned is "selective enhancement," the theory that predictable sensory inputs work to reinforce certain key nerve cell patterns at the expense of others. Hence, a single neuron's random firings gradually stabilize into patterns through an "associative process" (Fox, 1983b).

We do not yet know much about how information is stored in the brain. But what does seem clear is that it resides in flow patterns or pathways developed between such neurons, and not in individual cells per se (Evans, 1984). It is tempting, then, to think that metaphorical thought often involves the discernment of pattern similarities between widely separated neural sub-sets. The next question is, how do such comparisons get made? We know that neurons do not send out their signals along single pathways to specific receivers, as in a wiring diagram. Instead, neurons "broadcast" signals through hundreds of "feeler-like" arms (dendrites and axons). These touch other neurons at interface points called synapses. Effective communication must be considered the statistical result of complex interactions where, after many collisions, a proportion of colliding signals originating from many neurons handshake in some way (as in a chemical model). Neural pathways therefore act as electro-chemical media in which certain broadcast signals get picked up, if and when they encounter the right receivers (Lewin 1984b).

The physical processes that determine such communication patterns are not yet well understood. One hypothesis is that electromagnetic fields and wave patterns are important. In such a model, each new stimulus would create a pattern that might either resonate or interfere with previous patterns stored in memory, in a way similar to how a tuning fork or violin string responds to certain sound wave frequencies. These resonance patterns are no doubt nonlinear; that is, activity can occur even when an incoming wave is not identical to previous ones, but merely similar in some ways to already stored information (Learner, 1984). If the resonance concept proves accurate with further study, this idea could go a long way to helping us understand how information is sorted neurologically, and also how patterns can be compared across varied neural regions.

An intriguing and very new approach to computer programming by artificial intelligence experts is attempting to develop a mathematical version of this resonance idea by using a particular kind of algorithm called Boltzmann architecture. This idea builds on the mathematical work of an important 19th century figure in statistical mechanics, Ludwig Boltzmann. Described with the help of a thermo-chemical metaphor, Boltzmann programs allow a "lowering of temperature" within the computer's electrical networks by a randomization process. When a kind of "thermal equilibrium" is achieved, a particular input pattern can then be "floated" across it in a way such that prior patterns exhibiting a good match can "crystallize" around it. Apparently, this Boltzmann architecture can search or scan a large number of parallel sub-sets for such a "match," just as, in metaphor, one might wish to search various sensory storage domains.

In another description of the Boltzmann algorithm, this machine is said to change its equilibrium (in a given area) on the basis of weighted inputs received from other currently active processors. It will also compare new input values with previously set thresholds meant to model possible parallel values developed by neuronal synapses in the mind. Researchers are now developing a learning algorithm that would allow for self-activated changes in the strength of these input weights, and related threshold resistances (Tucker, 1984).

Apparently, this Boltzmann design works well even if there is "noise" in a system and even if the previous data stored is somehow incomplete (Waldrop, 1984f). Although such a new approach is still in the early stages of development, these principles fit in a promising way with what we can already say about metaphorical thought habits. In his new book on dreams, for example, Evans (1984) suggests that dreams involve a "condensation process." In condensation, "a new piece of input from our working life gets linked to older inputs already wired into the brain's memory circuits" (p. 167). Perhaps, for humans (as for a computer), waking experience is first stored in temporary memory. Sleep is then needed at a later point, in order to transfer that new material to a more permanent filing system. The mind must go "off line" at this point (refuse fresh input), because it cannot simultaneously cope with the body's need to catalogue data and also respond safely to external stimuli.

The above paragraphs draw many comparisons between the mind and a computer. But certain key differences must also be noted. Central to all such contrasts is the question of substance. Our brains are made up of neurons and synapses, a biological ground characterized by complex and shifting magnetic field patterns. Neuronal impulses do not encode digital information, but rather are characterized by frequency variations and complex resonance patterns. In the mind, more rapid firings and enhanced wave-like responses are the result of increasingly intense sensory input (Learner, 1984). Advances in hardware design are now beginning to narrow one obvious gap between digital computer electronics and natural brain structures: the amount of parallel processing. But still more radical developments in hardware are envisioned.

One interesting new idea uses an entirely new kind of physical basis for logic processors. A "computer" made of semiconductors and built out of alternating layers of gallium arsenide is now a technical possibility. Such an "optical system" would have a "multiple quantum well" structure (something like layered waffles). These "wells" could then be used to sort out streams of photons that would be generated by a laser beam. Such a system would be inherently parallel, because its input and output signals would have to travel in lines perpendicular to its conductor arrays. In addition to this advantage, such a system would utilize optical resonances in such a way that fundamental absorption patterns could be repeatedly changed by amounts proportional to the laser's electric field strength patterns (Robinson, 1984). This kind of computer hardware would have more of the properties of the biological mind that any electro-mechanical system currently available.

SENSORY KNOWLEDGE

In addition to developments in programming and in hardware that should soon allow for pattern searches across disparate domains, much additional work on sensory systems is needed before we can anticipate mechanical forms of metaphoric thought. I have already made clear that metaphoric reasoning rests (by its very nature) on sensory information. Intuition, likewise, appears to be heavily dependent on sensory-motor habits, or "flow" patterns. For this reason, it is interesting to note recent work suggesting that there are indeed two physically distinct memory systems in man, a procedural one that deals with habits or behavioral functions, and a declarative one that is cognitive or representational (Fox, 1983a). Much information, of course, is present in both systems at once, so that normal behavior stems from a combination of the two. The two systems are so physically distinct that amnesia only affects the latter.

There is plenty of evidence that the brain's procedural system can handle a certain amount of reasoning on its own. In sports, for example, one's muscles come to "know" what the right moves are. The athlete does not have to consciously think about much of what he or she does. Some lovely quotes from computer programmers and video machine addicts are provided by Turkle (1984) to illustrate this same idea. For example, one 50-year-old business man who plays video games extensively claims that they put him into the same state of mind he feels when he skis: In his words, "When I play the games I don't think. My fingers think. As in skiing, you know the terrain, you feel the terrain. My mind is clear . . . they say it is mindless, but for me it is liberating" (p. 85).

A new bridge can be built here, between neurophysiology and linguistic research. As pointed out earlier, language theorists are now using the idea of "activity signatures" for defining the words we use in everyday speech. They have studied the muscular habits associated with the word "chair" (what the body normally goes through to sit down in one, and to get up), for example. These motor habits help to define the concept of "chair" for us and help to subtly distinguish chairs from other objects that can be sat on (Rosch, Mervis, Gray, Johnson, & Boyes-Braem, 1976). Here is evidence for concept structures that must have some identity of their own, within our procedural or motor-memories. This part of the mind, furthermore, is clearly primary, in the sense that it develops faster and sooner, both in evolutionary terms and in the lives of individual human beings. Children acquire significant amounts of information at the motor-sensory level long before they leave the womb. At birth they can already recognize patterns that are surprisingly complex, even distinguishing one particular Dr. Seuss poem from another text when read by the same mother's voice (Kolata, 1984b).

Educators working with young children are, of course, well aware of the importance of motor learning. Logo, a special computer programming language well adapted to elementary school teaching, uses a "turtle" the child can move about with its hands. The novice is told "think of yourself as the turtle" or "play turtle." The technique clearly catches a child's imagination. Kids as young as three or four can use these "turtles" extremely well. Success with getting youngsters to program computers clearly rests on this sensory-motor approach, technically known as the "body syntonic relationship" (Turkle, 1984).

Vision, a particularly important sensory system, is also highly implicated in reasoning processes. Being able to picture one thing "before the mind's eye," and then to mentally compare it with some other situation or object, is by far the most common kind of metaphoric thought. Visual imagery is of equal and related importance in problem solving, as when Einstein reported imagining himself astride a sunbeam (at age 16), from which vantage point he was best able to think about general relativity (Guillen, 1984). Children are especially attracted to visual stimuli, of course, from just days after birth. Why else would parents go to such trouble to hang colored mobiles over their cradles? Later, the same phenomena emerges when kids encounter computers. One of the areas of programming children select most often is computer graphics. Later in life, we have plenty of evidence for the magnetic attraction of video games, television, and movies.

Computer-aided design (CAD) has shown itself to be extremely effective as a way for adults to design and analyze manufacturing components, or for engineers and architects to design buildings. This is because the CAD program communicates with the designer in pictures. The mind can absorb the content of such diagrams much faster than it can deal with an array of words or numbers. "Computer graphics seems to tap the way the brain is designed to work" (Fortune Magazine, 1982). Closer to everyday experience, we all know how much faster we can digest information about time when it is presented on an old-fashioned clock dial than in the numbers of a new digital watch.

Vision is also implicated, interestingly, as having a new kind of curative power in medicine. One creative researcher recently found, for example, that patients who have had a relatively stimulating view from their hospital windows recover from surgery faster than controls who can see only a brick wall (Ulrich, 1984). Norman Cousins similarly reports on the effectiveness of viewing movies as part of his regime to recover from an extremely debilitating illness. We know that vision is extremely important for our dream life, too, and we experience substantial periods of sleep each night in which the visual system is involved (Evans, 1984). During other periods of the night, we are more physically restless, but do not experience rapid eye movement. Perhaps programs get run through one brain system (declarative) and then the other (procedural), in alternation, as we sleep. Depriving the body of visual input during the day can also be a problem. Pilots flying at 40,000 or 50,000 feet in a featureless environment, for example, can experience severe disorientation.

Work on artificial vision systems for robots is progressing, but still has major hurdles ahead (Brown, 1984). One problem it would seem, is that the human visual system is fundamentally linked to our motor experience. When I had an infection in the semi-circular canals of my inner ear (one of the organs that determine body balance) a few years ago, any movement of things in front of my eyes made me profoundly dizzy. I could ride as a passenger in a car, for example, but only with my eyes closed. There was absolutely nothing wrong with my vision per se during this period, yet my representational system was so intimately connected to the procedural one determining balance that it seemed my visual apparatus had contracted the disease. Of course, these two mental systems are intimately intertwined. A child acquires its whole system of spatial orientation, and its concepts of object constancy, from linking motor movements to what it can see. This linking starts from the very first day we leave the womb.

If the connections between our visual and motor-sensate system(s) are so strong, then it appears unlikely that successful forms of artificial intelligence can be developed without first building robots that both see and move. This is already happening, of course, and the real question is how far such perceptual and mobile abilities must develop before metaphorical, cross-over thinking will be possible. A key additional ability here is the ease with which humans (and other higher animals) can imagine themselves in the role of the "other." Self–other interaction is fundamental to the development of a sense of personal identity, and indeed is a fundamental building block in any truly "social" system. Children must have "others" around them in order to grow into cognitively normal adults. And the role imitating others plays in childhood learning is widely appreciated. Indeed, some basic propensity for identifying with other humans, and for recognizing that one shares key features of their body form, seems present right from birth (Meltzoff & Moore, 1983).

This ability to recognize and to identify with another being, or even to imagine oneself as an object, has not yet been considered by artificial intelligence researchers. Yet it seems to me to be a key feature in any development of a truly "intelligent" system. The concept of kinship, something that anthropologists have studied extensively, is related to this same issue. All higher life forms have bonding patterns that link parents and children, and most seem to have systems for identifying other kinds of close kin as well. Something as lowly as the ground squirrel, for example, can tell its own full sibs from half sibs, even if the two litters concerned were raised in the same burrow (Lewin, 1984a). Human concepts of kinship, of course, are even more complex. Interestingly, however, humans lack the same subtle motor-sensory ability to identify siblings that have been raised apart. Kin recognition, for us, has largely moved over into the cognitive/representational side of the brain, away from the sensory-motor mind.

Man has been able to imagine himself in other human beings, and also in various elements of the natural environment, since the very beginnings of human time. Examples of a metaphoric link being drawn between the body and the earth, or between the body and the solar system, are present in the very earliest records we have of religious thought. Myths that attribute human thoughts to animals, or a human spirit to even less visible aspects of experience like wind or sound, lie at the very essence of early homo sapiens culture. This mode of thought, the ability to "presuppose a continuity between language, knowledge and body praxis" (p. 130) is fundamental both to our life experience and to our general mental makeup (Jackson, 1983). Turkle (1984) refers to a similar issue when she talks about how "mirrors, literal and metaphorical, play an important role in human development. In literature, music, visual art, or computer programming, they allow us to see ourselves from the outside, and to objectify aspects of ourselves we had perceived only from within" (p. 155). Work on artificial intelligence cannot afford to ignore this problem. The struggle for its solution will help draw us far closer than we are at present to a knowledge of what it really means to be human.

Another way to think about the importance of metaphorical mirroring is to consider the role which social interaction plays in the development of thought. Researchers, developers, inventors, and artists all appear to work in ivory towers. But recent research shows that such persons still have a strong need for face-to-face interaction (Gerola & Gomory, 1984). Even where creative imagination is not the issue, a highly personal social milieu is clearly of considerable importance to human well-being in general. For example, married people live longer, as do people with lots of friends. Even having a pet can help provide a "significant" other. To truly experiment with artificial intelligence, then, perhaps whole communities of robots that interact and get to know one another are needed.

CONCLUSION

An analysis of the properties of metaphorical thought leads us to consider the nature of human intelligence itself. As others have already observed, metaphors are ubiquitous in human language and a pervasive element in creative, innovative reasoning generally. They also function to enhance recall and to give direction or inspiration to many kinds of social activity. This paper has examined the potential that an understanding of metaphor has, to aid in the development of artificial intelligence. It has also reversed that central question, to ask what our current knowledge of neurophysiology, robotics, and computer systems might have to tell us about the nature of human thought. How much are men and machines likely to differ, as intelligent systems, in the forseeable future?

Key differences between living and artificial intelligence so far discussed have focused on the following traits:

1. the human ability to make comparisons as well as to combine information from disparate domains,
2. the human ability to link sensory input and known motor-sensory patterns with more abstract types of representation and reasoning,
3. the human ability to learn from experience so as to improve gradually on basic skills, and

4. the human ability to empathize with an "other" or nonself and thus to develop a sense of personal identity as reflected through others' perceptions.

None of these traits are exclusively human, one suspects, yet they are all well developed in our own species. Yet these four traits no longer belong exclusively to living beings. Computer-robot systems are now beginning to make advances in at least the first three areas.

There are other domains, of course, where human and machine intelligence face still greater differences, notably in the realms of emotion and general life-knowledge. One hardly need develop the significance of food, sexuality, birth, parenthood, domestic life, and death as key elements in the human experience. The nature of our "intelligence" is deeply linked to these elemental encounters. Our symbolic life, our social institutions, and our basic communication codes all rest on the fundamental biological constitution of the body. Intelligence, as we know it, is also linked to our immersion in particular cultural surrounds. Traditional Hawaiians, for example, makes a great deal out of fishing metaphors. Hindu philosophers find sublime insight in the contemplation of the simple earthen pot. The construction of such images rests on a combination of physical and cultural experiences, the latter being garnered from our infinitely particularized human networks and ecological milieus.

Though it does not seem that the logic of metaphoric reasoning is itself predicated on biology, the skills humans have access to are thoroughly and necessarily impregnated with life experience. If we do get to the point where robots can use metaphor, a peculiar output may result. Their images may well see "machine like," just as today's voice simulators have a mechanical "sound" because they cannot give sentences the proper stress patterns or tonal shaping. Similarly, it is hard to imagine a non-biology-based system that could really "feel" anger, become emotionally 'inspired," or "empathize" with a friend in trouble. Just where do we cross the human–nonhuman boundary anyway? Probably there will be no one place, a discovery similar to the one already emerging from recent controversies about beginning points for life and death. Yet the search for such boundaries is certainly worthwhile. The push towards this last great frontier is telling us, slowly but surely, more and more about ourselves.

Will electro-mechanical systems ever be able to fully "imitate" human intelligence, or is a electro-chemical model (the living cell) its necessary base? Does "hardware" determine "soft" outcomes? Does "intelligence" really rest on a process, so that the particular "substance" that sustains it becomes irrelevant? The jury will be out for some time on these key philosophical questions. Still, I find it hard to imagine fully "intelligent" (humanlike) systems that are not built of flesh and blood. The living cell has so much more going for it than do transistors and silicon chips, or even photons passing through semi-conductors made of gallium arsenide. In the former, we have an electrically sensitive structure that can send graded signals through a complex chemical environment, itself sensitive both to numerous "messenger" substances and to electromagnetic phenomena. Imagine all this packed in three dimensions. Each neuron enjoys thousands of different imput and output possibilities.

Signals in the cerebral cortex travel far slower than do the electrical impulses we can pass through silicon, yet for gradational subtlety the "hardware" of a celluar system has much greater potential. In the rush to discover "artificial intelligence," we ignore the obvious biological basis of human cognition at our peril. As a cultural anthropologist, I would have to agree with Merleau-Ponty when he wrote:

> Our body, to the extent that it moves itself about, that is, to the extent that it is inseparable from a view of the world and is that view itself brought into existence, is the condition of possibility, not only of the geometrical synthesis, but of all expressive operations and all acquired views which constitute the cultural world (1962, p. 388).

Metaphor, so central to human thought, is probably the prime example of an "expressive operation" that builds on our intelligence in its concrete form, a set of insights acquired, in the last analysis, only by living in our own human, culturally coded world.

REFERENCES

Beck, B. E. F. (1978). The metaphor as a mediator between semantic and analogic modes of thought. *Current Anthropology, 19,* 83–97.

Beck, B. E. F. (1982a). Root metaphor patterns. *Semiotic Inquiry, 2*(1), 86–97.

Beck, B. E. F. (1982b). *The three twins: The telling of a South Indian folk epic.* Bloomington: Indiana University Press.

Beck, B. E. F., & Moore, L. (1982). *Influence of corporate image on manager's styles: The example of five Canadian banks.* Paper delivered at a conference on Folklore and Organizational Culture at the University of California Los Angeles.

Beck, B. E. F., & Moore, L. (1984). *Shared images: Metaphor use and business style in Canada.* Paper presented at the First International Conference on Organizational Symbolism and Corporate Culture, Lund, Sweden.

Brown, C. M. (1984). Computer vision and natural constraints. *Science, 224*(4655), 1299–1305.

Bullock, T. H. (1984). Comparative neuroscience holds promise for quiet revolutions. *Science, 225*(4661), 473–478.

Dunbar, K. (1984). In-betweens and overlaps: Cognitive psychology and semiotics. *International Semiotic Spectrum, 2,* 2–3.

Evans, C. (with Evans, P. Ed.). (1984). In P. Evans (Ed.), *Landscapes of the night: How and why we dream.* New York: Viking Press.

Fortune Magazine, Editors of. (1982). *Working smarter.* New York: Viking Press.

Fox, J. L. (1983a). Debate on learning theory is shifting. *Science, 1983a, 222*(4629), 1219–22.

Fox, J. L. (1983b). Memories are made of this. *Science. 1983b, 222*(4630), 1318.

Fox, J. L. (1984). The brain's dynamic way of keeping in touch. *Science, 225*(4664), 820–21.

Gerola, H., & Gomory, R. E. (1984). Computers in science and technology: Early indications. *Science,* 225(4657), 11–18.

Guillen, M. A. (1984, May). Mind viewers. *Psychology Today,* pp. 73–74.

Harris, R., Lahey, M. A., & Marsalek, F. (1980). Metaphors and images: rating, reporting and remembering. In R. Honeck & R. Hoffman (Eds.), *Cognition and figurative language* (pp. 163–181). Hillsdale, NJ: Erlbaum.

Hoffman, R. R. (1983). Recent research on metaphor. *Semiotic Inquiry, 1,* 35–62.

Hunn, E. S. (1982). The utilitarian factor in folk biological classification. *American Anthropologist, 84,*(4), 830–42.

Jackson, M. (1983). Thinking through the body: An essay on understanding metaphor. *Social Analysis, 14,* 127–49.

Kay, P. (1978). Tahitian words for race and class. In *Rank and Status in Polynesia and Melanesia* (pp. 81–92). Paris: Musee de l'Homme, Publications de la Societe Oceanistes.

Kolata, G. (1984a). New neurons form in adulthood. *Science, 224*(4655), 1325–26.

Kolata, G. (1984b). Studying learning in the womb. *Science, 225*(4659), 302–3.

Learner, E. J. (1984). Why can't a computer be more like a brain?: *High Technology, 4*(8), 34–41.

Lewin, R. (1984a). Practice catches theory in kin recognition. *Science, 223*(4640), 1049–51.

Lewin, R. (1984b). Why is development so illogical? *Science, 224*(4655), 1327–29.

McLeod, B. (1984). Don't count on computers. *Psychology Today, 18*(9), 18.

Meltzoff, A. N., & Moore, M. K. (1983). The origins of imitation in infancy: paradigm, phenomena, and theories. In L. Lipsitt & C. Rovee-Collier (Eds.), *Advances in infancy research* (Vol. II). Norwood: Ablex.

Merleau-Ponty, M. (1962). *Phenomenology of perception.* Translated from the French by Colin Smith. London: Routledge and Kegan Paul.

Morantz, A. (1984, May). The nurturing of R & D: A good harvest takes management skill. *Executive,* pp. 21–23.

Ortony, A., Schellert, D. L., Reynolds, R. E., & Antus, S. J. (1978). Interpreting metaphors and idioms: Some effects of context on comprehension. *Journal of Verbal Learning and Verbal Behavior, 17,* 465–77.

Pavio, A. (1979). *Imagery and verbal processes.* Hillsdale, NJ: Erlbaum.

Peters, T. J., & Waterman, R. H. (1982). *In search of excellence.* New York: Harper and Row.

Poggio, T. (1984, April). Vision by man and machine. *Scientific American,* pp. 106–116.

Pratt, M. W., Luszcz, M. A., Mackenzie-Keating, S., & Manning, A. (1982). Thinking about stories: The story schema in metacognition. *Journal of Verbal Learning and Verbal Behavior, 21,* 493–505.

Rice, B. (1984, May). Imagination to go. *Psychology Today,* pp. 48–56.

Robinson, A. L. (1984). Multiple quantum wells for optical logic. *Science, 225*(4664), 822–24.

Rosch, E., Mervis, C. B., Gray, W. D., Johnson, D. M., & Boyes-Braem, P. (1976). Basic objects in natural categories. *Cognitive psychology, 8,* 382–439.

Shurcliff, W. A. (1984). Computers, intelligence and emotion. *Science, 224*(4654), 1158.

Thorndyke, P. W. (1977). Cognitive structures in comprehension and memory of narrative discourse. *Cognitive Psychology, 9,* 77–110.

Tucker, J. B. (1984). Computers and the brain: An A. I. perspective. *High Technology, 4*(8), 39.

Turkle, S. (1984). *The second self: Computers and the human spirit.* New York: Simon and Schuster.

Ulrich, R. S. (1984). View through a window may influence recovery from surgery. *Science,* 224(4647), 420–21.

Verbrugge, R. R. (1977). Metaphoric comprehension: Studies in reminding and resembling. *Cognitive Psychology, 9,* 494–533.

Waldrop, M. M. (1984a). Artificial intelligence (I): Into the world. *Science, 223*(4638), 802–5.

Waldrop, M. M. (1984b). Artificial experts. *Science, 223*(4642), 1281.

Waldrop, M. M. (1984c). The necessity of knowledge. *Science, 223*(4642), 1279–82.

CHAPTER TWO

What Does It Mean To Say That A Metaphor Has Been Understood? *

Raymond W. Gibbs, Jr.
University of California, Santa Cruz
Program in Experimental Psychology
Clark Kerr Hall
Santa Cruz, CA 95064

We all have experienced the "click of comprehension" when encountering metaphors. When Romeo comments that *Juliet is the sun,* there is a moment at which the meaning of this metaphor just pops out at us. Yet it is difficult to explain that apperception, for, although we sense something about what Romeo (or Shakespeare) means by his metaphorical statement, it is not easy to describe. One of the often-noted advantages of using metaphors is that they express meanings that speakers are unable to state using more "literal" language. For this reason, researchers interested in metaphor have had a difficult time explicating the meanings of metaphors. As Ricouer (1977, p. 66) puts it, "The paradox is that we can't talk about metaphor except by using a conceptual framework which itself is engendered out of metaphor."

This problem is complicated even more by the fact that metaphors do not necessarily express a single proposition but are often seen as being "pregnant" with numerous interpretations. Each of these alternative meanings may be equally plausible, and it is here where the trouble begins. For centuries now, literary scholars have discussed Shakespeare's metaphor *Juliet is the sun* without coming to a consensus as to what it really means. But at the same time, there is a sense in which we feel some intuitive grasp of what a metaphor means when we hear

---

*Preparation of this paper was supported by a Faculty Research Grant from University of California, Santa Cruz. I wish to thank Gayle Gonzales and Rachel Mueller for their comments on an earlier draft of this paper.

or read it. And it is just this feeling of "knowing" what a metaphor means that has spurred metaphor researchers on in their quest for a theory of metaphorical meanings.

My purpose in this paper is to consider the problem of specifying the meanings of metaphors. I will examine this issue from a psycholinguistic perspective, where the goal is to describe the mental processes that operate when we interpret metaphorical expressions and come to the magic "click of comprehension." More specifically, I attempt to deal with the apparent indeterminacy of metaphorical statements by showing that there is nothing inconsistent in suggesting that metaphors have specific meanings, yet are also open-ended in what they *could* possibly mean. To do this, I advocate an *intentionalist* approach to the study of metaphor which suggests that recognition of a speaker's intentions in making a metaphorical statement is the primary aim in understanding the meanings of metaphors.

This chapter has five parts. In the first section, I consider some of the current philosophical theories on the meanings of metaphors. Each of these differing approaches has attracted the attention of many metaphor researchers and has provided the fuel for psychologists' interest in metaphor. Following this, I discuss some additional problems for a theory of metaphor, and suggest that the current proposals are unable, for the most part, to account for these other aspects of metaphor. The third section describes the *intentionalist* approach, and suggests that this way of looking at metaphor should provide some important constraints on a psychological theory of what it means to say that a metaphor has been understood. The fourth section considers the relationship between metaphor comprehension and appreciation. In the final section of the paper, I make some concluding remarks.

THEORIES OF METAPHORICAL MEANINGS

Most traditional theories of metaphor have been somewhat vague about what it means to say that a metaphor has been understood. Nonetheless, there are three philosophical accounts of metaphor that dominate the metaphor literature, each of which attempts in some way to elucidate what metaphors appear to mean. These theories are those of Max Black, Donald Davidson, and John Searle. I have chosen to focus on their respective work since, together, they encompass a broad range of views on the issue of metaphorical meanings. My primary focus in describing these theories will be on the contributions each makes to the issue of what does it mean to say that a metaphor has been understood. I will also be concerned with how each respective theory deals with the apparent open-endedness of metaphorical meanings.

Black's View

Perhaps the most popular theory of metaphor is Max Black's *interactive* view. In his earliest contribution, Black (1954–55) criticized what he termed the *substitution* and *comparison* views of metaphor. These theories suggest that a metaphor is a comparison in which one term (the *tenor* or subject of the comparison) is asserted to bear a partial resemblance (the *ground* of the comparison) to something else (the *vehicle*). This approach, which dates back to Aristotle, holds that understanding metaphors, such as *Sam is a giant,* necessitated finding a category for which both the tenor and vehicle belong. This is done by constructing some analogy involving the tenor and vehicle, given that these share a set of features.

Black successfully argued that the *substitution* and *comparison* views are incomplete, since they do not tell us how we are to compute the meanings of any given metaphor. Almost any two objects are similar in some respect, and what is needed is a theory that specifies how we are to select the relevant similarities between the tenor and vehicle in each metaphorical statement. Furthermore, there are many cases where there is no basis for computing the similarity between the tenor and vehicle, yet we are still able to understand the metaphorical assertion. If someone said to me that *Manuel Felice is the Reggie Jackson of Mexico,* I could easily understand the metaphor despite my not knowing anything about Manuel Felice. This metaphor could not be comprehended by finding the relevant features that Jackson and Felice share.

The alternative, *interactive* view of metaphor Black proposed suggests that, in comprehending a metaphor, the vehicle of a metaphor is a template for seeing the tenor in a new way. This reorganization of the tenor is necessary because the features of the vehicle cannot be applied directly to the tenor. After all, the features that the tenor and vehicle share are often only shared metaphorically. For example, *Man is a wolf* is metaphorical in part because both men and wolves are predators, but they are so in very different senses. Understanding metaphor, according to Black's proposal, involves discovering the "system of commonplaces" associated with both the tenor and vehicle. These commonplaces are stereotypes which are widely agreed upon and may not be strictly true of either the tenor or vehicle. When we interpret metaphor we do not compare the tenor and vehicle for existing similarities, but view each in a new way to *create similarity* between them. The tenor and vehicle *interact* in the sense that the presence of the tenor incites the hearer to select some of the vehicle's properties, thus inviting the hearer to construct a parallel implication complex that can fit the tenor, which in turn induces parallel changes in the vehicle. Thus, Wallace Steven's remark that *Society is a sea* is not about the sea, but a "system of relationships" between society and sea signaled by the word *sea.*

Black (1979) illustrates his vision of the understanding process in the context of the example *Marriage is a zero-sum game.* Here *game* is seen as a contest between two opponents in which one player can win at the expense of the other. *Marriage* is then viewed as a sustained struggle between two contestants in which the rewards of one contestant are gained only at the expense of the other. However, we can also interpret this metaphor from the perspective of game theory, which implies that there is no rational procedure for winning in a single play. Which of these two interpretations is actually chosen depends on how much an understander knows about the nature of games and game theory. Black suggests that the difficulty in making a firm and decisive interpretation is present in all cases of metaphorical statements. People cannot set firm standards for deciding which are admissible interpretations, since metaphors are inherently ambiguous and suggestive of numerous meanings.

There have been many psycholinguistic studies that are derivative from Black's *interactive* theory of metaphor. These investigations have focused on the relationships between the tenor and vehicle in interpreting and appreciating metaphors. Some studies have found that the metaphorical relations between tenor and vehicle are apprehended by means of a feature-matching operation. In this model, the hearer determines the degree to which the semantic features of the tenor and vehicle nouns overlap. Presumably, the greater the degree of feature overlap, the more "apt" and "comprehensible" the metaphor (Johnson & Malgady, 1979; Marschark, Katz, & Paivio, 1983).

However, other studies have shown that people do not interpret metaphors by inferring grounds that consist of familiar features shared by the tenor and vehicle. Verbrugge and McCarrell (1977), for example, presented subjects with metaphorical sentences, such as *billboards are warts on the landscape.* Later on, subjects attempted to recall the metaphors with the aid of recall cues. Some subjects received the tenor ("billboards") as cues, others got the vehicle ("warts"), others got the relevant ground that linked the two terms ("are ugly protrusions on a surface"), and, finally, some subjects received irrelevant grounds as cues ("tell you where to find businesses in the area"). The results showed that the relevant grounds facilitated recall of the metaphorical sentences about as well as the tenor and vehicle terms themselves. Verbrugge and McCarrell argued that the grounds were good recall cues because subjects inferred them when they comprehended the metaphors and then formed an abstract representation in memory for the metaphor based on the tenor, vehicle, and ground. More recently, Camac and Glucksberg (1984) presented the results of a reaction-time study which suggested that good metaphors do not use preexisting associations to achieve their metaphorical effects. Rather, people use metaphors to create new associations between concepts.

It has also been suggested by a number of psychologists that the tenor and vehicle terms play asymmetrical roles in metaphor (Ortony, 1979a, b; Tversky, 1977). Generally, a statement of the form "A is like B" will be seen as a literal comparison if high-salient properties of B are also high-salient properties of A. For instance, *Encyclopedias are like dictionaries* is seen as a literal comparison, since the high-salient predicates or features of dictionaries are similar to the high-salient features of encyclopedias. If high-salient predicates of B are lower-salient predicates of A, while there are high-salient predicates of B that cannot be applied to A at all, then the statement will be seen as a nonliteral comparison. *Encyclopedias are like gold mines* is seen as a metaphorical comparison, since the high-salient features of gold mines are similar to the lower-salient predicates of encyclopedias. The key feature, then, of a nonliteral statement is the radical asymmetry of the comparison between the topic and vehicle. Ortony (1979b) reports empirical evidence to support this claim.

In sum, there is reasonably good empirical support for the idea that a metaphor has been understood when a hearer recognizes that the tenor and vehicle interact, perhaps via some asymmetrical relation which creates new associations between these terms. However, there remain a number of difficulties with the *interactive* view of metaphor that limit its usefulness as a general theory of metaphor. These problems will be discussed in the next section of the paper.

Davidson's Theory

Donald Davidson's (1979) theory of the meaning of metaphors is a radical challenge to Black's account. His theory rests on the distinction between what words mean and what they are used to do. Since metaphor exclusively belongs to the domain of use, Davidson argues, it is incorrect to believe that metaphor has a special message or meaning that must be deciphered in order to be understood. Metaphors mean only what they appear to mean on the surface in their most literal sense. Usually, then, metaphors state a patent falsehood or an absurd truth and thus need no paraphrases, as they are given in the literal meanings of the word themselves. Davidson recognizes that metaphor may induce new insights about things previously unnoticed. However, he believes that theorists are quite mistaken in their attempt to specify the contents of the thoughts or insights that a metaphor produces and read these contents into the meaning of the metaphor. The great difficulty we have in specifying the meanings of metaphors, Davidson suggests, lies precisely in the fact that there is really no limit to what a metaphor calls to our attention. But these additional insights should not be confused with the meanings of metaphors.

Part of the attractiveness of Davidson's account is that it explicitly recognizes that metaphors are open-ended and, in some sense, indeterminate in their meanings. It is indeed impossible in the absence of either a context or knowledge of the speaker to state conclusively what any metaphor means without drawing out all that it *could* mean. At the same time, Davidson's theory reduces the problem of specifying the meanings of metaphor to an account of these sentences' literal meanings, along with the usual set of truth conditions associated with them. From a philosophical perspective, this may be ideal, but it certainly does little to explain what people intend by their use of metaphorical expressions. When Black (1954–55) suggests that *Man is a wolf* he certainly does not intend for us to recognize this in its most literal form. Rather, he intends for us to see some metaphorical similarities between *men* and *wolves*. A psychological account of what metaphors mean, and of what it means to say that a metaphor has been understood, must recognize the role of the speaker's intention in using some metaphorical expression. As such, a psychological theory must take into account the *effects* metaphors have on us insofar as these effects are *intended* by speakers/authors. Searle's (1979) theory attempts, in part, to do just this.

Searle's Theory

In his rebuttal to Black (1979), Searle (1979) takes a very different approach to the study of metaphor, one which is similar to his earlier work on speech acts (Searle, 1969, 1975). Searle believes that the main problem with metaphor is that, in making a metaphorical statement, such as *Sally is a block of ice,* the speaker intends the utterance to have a different *speaker meaning* than its so-called *literal* or *sentence meaning*. Thus, the issue for Searle is, how can a speaker utter "S is P" and thereby mean that "S is R"? The task for the metaphor theorist is to characterize the relation between the three sets, S, P, and R, together with the principles and other information used by the hearer, so as to specify how it is possible to derive "S is R" from "S is P". In literal utterances, the speaker meaning and sentence meaning are identical, and so, stating that "S is P" means the same thing as "S is R". Understanding such literal utterances does not require any extra knowledge beyond a hearer's knowledge of the rules of language, his or her awareness of the conditions of the utterance, and a set of background assumptions shared by both the speaker and hearer. However, in the case of metaphorical utterances, the truth conditions of the assertion are not determined by the truth condition of the sentence itself. Consequently, in order to understand that, when a speaker says "S is P", he or she metaphorically means "S is R", the hearer requires something more than his or her knowledge of the rules of language, the condition of the utterance, and the shared background assumptions. The hearer must resort to some other set of principles or factual knowledge that permit him or her to figure out "S is R" from "S is P".

Searle proposes that understanding metaphor, or deriving "S is R" from "S is P", takes place in three steps. First, the hearer determines if the literal meaning of the sentence is defective. If so, the hearer looks for an utterance meaning that differs from the sentence meaning. In other words, if "S is P" is literally defective, the hearer must seek a different meaning "S is R". Second, the hearer should compute possible values of R by examining a variety of principles according to which the utterance of P can call to mind the meaning R in ways that are peculiar to metaphor. He suggests a number of principles for doing this. Some examples are:

(1) Things which are P are by definition R. So, R will be one of the salient defining characteristics of P. Thus, *Sam is a giant* will be taken to mean that "Sam is big" because giants are by definition big.

(2) Things which are P are contingently R. So, the property R should be a well-known property of P-type things, such that *Sam is a pig* will be taken to mean that "Sam is filthy, sloppy, etc.".

(3) Things which are P are not R, nor are they like R things, nor are they believed to be R. However, people often perceive a connection between P and R such that to utter P is to call to our mind R properties. Thus, *Sally is a block of ice* can be uttered to metaphorically mean "Sally is unemotional."

Searle lists eight principles, like the above, that are possibly evaluated when a hearer is seeking an alternative "S is R" interpretation. After these principles are examined and possible values of R generated, the hearer goes through the third step of going back to the S term to see which potential R value is likely to be a property of S.

Searle's approach is valuable, since there have been few detailed statements of the knowledge required for understanding a metaphor, nor has there been an account of how the relevant knowledge is brought to bear in specific cases. One of the advantages of his proposed three-step strategy is that it illustrates how it is possible for a speaker to say "S is P" and mean metaphorically an infinite range of meanings—"S is R1", "S is R2", "S is R3", etc.—since the possible values of R generated in step two can be equally applicable to the S term. Although Searle correctly advocates that understanding the meanings of metaphor involves understanding what speakers mean by their use of different utterances, similar to the comprehension of so-called special cases of metaphor like metonymy and synecdoche, as well as other nonliteral expressions such as irony, idioms, and indirect speech acts, there is reason to believe that his proposed account of the comprehension process does not adequately represent what people really do in comprehending metaphors. In particular, there is much psycholinguistic evidence indicating that people do *not* necessarily analyze the "literal" or "sentence" meaning of a metaphor either before or simultaneous to figuring out what the speaker intends (see Gibbs, 1982, 1984 for further details of this work).

For example, Ortony, Reynolds, Schallert, & Antos (1978) showed that the serial-process model does not explain normal processing strategies when people understand metaphors in appropriate social and linguistic context. They found that subjects take more time to understand utterances used metaphorically (*Regardless of the danger the troops march on*) than used as literal statements, when these are read in short story contexts. However, when subjects read these same sentences in longer story contexts, there was no difference in the time it took subjects to read metaphoric and literal statements. If people actually computed the literal meaning of the metaphor before deriving its nonliteral interpretation, then subjects should have taken longer to comprehend the metaphorical expressions than the literal ones. This, however, was not the case. Similar findings have been reported for understanding other kinds of metaphor (Pollio, Fabrizi, Sills, & Smith, 1984), idioms (Gibbs, 1980, 1985; Ortony et al., 1978; Swinney & Cutler, 1979), indirect speech acts (Gibbs, 1979, 1983), and proverbs (Kemper, 1981). It appears that people are able to grasp a speaker's intention in using a metaphor quite quickly without resorting to a bottom-up analysis of a metaphorical statement's literal structure. This is especially true when these nonliteral utterances are encountered in normal linguistic and social contexts. Something in the context makes it easy for the hearer/reader to determine a speaker/author's metaphorical intentions.

The psycholinguistic evidence, then, does not support the details of Searle's model of metaphor understanding. In particular, it does not seem to be the case that computation of a metaphor's literal meaning is an obligatory process if it is encountered in appropriate discourse contexts. Nevertheless, Searle's model correctly ties the meanings of metaphors to what speakers' mean by their use of such utterances. This puts the weight on a theory of metaphor to explain the correspondence between what words likely mean and what speakers mean when they use these words. At the same time, Searle's approach is better suited to explaining the open-endedness of metaphorical meanings, since there are as many meanings for a metaphor as a speaker intends.

ADDITIONAL PROBLEMS FOR A THEORY OF METAPHOR

There appears to be no common thread that can tie the different theories so as to provide a more unified account of what it means to say that a metaphor has been understood (but see Cooper, 1984; Davies, 1982–83). Each approach has its own advantages in either specifying what makes certain "A is like B" expressions metaphorical (Black), or in restricting a theory of the meanings of metaphors such that metaphors mean what their literal meanings specify, but that their possible uses are essentially innumerable (Davidson), or in suggesting a rationalistic account of what must be done in order to determine what speakers possibly mean by their use of a metaphorical expression (Searle). In this section, I present a number of additional problems for a theory of metaphor. Each of these difficulties are not easily handled by any of the existing theories, and demand an account of metaphor which is more context-dependent and sensitive to the presuppositions and mutual knowledge shared by speakers and hearers in using metaphor.

The first difficulty is that not all metaphors are of the "A is like B" or "A is B" form. Other kinds of metaphorical utterances, such as metonymy, oxymoron, hyperbole, and synecdoche, demand just as much theoretical explanation of their metaphorical meanings as do utterances that are more closely related to simile.

A second problem is that many metaphors do not violate selection restriction rules. In these cases, understanding the meanings of the metaphor does not involve recognition of the "system of commonplaces" between the tenor and vehicle, or in creating similarity between them. For instance, *The rock is becoming brittle with age* is metaphorical, not because any semantic violations within the sentence itself, but because of its relation to context. Although this sentence can be viewed as having strictly literal meaning in a geological context, it quickly becomes metaphorical in reference to a professor emeritus. Conversely, the deviant sentence is not necessarily metaphorical. Thus, the sentence *The tree asked Mervyn to direct it to London,* from the *Lord of the Rings,* is quite literal in a fantasy world where trees are animate. For many metaphors, then, there are no semantic features that need to be overridden to produce a metaphorical interpretation. Instead, the metaphorical nature of these utterances comes from their relation to a specific pragmatic context and not from any specific properties of the utterance itself.

Finally, even if a metaphor does violate selection restriction rules, and is in the "A is like B" or "A is B" form, it is not clear how the salient characteristics of the A and B (or tenor and vehicle) terms are determined. As mentioned earlier, various psychological works on saliency and the interaction of the A and B terms of a metaphor indicate that "A is like B" comparisons are most often seen as metaphorical when there is some degree of asymmetry between the terms. "A is like B" statements will be seen as metaphorical to the extent that high salient aspects of the A term match with low salient aspects of the B term (Ortony, 1979a, 1979b; Tversky, 1977). Still, there is no general consensus on how one determines which semantic properties of A or B are salient. Some theorists have argued that the study of metaphor can be made more precise by ranking the salient features of a concept or term. Thus, Cohen (1979) hypothesized that, in metaphor, "empirical" rather than "inferential" features are cancelled. Thus, for a sentence like *The legislative program is a rocket to the moon,* obvious empirical features of the tenor, such as "air-cleaving" and "cylindrical," are canceled, leaving the inferential features, such as "fast-moving" and "far-arriving." But Cohen found this notion unsatisfactory, preferring to argue that semantic features should be arranged in order of their decreasing semantic importance. The metaphorical interpretation of a sentence can be found, according to Cohen, by cancelling the most important, general, and obvious features and retaining the more distinctive and specific ones which are less probable and carry with them more information.

I have already reviewed some empirical studies which demonstrate that a feature matching procedure, such as proposed by Cohen, does not explain what people are doing when they comprehend metaphors. The failure of semantic feature theories has, in part, led to the adoption of a new *Contextualist* approach to the meanings of metaphors (Hoffman & Nead, 1981). This view makes no strong ontological claim about the physical or psychological status of the properties and relations that underlie semantic features. Hoffman and Nead argue that the creative aspect of metaphor must be described as a complex mapping operation, not a single map of topic and vehicle in terms of their shared features, whether or not salience weights are involved. The knowledge which permits the successful use of metaphor language is not static. One concrete example of this can be seen in Clark and Gerrig's (1983) work on understanding old words with new meanings.

They experimentally demonstrated that understanding old words with innova-tive meanings (e.g., *John did a Napoleon for the camera* meaning "John posed for the camera by putting his hand in his shirt pocket") requires both sense-selection and sense-creation processes. The creation of new word senses (i.e., that *Napoleon* can be used as an eponymous verb) demands that there be some sort of coordination between what a speaker and hearer know, if the hearer is to understand the speaker's innovative, often metaphorical utterance. There appears to be no clear way for determining the salient characteristics of any tenor or vehicle term. Which properties of a concept are activated during metaphor comprehension will depend on the specific context that is shared by speakers and hearers. Hobbs (1983) suggests that, even in interpreting a stock metaphor, such as *John is an ele-phant*, a hearer must use context to selectively determine which inferences apply to the intended meaning of the metaphor. By itself, the expression *John is an ele-phant* can activate a variety of meanings, such as "John is large" or "John has a good memory" or "John loves to eat peanuts." However, given some context, like *Mary is graceful, but John is an elephant,* or *Sam forgets everything, but John is an ele-phant,* we can see exactly which aspects of elephant should be attributed to John.

The search for the acceptable interpretations of a metaphor will involve a large range of cultural conventions and mutually held beliefs, some of which may be quite idiosyncratic to particular people and contexts. Suppose that you are upset with the high cost of auto insurance and that, because of recently paying your yearly insurance premium, you have no money to take a vacation. I recognize your point and add to the conversation by saying *Those tires are my vacation,* to indi-cate that I too am now unable to afford a vacation because of the price of the new tires. Your understanding of this metaphorical expression can only occur if you share the same presuppositions I have at that moment about the high cost of tires and about how my buying tires prevents me from taking a vacation. It is clear that the interpretation of this metaphorical expression can only be accomplished if the speaker and hearer share certain assumptions. That is, which properties of a metaphor are the salient ones depends precisely on what knowledge is shared by the speaker and hearer on any given occasion. The properties of any given terms in a metaphor may be *ephemerally* rather than eternally salient (Bergmann, 1982). The anecdote about the cost of auto insurance and vacation makes the "high cost of buying" a salient characteristic of *tires*. Of course, this piece of knowledge may soon be forgotten by both speaker and hearer. And what is salient for one person may not be salient for another.

This argument strongly suggests that determining which are the salient char-acteristics of something demands a pragmatic solution, one which accounts for a speaker–hearer's coordinated knowledge and beliefs. Specifying what it means to say that a metaphor has been understood requires that some notion of this shared knowledge be brought into a theory of metaphorical meanings. The "shared knowledge" solution also provides an answer to the issue of reconciling the idea that metaphor generates further and further readings with the claims that metaphor can convey a specific cognitive content. The shared knowledge will constrain a hearer's interpretation of what a speaker means by his or her use of a metaphorical statement. Speakers usually have some specific intention in mind when using a metaphor, and typically do *not* assert everything that we can read into a metaphor (Bergmann, 1982). At the same time, it may very well be that understanders are able to recognize what is and is not intended by a speaker's use of a metaphor.

Consider an example from Bergmann (1982), where a speaker says to you *Nuclear reactors are time bombs*. You correctly comprehend the speaker's comment as an assertion to the effect that nuclear reactors are likely to fail with disastrous consequences at an unexpected moment. Later on, however, you reflect further on the metaphor and recognize something quite interesting. Although the people responsible for the building of nuclear reactors don't want people to get killed by them, it seems that they have a terrible disregard for other people's lives just like those responsible for building time bombs. Of course, the speaker may have actually intended you to understand this. Yet it is not necessarily the case that, when a speaker says *Nuclear reactors are time bombs,* he or she wants you to recognize all of these possible meanings. The richness of metaphor does not preclude the possibility that a speaker, in making a metaphorical statement, is actually making a very specific assertion. You and the speaker both acknowledge that the speaker could have stated the metaphor to make a specific comment about the people responsible for nuclear reactors, and still understand that the speaker was not intending this.

INTENTION AND METAPHOR

The problem with all of this is that it is nearly impossible to state conclusively what a metaphor "means," and to say that a metaphor has been "understood," without reference to the speaker who produced the metaphor and the social/ linguistic context in which it was done. Otherwise, understanders could go on endlessly drawing all sorts of inferences about what a metaphor *might* mean. What is needed here is some recourse to what speakers' intentions are in using metaphors. Many studies have demonstrated that people can't avoid interpreting the intentions behind a speaker's utterance, and will make false recognition responses to the pragmatic implications of a sentence, even when told to focus on the words themselves (cf. Harris & Monaco, 1978). But how do we characterize a speaker's intentions or meanings?

Grice's (1957) celebrated analysis proposed one sense of the notion of "meaning." According to Grice, to say that a speaker meant something by X is to say that the speaker intended the utterance of X to produce some effect in the listener by virtue of the recognition of this intention. Thus, in speaking a language, the speaker attempts to communicate things to a listener by means of getting the listener to recognize the speaker's intentions to communicate just those things. This reflexive intention, an intention that is intended to be recognized, is called an *m-intention* (Grice, 1968).

Understanding metaphor can be viewed, not simply as dividing a sentence into its A and B, or tenor and vehicle, parts, and then inferring a ground that relates them, but as identifying the goals or *m-intentions* the speaker had in making the utterance. This *intentional* approach to comprehension states that utterances are comprehended with reference to the knowledge, beliefs, and suppositions shared by speakers and hearers. Hearers can determine which aspects of the A and B terms are salient ones (if the metaphor is in the "A and B" form), and which of the possibly innumerable meanings a metaphor has, by consulting this information which constitutes the *common ground* between speakers and their addressees (Clark & Carlson, 1981).

Consider again the metaphorical assertion *Those tires are my vacation*. Understanding what is meant by this expression necessitates referring to the common ground information that has been established by the context and the previous conversation. In producing such a metaphor, the speaker (say Al) assumes that the hearer (say Bob) recognizes (a) that Al is using *tires* to denote the buying of new tires for the car, (b) that Al wants Bob to believe that he is asserting something about the tires which Al has got reason to believe that, on this occasion, Bob can readily compute, on the basis of their common ground, such that the mention of tires is relevant to vacation; and (c) that Al wants Bob to recognize that he is mentioning the buying of tires in relation to his vacation to mean that having bought the tires does not leave enough money for Al to pay for his vacation.

This, of course, is only a rough approximation of the set of goals Al has in uttering *Those tires are my vacation*. Nonetheless, these goals, or *m-intentions*, are exactly what Al wants Bob to recognize, and the metaphor could not possibly be understood without Bob's recognition of these goals. Figuring out what is salient about the tires and what relation these have to Al's vacation could not be accomplished unless some reference is made to what Al possibly wants Bob to recognize in the context in which the metaphor is spoken. It is this coordination between speaker and hearer wherein the meaning of metaphor lies.

Clark and Gerrig (1983) demonstrated that people comprehend novel words based on proper nouns, such as *After Joe listened to the tape of the interview, he did a Richard Nixon to a portion of it* (i.e., he erased a portion of it), against a hierarchy of information assumed to be in the common ground shared by the speaker and hearer. This hierarchy included information about Nixon's identity, acts associated with Nixon, specific acts done by Nixon appropriate to the utterance, and the specific act intended. Listeners evaluate the salience and coherence of potential interpretations for these contextual expressions against the common ground, and do so quite easily.

All metaphors, then, can be assumed to be comprehended against a hierarchy for some cases than for others, but even in understanding the most cliched, stock metaphor (e.g., *Sally is a block of ice*), there must be some presupposition about the of common ground information. This information may have to be more specific context of its utterance. But how is context defined here? Does it include everything that the speaker and hearer individually know?

One solution Clark and Carlson (1981) propose is that, for a hearer to understand a speaker's meaning, he or she can confine himself or herself to a certain limited domain of information, namely the speaker and his or her listener's common ground, i.e., that part of the speaker's and his or her listener's knowledge, beliefs, and assumptions that are shared. Clark and Carlson point out that this shared information can be divided into three parts. The first source is linguistic co-presence. Here the listener takes as comon ground all of their conversation up to and including the utterance currently being interpreted. A second source for common ground is physical co-presence. Here the listener takes as common ground what he and the speaker are currently experiencing and have already experienced. The final source of evidence is community membership. This includes information that is universally known in a community, and covers mutually known conventions governing the phonology, syntax, and semantics of the sentence uttered.

This view of comprehension provides some necessary constraints on what it means to say that a metaphor has been understood. When a speaker says something to a listener, he or she only intends the listener to interpret what is meant within the limits of their common ground. Clark and Carlson (1981) call this the *intrinsic* context of his utterance, and all other aspects of knowledge and the situation are *incidental* context. By focusing on those parts of the *intrinsic* context, a hearer should be able to interpret what a speaker says without having to first examine the putative literal meanings of metaphorical utterances (Gibbs, 1984). Moreover, by focusing on aspects of the *intrinsic* context, the hearer should be able to make only those inferences about what the speaker intends that are *authorized* (cf. Clark, 1977). These inferences are those the speaker intends the hearer to draw as an integral part of the message being conveyed. An *unauthorized* inference is one that a hearer draws without the speaker's authorization. Thus, when Al says *Those tires are my vacation,* he intends Bob to recognize only the authorized inference that buying the tires left little money to pay for a vacation. Bob, however, could have made an *unauthorized* inference, perhaps that Al bought the new tires so that he *could* take a vacation in his car. But, if Al and Bob have a good sense of what is in the common ground, drawing such *unauthorized* inferences about the meaning of a metaphor is unlikely.

The distinction between *authorized* and *unauthorized* inferences suggests one way of dealing with the idea that metaphors are unlimited in what they possibly could mean, but can actually be used on any one occasion to convey a specific meaning. By restricting themselves to that information which is in the common ground with speakers, hearers should be able to determine which of the many possible meanings of a metaphor are actually intended or *authorized*. The "click of comprehension" usually associated with understanding metaphor occurs when a hearer has recognized what he or she believes are the *authorized* meanings intended by a speaker.

There still exists the possibility, however, that a speaker can utter a metaphor and actually intend the hearer to recognize a number of equally plausible inferences. Is it possible for hearers to figure out which of all the possible meanings of the metaphor are *authorized*? Let me discuss this in the context of a personal example. When I was a teenager, my father would often come into my admittedly messy room and say to me *This room is a toilet*. Each time he said this over the years I always felt as if I understood his intended meaning, which to me implied that he thought the room messy and in dire need of cleaning. However, his metaphorical utterance *This room is a toilet* struck me differently each time he said it. Certainly, my room in no way resembled a porcelain container with the shape of a toilet, nor did the metaphor suggest that my room was antiseptic and deserving of a write-up in *Better Homes & Gardens*. Either of these inferences about the meanings of my father's statement would have been *unauthorized*. I don't believe that I had any tendency to derive such erroneous inferences, given what I sensed was in the common ground between us, namely that he didn't usually make compliments about my room even when it was tidy, and because he usually made some kind of critical comment when my room was in the state that it was.

What I did sense each time he said *This room is a toilet* was some kind of negative association with toilets, as that toilets sometimes smelled unpleasant, or were unpleasant to look at on occasion. Each of these inferences seemed to be a part of the meaning of my father's metaphorical statements, and I always sensed that these were indeed *authorized*. The question, though, is whether my father truly intended each and every one of these inferences to be made, or did he only intend *one* specific implication (e.g., that my room was like a toilet in that both smelled unpleasant). My feeling now, and this is my argument, is that my father probably wanted me to see that my room was a mess and so he uttered a metaphorical statement which he *m-intended* me to recognize as having a range of *authorized* meanings. As far as he was concerned, it didn't especially matter which *authorized* inferences within this set I made, as long as I recognized one of them. In this way, the metaphorical assertion that *This room is a toilet* was deliberately ambiguous, such that any one of a range of meanings was acceptable. Metaphors are often viewed as open-ended precisely because their ambiguity resists a single, definitive propositional meaning. However, this does not mean that a metaphor can never be used with a specific intention in mind. The meanings of metaphors are anchored in this intention, and a metaphor can be said to have been understood, the "click of comprehension" sensed, when a listener recognizes this very intention.

METAPHOR COMPREHENSION AND APPRECIATION

One could argue that many of the metaphors I have considered, such as *Those tires are my vacation* or *This room is a toilet,* are not particularly "good" or "apt" and, as such, lie outside the proper domain of a theory of metaphorical meanings. I do not want to suggest that our understanding that "good" metaphors are seen as having an asymmetrical interaction between the tenor and vehicle, or that the tenor and vehicle do not usually share common features, tells us nothing about the meanings of metaphor. Such information is quite useful in understanding people's aesthetic responses to metaphors and in showing how metaphors reveal aspects of the world previously unknown to us.

Nevertheless, judgments of "aptness" or "goodness" are not a part of the moment-by-moment processes used in comprehending metaphors. There may not be a direct correspondence between the literary quality and the on-line comprehensibility of a metaphor (Gerrig & Healy, 1983). Although a number of empirical studies (Malgady & Johnson, 1980; Tourangeau & Sternberg, 1981, 1982) have suggested a possible correlation between subjects' ratings of goodness and comprehensibility, other research (Gerrig & Healy, 1983) has demonstrated that the processing time needed to interpret metaphors does not generally correspond with subjects' goodness ratings. This latter finding indicates that a theory of metaphoricity is not similar to a theory of how people actually understand metaphors.

More important, perhaps, is that there are many instances of what we would normally judge as "bad" metaphors which are easily understood. The *New Yorker* magazine has published many of these in their little filler section titled *Block that Metaphor!*. For instance, consider the following originally published in the *Nashville Banner.*

> Like a rare fish heaving with delicate roe, premiere recording artist Willie Nelson has more music in the oven than a snow has rumors of falling.

This example is understandable, I believe, in that there is a "click of comprehension" related to our recognizing what the writer intends, even though few people would judge this metaphorical utterance as being particularly "good" or "apt". Of course, the "goodness" of any metaphor, like the salience of its internal terms, depends on the context in which it is given (cf. McCabe, 1983). In any event, specifying what it means to say that a metaphor has been understood does *not* require that we explicate whether or not the metaphor that has been comprehended is a good one or not.

CONCLUDING REMARKS

What does it mean to say that a metaphor has been understood? I have taken a psycholinguistic approach in answering this question and suggested that the meanings of metaphors are inextricably tied to speakers' intentions in making metaphorical statements. The "click of comprehension" associated with understanding metaphor can not be reduced to a specification of the ways the terms of a metaphor contrast, interact, etc., but must be seen as a recognition of a speakers' intention in using the words they do. This requires that the speaker and hearer coordinate what they mutually believe and know, in order to determine which of the potentially innumerable meanings associated with a metaphor are actually *authorized* and intended.

This approach to the meanings of metaphors differs from more traditional philosophical and psychological theories. The ordinary use of "meaning" involves an implicit appeal to *language* conceived as something which determines meanings in general, independent of the intentions of particular speakers. This view stems from the Fregian principle that the meaning of an expression in a language must be independent of the psychological states of the individual speakers. My abandonment of this view suggests that the meanings of metaphors are tied inextricably to speaker's intentions, and there may be no limit to the kinds of sentences people will judge as metaphorical. Although some theorists have proposed that certain ontological constraints operate to make certain combinations of words anomalous (cf. Keil, 1979), other studies demonstrate that the acceptability of a sentence as being metaphorical depends on the contexts in which it is judged (Pollio & Burns, 1977; McCabe, 1983) and the instructions given to subjects making the judgments (Gerard & Mandler, 1983; Hoffman & Honeck, 1979). I argue that a *radical indeterminacy* exists in language, such that almost any combination of words can be used to express almost any kind of intention, including those traditionally thought to be metaphorical.

Such an emphasis of the role of common ground and intentions in determining the meanings of metaphors partially explains the paradoxical feeling that metaphors are somewhat indeterminate in what they possibly could mean, yet at the same time also have specific content. Metaphors can be deliberately ambiguous, in that a speaker can wish the hearer to recognize a specific intention, but does so through their recognition of any number of possible *authorized* inferences. This does not mean that the *authorized* inferences and the speaker's intentions can be separated, with the meaning of the metaphor being the main cue to the speaker's original intentions. Such a view creates the illusion of a choice between alternative notions of what it means to understand. But there is no choice. The speaker's intention is already present at every moment of interpretation. The psychology of metaphorical transformations is unlimited in this way, constrained only by the pragmatic, communicative purposes of the speakers who use metaphor.

REFERENCES

Black, M. (1954–55). Metaphor. *Proceedings of the Aristotelian Society, 55,* 273–294.

Black, M. (1979). More on metaphor. In A. Ortony (Ed.), *Metaphor and thought.* London: Cambridge University Press.

Bergmann, M. (1982). Metaphorical assertions. *Philosophical Review, 91,* 229–245.

Camac, M., & Glucksberg, S. (1984). Metaphors do not use associations between concepts, they are used to create them. *Journal of Psycholinguistic Research, 13,* 443–455.

Clark, H. (1977). Inference in comprehension. In M. Just & P. Carpenter (Eds.), *Cognitive processes in comprehension.* Hillsdale, NJ: Erlbaum.

Clark, H., & Carlson, T. (1981). Context for comprehension. In J. Long & A. Baddeley (Eds.), *Attention and performance, IX.* Hillsdale, NJ: Erlbaum.

Clark, H., & Gerrig, R. (1983). Understanding old words with new meanings. *Journal of Verbal Learning and Verbal Behavior, 22,* 591–608.

Cohen, L. J. (1979). The semantics of metaphor. In A. Ortony (Ed.), *Metaphor and thought.* New York: Cambridge University Press.

Cooper, D. (1984). Davies on recent theories of metaphor. *Mind, 93,* 433–439.

Davidson, D. (1979). What metaphors mean. In S. Sacks (Ed.), *On metaphor.* Chicago: The University of Chicago Press.

Davies, M. (1982–83). Idiom and metaphor. *Proceedings of the Aristotelian Society, 83,* 67–85.

Gerard, A., & Mandler, J. (1983). Ontological knowledge and sentence anomaly. *Journal of Verbal Learning and Verbal Behavior, 22,* 105–120.

Gerrig, R., & Healy, A. (1983). Dual processes in metaphor understanding: Comprehension and appreciation. *Journal of Experimental Psychology: Learning, Memory, & Cognition, 9,* 667–675.

Gibbs, R. (1979). Contextual effects in understanding indirect requests. *Discourse Processes, 2,* 1–10.

Gibbs, R. (1980). Spilling the beans on understanding and memory for idioms in conversation. *Memory & Cognition, 8,* 449–456.

Gibbs, R. (1982). A critical examination of the contribution of literal meaning to understanding nonliteral discourse. *Text, 2,* 9–27.

Gibbs, R. (1983). Do people always process the literal meanings of indirect requests? *Journal of Experimental Psychology: Learning, Memory, and Cognition, 9,* 524–533.

Gibbs, R. (1984). Literal meaning and psychological theory. *Cognitive Science, 8,* 275–304.

Gibbs, R. (1986). Skating on thin ice: Literal meaning and understanding idioms in conversation. *Discourse Processes, 9,* 17–30.

Grice, H. P. (1957). Meaning. *Philosophical Review, 66,* 377–388.

Grice, H. P. (1968). Utterer's meaning, sentence-meaning, and word-meaning. *Foundations of Language, 4,* 1–18.

Harris, R., & Monaco, G. (1978). Psychology of pragmatic implication: Information processing between the lines. *Journal of Experimental Psychology: General, 107,* 1–22.

Hobbs, J. (1983). Metaphor interpretation as selective inferencing: Cognitive processes in understanding metaphor. *Empirical Studies of the Arts, 1,* 17–33 (part 1), 125–142 (part 2).

Hoffman, R., & Honeck, R. (1979). She laughed her joy and she cried her grief: Psycholinguistic theory and anomaly. *Psychological Record, 29,* 321–328.

Hoffman, R., & Nead, J. (1981). *The metaphors of cognitive science.* Unpublished manuscript.

Johnson, M., & Malgady, R. (1979). Some cognitive aspects of figurative language: Association and metaphor. *Journal of Psycholinguistic Research, 8,* 253–265.

Keil, F. (1979). *Semantic and conceptual development.* Cambridge, MA: Harvard University Press.

Kemper, S. (1981). Comprehension and the interpretation of proverbs. *Journal of Psycholinguistic Research, 10,* 283–296.

Malgady, R., & Johnson, M. (1980). Measurement of figurative language: Semantic features of models of comprehension of appreciation. In R. Honeck & R. Hoffman (Eds.), *Cognition and figurative language.* Hillsdale, NJ: Erlbaum.

Marschark, M., Katz, A., & Paivio, A. (1983). Dimensions of metaphor. *Journal of Psycholinguistic Research, 12,* 17–40.

McCabe, A. (1983). Conceptual similarity and the quality of metaphor in isolated sentences versus extended contexts. *Journal of Psycholinguistic Research, 12,* 41–68.

Ortony, A. (1979a). Beyond literal similarity. *Psychological Review, 86,* 161–180.

Ortony, A. (1979b). The role of similarity in similes and metaphors. In A. Ortony (Ed.), *Metaphor and thought.* London: Cambridge University Press.

Ortony, A., Reynolds, R., Schallert, D., & Antos, S. (1978). Interpreting metaphors and idioms: Some effects of context on comprehension. *Journal of Verbal Learning and Verbal Behavior, 17,* 465–477.

Pollio, H., & Burns, B. (1977). The anomaly of anomaly. *Journal of Psycholinguistic Research, 6,* 247–260.

Pollio, H., Fabrizi, M., Sills, A., & Smith, M. (1984). Need metaphoric comprehension take longer than literal comprehension? *Journal of Psycholinguistic Research, 13,* 195–214.

Ricouer, P. (1977). *The rule of metaphor.* Toronto: University of Toronto Press.

Searle, J. (1969). *Speech acts.* Cambridge: Cambridge University Press.

Searle, J. (1975). Indirect speech acts. In P. Cole & J. Morgan (Eds.), *Syntax and semantics: Speech acts,* (Vol. 3). New York: Academic Press.

Searle, J. (1979). Metaphor. In A. Ortony (Ed.), *Metaphor and thought.* Cambridge: Cambridge University Press.

Swinney, D., & Cutler, A. (1979). The access and processing of idiomatic expressions. *Journal of Verbal Learning and Verbal Behavior, 18,* 523–534.

Tversky, A. (1977). Features of similarity. *Psychological Review, 84,* 327–352.

Tourangeau, R., & Sternberg, R. (1981). Aptness in metaphor. *Cognitive Psychology, 13,* 27–55.

Tourangeau, R., & Sternberg, R. (1982). Understanding and appreciating metaphors. *Cognition, 11,* 203–244.

Verbrugge, R., & McCarrell, N. (1977). Metaphor comprehension: Studies in reminding and resembling. *Cognitive Psychology, 9,* 494–533.

CHAPTER THREE

Sensory Similarities: Classes, Characteristics, and Cognitive Consequences*

Lawrence E. Marks
John B. Pierce Foundation Laboratory and Yale University

Marc H. Bornstein
New York University

Similarity is a primary psychological principle that for centuries has played a major role in explaining associations of ideas with ideas, associations of stimuli with responses, transfer of learning, and other cognitive processes. But similarity is also an important psychological phenomenon in its own right: Similarity itself needs study and explanation. In the present chapter, we delve into the nature of similarity, focusing on sensory similarities. At the same time, we explore correspondences between sensory similarities and verbal metaphors, for we believe that the recognition of similarity underlies many instances of people's understanding of figurative language, especially of metaphoric expressions.

At base, all things are different, yet there are innumerable ways in which we perceive or conceive of different things as being similar. Similarity ranges from the concrete and direct to the abstract and abstruse; it encompasses such commonplaces as the recognition of facial resemblance in homozygotic twins as well as such esoteric tropes of poetry as John Donne's analogy (in "A Valediction: Forbidding Mourning") between parting lovers and the two feet of a compass. Abstract, conceptually based similarities are typically verbal, and often they are

---

*Lawrence E. Marks was supported by grants from the National Institutes of Health (NS21326) and from the National Science Foundation (BNS 84-20017). Marc H. Bornstein was supported by a Research Career Development Award from the National Institute of Child Health and Human Development (K04HD00521), and by a Guggenheim Foundation Fellowship.

conveyed through metaphor. However, many simpler and equally important forms of similarity have roots closer to biological and sensory-perceptual function. Sensory similarities commonly rely on directly given perceptual equivalences rather than on conceptualized or constructed verbal analogies.

Sensory similarities come in several kinds. Our first job in this chapter will be to delineate sensory similarity, and to distinguish its several classes. Afterwards, we focus in detail on our main interest, which is the class of sensory similarities known as cross-modal or synesthetic. We argue that certain synesthetic expressions are metaphors that rely on primitive and basic cross-modal similarities given in sensory experience, whereas other synesthetic expressions derive from observed associations and are more properly considered metonymies than metaphors.

Three psychological questions arise out of our considerations of cross-modal similarities. First, what are the origins or bases of synesthetic metaphors as compared to metonymies? That is, does one or the other rest on innate cross-modal resemblances? on experienced perceptual or verbal connections? or perhaps on cultural conventions? Second, are synesthetic metaphors and metonymies discovered or are they created? That is, does one or the other exist independently, outside of the mind or the nervous system? And third, to what extent do synesthetic metaphors serve as a model for more common conceptual and verbal metaphors?

PRINCIPAL CLASSES OF SENSORY SIMILARITY

Similars comprise those entities conceived of or treated as alike by decision rules. One example of a relatively high-order decision rule would state that entities are similar if they have been defined as equivalent by convention or if they bear some specifiable logical relation. In "A Valediction: Forbidding Mourning," Donne sees the soul of his lover as the fixed foot of the compass that holds him near, the foot whose "firmness drawes my circle just,/ And makes me end, where I begunne." An example of a lower-level decision rule would state that entities are similar because (or to the extent that) they share perceptual attributes or elements (violet is similar to aqua, in that both contain blue) or merely as they are located on the same perceptual continuum (a 100-Hz tone resembles a 110-Hz tone). In short, similars are those entities that themselves are different but are perceived and treated on some basis as the same.

Classes of Sensory Similarity

Bornstein (1984) has distinguished several classes of similarity that have a sensory basis. Here, we note five.

(1) When we see the same stimulus from different perspectives, the proximal

sensations differ, but, in the very process of perceiving that the source is the same, we treat the different sets of proximal sensations alike. Perceptual constancy is one aspect of this sort of sensory similarity.

(2) A second kind of sensory similarity operates when we recognize a three-dimensional object in a two-dimensional representation, or vice versa. Here again, the sensations roused by the two stimuli are different, but still we conceive or respond to them as similar. In both class (1) and class (2), the reference (that is, the original stimulus) is physically constant, and its several manifestations are, in many instances, equally representative of the reference: Consider the sculpture that we appreciate as the same from different perspectives, or the person whom we recognize both in life and in a picture. Moreover, in both examples, stimulation arrives via a single modality.

(3) A third kind of sensory similarity operates when we recognize the same reference stimulus through two (or more) modalities. For example, if we touch something without being able to see it and we are later shown the tactually familiar object together with a novel object, we might easily recognize the familiar object by sight alone, without touching it.

(4) In the first three types of sensory similarity, the original reference stimulus is the same; in the fourth type, the reference stimuli differ, but the distinguishable sensations they provoke are nevertheless perceived or responded to as similar. For example, different short wavelengths of light give rise to discriminably different yet nonetheless related perceptions of blue.

(5) Finally, there is the kind of sensory similarity on which we focus here; this is cross-modal similarity, where physically different stimuli, acting via different sensory systems, yield sensations that are perceived and treated as similar. Among the best-known examples are Köhler's (1979) two line drawings, one a globular, rounded form, readily matched to the name "maluma," and the other a straight-edged, pointed form, readily matched to "takete."

Characteristics of Sensory Similarity

Sensory similarities of the kinds we have just described share a variety of characteristics that help distinguish them from other, nonsensory similarities. Of these characteristics, two are significant. First, sensory similarities are present in early infancy. Second, and related to the first characteristic, their substrates are typically congenital, even innate, or the product of very early experience. Consequently, we would expect to locate their underlying mechanisms within primary sensory areas or sensory association areas of the cerebral cortex, rather than in cortical areas subserving, say, verbal processes.

With regard to the first characteristic, we note the following: Human infants in the first 6 months of life treat as similar displays of the same stimulus that vary in size or shape (e.g., Bornstein, Gross, & Wolf, 1978; Day & MacKenzie, 1977); infants treat as similar two-dimensional and three-dimensional representations of the same stimuli (e.g., DeLoache, Strauss, & Maynard, 1979; Dirks & Gibson, 1977; Rose, 1977); infants treat objects they see as familiar when the infants have previously felt the objects but have not seen them (e.g., Gottfried, Rose, & Bridger, 1977, 1978; Rose, Gottfried, & Bridger, 1981); and, finally, infants treat certain different wavelengths as similar in hue (Bornstein, Kessen, & Weiskopf, 1976). Babies do all these things, even though they can very well tell the difference between different perspectives of the same stimulus, even though they can tell the difference between two- and three-dimensional versions of the same object, even though they can tell the difference between seeing an object and touching it, and even though they can tell the difference between different wavelengths.

As far as neural mechanisms are concerned, many of these sensory similarities seem to be associated with identifiable neurophysiological substrates located in a primary sensory area or in a sensory association area of the cerebral cortex. For example, Gross and Mishkin (1977) identified, in higher primates, cortical neurons that respond similarly to a given visual stimulus anywhere within the neurons' receptive fields. That is, these neurophysiologists may have located some of the neural mechanisms that subserve shape constancy, or stimulus equivalence across retinal translation. Likewise, there is evidence from studies of the functioning of the visual system in higher primates that the classification of similar colors (categories of wavelength) may relate directly to the sensitivities of visual cells (DeValois & DeValois, 1975). Of course, neurophysiological substrates have not been identified for all sensory similarities, but the fact that substrates in sensory areas of the brain have been identified for some of the most prominent is consistent with the thesis we wish to develop, namely that sensory similarities have psychological primacy.

We now turn to discuss in detail one especially powerful kind of sensory similarity: cross-modal or, as it is sometimes called, synesthetic similarity. Although cross-modal similarities are more complex than many intramodal resemblances (because they arise from physically different stimuli, acting on different modalities), like their intramodal kin many of them also have early ontogenetic origins, as well as probably innate neurophysiological substrates. These characteristics – early origin and sensorineural basis – elevate cross-modal similarities to join other sensory similarities in the status of psychological primitives. Cross-modal similarities are particularly interesting, of course, because they may foretell sophisticated, verbal forms of metaphor.

CROSS-MODAL OR SYNESTHETIC METAPHORS

If you ask the metaphorical question, "Which is brighter, a sneeze or a cough?" most people readily respond that sneezes are brighter. People think that sneezes are higher in pitch than coughs, and they think that high-pitched sounds are like bright lights (Marks, 1982a). People also think sneezes have a more rapid, "sharper" onset, and that sharp and bright are similar to each other. If you present to young children – say of about 4 years – a high-pitched sound and a low-pitched sound, and ask which is similar to a bright light and which to a dim light, virtually all match the high-pitched sound to the bright light and the low-pitched sound to the dim one (Marks, Hammeal, & Bornstein, in press). These two findings show, first, that young children have an implicit perceptual knowledge of cross-modal similarities and, second, that this knowledge parallels to a large extent the implicit verbal knowledge of cross-modal similarities that adults use in comprehending certain important kinds of metaphors.

Perceptual events in different sensory modalities can be linked by shared qualities or attributes. It is possible on the basis of shared qualities to translate the language of one kind of sensory experience into that of another. "There are," wrote Baudelaire in his sonnet on "Correspondences," "odors as fresh as children's skin/ As sweet as oboes, as green as prairies." The poet thereby proposed or defined an equivalence across smell, taste, and vision, as if freshness, sweetness, and greenness alike represent a single attribute common to the three modalities.

Another, more obvious, example of a common attribute is intensity, which reveals itself as loudness in sound and as brightness in light. Contrast Browning's "quiet-coloured end of evening" ("Love Among the Ruins") with Swinburne's "loud light of thunder" ("Birthday Ode"): The metaphorical differences between the two expressions rely almost explicitly on the connections between dim and soft in the former, and between bright and loud in the latter, as if the visual and auditory dimensions of intensity in both are aligned in strict correspondence.

SYNESTHETIC METAPHOR AND SYNESTHETIC PERCEPTION

Marks (1975, 1978) has shown that many such synesthetic metaphors – especially those found in French and English poetry – actually rest on just a few cross-modal resemblances found in synesthetic perception, and that these very same cross-modal resemblances are special, in that they are general properties of perceptual responses, they are essentially universal, and they may be innately given. Rather than repeat the arguments in detail, we highlight three salient points.

First, a small portion of the population actually perceives the world synesthetically: There are people for whom stimulation of one modality, say hearing, produces not only the usual auditory qualities, such as pitch and vowel quality or timbre, but also some kinds of secondary qualities or images typically deemed appropriate to another modality, such as color or shape. A significant point for the present argument is that there are several universal dimensions to synesthetic perception. Notable within the realm of visual–auditory synesthesia are cross-modal translations by means of common intensity (as we have noted), by means of common brightness, by means of common volume, and by means of common spatial and temporal aspects of perceptual experience. To a synesthetic individual, sounds may produce visual images that follow the sounds in space, that follow the sounds in temporal patterns, and that wax and wane in brightness and size as pitch and loudness shift. These cross-modal relations are virtually sine qua non to synesthesia.

Second, synesthetic sensitivities generally have an early origin, and are found more often among children than adults in the normal population. Moreover, most synesthetic adults report having been synesthetic since childhood.

Third, and perhaps most important, nonsynesthetic perceivers readily display the same connections or equivalences between sense modalities that synesthetic perceivers "naturally" make in their phenomenal experience. That is, nearly everyone (adults, older children, and even relatively young children) reliably matches dim lights to soft and low-pitched sounds and bright lights to loud and high-pitched sounds, just as synesthetics perceive soft, low-pitched sounds to be dim, and loud, high-pitched sounds to be bright. Adults and older children match larger-sized objects to low-pitched sounds and smaller objects to high-pitched sounds. Those who are not synesthetic may not be able to perceive as synesthetics perceive, but nonetheless they readily assent to the "appropriateness" of these cross-modal, synesthetic associations.

The recognition of sensory similarities, we believe, bears directly on the comprehension of sensory metaphors. We suspect that people can readily and uniformly interpret verbal expressions such as "the quiet-coloured end of evening," "the murmur of the gray twilight" (Edgar Allen Poe, "Al Aaraaf"), "Sunlight above him/ Roars like a vast invisible sea" (Conrad Aiken, "The Divine Pilgrim. III. The House of Dust") and "loud light of thunder" because people naturally perceive normative sensory equivalences between softness and dimness, and between loudness and brightness. In semantic memory, a "murmur" is coded as prototypically soft, and "twilight" is coded as prototypically dim; in addition, the synesthetic undercurrent to perception draws an equivalence between soft and dim, thereby equating "murmur" and "twilight." Indeed, in the four metaphors we have just quoted, the levels of both loudness and brightness are at least roughly specified within the text themselves. So it is not even necessary for a reader or a listener to compute equivalence levels between modalities to interpret expressions like "the murmur of the gray twilight"; it suffices merely to acknowledge that soft sounds (murmurs) are akin to dim illuminations (twilights).

Other metaphors do require active calculation on the part of the reader or listener. It is instructive to note that, with respect to loudness, at least, "the sound of coming darkness" is judged virtually identically to "the murmur of the gray twilight" (Marks, 1982b). While the latter metaphor defines the sound level literally—as a murmur—the former defines it only metaphorically—as a sound whose softness comes through analogy with coming darkness. Despite rhetorical and psychological differences between these two metaphors, an identical cross-modal relationship underlies their interpretations. And in both cases, the relationship is normative: The sound of coming darkness is intrinsically soft, just as gray twilight may murmur but does not scream.

Origins of Synesthetic Metaphors

If synesthetic metaphors appeal to normative cross-modal relations that emerge from sensory processing, it should be possible to show their functioning or operation in children of a very young age. Our own findings with 4- to 13-year-old children (Marks et al., in press) suggest that there are equivalences between brightness and loudness, and between brightness and pitch, at least in children as young as 4 years of age (the youngest so far tested). We have found that young children reliably match the louder of two tones and the higher-pitched of two tones to the brighter of two lights. However, we have also found that young children do not reliably associate the higher-pitched of two sounds with the smaller of two objects: Recognition of the metaphoric similarity between pitch and size does not appear until about 11 years of age. (Our overall findings are tabulated in Table 1.) Gardner (1974) reported findings that are related: Children as young as 3.5 years of age evidenced some understanding of cross-modal metaphors. Clearly, some synesthetic metaphors are present in early childhood and seem not to require much experience in developing, whereas others emerge later and may be based on experience.

To answer the question of how much, or how little, experience is necessary, we have to turn to studies of infancy. In one such study of synesthetic connection, Wagner, Winner, Cicchetti, and Gardner (1981) found that 1-year-old infants "matched" visual and auditory stimuli on the basis of direction (upward pointing arrow matching ascending tone; downward pointing arrow, descending tone). In another intriguing study, Lewkowicz and Turkewitz (1980) presented data indicating absolute equivalence between loudness and brightness in

TABLE 1

Percentages of Children and Adults Who Matched Visual and Auditory Stimuli in the "Normative" Manner (Defined as the Rule Used by a Majority of Adults)

Age (years)	Pitch–Brightness low-dim high-bright	Loudness–Brightness soft-dim loud-bright	Pitch–Size low-large high-small
4-5	88% (N = 51)	76% (N = 50)	
6-7	97% (N = 63)	74% (N = 65)	
8-9	100% (N = 35)	91% (N = 32)	53% (N = 32)
10-11	98% (N = 51)	94% (N = 33)	78% (N = 27)
13			91% (N = 33)
Adult	100% (N = 16)	100% (N = 16)	90% (N = 50)

infants as young as 3 weeks of age. When shown a stimulus such as a light, infants respond in several ways, one of which is with a change in their heart rate. Repeated presentation of a light of fixed luminance, however, leads to habituation; that is, eventually, the changes in heart rate are minimal. Lewkowicz and Turkewitz brought groups of babies to the point where the babies showed minimal change in heart rate to repeated visual stimulation, at which time the experimenters played sounds of various intensity levels to the different groups. Most new sounds naturally provoke a change in the babies' heart rate, just as the first presentation of the light changed heart rate. But, after habituation to the light, one particular sound level yielded minimum change in heart rate. Lewkowicz and Turkewitz interpreted this level as having a loudness most similar to the brightness of the repeated light. Especially important was the finding that the matching values of loudness and brightness for infants agreed well with adults' cross-modal matches between loudness and brightness.

If we are willing to treat cross-modal equivalences in perception, of the sort uncovered by Lewkowicz and Turkewitz, as examples of metaphors, then it is clear that some synesthetic metaphors are present very early in life, and require little or no experience to develop. But how could human infants as young as 3 weeks postpartum accomplish such seemingly sophisticated intermodality matching?

Neurophysiological Substrates for Synesthetic Metaphors

One interpretation of these findings – that cross-modal equivalences are appreciated by young children, even by infants – is that a handful of cross-modal connections are "built into" our sensory systems, perhaps by dint of some common modes of neural coding or by the sensitivities of single cells to information arriving via different modalities. This seems to us at least plausible. For example, brightness is presumably coded in the visual system by the tonal magnitude of the neural response within a particular subset of visual neurons, that is, in terms of the number of active neurons and their average rate of discharge (for a discussion of neural coding, see Uttal, 1973). Just the same kind of neural pattern is likely to be used by the auditory system to code loudness. Hence we have the ground for a direct correspondence of perceived intensity, the basis being an equivalent neural response or a common neural code.

At least in part, the code for sensory intensity is temporal in nature: The rate of discharge of a nerve cell is, by definition, the average number of impulses per unit time. In the auditory system, at all but very high sound frequencies, neurons respond to pure tones with a pattern of discharges whose interpulse intervals are even multiples of the reciprocal of frequency. For example, a 200-Hz tone at a sufficiently high sound pressure level may virtually "follow" the temporal waveform of the sine wave stimulus, producing 200 impulses per second – one impulse every 5 milliseconds. At lower sound intensity levels, however, some of these impulses drop out, so that, while many impulses come at intervals of 5 milliseconds, sometimes 10 or 15 or 20 milliseconds will separate successive impulses, and thus the overall response shows fewer than 200 impulses per second (e.g., Rose, Brugge, Anderson, & Hind, 1967). In this manner, while the pattern of neural discharge maintains some of the temporal characteristics of the stimulus frequency, the pattern also reveals a correspondence between stimulus intensity and the average response rate. In short, the auditory nerve can use time to code both loudness and pitch (see Moore, 1982; Uttal, 1973). For this reason, auditory pitch as well as loudness should bear a resemblance to visual brightness, and both do. The coding model accounts nicely for this instance of multiple perceptual parallelism between the senses (see Karwoski, Odbert, & Osgood, 1942): One dimension on a given modality (here, brightness) may in this way align itself synesthetically with more than one dimension in another modality (here, loudness and pitch).

Perhaps other aspects or qualities of perceptual experience have neural codes that behave in this fashion – codes that function at the physiological level in ways that parallel their functioning at the perceptual level. Opponent-process cells or networks, which are well known in sensory systems such as the visual (DeValois & DeValois, 1975) and which can provide both discrete and graded information, may serve as a general mechanism for perception and perceptual metaphors. Opponent-process cells have the particular virtue of being able to provide both continuous (graded) and categorical (discrete) information. Consider, in the visual system, an ideal opponent-process cell that codes the colors green and red. When the eye sits in darkness, or is adapted to a light of neutral color, the cell fires at its steady, baseline rate, indicating neither green nor red. Lights that appear green cause this particular cell to increase its firing rate, whereas lights that appear red cause a decrease. Thus the direction of change provides a single, discrete bit of categorical information. Moreover, the magnitude of the change in firing rate correlates with how green-appearing or how red-appearing the light is. Thus the overall change in activity provides graded, continuous information.

Might opponent-process mechanisms provide a general model for the neural activity that underlies perception? Green-vs.-red, yellow-vs.-blue, dim-vs.-bright, peaked-vs.-rounded, soft-vs.-loud, high pitched-vs.-low pitched – all of these and other sensory dichotomies, as well as their semantic representations, could rely on opponent-process mechanisms. Might opponent mechanisms provide a code for "distinctive features," whose contrasts, positive and negative, could serve as the labels (vehicles and tenors) that are made equivalent in perceptual metaphors? According to such a view, some semantic features are stored in memory in terms of positive and negative poles of opponent processes, so that sensory terms with corresponding polar values (for instance, positive values for high pitch, loud, and bright) would be semantically as well as perceptually equivalent.

Are there other neural mechanisms that could mediate cross-modal similarities, especially similarities in the spatial and temporal properties of percepts? Wilson (1965) has pointed out two classes of relevant mechanism that may subserve cross-modal transfer. First, it is known that some cortical neurons are polysensory; that is, they respond in similar ways to specific inputs from more than a single sense modality. Second, it is known that information from modality-specific cortical projection regions is integrated at particular cerebral association areas; cortical damage in these areas results in deficits in cross-modal perception. In short, there are several types of mechanism identifiable in the central nervous system that could subserve cross-modal similarity, and, insofar as they may be "wired" innately to do so, would enable the young infant to match across modalities, in the absence of learning or experience.

Let us summarize: It seems that many cross-modal similarities rely on neural mechanisms found in primary sensory cortex or sensory association cortex. It also seems that mechanisms operating in primary and secondary sensory areas are largely innate or established very early in life. Given both of these, we should not be surprised to find that the perception of cross-modal similarities is virtually universal and evident in childhood, even in infancy. That young children not only perceive cross-modal similarities but can respond to their verbal equivalents implies further that a sensorineurally based, perceptual knowledge readily makes itself available to the abstract structures of language. This perceptual knowledge reveals itself in "preformed" synesthetic metaphors.

SYNESTHETIC METONYMIES

Not all synesthetic metaphors have this preformational character. Nor are all normative. And even when metaphors do rely on normative relations, they need not have an innate or intrinsic basis. A metonymy is a relationship based on association rather than on equivalence (see Wellek & Warren, 1956); most metonymies are probably learned. As we shall see, some synesthetic metaphors are perhaps better characterized as metonymies.

We have found that comprehension of pitch–size metaphors, unlike the comprehension of loudness–brightness and pitch–brightness metaphors, does not rely on an intrinsic perceptual similarity (Marks et al., in press). That is, young children do not demonstrate any uniform understanding of pitch–size metaphors, nor do young children normatively match small-sized objects with high-pitched sounds and larger sizes with lower sounds, as adults do (see Table 1). Only around age 11 years do we find evidence for the reliable recognition of pitch-size similarity. By contrast, with loudness–brightness and pitch–brightness similarities we have found both verbal and perceptual recognition to be evident in children at least as young as 4–6 years.

It seems likely, as Osgood, Suci, and Tannenbaum (1957), Brown (1958), and others have suggested, that people learn to associate larger objects with lower sound frequencies, and smaller objects with higher frequencies, perhaps through the natural resonance properties of actual objects. Other things being equal, the larger an object, the lower its resonance frequency and thus the lower the pitch. Large objects thud, while small ones ping; and adults have voices with pitches generally lower than the voices of children. When Wallace Stevens wrote (in "Parochial Theme") of "sounds blown by a blower into shapes,/ The blower squeezed to the thinnest 'mi' of falsetto," he produced a synesthetic figure of speech that is normative, but one probably based on a learned norm, an experienced association. In other words, a metonymy.

By far the best known of all synesthetic metonymies are the warm and cool colors: Reds, oranges, and yellows are warm; blues and greens are cool. Why do these relationships obtain? Wavelengths that are the physical correlates of perceptible hues do not themselves usually provoke thermal sensations. As widespread and generally acknowledged as these connections are, it is notable that young children have little systematic or reliable conception of them. These "norms" are not usually established or accepted until adolescence (Morgan, Goodson, & Jones, 1975). But there is one exception; we have observed that some young children are explicitly taught – in art classes, for instance – which colors are warm, and which are cool. Of course, this means that even the connections between color and temperature can be established earlier in life than they usually are; however, we suspect that they may still have a lower age bound. Unlike the sensory synesthetic similarities between loudness and brightness and between pitch and brightness, color–temperature connections are most probably learned; even so, the comprehension of color–temperature connections may nonetheless be widespread, probably because the associations they reflect represent universal experiences: with fire and flames, with the warmth of the sun, the cool lakes and rivers, and so forth. Throughout the world, the sun appears yellow, whereas oceans and other large bodies of water appear blue and green, and these associations transcend specific cultures (see Osgood, May, & Miron, 1974).

Metonymically, it is not at all surprising to find black, the color of nighttime, closely associated with coolness or cold; Shelley (in "Alastor") noted:

When the heaven remained
Utterly black, the murky shades involved
An image, silent, cold, and motionless.

The relative cold of night contrasts with the warmth of day, the one marked by pale white moonbeams, the other by deeper golden rays of the sun, or as Swinburne (in "The Masque of Queen Bersabe") wrote:

The sun thou madest of good gold,
Of clean silver the moon cold.

These are metonymies, plain and simple. And they are metonymies, we argue, because the sensory pairings are informed by associations experienced between certain events. Metonymy, like metaphor, is first and foremost a psychological concept: Synesthetic metaphors and metonymies alike rely on relationships determined by the percipient organism, in the one case being innately given and in the other learned. Moreover, both the metaphors and metonymies usually obey normative rules, though this is not universally true.

METAPHORS AND NORMS

The range of metaphors is rich and varied. The norms of perceptual synesthesia are, by comparison, impoverished and limited, a bare-bones structure that can hardly support even a small range of cross-modal metaphors. A goodly number of verbal metaphors cannot be reduced to implicit sensory norms. This is true even for synesthetic metaphors.

Consider Kipling's "dawn comes up like thunder" (in "Mandalay"). Not all dawns come up like thunder. Presumably, Kipling aimed at suggesting a particular kind of Oriental sunrise, specifically, one at Mandalay. Kipling, unfortunately, never reached Burma itself, and thus never saw the sun rise up "outer China 'crost the Bay"; but surely he had many times seen Aurora's sun hurled up in the East, and we conjecture that—assuming he was not merely engaging in verbal exercise—Kipling sought to indicate the rich, rapid display of deep color and growing luminous intensity. Dawn does not reach especially high on the scale of brightness. Thunder, on the other hand, is loud. When the "dawn comes up like thunder," the metaphor takes disparate values of intensity from the visual and auditory realms and puts them together in a new way—a way that changes both. The dawn that comes up like thunder is judged brighter than plain dawn, whereas its thunder is less loud than plain thunder (Marks, 1982a). There is a mutual attraction, an assimilation, between members of a metaphorical equation, in this instance augmenting one and diminishing the other. Although Kipling's metaphor qua metaphor does not use a normative relation, readers or listeners who interpret the metaphor do.

This is one way by which synesthetic metaphors can far transcend cross-modal norms, even as metaphor can far transcend synesthetic similarity. Metaphors need not rely exclusively on cross-modally equivalent levels. Still, it may well be that within the realm of intrinsic resemblances amongst the senses there resides a core that can tell us much about figurative language in its many aspects—though undoubtedly not in all aspects, for it is unlikely that metaphor is one kind of "thing," and therefore unlikely that metaphor has a unitary core.

IMPLICATIONS FOR A DEVELOPMENTAL
THEORY OF SYNESTHETIC METAPHOR AND METONYMY

Metaphors and Metonymies as Discovered

In comparing synesthetic metaphors and synesthetic metonymies, we have suggested that synesthetic metaphors are based on normative, and probably congenital or even innate, perceptual similarities, in that they probably rest on innate neurophysiological substrates. By contrast, metonymies seem to reflect our experiences in the world; nevertheless, to the extent that the experiences are universal, metonymies too will be normative. Presumably these too have neural substrates, but substrates that become organized through experience.

This central difference between synesthetic metaphors and metonymies suggests to us that although both the metaphors and metonymies may be "discovered" rather than "created" by perceivers, the nature of the "discovery" in the two cases is rather different. In the case of synesthetic metonymies, such as pitch–size and color–temperature, the perceiver discovers something about contingencies in the world. In the case of synesthetic metaphors, however, the perceiver discovers something not about relationships between physical objects or events, but instead about phenomenological – or psychophysical – experience, and, therefore, in an indirect, a priori manner, something about his or her own nervous system. Similarities given by the nervous system are available to be discovered (unlike linguistically based metaphors, which, reversing the logical order, are created – and thereby established in the nervous system). These intrinsic, sensory similarities are "created," to be sure, in the sense that – as all behavior is created – they are contingent upon the particular structure and function of the nervous system; but, given the interaction of the nervous system and the world, the similarities become available to discovery.

The two kinds of connection – metaphor and metonymy – also imply differences in developmental timetables. Insofar as synesthetic metaphor presumably reflects the intrinsic functioning of the nervous system and metonomy reflects the role of experience, synesthetic metaphor ought to antedate metonomy ontogenetically. Our data (Table 1), along with those of others, support the view that these two types of cross-modal relation differ indeed in developmental appearance.

What Cognitive Skills Does the Metaphorical Infant Require?

The mapping of similars entails a small series of requisites. It is necessary first, to establish order among elements; second, in the case of continua such as brightness and loudness, to establish gradation of the elements; and, third, to establish polarity or directionality ("which end is up"). Order, gradation, and polarity together make it possible for the perceiver to observe that one modality's Stimulus

A is more like another modality's Stimulus *a* than it is like Stimulus *b*. Thus, the acquisition of order, gradation, and polarity is of prime developmental significance. How does the infant or young child come to acquire these requisite features of metaphoric mapping?

Three schools of thought compete to explain the origins of sensory comparison and integration early in life. An empiricist position maintains that resemblances are acquired through the child's experience in the environment. Piaget (1952), for example, argued that infants first perceive stimuli as meaningless patterns of sensation, then gradually differentiate the sensations and finally integrate and align them; thus only beyond the second half of the first year of life do infants recognize associations between particular sounds and particular visual patterns. Bower (1982) argued an alternative nativist position, describing the senses as coordinated at birth, with perception even in the newborn being integrated over multimodal features. In infancy, according to the nativist account, visual events automatically imply auditory components, and auditory events, visual ones. A third view, proposed by Gibson (1979), transports to infancy the notion that perception involves detection of invariances; Gibson argued that infants directly perceive intermodal relations between, say, visual and acoustic sources of information that specify a single event. Insofar as stimulus invariance is concerned, this theory specifies that infants, even newborns, will actually perceive bimodal events as unitary. The availability in early infancy of cross-modal similarities based on common information (spatial and temporal features) is compatible with the stances of both Bower and Gibson. The more metaphorical similarities, however, such as that between loudness and brightness, imply a causal theory of perception – a Lockean theory of secondary qualities – less compatible with Gibson's view (see Marks, 1978, Ch. 2).

Synesthesia as a Model for Metaphor

We have discussed the probable developmental priority of synesthetic metaphors over metonymies and the probable foundations of synesthetic metaphors in neurophysiological functioning. If synesthetic metaphors have their basis in inborn neural mechanisms, then those mechanisms could automatically supply some requisite steps in metaphorical matching. In the example of loudness and brightness, neural mechanisms in two sensory systems, vision and audition, provide both polarity and gradation. Furthermore, equivalent processing of sensory information in different modalities implies that the underlying neural equivalence provides normative rules for mapping the polarities of attributes from one modality to another.

On the basis of these conclusions, we argue that synesthetic equivalences themselves provide a starting point for transforming the infant into the mature, metaphorical adult. The ability to assess similarity is, we believe, essential to the comprehension and creation of metaphor (cf. Miller, 1979). In the progression from mute infancy to loquacious childhood, as the scope of metaphor both broadens and deepens, perceptual equivalences are made available to language; that is, some linguistic labels map onto preformed sensory equivalences. This view tends to resolve the nature–nurture question for synesthetic metaphors in terms of nature, but it leaves open the question of whether metonymies are verbal structures overlaid on pre-existing nonlinguistic correspondences or, alternatively, whether verbal correspondences are learned and responded to in and for themselves. Following either process to its conclusion represents a major step of childhood; that is, to develop from fully analogue, isomorphic structures to adaptable, abstract, verbal ones implies an enormous developmental stride.

We note that mapping in this sense is metaphoric in and of itself. Innate perceptual similarities based on equivalences in the activity of neural mechanisms may provide an initial framework, but further "figurative extension" must represent a metaphorical élan whose model is itself the original similarity. This succession exemplifies the extraordinary case where the second term of a metaphoric equivalence is itself a metaphorical extension of the first term.

The implications of this deduction bear some significance. Once children know that they can map one (sensory) opponent process onto another, they presumably can extend the process to nonsensory categories, rendering such information bipolar and, where appropriate, graded. Physiological mechanisms of the same sort that subserve sensory dichotomies can also mediate more abstract semantic features, to which the properties of order, gradation, and polarity may also apply. Polarity has special import, for it is conceivable that a nonsensory feature can be represented by two opponent processes, with reversed polarities (one +/−, the other −/+). The availability of polarities in both directions would make it possible for the person, child or adult, to manipulate the feature's direction – either pole could be "up" or "down" – and thereby construct an original metaphor. Discovering or constructing or creating analogies, transferring elements or relationships from one domain to another, naturally follows suit. Of course, how children come to be able to do this remains a question.

Metonymies follow metaphors, which in turn follow synesthetic polarities; tracing this regression back to its logical beginnings, we construe the comprehension and construction of metaphor – the genus of metaphor – to rely ultimately on neurophysiological equivalence. That is, the origin of similarity-as-created lies in similarity-as-discovered. We have in this way arrived at a view of metaphor that sees its beginnings in sensory similarities: similarities that are based on intrinsic and primitive neural processes; similarities that are fixed and determined as regards order, direction, and polarity; similarities that spawn other associative equivalences, many of which, even in childhood, are based on experience and are considerably more abstract and flexible than their progenitors.

CONCLUSIONS

As mental activity, the attribution of similarity serves many purposes. Because we and the world that we inhabit are in constant flux, by perceiving similarity or treating different entities as similar we reduce variation and increase order and coherence. Further, similarity enhances memory by facilitating our recognition of new information. Finally, perceiving similarity is incipient information processing. In short, similarity is a primary psychological phenomenon.

There are many modes and expressions of similarity, from those entities that are given as perceptually identical to those whose equivalence is learned and wholly ad hoc. Among the former are sensory similarities; these occupy a position of primacy, first, because infants and very young children are capable of recognizing them, and, second, because many have identifiable, hard-wired neurophysiological substrates.

Among various sensory similarities, we have focused on one class, namely cross-modal similarity. Cross-modal similarities are of special interest because they come in two distinctive types. Some similarities, such as that between brightness and loudness, appear early in development and perhaps are innate; these give rise to synesthetic metaphors. Other similarities, such as that between color and temperature, seem to develop later and to be based in experience; these give rise to synesthetic metonymies. Despite the differences between them, synesthetic metaphors and metonymies together share several characteristics; for instance, most seem better characterized as "discovered" than as "created."

But perhaps most importantly of all, synesthetic metaphor provides a developmental starting point: The processes that underlie our understanding of synesthetic metaphors may contribute to our achieving higher conceptual and linguistic forms of metaphor. On this account, the structures of synesthetic metaphors that are shown to be present in the earliest months after birth would constitute *Anlagen*, or primitive forms, for the plethora of more sophisticated, figurative expressions we commonly encounter and create in language and literature.

REFERENCES

Bornstein, M. H. (1984). A descriptive taxonomy of psychological categories used by infants. In C. Sophian (Ed.), *Origins of cognitive skills.* Hillsdale, NJ: Erlbaum.

Bornstein, M. H., Gross, C. G., & Wolf, J. Z. (1978). Perceptual similarity of mirror images in infancy. *Cognition, 6,* 89–116.

Bornstein, M. H., Kessen, W., & Weiskopf, S. (1976). Color vision and hue categorization in young human infants. *Journal of Experimental Psychology: Human Perception and Performance, 2,* 115–129.

Bower, T. G. R. (1982). *Development in infancy.* San Francisco: Freeman.

Brown, R. (1958). *Words and things.* New York: The Free Press.

Day, R., & McKenzie, B. E. (1977). Constancies in the perceptual world of the infant. In W. Epstein (Ed.), *Stability and constancy in visual perception: Mechanisms and processes.* New York: Wiley.

DeLoache, J. S., Strauss, M. S., & Maynard, J. (1979). Picture perception in infancy. *Infant Behavior and Development, 2,* 77–89.

DeValois, R. L., & DeValois, K. K. (1975). Neural coding of color. In E. C. Carterette & M. P. Friedman (Eds.), *Handbook of perception* (Vol 5). New York: Academic Press.

Dirks, J., & Gibson, E. J. (1977). Infants' perception of similarity between live people and their photographs. *Child Development, 48,* 124–130.

Gardner, H. (1974). Metaphors and modalities: How children project polar adjectives onto diverse domains. *Child Development, 45,* 84–91.

Gibson, J. J. (1979). *The ecological approach to visual perception.* Boston: Houghton Mifflin.

Gottfried, A. W., Rose, S. A., & Bridger, W. H. (1977). Cross-modal transfer in human infants. *Child Development, 48,* 118–123.

Gross, C. G., & Mishkin, M. (1977). The neural basis of stimulus equivalence across retinal translation. In S. Harnad (Ed.), *Lateralization in the nervous system.* New York: Academic Press.

Karwoski, T. F., Odbert, H. S., & Osgood, C. E. (1942). Studies in synesthetic thinking. II. The role of form in visual responses to music. *Journal of General Psychology, 26,* 199–222.

Köhler, W. (1979). *Gestalt psychology.* New York: Liveright.

Lewkowicz, D. J., & Turkewitz, G. (1980). Cross-modal equivalence in early infancy: Auditory-visual intensity matching. *Developmental Psychology, 16,* 597–607.

Marks, L. E. (1975). On colored-hearing synesthesia: Cross-modal translations of sensory dimensions. *Psychological Bulletin, 82,* 303–331.

Marks, L. E. (1978). *The unity of the senses: Interrelations among the modalities.* New York: Academic Press.

Marks, L. E. (1982a). Bright sneezes and dark coughs, loud sunlight and soft moonlight. *Journal of Experimental Psychology: Human Perception and Performance, 8,* 177–193.

Marks, L. E. (1982b). Synesthetic perception and poetic metaphor. *Journal of Experimental Psychology: Human Perception and Performance, 8,* 15–23.

Marks, L. E., Hammeal, R. J., & Bornstein, M. H. (in press). Children's comprehension of cross-modal similarity: Metaphor and perception. *Monographs of the Society for Research in Child Development.*

Miller, G. A. (1979). Images and models, similies and metaphors. In A. Ortony (Ed.), *Metaphor and thought.* Cambridge: Cambridge University Press.

Moore, B. (1982). *An introduction to the psychology of hearing.* New York: Academic Press.

Morgan, G. A., Goodson, F. E., & Jones, T. (1975). Age differences in the associations between felt temperatures and color choices. *American Journal of Psychology, 88,* 125–130.

Osgood, C. E., May, W. H., & Miron, M. S. (1974). *Cross-cultural universals of affective meaning.* Urbana, IL: University of Illinois Press.

Osgood, C. E., Suci, G. J., & Tannenbaum, P. M. (1957). *The measurement of meaning.* Urbana, IL: University of Illinois Press.

Piaget, J. (1952). *The origins of intelligence in children.* New York: International Universities Press.

Rose, J. E., Brugge, J. F., Anderson, D. J., & Hind, J. E. (1967). Phase-locked response to low-frequency tones in single auditory nerve fibers of the squirrel monkey. *Journal of Neurophysiology, 30,* 769–793.

Rose, S. A. (1977). Infant's transfer of response between two-dimensional and three-dimensional stimuli. *Child Development, 48,* 1086–1091.

Rose, S. A., Gottfried, A. W., & Bridger, W. H. (1981). Cross-modal transfer in 6-month-old infants. *Development Psychology, 17,* 661–669.

Uttal, W. (1973). *The psychobiology of sensory coding.* New York: Harper & Row.

Wagner, S., Winner, E., Cicchetti, D., & Gardner, H. (1981). "Metaphorical" mapping in human infants. *Child Development, 52,* 728–731.

Wellek, R., & Warren, A. (1956). *Theory of literature.* New York: Harcourt.

Wilson, W. A. (1965). Intersensory transfer in normal and brain-operated monkeys. *Neuropsychologia, 3,* 363–370.

CHAPTER FOUR

Giambattista Vico and the Discovery of Metaphoric Cognition

Robert E. Haskell
University of New England

In 1725, or thereabout, Giambattista Vico (1668–1744), the Italian philosopher and rhetorician, discovered the cognitive function of metaphor. He set forth his views in what he called his *New Science* (1948). Of course, metaphor as-a-figure-of-speech was known long before Vico, but not metaphor as a fundamental cognitive operation. What is more, he discovered it without significant antecedent. It is not often in the history of science or of philosophy that one can trace the first historical conceptual moment in the birth of a discovery. Certainly such is not the case with Darwin's theory of evolution, nor with the Copernican theory of the sun centered universe, nor with Freud's discovery of the unconscious.

The translators of Vico's abridged *New Science* call it "one of the few works of original genius in the entire history of social theory. (p. xiii). While the *New Science* is in fact a social history and theory, its entire edifice is made possible by his cognitive theory of metaphor. As Vico and his translators point out, it is Book Two, what Vico calls "Poetic Wisdom," which is the foundation for his social theory. More importantly, it is the tour de force for his cognitive theory of metaphor. Whatever else Vico may have been–philosopher, social theorist, rhetorician, professor of eloquence–he was most certainly one of the first cognitive psychologists.

In this chapter, I will confine myself to Vico's cognitive concept of metaphor per se, and not to his social transformations which give issue to his developmental social theory. I shall also limit myself to pointing out his general principles, and not burden the reader with the details of his discovery. The latter have been explicated clearly by Vico himself, as well as by others (Verene, 1976; White, 1973, 1976). In addition, I will introduce some of my own empirical data that seems to confirm Vico's theory of metaphor. Finally, I will suggest a view of

Vico's writing that has implications for a new epistemology and consequences for a new area of research for cognitive psychology.

I should mention here that, while portions of this chapter were presented at the International Vico-Venezia Conference held in Venice, Italy in 1978, I make no pretense at being a Vichian scholar. I am simply interested in metaphor and cognition, and consider it important for Vico to become more widely recognized. Vico's theory of metaphor is not widely known in metaphor research. Hence the reason for this chapter.

Vichian Metaphor: The Master Trope

Metaphor is still considered by many to be simply a figure of speech, as a simple linguistic comparison. Such is the legacy to modern times bequethed by the Greek philosopher Aristotle (see Cooper, 1960). In Vico's time, as well as our own, the prevailing epistemological Zietgeist was that of Aristotelian and Cartesian theories of "cognition," which hold that *categorical, clear and distinct ideas* are at the basis, and are the only valid mode, of cognition and knowledge (Verene, 1976). Only *logically precise* methods, leading to *necessary relations*, are significant indicators of the true and rational.

Unlike Aristotle and Descartes, however, Vico was not primarily a man of the logical, but of the rhetorical; not a man of the syllogism, but of the enthymeme; not a man of the necessary, but of the probable; not a man of grammar, but of speech. The significance of these differences speak to cardinal issues in the psychology of language. The Aristotelian "intelligible" or rational concept, the Cartesian clear and distinct idea, and indeed the very rules of logic and grammar by which they are expressed, says Vico, are merely abstracted and reified products of a more primary metaphorical process of cognition, that of a developmentally earlier mode of "poetic cognition."

To develop this theory of metaphoric cognition, Vico had to perform a virtual autopsy on an entire epistemological body. What he found was that rigor mortis had set in. In Vichian epistemology, metaphor is fundamental and necessary to cognition. But it is not the Aristotelian, rationalized metaphor which is reduced to a mere linguistic figure of speech, a mere rhetorical trope; rather it is a primary psycho-somato-sensory process of cognition generating the entire edifice of language and thought.

It should be noted, too, that Vico's theory is not idle philosophical speculation. It is grounded in an empirical data base. His data were the ancient fables, myths, and homeric epic poetry of early history. His method was the linguistic analysis of that vast body of data. He saw in that data a series of cognitive, structural, and linguistic transformations extending through time, the assumption being that the developmental changes he observed in the surface linguistic processes of that body of data were indices of changing psychological functions. It was a method not too different from that of many behavioral scientists and linguists today in their analysis of verbal protocols (Foulkes, 1978), and not so different at all from the work of hermeneuticists (Palmer, 1969; Ricoeur, 1977), structural anthropologists (Levi-Strauss, 1963), and others (Jaynes, 1976; Snell, 1960).

According to Vico (1948, pp. 87–91), all tropes can be reduced to four: metaphor, metonymy, synecdoche, and irony, with metaphor being the master trope. All the tropes, says Vico, are corollaries of a poetic logic, and, as White (1976) points out, they are "mental operations," not rationalized rhetorical figures of speech. Moreover, the tropes, for Vico, serve as models for demonstrating the transformations of consciousness. The tropes *represent* a set of logico-cognitive operations existing in that time before logic. Poetic logic is a nonconscious set of cognitive operations which only later became abstracted into what we now understand as logic.

Through a structural and transformational analysis of the language of fables, myths, and epic poetry, Vico enters into the mind of what he metaphorically calls the "first men," to a time before the dawning of conscious rationalism. The journey to this time, however, is difficult, because as he says, "with our civilized natures we [moderns] cannot at all imagine and can understand only by great toil the poetic nature of these first men" (p. 5). This discovery that primitive men could *only* speak in "poetic sentences," and that the fables, myths, and allegories were the original and "true speech," cost him 20 years of research.

The "first men," he says, did not think with clear and distinct ideas; they had to learn the "power of ratiocination" (p. 74). They were primal poets. The precursors of modern logico-cognitive operations are to be found, he says, "hidden in the fables" (p. 6). Moreover, these first ideas and categories were "felt and imagined" (p. 74). Only "later as this imagination shrank and the powers of abstraction grew these vast imaginations were reduced to diminutive signs" (p. 86). First there was metaphor, not by analogy or similarity, but by identity. Original metaphor is based on identity not similarity relations; there is no differentiation of tenor and vehicle. Then, as abstraction developed, came metonymy, then synecdoche, as part standing for the whole, then irony. It is only in the development to irony that true consciousness arose. With irony, the separation of object and subject, the awareness of true difference and opposition, is represented.

Thus one can trace, in the progressive development of these tropes within the fables and myths, the slow differentiation of the "felt and imagined" to the abstraction of consciousness. This cognitive reduction was accomplished by a series of operations we now, but with a different understanding, call metaphor. The protoexemplar or model used by Vico to illustrate this transmutational process from the "felt and imagined" to the "clear and distinct" was the response of primitive men to the natural phenomenon of thunder.

In some distant and dim past, says Vico, groups of men huddled together and *identified* a sudden and loud clap of thunder as *anger*. Thus was created the first metaphor, what we now might call synesthetic or sensory metaphor. According to this Vichian big bang theory of metaphor, the affective identification by these first men, on the basis of tone volume, and power of the sudden clap of thunder with the human emotion *anger,* constitutes paradigmatically a demonstration of the primal transmutation of sensory experience into the abstraction of imagery and language. It is the origin of consciousness. In effect, thunder was the first word.

Verene (1976) recognized and cites a piece of anthropological data that could be considered evidently supportive of what I have above termed Vico's big bang theory of metaphor. Nance (1975), reporting on the Tasaday, a stone age tribe discovered in the Philippines in 1971, asked them, "What is the worst thing in the forest?" The "Big Word is the worst thing," they said. "We are afraid of it. Our ancestors were also afraid." According to the interpreter who was sensitive to the Tasaday's use of "metaphor," the Big Word was thunder.[1]

In like manner, that is, by successively abstract and transformative operations, e.g., identification of part for whole, were all the so-called rhetorical tropes, as indeed the phonetic, semantic, and syntactic parts of language, developed. "Our theory, says Vico, "gives us moreover, the order in which the parts of speech arose and, consequently, the natural causes of syntax" (p. 110). What Vico describes as metaphoric cognition reads very much like the processes found in dreaming. Sound or primitive phonetic relations like puns are significant. In addition, sentences are generated from an affective or sensory base or "sensory topics" leading to "poetic sentences" that are felt and based on imaginal processes.

Vico's Significance to Cognitive Psychology

Vico's significance in the history of cognitive psychology has not been recognized. The reason for this is that cognitive psychology has not as yet caught up with him. Only recently has cognitive psychology begun to research metaphor, affect, and imagery production, and the analysis of narrative forms (see Martindale, 1981; also Bruner, in Cordes, 1984). Vico was concerned with the structural and transformational relations among affect, imagery, and language. And his interest had a developmental perspective. More modern researchers, both philosophical and psychological, seem pertinent to Vico's work, among them Arieti (1976), Cassirer (1946), Jaynes (1976), Marks (1978), Piaget (1962), and Werner and Kaplan (1963).

The psychiatrist Arieti has suggested, as has others, that Vico's metaphoric or poetic cognition bears a distinct similarity to what Freudians have called "primary process," and Arieti has pointed out the similarity to his own work with schizophrenic language and logic, what he calls "paleologic" or "archaic

---

[1]Since these pages went to press, it has been suggested that the Tasaday Culture is a hoax; perpetuated by a Philippine official. I have elected to retain the reference as the validity of the informant's report is not out of line with similar historical anthropological reports of pre-literate people's anthropomorphizing of natural phenomena. In any event the *perception* of the informant reporting his reaction to thunder does not necessarily depend on the validity of a "Tasaday" Culture.

logic," a re-emergent form of archaic rationality. Mora (1976) has pointed out the similarity of Vico's work to the genetic epistemiology of Piaget, of the cognitive development from sensory motor and pre-operational to fully operational thought. If Vico's theory of a primitive, poetic logic is correct, then cognitive psychologists could profit from studying so-called anomolous data such as myths, poetry, and dream imagery, all of which bear a striking resemblance to Vico's "first language."

One would suspect, as in schizophrenic metaphors, that one would find other linguistic situations where "poetic logic" can be found, and Vico's theory confirmed. Since history, by definition, is lost in an unrecognizable past, empirical confirmation of hypotheses regarding that past is difficult. This is especially true for cognitive hypotheses regarding historical states of mind. A Vichian researcher, Berlin (1976) asks how the poetic logic works on which the *New Science* is based. Further, he asks, how does one enter or descend into the minds of these "first men"? This is an important question if Vico's theory of metaphor is to be confirmed. But it is a task which, as we have seen, Vico himself recognized is difficult, "because with our civilized natures we [moderns] cannot at all imagine and can understand only by great toil . . . (p. 5) the thought processes of these first men. I would like to now suggest that the opportunity for studying the cognitive processes of Vico's "first men" is possible. To further explicate Vico's theory of metaphor, data from my own research will be presented. In this way, I hope to bring Vico closer to the modern mind. In so doing, Vico's theory and data will not only be confirmed but will be extended.

THE VICHIAN LABORATORY

Vichian theory is not only concerned with individual cognition, but with the historical evolution of cognition, along with collective cognition. His schema for this historical evolution is a genetic schema of cyclic recapitulation. Just as ontogeny recapitulates phylogeny, it follows that modern man retains, on a different turn of the cycle, some of those same early cognitive processes of Vico's "first men." He already has suggested that poets are such an instance of this recapitulation. But poets are a peculiar instance, as are the schizophrenics of Arieti. If Vico's theory is valid, then I would suspect such instances from everyday discourse. According to Vico, in the cycle of history there are reversions to earlier more primitive states, revealing historically earlier modes of functioning.

The laboratory study of small group interaction may be considered an analogue of the "first men huddled together." If, as some have suggested (Slater, 1966), the developmental stages of the small group are a microcosm of social processes, then we may consider research into the small group as a Vichian laboratory in which to study, not just language processes, but what Vico termed "true speech." The ancients were more aware of the distinction between written language and "speech" (see Baldwin, 1959). The analysis of speech yields different information from written language. Merely reading a written report is not speech. Speech is spontaneously creative and not always grammatically correct. What Vico calls "true speech" is more "poetically" constructed. Speech is closer to inner thought and cognition than is written language, with meaning being more clearly tied to sensory processes, rhythm, tone, and sound. Spontaneous speech, or what linguists call *parole,* is thus more closely linked to inner psychological processes (see Edie, 1976; Gadamer, 1975; Ricoeur, 1970).

There is an ironic aspect to the fact that, when modern researchers analyze verbal protocols, they do so as if they were written language, neglecting the fact that they are oral documents. Too often, protocols are analyzed from an Aristotelian/Cartesian epistemology of clear and distinct ideas. One of the founding principles of the *New Science,* however, suggest a fundamentally different approach; namely, Vico's principle that "doctrines must take their beginnings from that of the matters of which they treat" (p. 49). Vico means by this principle that the methods used to study a subject must themselves be based on the characteristics of the subject matter the methods are to investigate. Thus a researcher does not study poetry with the methods of traditional linguistics, but rather with methods which themselves have the characteristics of poetic thought. This principle leads linguistic research into the "psycho"-linguistic and cognitive structure of verbal protocols, into the study of what Vico calls "poetic sentences" (p. 33), which are formed by feelings of passion and emotion, as opposed to "philosophic sentences," which are formed by reflection and reason. In modern rationalized terminology, the distinction made by Vico here is the distinction between figurative vs. literal sentences. It must be recalled that, for Vico's "first men," figurative language was the literal language. They were one and the same; only later, as these powers of abstraction grew, did the literal become clear and distinct.

The "poetic sentences" of the "first men," however, are not to be confused with the works of modern poets, for modern poets know they are speaking figuratively or poetically, whereas according to Vico the "first men" did not. Outside of poetry or of Arieti's archaic or paleo logic of schizophrenic language, then, is it possible to find the analogue of the "poetic sentences" of these "first men," which are uttered without the awareness of their poetic nature? If there is such an analogue, or if a cyclic recapitulation of this primal cognition exists, then there would exist the opportunity to study first hand Vico's theory. A Vichian laboratory.

According to the above principle that "doctrines must take their beginnings from that of the matters of which they treat," it would suggest that researchers apply a "poetic" methodology. Vico's principle brings to mind A. N. Whitehead's dictum that every science must create its own methods. With a specifically developed methodology (Haskell, 1978a, 1978b, 1982, 1984), I have been analyzing small group verbal reports "poetically."

Instances of "poetic" or "symbolic" speech have occasionally been observed and sporadically reported throughout some of the small group literature, but no theoretical framework has existed explaining the phenomena. Moreover, when such tropological discourse has been recognized, it has been only in the most general of terms. This Vichian tropological discourse is what in psychological terms I have called "analogic talk" and "analogic cognition," a process which has been overlooked in the field of cognitive psychology.

The Vichian account of the psychological conditions underlying the production of poetic sentences of these "first men" would, in modern psychological vernacular, be called a "hypnogogic state," not yet fully conscious. Thus, if the small group is to yield pertinent data as an analogue of this psychological state of the "first men," then it must simulate or replicate as closely as possible this first state of being. Such conditions are to be found in the classical style of conducting T-Groups.

Typically, the classic T-Group ("T" = training) conditions are unstructured, nondirective, and ambiguous; relative strangers find themselves in an uncertain and threatening situation. As a consequence, "imaginations" and affective feelings are intense with regard to the open-ended range of possible interactions, especially toward the trainer, who is typically perceived as a powerful and threatening authority figure. Perceptions, therefore, are only partially "rational"; mostly the situation is "felt and imagined."

Thus, there abound in Vichian terms what are called "sensory topics," i.e., affective concerns. These sensory topics become transmuted into the ostensibly literal group discourse. But how is it done? Consider the following pieces of discourse from the author's group training laboratory.

A newly formed group with no explicit structure, and unable to rationally cope, understand, and otherwise make sense out of the situation and out of a trainer who says nothing, is full of sensations. Every move others make, especially the authority, is "imagined" to be significant; every move and word is "felt," and thunders through the participants' being. One such group began to discuss "journalists." Out of a nearly infinite number of possible topics, why the topic of journalists? If asked, the group responds that they do not know why they are discussing journalists. It is no coincidence, however, that the trainer is sitting silently and *writing* notes on their behavior.

The group's affective concern (sensory topic) with the trainer writing about them is transmuted into the ostensibly rational-literal (philosophic) discourse about authorities who write about people, i.e., journalists. The discourse on journalists, then, is a "metaphor," a tropological transformation of their sensory concerns, just as thunder was transmuted into the feeling of anger. During the course of the talk, all of the here-and-now aspects of this sensory topic are transmuted into the various felt elements of the subject. The discourse is indeed "fabulous speech."

The above example of tropological discourse is not anomalous. A group affectively concerned with having *two trainers* instead of one "just happened" to begin talking about *identical twins*. This transformational talk was so detailed in its various aspects and isomorphic to the concrete here-and-now sensory topics that it was clear which twin in the discourse analogically (poetically) corresponded to which trainer. In a similar co-trainer situation, the trainers were tropologically transformed into discourse about "pilots and co-pilots."

Words spoken by any significant Other thunders tropologically through the group's ears. Just as the first men *identified*, on the basis of similarity relations, the thunder in the sky as the Big Word eminating from a great animated body, in like manner, after a trainer intervenes with what is perceived to be a *deep psychological analysis* of the group behavior, the topic to be *selected-in* may be about *skin diving* or the *exploration of caves*. In the initial stages of a group, where members are concerned about what is perceived to be an anomic and therefore threatening situation, the discourse may be about *traffic problems* and the *need for rules to regulate the traffic flow* (i.e., need for rules to guide group interaction). After a silence following a discussion of competition and conflict involved in the emerging leadership structure of the group, the movie *Star Wars* was selected-in as a topic. The *Stars* = the emerging leaders, and *Wars* = the abstract tropological transformation of sensory topic of the "felt" conflict. A "felt" verbal insult led immediately to the topic of "pierced ears." This latter type of poetic discourse is what may be considered a kind of holophrastic transformation (see Werner and Kaplan, 1963), where a felt insult, for example, is expressed transformationally as a "slap in the face."

The data presented so far can be considered true poetic "fables" similar to Vico's first men in that the speakers are not aware of their metaphorical nature. Figurative and literal are fused. It is metaphor based on identity, not similarity. Actual fables are also used metaphorically. For example, after a trainer's analysis of the group which was perceived by members as being magical, the *Wizard of Oz* fairy tale was selected-in for discussion. Similarly, affective feelings toward a young female member who said *she worked as a co-therapist in a psychiatric clinic* were transmuted into the fairy tale *Alice Down the Rabbit Hole*. The "rabbit hole," of course = the stereotype of working on the "unconscious" in psychiatric therapy.

Since analogic talk and cognition, in Vichian terms poetic or fabulous speech, belong not to the class "intelligible genera" (i.e., rational) but to the class "sensible genera" (i.e., felt), the analysis of such speech using rationalized, Aristotelian logic necessarily leads to the filtering out of certain aspects of speech production – for example, ostensible "mistakes" and other "illogical" aspects of speech, like "puns." From the author's research into analogic talk and cognition, "mistakes," like "puns," "repetitiveness," and "misremembering," are frequently meaningful *psycho*linguistic forms of communication.

To illustrate: In a group where there were two trainers, the discussion of journalists was augmented by a member insisting on telling a story about a journalist by the name of Harry Harris who was supposed to be well known. As it happened, the member had misremembered" the journalist's correct name. In fact, it was Sidney Harris. The misremembering, however, made it possible for certain sensory concerns to be transmuted into the literal talk that using the (f)actual name would have precluded.

First, the name *Harry Harris*, unlike the correct name of Sidney Harris, made it possible to analogically comment, to tropologically transform the member's affective concern with the two trainers, each of whose last names began with "H," (i.e., *Haskell* and *Heapes*). Secondly, by misremembering the name as Harry Harris, it was possible to "metaphorically" describe certain sensory concerns the member had regarding the two trainers' physical looks. *Harry Harris* "phonologically" describes the two trainers' one with a beard, the other without; i.e., one is *Hairy*, the other *Hairless*. (See Haskell, 1978, 1982) Vichian punning is clear here. Vichian puns reverberate through group discourse. It is no accident that a group concerned with the trainer being relatively *inactive* talks about a man who is "semi-retired", or that a 60-year-old woman in a group of *much younger females* constantly talks of her granddaughter. She is the group's "grand" daughter.

This kind of talk is at once rational and poetic. It may aptly be considered an instance of what one writer in describing James Joyce's work calls "ratiocinative poetry" (Hampshire, 1976). Joyce, (in Litz, 1972) of course, wrote *Finnegans Wake* based on Vico's cycles and theory of language.

Common Sensory Topics in the Vichian Laboratory

According to the Vichian theory, sensory topics have a common ground for all nations (in our terms, groups). A "common sense," says Vico, "is judgment without reflection, shared by an entire class, an entire people, an entire nation, or the entire human race" (p. 21). In group dynamics vernacular, this common sense has been referred to as "unconscious group assumptions," "group focal conflict," "common group tension," and "the group mind" (see Bion, 1959; Durkin, 1984). That this common sense is shared by the "entire human race" is perhaps indicated by research suggesting that small groups in general tend to be concerned with certain "topics" at certain stages of their development. From these common sensory topics, tropological transformations are generated.

It is this common ground that creates a *"mental language common to all nations, which uniformly grasps the substance of things feasible in human social life and expresses it with as many diverse modifications as these same things may have diverse aspects. A proof of this is afforded by proverbs or maxims of vulgar wisdom, in which substantially the same meanings find as many diverse expressions as there are nations ancient and modern"* (p. 25, emphasis added). Small groups exhibit such a common sense, which is unreflectively shared by members.

Furthermore, this common sensory language of groups seems to uniformly grasp the substance of things, which, however, may be expressed diversely according to their diverse aspects. The common sensory topic (concern) over a trainer's note taking is probably present in groups conducted under similar conditions to those described here, but will be expressed diversely according to their diverse aspects. An indication of this is afforded by the various permutations of this common sensory topic, produced by the diverse aspects of the topic present in a given group.

The common sensory topic of an authority taking notes is diversely permuted into (a) talk of *journalists*, if the aspect of concern is an authority collecting information for *publication*; (b) talk of *F.B.I. and C.I.A. files*, where the aspect of concern is authority (government) *spying on them*; (c) *talk of novelists*, where the concern is what is being written about them is untrue, i.e., "novel" = fiction; (d) talk of *archivists*, where the aspect of concern is that what is being written about them is to be stored away for future researchers; and, finally, (e) talk of a *Dr.'s writing prescriptions that patients cannot read*, where the aspect of concern is the feeling of being diagnosed, and that if they had the trainer's notes (i.e., prescription) they would then be made healthy (i.e., a correctly functioning group). The prescriptions that the patients *cannot* read, on the literal level, are a reference to the fact that medical doctors' handwriting is unreadable. On an analogic or poetic level, it is a reference to the fact that the trainer's notes are unavailable to them; indeed, they "cannot" read them. Thus, the subject or sensory topic of "being written about" is expressed in various groups (nations) with as many diverse modifications as it may have diverse aspects.

The significance of such research is that it can extend original ideas, methodologically in terms of the range of phenomena not originally hypothesized. I have found (Haskell, 1983), for example, that numbers in discourse also function as "sensory topics"; that sensory topics are further transmuted into the higher order abstractions of "Number." A group affectively concerned over *eight extremely active* members talked of *eight automobiles* in a parking lot. In the same group session, in discourse about an airfield, it "just happened" to be said that *eight airplanes* were parked there.

In a group where the leadership structure was dominated by *three* members, the various topics of conversations tropologically reflected the group's affective concerns with the *three* leaders. Since members were being evaluated on their leadership abilities, to be a leader was an enviable position. Thus, when the group talked about popular musical groups, the one most discussed was called "The Three Lucky Spots." When the group discussed *travel*, much was made by certain members of "three old Greyhound buses." Similarly, in talk of high school class trips, it was explained that "three seniors" were drunk. Significantly, the *three leaders* were all older than the rest of the group; hence, the "three *old* Greyhound buses," and "three seniors" as opposed to *juniors*.

There was, moreover, considerable talk about a group of people in a bar (= group), with particular emphasis on "this *one girl* who was *with two guys*." Once again, it is no coincidence that the three dominant leaders were *one female* and *two males*. Other aspects of the various discussions tropologically reflected the group sensory concern with the number three. There was talk about having to wait *"about* 3 hours" in an airport; the phrase *"about* 3 days later," in another discussion, was also tropologically significant.

Implications of a Vichian Laboratory

A Vichian laboratory of the kind suggested here would seem to indicate a productive and *"New Science," a new interdisciplinary interfacing of philosophy and behavioral science. While the author cannot speak for philosophy with any authoritative voice, a group training laboratory could, at the least, offer an empirical/*experimental hand to philosophical hypotheses. Though the hand would be a secular one, to be sure, it would render the fact more visible that ideas have consequences.

For behavioral science, a new paradigm is introduced. With the Vichian principles of language analysis, of the principle of *verum factum,* i.e., of the convertibility of the *true* and the *made,* of a science which takes its beginnings from the matters of which it treats, a new epistemology and methodology is suggested. These principles dictate that the behavioral scientist recognize that he or she is a part of his or her own subject matter; that, in studying others linguistically, his or her own language, which is also the language of the Other he or she is studying, is integral to any "scientific" construction he or she may *make;* that his or her person is in dialectical relation to the Other. Hence, the convertibility of the *true* and the *made.*

A Vichian laboratory leads a researcher to treat quite differently that peculiarly human institution called language, but more importantly that psychosocial linguistic process called speech. From the research suggested here as it articulates with Vichian theory, it is not by chance that a particular piece of "literal" discourse occurs; neither is it to be totally explained and studied on a "rational" basis. Discourse does not develop simply as one literal topic leading "naturally" into the following piece of talk; nor does discourse develop by being merely logically related to a previous piece of talk. Rather, to understand discourse, one must understand its metaphoric "deep structure" of sensory topics and the tropological transformational process.

To understand a piece of discourse, it is necessary to understand the sensory basis of why a particular word is selected-in to a particular arrangement of words with particular sounds. Discourse is shaped by the psycho-socio-physical environment in which it is embedded, and the speaker's sensorial response to these factors. "Sensory topics" are the "deep structure" generating the surface order of discourse.

A Vichian laboratory returns empiricism to its original sensory state. The kind of data presented in this chapter would seem to call for a reversal of one writer's dictum (Leach, 1974) that there is no place in the laboratory for the poet. Moreover, the application of a Vichian research laboratory leads to important and far-reaching implications into the nature and interrelations between language, discourse, and cognition, which in turn should yield valuable data on the nature of Mind.

Finally, it follows that, if the Vichian hypothesis of tropological transformation is valid – that literal and rational discourse is a transmutation of sensory "thinking" – then a great deal, if not all, of what has normally come to be seen as the distinction between literal language and figurative language fades, fundamentally, into a mere analytical convenience; it is a "reconstruction." Literal language, in fact, is the real figure of "speech."

It is clear that for Vico, sensation or feeling *is a form of thinking.* Others have more recently suggested a similar nonconscious form of cognition and thought. The Swiss psychologist J. Piaget has suggested an "affective and cognitive unconscious" (1973). Werner and Kaplan (1963), in their classic Clark University studies on micogenesis of thought, have also suggested a similar notion, as has Dixon (1981). In addition, the empirically based philosophy of Ernst Cassirer (1955) and Susanne Langer (1942) suggest a similar cognitive process. In this regard, Cassirer quotes Goethe's assertion that there exists an "exact sensory imagination." The symbolist poets, too, maintained a similar idea (Boon, 1972), as do the hermeneuticist Hans Gadamer's (1975) theories about the existence of an inner linguistic form. More recently, the psychologist Charles Osgood's (Osgood, May, & Miron, 1975) work on affective universals directly relates to Vico. Osgood was one of the first academic psychologists to recognize the significance of the sensory basis of metaphoric production.

THE NEW SCIENCE AS A STRUCTURAL METAPHOR

The epistemology of the *New Science,* as I have already indicated is one quite different than Aristotelian–Cartesian minds are used to, but one quite familiar to those versed in the language of poetry, where writers practice what they preach, where they do indeed what they say they do, where form copies or mimics content. "Mimesis" is the general term in literature given to what I am referring to as structural metaphor (Haskell, 1978a). Is it possible that the *New Science,* whose author's mind was soundly based in the poetics of language, and who in fact discovered metaphor as a mental operation, was written as a metaphorical recapitulation of its own theory.

When first reading the *New Science,* it seemed to me that this is what Vico was indeed doing. Part of Vico's epistemology is the principle of *verum et factum convertuntur,* or the convertability of the *true* and the *created or made,* and/or the *actually performed.* It would therefore, follow, at least for a mind such as Vico's, that he would indeed carry out the function he is explaining.

Verene (1976) has cautiously suggested a similar thesis. The thesis, he says, would account for it seeming to be such a strange book. The table of contents appears more like a mosaic of words than an outline. In the text, nothing is explained in sequential order; it is woven and interwoven, with constant repetition. I would like to suggest, somewhat less cautiously than Verene, and with somewhat more augmentive detail, that the New Science is indeed a structural metaphor (see Chapter 13, this volume) of its very thesis.

While I believe a complete hermeneutic explication of this hypothesis would require a line by line analysis of the New Science, a more modest and general explication will have to suffice here. The author who perhaps understood what Vico was doing in the New Science was James Joyce (see Hampshire, 1976; Litz, 1972) in his Finnegans Wake. To begin at the beginning, Vico himself says of poetic speech that 'as far as our small erudition will permit, we shall make use of this vocabulary in all the matters we discuss" (p. 5). It is congruent with Vico's principles to do no less. Puns reverberate through the text. For example, in using the phrase "hereinbefore" (p. 18), he is setting the reader up for the topic of rumor, i.e., "hearing before." One writer (Leach, 1976) says, "of course one can get alot of fun out of Vico's puns, so long as he does not take them too seriously" (p. 812). But this is to miss the bottom line of Vico's discovery of the movement of poetic cognition. The pun, or sound symbolism, is not generally understood by Aristotelian minds. Poetic puns are the work of a sound mind (see Boon, 1972; Brown, 1958; French, 1977; Fromkin, 1973; Haskell, 1982, 1987).

The translators and editors of the New Science (Vico, 1948) maintain that, in Vico's original text, he "misremembers," "misquotes," and "distorts." Some of these "errors" the translators have corrected. Further, the editors reduced the "excess repetition" and rendered more "literal" meanings to some of Vico's writing. Moreover, the editors lament that Vico's writing style is loaded with forward and backward references. I am suggesting that it is quite probable that many of these "stylistic problems" were strategic rhetorical devices with which to "poetically" demonstrate his thesis—what I have termed "semantaphors" and "structural metaphors" (Haskell, 1978a). It will be recalled that, in the group language data presented above, speakers' misrememberings were in fact a natural cognitive operation performed nonconsciously in order to render the conversation isomorphic to the concrete situation.

If, indeed, Vico is engaging in poetically or metaphorically demonstrating his thesis, then it is unfortunate that the editors of the New Science may have edited out much of the structural meaning of Vico's work, for the New Science was translated within the very Aristotelian and Cartesian epistemology that Vico sought to break through. This leads to an inevitable question: what would the New Science look like translated within its own framework?

Speaking to a related aspect of Vico's work, Hughes (1976) suggests that Vico's rhetorical ironic form is somewhat similar to Plato's Phaedrus, where Plato tries to bring the reader to a point where he is no longer involved in the issues because the reader comes to see that the real issue exists at a higher level of generality which, if recognized, brings the reader to a state of enlightenment. This is known as the

"Platonic ascent." But, as Hughes points out, in aspiring to the wisdom of Socrates, the reader is at the mercy of his editor, Plato.

Cornford (1957, p. 176) advances a thesis about Plato similar to the one I am here suggesting about Vico. He maintains that widespread confusion has resulted from interpreting Plato in Aristotelian terms. According to Cornford, Plato was not a man of the Aristotelian "intelligible concept." Unlike the Aristotelian categories "genus" and "species," Plato's category "kind" was not mutually exclusive with other "kinds"; rather, it blended and pervaded every other "kind." This would perhaps explain the ostensible rationalist, Plato, being one of Vico's "readers." That is, Vico read Plato differently. Vico evidently understood Plato from a pre-Aristotelian epistemology, for, in speaking of Plato's *Cratvlus,* where Plato expands the theory of a time before men spoke a "natural speech," he also points out that Aristotle opposed this view, so it was put to rest. Perhaps, with Vico, there is the end of an epistemological error. As with the Platonic ascent into what Vico calls true knowledge, praxis makes perfect.

The question is, why would Vico write in structural metaphor? The answer is two-fold. First, as with Plato, it is perhaps considered a higher form and more effective communication (see Chapter 13, this volume). Second, Vico believed that some cognitive-linguistic processes functioned in this manner; it was appropriate and congruent with what he would consider true knowledge. For Vico, true knowledge is not real unless it leads to action.

Conclusion

What is to be gleaned from Vico by modern cognitive psychologists? First and foremost is that literal language is a secondary development of a more "psycho"-linguistic mode of poetic speech, and that what we call figurative language is in fact the primary linguistic mode. Second, metaphor is a primary cognitive function, integral to so-called rational thought and concept formation. Third, more cognitive research should be directed at areas that exhibit metaphoric processes, such as poetry, schizophrenic utterances, and dream processes. Cognitive psychologists may discover at least as much about the operation and transformation of the cognitive processes by investigating and devising new methods to study such areas, as by studying so-called rational processes.

REFERENCES

Arieti, S. (1976). Vico and modern psychiatry. *Social Research, 46,* 737–752.
Baldwin, C. S. (1959). *Ancient rhetoric and poetic.* Glouchester, MA: Peter Smith Pub.
Berlin, I. (1976). Vico and the ideal of the enlightenment. *Social Research, 43,* 640–653.
Bion, W. R. (1959). *Experience in groups.* New York: Basic Books.
Boon, J. (1972). *From symbolism to structuralism.* New York: Harper Torchbooks.

Brown, R. (1958). Phonetic symbolism and metaphor. In R. Brown (Ed.). *Words and things.* Glencoe, IL: The Free Press.

Cassirer, E. (1946). *Language and myth.* New York: Dover.

Cassirer, E. (1955). *The philosophy of symbolic forms: Vol. 1. Language.* New Haven: Yale University Press.

Cooper, E. (1960). *The rhetoric of Aristotle.* New York: Appleton-Century-Crofts.

Cordes, C. (1984). Narrative thought neglected, *American Psychological Association Monitor.* 15, (11). p. 12.

Cornford, F. (1957). *Plato's theory of knowledge.* New York: Bobbs-Merrill.

Dixon, N. F. (1981). *Pre-conscious processing.* New York: Wiley.

Durkin, H. F. (1984). *The group in depth.* New York: International Univ. Press.

Edie, J. (1976). *Speaking and meaning: the phenomenology of language,* Bloomington, IN: Indiana Univ. Press.

Foulkes, D. (1978). *A grammar of dreams.* New York: Basic Books.

French, P. (1977). Toward an explanation of phonetic symbolism, *word,* 28, 305–22.

Fromkin, V. A. (1973). *Speech errors as linguistic evidence.* The Hague: Mouton.

Gadamer, H. (1975). *Truth and method,* New York: The Seabury Press.

Hampshire, S. (1976). Joyce and Vico: the middle ways. In G. Tagliacozzo & D. P. Verene (Eds.), *Giambattista Vico's science of humanity. Baltimore, MD: Johns Hopkins Univ. Press.*

Haskell, R. E. (1978a). Lacanian pscholinguistics: The way in. *Interfaces, 9,* 3–10.

Haskell, R. E. (1978b). An analogic model of small group behavior. *International Journal of Group Psychotherapy, 28,* 27–54.

Haskell, R. E. (1982). The matrix of group talk: an empirical method of analysis and validation. *Small Group Behavior, 13,* 165–191.

Haskell, R. E. (1983). Cognitive structure and transformation: an empirical model of the psycholinguistic function of numbers in discourse. *Small Group Behavior, 14,* 419–443.

Haskell, R. E. (1984). Empirical structures of mind: cognition, linguistics, and transformation. *The Journal of Mind and Behavior, 5,* 29–48.

Haskell, R. E. (1985). "Thought-things: Levi-Strauss and the modern mind, *Semiotica, 55,* 1–17.

Haskell, R. E. (1987). Social cognition and the non-conscious expression of racial Ideology. *Imagination, cognition and personality, 6,* (1) 75–79.

Hughes, P. (1976). Creativity and history in Vico and his contemporaries. In G. Tagliacozzo & D. P. Verene (Eds.), *Giambattista Vico's Science of Humanity.* Baltimore, MD: John Hopkins Univ. Press.

Jaynes, J. (1976). *The origins of consciousness in the breakdown of the bicameral mind.* Boston: Houghton Mifflin Co.

Langer, S. (1942). *Philosophy in a new key.* New York: Mentor Books.

Leach, E. (1974). *Claude Levi-Strauss.* New York: Viking Press.

Leach, E. (1976). Vico and the future of anthropology. *Social Research, 46,* 807–817.

Levi-Strauss, C. (1963). *Structural anthropology.* New York: Basic Books, Inc.

Litz, A. W. (1972). *James Joyce.* Princeton, NJ: Hippocrene Books.

Marks, L. E. (1978). *The unity of the senses: interrelations among the modalities.* New York: Academic Press.

Martindale, C. (1981). *Cognition and consciousness.* Homewood, IL: Porsey Press.

Mora, G. (1976). Vico and Piaget: parallels and differences. *Social Research, 46,* 698–712.

Nance, J. (1975). *The gentle Tasaday.* New York: Harcourt, Brace, and Jovanovich.

Osgood, C., May, W. H., & Miron, M. S. (1975). *Cross-cultural universals of affective meaning.* Chicago: University of Illinois Press.

Palmer, R. (1969). *Hermeneutics.* Evanston, IL: Northwestern University Press.

Piaget, J. (1962). *Play, dreams and imitation in childhood,* New York: W. W. Norton.rk: W. W. Norton.

Piaget, J. (1973). The affective and the cognitive unconscious. *Journal of the American Psychoanalytic Association, 21,* 249–61.

Ricoeur, P. (1970). *Freud and philosophy: An essay on interpretation.* New Haven, CT: Yale University Press.

Ricoeur, P. (1977). *The rule of metaphor.* Toronto: Toronto Univ. Press.

Slater, P. (1966). *Microcosm: Structural, psychological and religious evolution in groups.* New York: Wiley.

Snell, B. (1960). *The discovery of the mind: the Greek origins of European thought.* New York: Harper Books.

Verene, D. (1976). Vico's philosophy of imagination. *Social Research, 43,* 410–429.

Vico, G. (1948). *The new science,* (trans. T. G. Bergin & M. H. Fisch). Ithaca, NY: Cornell University Press.

Werner, H., & Kaplan, B. (1963). *Symbol formation: An organismic developmental approach to language and the expression of thought.* New York: Wiley.

White, H. (1973). *Metahistory: The historical imagination in nineteenth-century Europe.* Baltimore, MD: Johns Hopkins University Press.

White, H. (1976). The tropics of history. In G. Tagliacozzo & D. P. Verene (Eds.), *Giambattista Vico's science of humanity.* Baltimore, MD: Johns Hopkins Univ. Press.

PART II
Cognition and Categorization

CHAPTER FIVE

Cognitive Psychology and the Problem of Symbolic Cognition

Robert E. Haskell
University of New England

In this chapter, I would like to explore the tenuous and uneasy relationship that exist between cognitive psychology, on the one hand, and metaphor and symbolic cognition on the other. In so doing, I will outline what I consider to be the main problems in both areas. The format will be as follows: (a) The Problem. This section will explore the selective bias of mainstream cognitive psychology toward the conscious, "rational" aspects of cognition. (b) What Does the "Cognitive" Mean in Cognitive Psychology? This section will outline mainstream and nonmainstream approaches to cognition. (c) The Problem of Symbolic Structures section examines differing conceptions of "unconscious" cognition. (d) The Metaphor and Symbolic Structures section will briefly suggest that metaphoric language is symbolic language. (e) Neurocognitive Data. This section will review data that can be seen as explaining symbolic cognition. Finally, (f) in the section Symbolic Cognition and Cognitive Psychology, I will return to the initially stated problem.

THE PROBLEM

Mainstream cognitive psychology is half out of its mind. Still largely dominated by a simplistic conception of the human brain and nervous system as an information-processing computer, cognitive psychology has refused to compute other than easily controllable surface mental functions. As Church (1961) pointed out years ago, psychologists have a tendency to assign organisms laboratory tasks which artificially limit the range of the organism's natural repertoire of functions, thus limiting observations to that restricted portion of behavior, and then, on the basis of what are in effect artifactual outcomes "draw sweeping conclusions" about the organism's capacity.

In addition to cognitive psychology researching short term memory, associative clustering, nonsense syllables, and what is considered rational and logical processes, there is another half of the mind and brain that needs scientific illumination. Despite mainstream cognitive research, there are signs of some cognitive psychologists attempting to find their way in to that other half of the mind. "We need to understand," says Martindale (1981), "the 'irrational' thought of the poet as well as the rational thought of the subject solving a logical problem" (p. viii). Along with the "cold cognition" of logical thought, we need to know what has been termed "hot cognition" (Abelson, 1963), the emotional-affective aspects of cognition and how they influence rational thought, decision processes, language use, and problem solving sequences; we need to know, if we are not to remain half out of our minds, not just the function of literal language, but of figurative-metaphoric language and its influences on cognition; we need to know the functioning of so-called "symbolic" thought, in the sense that poets and psychoanalysts use the term, and its influence on the cognitive processes. Only when we understand such cognitive operations will cognitive psychology be left completely in its *right* mind.

To use a line from Weimer's (Weimer & Palermo, 1974) now classic volume, having stated the problem, "The enormity of our ignorance conspires against us all. Perhaps the most important thing we can learn from this volume is how little we know about the mind and its place in nature" (p. 440). The question remains: how are we to get into these cognitive processes? While no firm answer can be offered, at least the question will have once again been asked and some further direction suggested. Whatever future findings may yield, what is now termed metaphoric thought, and symbolic cognition and its transformational processes, will figure prominently in our understanding of the other half of our cognitive capacities.

Current "stage" models of information processing in cognitive psychology are not sufficiently concerned with the person as a source of meaning (Lazarus, 1982). Current "process" models, where cognition is viewed as the activation of pre-existing "analyzers" (Martindale, 1981), come closer to seeing the subject's cognitive activity as selective as opposed to passive. The process model is a more "constructivistic" approach, to use Neisser's (1967) term. As Neisser (1976) has commented, the information processing paradigm has a great deal of momentum and prestige, but it has no conception of human nature that applies beyond the restricted tasks found in laboratory research. What is needed, says Neisser, is a cognitive psychology with a more "realistic turn", one with what he calls "ecological validity," that is, a relevance to everyday life.

I do not wish however to lament en toto the inadequacies of an information processing paradigm as others have and continue to do. It is often too simplistic a negation. Certainly, the information processing model as practiced by most mainstream cognitive psychology is often ecologically inadequate. But it does not follow that an information processing framework per se is inadequate. The problem of most current information processing models is fivefold: (a) the particular way they are conceptualized, (b) the content of the cognitive tasks studied, (c) a lack on researchers' and critics' part to see the everyday analogues of laboratory findings, (d) the assumptions underlying the models, and (e) the view that logical and rational processes are the only essential elements of thought. Let me briefly comment on these problems.

First, there are no inherent limitations in the information processing framework that necessarily exclude the functional conceptualization of motive, volition, affect, symbolic processes, or other related "phenomenological" structures. If there were such limitations, then the very term "cognition" would be, in my judgment, a contradiction in the system just as the term "thought" was a contradiction to classical stimulus–response paradigms. Second, the content of information processing research need not be restricted to nonsense syllables, static stimuli, and other nonecologically relevant tasks. Third, when research is limited to laboratory-created stimuli for purposes of control, the problem is often not in the constrained parameters of the research, but rather in the cognitive processes of the researchers and critics who appear to be unable, or at least refuse, to generalize or discover phenomenological analogues of the research. In the early days of so-called "rat psychology," similar charges of nonrelevance were heard about the stimulus–response paradigm. Today, there are perhaps only a few who would not admit the significant ecologically valid analogues of laboratory findings with rats, just as there still may somewhere be a few who would deny the importance of wind-tunnel modeling on the practical engineering of aerodynamics.

The fourth problem of most current information processing models is certain assumptions about (a) human cognitive processes, and (b) the nature of science, both assumptions being related. Partly as an outgrowth of stimulus–response psychology, where human behavior is viewed as reactive in the cause–effect sense, and of an antiquated view of physics as the paradigm of science, information processing in its quest for scientific status assumed that cause–effect model of science. It thus follows from these assumptions that, just as physics does not endow meson particles with internal volition, so cognitive psychology does not imbue cognitive processes with volition. Anyone familiar with modern physics, however, does not give tribute to the old simplistic cause–effect assumptions, at least outside of macro physical phenomena. Not only is there the world of quantum probability equations, but physics has been talking scientifically for some time now about "matter" being glued together by "quarks" that bear "charm." More recently, the universe has been described as functioning "holographically" (Bohm, 1980). And Pribram (1971, 1977) has suggested the brain may work holographically.

I am not suggesting that cognitive psychology abandon a cause–effect paradigm. Newtonian physics still finds cause–effect a useful paradigm. What I am suggesting is, like physics, human cognition is sufficiently complex to warrant multiple methods and paradigms.

The fifth problem is an epistemological one, bearing directly on the issue of figurative or metaphoric processes. Cognitive psychology has taken on the Aristotelian and Cartesian assumption that valid thought and perception of the external world is to only be found in the "clear and distinct" ideas of what we call the logical and the rational. Metaphoric, figurative, poetic, and nonconscious thought and language have been considered "irrational" modes, not therefore significant enough to merit serious research. The rest of this chapter will continue to deal with these five problems.

WHAT DOES THE "COGNITIVE" MEAN IN COGNITIVE PSYCHOLOGY?

At this point, cognitive psychology is in need of some further meaning and definition. The term "cognitive psychology" came into usage as a reaction to behavioral stimulus–response psychology, by Neisser (1967). To behavioral psychology, the "mind" was considered a hermetically sealed "black box." The behaviorist view was, in turn, a reaction to psychoanalytic theorizing about the nature of "mind." With the development of cognitive psychology, the black box was once again opened. Theoretically, everything that relates to perception, memory, imagery, and "thinking" in general is the purview of cognitive psychology. The fact of the matter is, however, that mainstream cognitive psychology has confined itself, not only to (a) certain limited contents of the black box, but (b) to certain conceptions about that content, and (c) to certain procedures of dealing with that content, all of which have precluded research into a large and significant portion of the black box. It is these three general attributes, it seems to me, that characterize mainstream cognitive psychology, and its approach to cognitive processes. Granted, the field had to start in some limited sphere. The problem, however, is that it has not developed much beyond its initial point of departure. While pragmatically it is true that it had to start somewhere, it is equally true that epistemologically it could have started anywhere.

Given the possible range of cognitive phenomena and modes of conceptualizing them, three cognitive psychologies can be generally delineated. The first is the mainstream approach just mentioned. This approach utilizes an information processing framework that deals largely with linear sequences of information that presumably "flow" from one "place" to another, as in computer circuitry. But as Marcel (1983a, b) has made clear, the phenomenal experience of a subject "cannot be identified with and bears no simple relationship to information processing" (p. 281) frameworks as now constituted in mainstream computer psychology. Mainstream cognitive methodology yields a great deal of control over experimental variables, but at the same time it yields little phenomenological relevance.

Unlike many critics, however, the above description of the mainstream view is not intended to turn into an unqualified indictment. My own criticism of the mainstream information processing approach – as historically constituted – is not with its artificial tasks and nonphenomenological conception, but with the tyranny and power it exerts in invalidating deviating and competing approaches to the study of cognition. It is this tyranny and power that many critics – in my judgment – are in large measure reacting to, but which is displaced onto the very notion of information processing itself.

The second cognitive psychology, as I see it, is that exemplified by Neisser (1967, 1976). Instead of seeing subjects as passive receptacles of the flow of information, Neisser sees subjects as internally "constructing" and ordering inputs. For Neisser, cognition is an active and constructive process with "executive" or higher order cognitive processes channeling inputs, not simply an associative linear process. He is much more in line with the earlier classic work by Miller, Galanter, and Pribram (1960), where "plans" and "motives" determine both input and output. Neisser's view is somewhat more phenomenological, in the sense of everyday experience, than the mainstream approach.

In his early work, Neisser (1967) attempted to integrate what Freudian's call "primary process" thinking, and he theorized about cognitive functioning in dreams, an area that mainstream cognitive psychology has left virtually unexplored (see Haskell, 1986). Despite Neisser's more phenomenological stance, he still remains largely within mainstream thinking (since he did, in effect, create it). Nevertheless, Neisser can be seen as standing between the mainstream approach and a third view of cognition.

The third cognitive psychology I will tag the "deep cognition" view. The main difference between this approach and the two approaches mentioned above is that the deep cognition view holds that there are cognitive processes similar to *conscious* operations operating below or outside conscious awareness. It is this third force in cognitive psychology that has direct relevance for the study of metaphor and symbolic structures. It can be seen as composed of three areas of research, one of which has been interstitial within cognitive psychology, and has been called "the new look" (Erdelyi, 1974). Another has held views psychoanalytic in nature, but which have been based in experimental findings, and a third is based in a developmental framework.

Within this third force, the first group can be exemplified by the work of Bowers and Meichenbaum (1984), Broadbent (1958), Bruner and Postman (1949), Deutsch and Deutsch (1963), Dixon (1981), Erdelyi (1974), Hilgard (1977), Nesbett and Wilson (1977), Norman (1976), Posner (1973), Spence (1964), and Treisman (1964). What ties this research together is their work on nonconscious cognition or pre-conscious processing within cognitive psychology. The second group can be exemplified by the work of Fisher (1976), Shevrin and Dickman (1980), and Silverman and Silverman (1964). What ties this group together is their *experimental* psychoanalytic approach. The third group can be exemplified by the work of Piaget (1973) and Werner and Kaplan (1963). What ties this latter group together is their developmental approach to cognition and pre-conscious processing.

Perhaps the most systematic statement and comprehensive compendium of research demonstrating nonconscious cognition, in information processing terms, is the work of Dixon (1981). Dixon's work has not as yet received the attention it deserves in cognitive psychology. He brings together hard experimental data from the fields of neurology, signal detection theory, dichotic listening, brain lateralization, perception, and experimental psychoanalytic data, and frames it within an information processing perspective. His work suggest nonconscious cognitive processing at a level of complexity not only equal to but perhaps exceeding the complexity of conscious processing. From his own research and from the findings he has integrated Dixon concludes that there are multiple neurocognitive levels of nonconscious cognitive processing. He, like Spence (1964), further concludes that conscious cognition is a restricting and limited-capacity information processing channel; that the largest portion of cognition occurs prior to conscious recognition.

The first group within this third force in cognitive psychology conceptualizes nonconscious cognition in terms congruent with the information processing paradigm, of "multiple channels"; the second group uses terms congruent with the psychoanalytic paradigm, of "unconscious motives"; the third group uses terms congruent with early notion in cognitive psychology, of "schemata." As Kihlstrom (1984) has suggested of the "new look" movement, the implications of this entire third force will no doubt be an integration or accommodation within mainstream cognitive psychology. There are already indications (see Marcel, 1983a, 1983b). Indeed, Piaget (1973) has suggested, in an article appropriately entitled "The Affective and the Cognitive Unconscious," that, eventually, the concepts in cognitive psychology and some of the psychoanalytic concepts will have to merge. One can foresee a Kuhnian (1962) "paradigm shift." I see the growing research into metaphoric cognition and figurative language as a part of this incipient shift.

Why, it might be asked, has mainstream cognitive psychology been so resistant to nonconscious cognition? Part of the answer lies in the assumption that logical, rational, "aware" thought is the primary mode of thought. Coupled with this assumption is the fact that most of us link our sense of who we are by identifying our personal identity with conscious cognition. Thus any concession to nonconscious, and therefore to what has been considered irrational, processes undermines the Western notion of personal autonomy and rationality. The belief of conscious determination of behavior is a phenomenological and common-sense stance; it is thus ironic that cognitive science, whose goal it is to separate itself from common sense, should find itself founded on it.

As not only psychoanalysts, but anthropologists, have been attempting to demonstrate for years, the edifice of human behavior and culture, of language and symbolism, rests upon processes of which we are not aware. To many, this is an insulting proposition. Freud, of course, assumed a large measure of the ensuing wrath of this ostensible insult. He still does. But Freud's "unconscious" is not the same "unconscious" as the "nonconscious" information processing view of the third force. The latter is not an irrational pool of id impulses and pathological motives; it is rather a set of Learned processes and cognitive operation very much like conscious cognition. With this said, it is time to more closely examine the concepts of nonconscious cognition and symbolic structures.

THE PROBLEM OF SYMBOLIC STRUCTURES

Since the view of symbolic structures presented here is predicated on meaningful cognitive processes below the level of conscious awareness, it is important to review the concept of the unconscious. I will first briefly explicate Freudian and neo-Freudian conception, and then explore information processing and neurological data that can be used to more clearly understand nonconscious processes giving rise to symbolic cognition.

As indicated above, mainstream cognitive psychology has not brought its information processing methods to bear on the problem of symbolic cognition as understood, not by logicians, but by poets and psychoanalysts. Yet the problem of symbolic cognition pervades everyday thought and is a constant concern to many disciplines, such as clinical psychology, anthropology, sociology, psychohistory, and the study of language. By and large, this omission is due to a variety of reasons.

First, historically the interpretation of symbols derived from the study of religious texts, from which the modern discipline of hermeneutics or the interpretation of textual material is descended. Modern science has justifiably separated itself from investigating phenomena that have quasi-religious explanations. Second, symbolism has been considered to be the modern province of literature and poetry, another area from which cognitive psychology in its quest for scientific status has separated itself, though, as we shall see, not so justifiably. Third, in more contemporary times, symbolism has been considered to be outside the realm of scientific investigation. Fourth, no scientific method has seemed to be available for the investigation of so-called symbolic phenomena. Fifth, the symbolic process is considered to be an "irrational" process, and cognitive psychology is overwhelmingly founded upon the "clear and distinct idea" notion of rationality as posited by Aristotelian and Cartesian philosophy and epistemology.

Finally, the very definition of what constitutes "symbolic" has been and continues to be in question.

The term "symbol" is used in two contrathetical senses. The first is in the sense of symbolic logic, as a logico-mathematical notation, where it is used as a sign to substitute for a clearly defined set of meanings or functions. The second sense in which the term symbol is used is as a poetic or dream symbol, where its full meaning is largely unconscious and undefined. Perhaps the most well-known labels for these two senses of the term symbol are those of Langer (1942), who follows the work of Cassirer (1955a, b, 1959) on symbolic forms. The logical symbol or "sign" she calls a "discursive" symbol; the poetic type symbol she calls a "presentational" symbol. I will be using the term symbol in this second sense. Cognitive psychology has worked with the first definition of symbol, but not with the second definition.

By and large, this second view of "symbol" has been haunted to one degree or another by a Freudian framework where the symbol derives its powerful, affective, "hidden" meaning from repressed unconscious material (see Jones, 1948). According to this view only repressed material needs to be symbolized. In this view, the relation of the external referent is indeterminate with respect to the repressed material. A dream image, for example, is said to be "overdetermined," that is, to have multiple unconscious meanings.

From a Piagetian (1962) point of view, the symbol is a result of external reality not being accommodated, adopted, or fit into the internal reality. For Piaget, the unconscious character of symbolism derives entirely from the primacy of assimilation (or internal schemata) over accommodation, thereby excluding consciousness awareness of the complete set of meanings attached to the symbol.

Werner and Kaplan (1963), in their classic work on *Symbol Formation,* see the symbol as a cognitive developmental process. At the early end of a developmental continuum, they, like Piaget, maintain that internal affective schemata are egocentrically apprehended and are not differentiated. Vehicle and referent are fused. Later, vehicle and referent become increasingly detached, resulting in the abstract symbols of logic and mathematics, the one-to-one relation of "sign" to object, instead of the many-to-one relation of "symbol" to referent, as in dream and poetic symbols.

In sum, Langer, Freud, Piaget, and Werner and Kaplan all view symbolic structures as issuing from multiple nonconscious relations, though the nature of what constitutes "nonconscious," and its dynamics, are different for each of them. Each of these researchers, however, can be seen to hypothesize sets of interacting nonconscious schemata, affective meaning structures which function as nonconscious levels of thinking.

Traditionally, mainstream cognitive psychology has not dealt with this level of cognition. Unconscious or nonconscious thought was considered to be not amenable to scientific investigation. Recently, however, researchers have begun to reconsider nonconscious cognitive processing. Reacting against a Freudian unconscious (the pre-conscious notwithstanding), a move to reconceptualize nonconscious processes has been present for some time. The psychiatrist, H. S. Sullivan (See Mullahy, 1970) suggested that a feeling or idea was not necessarily repressed into the unconscious, but may be simply "unformulated" so as to be not clearly in awareness. Whitman (1964), suggesting a similar view of so-called "unconscious defense mechanisms," put forth the following: If a person driving into a town in need of food and gas immediately saw a restaurant and gas station, one would not say the person was defending against the barber shop next door that the person did not see. Similarly, Foulkes (1978) maintains that the "unconscious" simply designates a set of verbally formulated propositional structures of which a person is not aware.

Piaget (1973) sees the "unconscious" as a set of nonconscious affective schemata which organize action. The structural anthropologist Levi-Strauss (1963) sees the "unconscious" as a set of combinatory and categorizing processes which are relatively independent of conscious thinking.

More recently, Marcel (1983a, b) has challenged what he terms the "identity assumption" of mainstream cognitive research. Specifically, the mainstream assumption has been that, by studying micro-perceptual and sensory input, eventually an additive picture of the elements of conscious cognition will emerge. From his research, Marcel suggest there is no necessary identity between perceptual input and conscious phenomenal experience, that the two levels are probably coded quite differently. Like Dixon (1981), Marcel suggests that consciousness is a limited capacity channel, and that previous nonconscious coding is necessary for conscious cognition. The mainstream view has been that consciousness is primary. From Marcel's and Dixon's view, nonconscious processing is a *precondition* for much of conscious cognition. Neisser (1967) has, in fact, suggested a similar view from his constructivistic perspective. He maintains only the products of cognitive construction are in consciousness, not the constructive processes themselves.

Piaget's (1973) phenomenalistic and developmental approach to cognition more strongly suggests that a large part of what we call conscious thinking is in fact the product of nonconscious constructive (thinking) processes. He says this is especially apparent in studying 6- and 7-year-old children. They are, he says, "conscious of the results, but not of the innermost mechanisms which transformed" the thinking, "the structures of which remain unconscious." It is those structures that he calls the "cognitive unconscious." That is why, says Piaget, becoming conscious is largely a reorganization process and not merely a translation or simple retrieval process. Conscious thought is a reconstruction on a higher level, of structures already organized on a lower level. Piaget (1962) likens this process to mathematical construction, where the "stronger" or higher order mathematical structures are not capable of elaboration until the "weaker" or more elementary structures are elaborated, though the higher systems facilitate the "weaker" structures as well (p. 140).

In another context, Foulkes (1978) makes a similar point that can be adapted here. Writing on the cognitive process in the dream state, he suggests that what "wakefulness" (i.e., conscious thought) means is that the mind is no longer "encumbered by the constructive task with which it was occupied during sleep" (p. 165). Foulkes is suggesting here that dream sleep is cognitively constructive. What the "cognitive unconscious" is to Piaget, the "dream state" is to Foulkes. The implications of this perspective are multiple, and bear directly on metaphoric cognition and so-called symbolic structures.

METAPHOR AND SYMBOLIC COGNITION

A metaphor is a symbol. Metaphors are symbolic in both senses of the terms outlined above. First, it can stand in a one-to-one relationship representing something else, as in the case of a simple sign notation, and is therefore a discursive symbol. Second, it can stand in a one-to-many relationship with what it represents. As Piaget (1971) points out, a metaphor is a symbol "because there is a relationship between the image used and the object to which it refers" (p. 169). Moreover, as Ricoeur (1978) has indicated, the polysemic feature of words, that is, their ability to mean in different ways, is basic to the notion of symbolism. And, as Urban (1961) has adequately demonstrated, since all language is metaphorical, all language is symbolic to one degree or another.

Ricoeur (1978a,b) defines symbol "as any structure of signification in which a direct primary, literal meaning designates in addition another meaning which is indirect, secondary and figurative and which can be apprehended only through the first" (p. 98). Werner and Kaplan (1963) also note that the mark of the symbol is its "inherent duality." All metaphor, then, is inherently symbolic, being, at one end of the continuum, a single sign standing for a single referent, as in mathematical symbols, and, at the other end of the continuum, a single vehicle of reference, as in a figurative word, gesture, or dream image which stand for multiple referents. As indicated earlier, I am using "symbol" in this latter sense.

In addition, the referents to which the symbol refers are largely nonconscious, indicating a felt apprehension of the constructive cognitive processes underlying the vehicle. It is this latter quality that often gives the symbol its affectively powerful meaning. In short, a dense symbolic metaphor will evoke strong affect derived from the nonconscious schemata connected to it. Poetic symbols or the words used in poetry are examples, as are dream images. The referential meaning of a symbolic vehicle remains consciously unformulated; its nonconscious "propositional structure" (one aspect of its meaning) is not available to conscious awareness.

So far, the general perspective of the symbol presented here is not a novel one. That metaphor is symbolic is not novel either. To reformulate them, however, into a cognitive psychology framework is a somewhat fresh and hopefully productive approach, as, until very recently, cognitive psychology has been largely mute regarding both metaphor and symbolism. The question is: How would symbolic cognitive processes work, and what might such cognitive data look like? A number of different but related fields of research lend themselves to an answer.

NEURO-COGNITIVE DATA

The answer to the above question in fact entails two related issues. The first is the veridicality of the very notion of nonconscious cognition (not just perception or the registration of stimuli). The second is how it is possible, or how it works. I would like to suggest two types of data relative to this issue, one I will call macro or phenomenological/clinical data, the other micro or experimental data. The former relates more to the existence of nonconscious cognition, the latter both to its existence and its workings. In order to understand metaphor and symbolic cognition, we need to look at other than laboratory cognitive data. As Norman (1980) has suggested, cognitive psychology needs to look at the fields of neurology, and even at clinical data.

On the macro level, a number of phenomena suggest nonconscious cognition. In recent years, there has been an increasing awareness of the reality of such "clinical" entities as multiple personalities, fugue states, hypnotic phenomena, and hysterical blindness, where people function "normally" but have no "awareness" of their thoughts, actions, or motivations while in these states. Perhaps the exemplar of these cognitive states is the phenomena, discovered by Hilgard (1977), at Stanford University known as the "hidden observer" effect. Hilgard discovered through hypnotic procedures that some subjects, while hypnotically deaf, or while hypnotically analgesic for pain, exhibited a dissociated cognitive structure that was aware and could feel and hear, even though they had no conscious awareness of sound or pain. The "hidden observer" structure can process information outside of awareness. Hilgard explains the phenomena in cognitive information processing terms of parallel channels.

Much less well known is the work of Cheek (1959, 1964, 1966, 1981). Cheek established that surgical patients, while under deep general anaesthesia, not only hear but cognitively process certain conversations in the operating room. Through experiments involving tape recorders during an operation, Cheek has later retrieved, through the use of hypnosis, the conversation of operating room personnel. More importantly, patients have been known to later act on what they heard, just as if they had been given a post-hypnotic suggestion. Under general anaesthesia patients are clearly "not conscious," but are cognitively processing information.

From micro research into neurological and related visual data, it appears clear that a great deal of cognitive processing occurs outside of conscious awareness.

For example, in the neurological disorder known as the "neglect syndrome" (Heilman & Watson, 1977) that seems to be the consequence of damage to certain neurological tissue involved in visual functioning, subjects with lesions on the left side of their brains do not "see" objects on their right sides. When asked to describe a room, such patients will only describe the left side of the room, or, when shown the word "baseball," will see only "base" and not "ball." But these patients are not in fact completely blind on their right side, for when they are forced to select from an array of objects some of which were located on the right half of the room, they achieve better than chance levels of correct selection. The patients are not in fact consciously "seeing" the right side of the room. Nevertheless the information is received and transmitted to some neurological level of processing prior to consciousness.

Similar nonconscious visual neurological deficits have been observed in what are called "blindsight" and "binocular rivalry" and "cortical blindness" deficits. The "blindsight" research of Weiskrantz, Warrington, Sanders, and Marshall (1974, cited by Dixon, 1981, p. 14) with patients who are "blind" on both left halves of their visual fields as a consequence of brain lesions demonstrates that these "blindsight" patients are, like the above neglect syndrome patients, nonconsciously receiving, transmitting, and processing information in their left visual fields. Again, when forced to describe or "guess" what was presented to their left visual field, subjects said they just had a "feeling" that the object they located was "there."

Research into binocular rivalry, where under certain conditions information from only one eye attains conscious awareness, demonstrates that information to the suppressed eye, while not attaining conscious awareness, is neurologically registered (Riggs & Whittle, 1967; Cobb, Morton, & Ettlinger, 1967, in Dixon, 1981). Citing the work of Walker (1978), Dixon (1981) when a red patch was shown to one eye and a green patch to the other, while at the same time presenting a subliminal array of black and white squares to the suppressed eye, the latter immediately assumed dominance as the result of the additional (but subliminal) stimuli, demonstrates unequivocal evidence of non-conscious perception. Similar findings have been demonstrated in what is called "cortical blindness," caused by damage to central visual pathways, rendering the patient "consciously" blind.

In short, what this kind of data suggests is that, in vision at least, there are multiple neurological pathways that can cognitively process information on a nonconscious level and can be felt and acted upon without consciously knowing, or knowing why. Similar findings have been demonstrated in other than visual modes. The findings from so-called split brain (Myers & Sperry, 1958; Sperry, 1968) is one example.

People who, because of intractable epilepsy, have had a portion of their brain, called the corpus callosum, partially or totally severed, process information outside their conscious awareness. In general, the function of the corpus callosum is to transfer information received by one cerebral hemisphere to the other hemisphere. When the corpus callosum is cut, new information in one hemisphere is not transfered to the other. While some of the details of the processes underlying the findings from such research are somewhat controversial, the findings are not. In a now well-known experiment by Sperry (1968), a split-brain patient was shown pictures to the left visual fields, information from which was ostensibly going to only the right hemisphere. One of the pictures was of a nude body. The patient giggled and blushed, but did not consciously have any idea why, the explanation being that, since the information went only to the right hemisphere, which does not appear to have an active language function (at least for about 95% of people), the patient could not report it. Here we have an example of *felt meaning,* a nonconscious cognitive processing on a meaningful level, but no conscious awareness or formulation of it.

In an experiment by Gazzangia and LeDoux (1978, also in Springer & Deutsch, 1981), a split-brain patient was presented with a snow scene to the right hemisphere and a chicken claw to the left hemisphere. From an array of pictures, the patient selected a picture of a chicken with the right hand (controlled by the left hemisphere), and a picture of a shovel with the left hand. When the patient was asked, "What did you see?" the verbal response from the left hemisphere was, "I saw a claw and I pictured the chicken, and you have to clean out the chicken shed with a shovel." As the snow scene went to the right hemisphere, little or no experience of it was available for the left hemisphere, and thus the patient could not report the experience of it.

Shevrin and Dickman (1980), in reviewing the literature on cortical evoked responses (CER) that indicate nonconscious cognitive processing, cite the work of Riggs and Whittle (1967), as well as that of Lehmann, Beeler, and Fender (1965). Using retinal image stabilization procedures, where an image projected on to the retina of the eye is held stable relative to given cells on the retina, resulting in the perceived disappearance of the image, it was found that no cortical evoked response was produced when the conscious perception of the image disappeared. The *retinal* cells, however, were still responding to the image stimulus, and, therefore the stimulus was being transmitted along the optic nerve. The authors concluded that there was a cortical "turn off" of consciousness involved.

It has also been found (Dixon 1981), that a GSR (Galvanic Skin Response) is elicited by emotionally meaningful words, but not by emotionally neutral words presented subliminally. It has further been found (Von Wright, Anderson, & Stenman, 1975) that stimulus generalization occurs to a word which has been conditioned to a GSR. Associated or similar words *embedded* in an unattended message elicited a GSR. Other research (Eagle, Wolitzky, & Klein, 1966) also suggest similar findings. Shevrin and Fritzler (1968) found a larger CER to meaningful stimuli than for meaningless subliminal stimuli. Dixon and Lear (1963) found heart rate changes related to subliminal stimuli. Hartley (1969) found amplitude of a visual evoked response produced by a flash of light into one eye is reduced by presenting a subliminal emotional word to the other eye. Emotional neutral words did not have the same effect. A compendium of such research is presented by Dixon (1981).

For present purposes, the significant point to be derived from the above cited research is two-fold: first, that information is cognitively processed, not just perceptually received, on nonconscious levels as indicated by little or no response to subliminal neutral stimuli, but a response to emotional meaningful stimuli; second, that nonconscious information received by neurologically impaired patients influences conscious cognition and responses in clearly distinct ways, as indicated by the forced-choice correct selection of data not attaining conscious awareness.

In the above cited research nonconscious information was either "felt" to be present, or it was incorporated into an otherwise conscious explanation, as in the case of the split-brain patient who chose a shovel. The snow scene seemed to influence the patient's conscious selection without the patient's awareness of why the shovel was chosen. The patient did, however, "rationalize" why it was chosen by relating it to the chicken claw by way of circuitous associative reasoning.

Similar effects have been found in the hysterical or functional syndromes (see Sackeim, Nordlie, & Gur, 1979). Hysterical subjects, like the above cited neurological subjects, often can also "guess" what is present. Interesting to note here is the fact that many neurological deficit and hysterical patients often seem indifferent to their problem, a phenomenon known as *la belle indifference*. I have suggested (Haskell, 1984) that the common symbolic deficits of neurological, functional syndrome patients, and indeed of hypnotic patients, may point to a productive area of cognitive research on the cognitive processes involved in symbolism.

It may be objected that data from split-brain subjects is not appropriate, since their hemispheres are not intact. Split-brain data can be seen, however, as an extreme case of normal cognitive functioning. Galin (1974) has suggested that corpus callosum activity may be inhibited in other psychological ways, a kind of functional severing of the corpus callosum. It should be noted that, even in surgical severing of the commissure, certain kinds of information may reach the opposite hemisphere by other pathways, a sort of cross cuing (see Gazzaniga & Hillyard, 1971, in Springer & Deutsch, 1981), thus giving to the language dominant hemisphere information that can be only indirectly used leading to "rationalizing" the response (see Haskell, 1984). Similar rationalization can be observed with hypnotic subjects who are given a post-hypnotic suggestion. It is also observed in patients with hysterical or functional blindness.

As Dixon (1981) points out, the support for the veridicality of nonconscious cognition comes, not just from each piece of research, but from the fact that the evidence comes from so many different pieces of research and from different areas using different methods. In addition to the research cited here from neurological findings of the neglect syndrome, blindsight, binocular rivalry, cortical blindness, cortical evoked responses, and split brain, along with a subliminal perception, multiple personality, the "hidden observer" effect, and functional or hysterical disorders, there is also similar findings from cognitive paradigms involving perceptual defense, dichotic listening, masking and shadowing procedures, selective perception, and attention studies (see Dixon, 1981).

Once the veridicality of nonconscious cognition is accepted and explained on the basis of the above kind of data, then it seems to me that the concept of "symbolic" cognition can also be explained by that same data. There is no need to invoke psychoanalytic or otherwise obscure explanations, at least for "how" questions. The concept of symbolic cognition becomes open to mainstream cognitive research.

SYMBOLIC COGNITION AND COGNITIVE PSYCHOLOGY

What the above findings point toward is a conception of information processing that the new look movement in cognitive psychology research has been positing, in reaction to traditional mainstream research, namely, that data need not be processed consciously before it is stored in secondary or long term memory, that there are nonconscious "attentional" processes prior to conscious processing. Secondly, that there exist at least two, and most likely more cognitive pathways, one for information transmission, and another for determining conscious access to that information. Using results of research on vision as a model, there would be multiple neurological pathways for the transmission of stimuli, both on a cortical and subcortical level, and that information may be processed ("seen") before being accessed to consciousness. The way all of this relates to symbolism can now be generally summarized.

At the very center of theories of symbolism (in the sense it is used here) are the following four propositions: (a) that there is nonconscious meaning connected to the symbolic vehicle, (b) that the meaning is multi-leveled, (c) that these nonconscious levels of meaning are manifested in conscious cognitive structures and behaviors, and (d) that symbolic vehicles have attached to them affective components. There is thus an "inherent duality" to the symbol; its conscious dimension and its multi-leveled, nonconscious dimension.

If the explanatory framework of the new look theorists, and the entire third force conception outlined in this chapter, is accepted, then the type of neurocognitive evidence cited here can integrate the workings of so-called symbolism positioned by the, more psychoanalytic and unconscious schemata theories, and in fact can be demonstrated using the research paradigms of "information processing."

From this perspective, a symbolic vehicle is "pregnant" with meaning due to the multiple neurocognitive channels of information related to the vehicle that have not been accessed to consciousness. The full meaning remains "unformulated." In Freudian terms, the symbol is "overdetermined." Such meaning was seen in the above experiments with subliminal cognition, blindsight, the neglect syndrome, etc., where subjects were not consciously aware but were processing the data. In addition, some of them had "feelings" about the data not consciously perceived, and in fact were reacting to it, as indicated by GSR and CER measures, even when no conscious feelings were evident. Fourth, the nonconscious data were influencing conscious thought and behaviors.

Using the situations and methods of the above cited research, it should be fairly easy to control and create the production of "symbolic" behavior and responses in the laboratory, including the generation of metaphors, the latter being a special case of symbols. This has been done with varying degrees of success by researchers outside of mainstream cognitive psychology, using hypnosis and pre-sleep stimulation to produce particular content in the dream state (see Tart, 1979). Such research is valuable, not only because it can tell us about symbolic cognition and its transformations, but can also lead to a deeper understanding of cognition in general. We need to study more so-called "anomalous" data, such as neurological deficits, poetry, dreams, and metaphoric production. We also need to integrate research methodologies, relating the more micro, traditional laboratory procedures with the more phenomenological everyday methods.

REFERENCES

Abelson, R. P. (1963). Computer simulation of "hot cognitions" in S. Tomkins & S. Mesick (Eds.), *Computer simulation of personality.* New York: Wiley.

Bohm, D. (1980). *Wholeness & the implicate order.* London: Routledge & Kegan-Paul.

Bowers, K. S., & Meichenbaum, D. (Eds.). (1984). *The unconscious reconsidered,* New York: Wiley-interscience.

Broadbent, D. (1958). *Perception and communication.* Oxford, England: Pergamon Press.

Bruner, J. S., & Postman, L. (1949). Perception, cognition and personality. *Journal of Personality, 18,* 14–31.

Cassirer, E. (1955a). *The philosophy of symbolic forms: Vol. I. Language,* New Haven: Yale University Press.

Cassirer, E. (1955b). *The philosophy of symbolic forms. Vol. II: Mythical thought.* New Haven: Yale University Press.

Cassirer, E. (1959). *The philosophy of symbolic forms. Vol. III: The phenomenology of knowledge,* New Haven: Yale University Press.

Cheek, D. B. (1959). Unconscious perception of meaningful sounds during surgical anesthesia as revealed under hypnosis. *American Journal of Clinical Hypnosis, 1,* 1010–113.

Cheek, D. B. (1964). Surgical memory and reactions to careless conversations. *American Journal of Clinical Hypnosis, 6,* 237–40.

Cheek, D. B. (1966). The meaning of continued hearing sense under chemo-anaesthesia: A progress report and report of a case. *American Journal of Clinical Hypnosis, 8,* 275–280.

Cheek, D. B. (1981). Awareness of meaningful sounds under general anaesthesia: Considerations and a review of the literature 1959–1979. In H. J. Wain (Ed.), *Theoretical and clinical aspects of hypnosis,* (pp. 87–106). Miami, FL: Symposia Specialists, Medical Books.

Church, J. (1961). *Language and the discovery of reality.* New York: Vintage Books.

Cobb, W. A., Morton, H. B., & Ettlinger, G. (1967). Cerebral evoked potentials evoked by pattern reversal and their suppression in visual rivalry. *Nature, 216,* 1123–1125.

Deutsch, J., & Deutsch, D. (1963). Attention: some theoretical considerations. *Psychological Review, 70,* 80–90.

Dixon, N. F. (1981). *Pre-conscious processing.* New York: Wiley.

Dixon, N. F., & Lear, T. (1963). Electroencephalograph correlates a threshold regulation. *Nature, 198,* 870–872.

Eagle, M., Wolitzky, D. L., & Klein, G. S., (1966). Imagery: effect of a concealed figure in a stimulus. *Science, 151,* 837–839.

Erdelyi, M. H. (1974). A new look at the "new look": Perceptual defense as vigilance. *Psychological Review, 81,* 1–25.

Fisher, S. (1976). Conditions affecting boundry response to messages out of awareness. *Journal of Nervous and Mental Disease, 162,* 313–22.

Foulkes, D. (1978). *A grammar of dreams.* New York: Basic Books.

Galin, D. (1974). Implications for psychiatry of left and right cererbral specialization. *Archives of General Psychiatry, 31,* 572–583.

Gazzaniga, M. S., & Hillyard, S. A. (1971). Language and speech capacity of the right hemisphere. *Neuropsychologia, 9,* 273–280.

Gazzaniga, M. S., & LeDoux, J. E. (1978). *The integrated mind.* New York: Plenum Press.

Hartley, L. (1969). *The influence of information and meaning on the electrical activity of the brain.* Unpublished Ph.D thesis, University of London.

Haskell, R. E. (1984). *Hypnosis and cognitive psychology: neurocognitive implication.* Paper presented at the American Society of Clinical Hypnosis Conference, San Francisco, CA., Nov.

Haskell, R. E. (1986). Cognitive psychology and dream research: historical, conceptual and epistemological considerations, In R. E. Haskell (Ed.) Cognition and dream research, N.Y. Institute of Mind and Behavior (special double issue of The Journal of Mind and Behavior) 1–30.

Heilman, K. M., & Watson, R. T. (1977). The neglect syndrome–a unilateral defect of the orienting response. In S. Harnad, R. Doty, L. Goldstein, J. Jaynes, & G. Krauthamer, (Eds.), *Lateralization in the nervous system* (pp. 285–302). New York: Academic Press.

Hilgard, E. E. (1977). *Divided consciousness: Multiple controls in human thought and action.* New York: Wiley Interscience.

Jones, E. (1948). The theory of symbolism. *In Papers on psychoanalysis.* (5th ed.) (pp. 87–144). Baltimore, MD: Williams & Williams.

Kihlstrom, J. F. (1984). Conscious, subconscious, unconscious: A cognitive perspective. In *K. S. Bowers & D. Meichenbaum (Eds.), The unconscious reconsidered* (pp. 149–211). New York: Wiley.

Kuhn, Thomas S. (1962). *The structure of scientific revolutions.* Chicago: Phoenix Books.

Langer, S. (1942). *Philosophy in a new key.* New York: Mentor Books.

Lazarus, R. (1982). Thoughts on the relations between emotion and cognition. *American Psychologist, 37,* 1019–1024.

Lehmann, D., Beeler, G., & Fender, D. (1965). Changes in pattern of the human electroencephalogram during fluxuation of perception of stabilized retinal images. *E.E.G.: and Clinical Neurophysiology, 19,* 336–343.

Levi-Strauss, C. (1963). *Structural anthropology.* New York: Basic Books.

Marcel, A. (1983a), Conscious and unconscious perception: Experiments on visual masking and word recognition. *Cognitive Psychology, 15,* 197–237.

Marcel, A. (1983b). Conscious and unconscious perception: An approach to the relations between phenomenal experience and perceptual processes. *Cognitive Psychology, 15,* 238–300.

Martindale, C. (1981). *Cognition and consciousness.* Homewood IL: Porsey Press.

Miller, G. A., Galanter, E., & Pribram, K. (1960). *Plans and the structure of behavior.* New York: Holt, Rinehart and Winston.

Mullahy, P. (1970). *Psychoanalysis and interpersonal psychiatry: The contributions of Harry Stack Sullivan.* New York: Science House.

Myers, R. E., & Sperry, R. W. (1958). Interhemispheric communication through the corpus callosum mnemonic carry-over between hemispheres Archives of Neurology and Psychiatry, 80, 298–303.

Neisser, U. (1967). *Cognitive psychology.* New York: Appleton-Century-Crofts.

Neisser, U. (1976). *Cognition and reality: principles and implications of cognitive psychology,* San Francisco: W. H. Freeman & Co.

Nesbett, R. E., & Wilson, T. D. (1977). Telling more than we can know: verbal reports of verbal processes. *Psychological Review, 84,* 231–259.

Norman, D. A. (1976). *Memory and attention: An introduction to human information processing.* New York: Wiley & Sons.

Norman, D. A., (1980). Twelve issues for cognitive science. *Cognitive Science, 4,* 1–32.

Piaget, J. (1962). *Play, dreams and imitation in childhood.* New York: W. W. Norton.

Piaget, J. (1973). The affective and the cognitive unconscious. *Journal of the American Psychoanalytic Association, 21,* 249–261.

Pribram, K. (1977). Some comments on the nature of the perceived universe. In Robert Shaw & J. Bransford (Eds.), *Perceiving, acting and knowing: Toward an ecological psychology,* Hillsdale, NJ: Erlbaum.

Reagan, C. & Stewart, D. (Eds.). (1978). *The philosophy of Paul Ricoeur.* Boston: Beacon Press.

Ricoeur, P. (1971). *Languages and the brain: Experimental paradoxes and principles in neuropsychology.* Englewood Cliffs, NJ: Prentice-Hall.

Ricoeur, P. (1978a). Existence and Hermeneutics. In C. Reagan & D. Stewart, (Eds.), *The philosophy of Paul Ricoeur.* Boston: Beacon Press.

Ricoeur,. P. (1978b). From existentialism to the philosophy of language. In C. Reagan & D. Stewart, (Eds.), *The philosophy of Paul Ricoeur.* Boston: Beacon Press.

Riggs, L. A., & Whittle, P. (1967). Human occipital and retinal potentials evoked by subjectively faded visual stimuli. *Vision Research, 7,* 441–451.

Sackeim, H. A., Nordlie, J. W., & Gur, R. C. (1979). A model of hysterical and hypnotic blindness: Cognition, motivation, and awareness. *Journal of Abnormal Psychology, 88,* 474–489.

Shevrin, H., & Dickman, S. (1980). The psychological unconscious. *American Psychologist, 35,* 421–434.

Shevrin, H., & Fritzler, D. (1968). Visual evoked response correlates with unconscious mental processes. *Science, 161,* 295.

Silverman, L. H., & Silverman, D. K. (1964). A clinical-experimental approach to the study of subliminal stimulation. *Journal of Abnormal and Social Psychology, 69,* 158–172.

Spence, D. D. (1964). Conscious and unconscious influences on recall: another example of the restricting effects of awareness. *Journal of Abnormal Psychology, 68,* 92–99.

Sperry, R. W. (1968). Hemispheric disconnection and unity in conscious awareness. *American Psychologist, 23,* 723–733.

Springer, S. P., & Deutsch, G. (1981). *Left brain, right brain.* San Francisco: W. H. Freeman.

Tart, C. (1979). From spontaneous event to lucidity: a review of attempts to consciously control nocturnal dreaming. In B. Wolman (Ed.), *Handbook of dreams: Research theories, applications* (pp. 226–268). New York: Van Nostrand Reinhold.

Treisman, A. (1964). Selective attention in man. *British Medical Bulletin, 20,* 12–16.

Urban, W. N. (1961). *Language and reality.* London: Allen and Unwin; New York: Macmillan.

Von Wright, J., Anderson, K., & Stenman, U. (1975). Generalization of conditioned GSR's in dichotic listening. In P. Rabbitt & S. Dorric, (Eds.), *Attention and performance.* New York: Academic Press.

Walker, P. (1978). Binocular rivalry: Central or peripheral selective processes. *Psychological Bulletin, 85,* 376–389.

Weimer, W., & Palermo, D. S. (Eds.). (1974). *Cognition and the symbolic processes.* Hillsdale, NJ: Erlbaum.

Weiskrantz, L., Warrington, E., Sanders, M., & Marshall, J. (1974). Visual capacity in the hemispheric field following a restricted occipital ablation. *Brain, 97,* 709–728.

Werner, H., & Kaplan, B. (1963). *Symbol formation: An organismic developmental approach to language and the expression of thought.* New York: Wiley and Sons.

Whitman, R. M. (1964). Psychodynamic principles underlying T-group processes. In P. Bradford, J. R. Gibbs, & D. Benne (Eds.), *T-Group theory and laboratory method.* New York: Wiley.

CHAPTER SIX

Figurative Language and Psychological Views of Categorization: Two Ships in the Night?

Richard P. Honeck
University of Cincinnati

Clare Kibler
IBM Corporation at Endicott

Michael J. Firment
University of Cincinnati

There have been few attempts in experimental psychology to link figurative language with categorization. This is somewhat surprising, since these areas share some theoretical issues. To say *Man is a wolf*, for example, is to assert that man (i.e., people) is a subset of the wolf category. Similarly, if two people are discussing the case of a missionary who failed to convert some natives because he did not speak their language, one person might say, *A net with a hole in it won't catch any fish*. Here, the speaker has categorized a complex social situation via a proverb's figurative meaning. If the use of the term "category" in these two examples, and innumerable others like them, is not to be taken lightly, but rather as having some theoretical import, then there is good reason to expect that figurative language and categorization should be linked.

Philosophers such as Black (1962), Goodman (1968), and Turbayne (1970) have noted the link. In psychology, however, the rather voluminous traditional literatures on categorization and figurative language have remained relatively separate. The categorization literature (e.g., Bourne, 1966; Rosch, 1978; Scholnick, 1983; Smith & Medin, 1981), in particular, contains no discussion of figurative language. On the other hand, some investigators of figurative language have begun to seriously consider the two topics jointly. The purpose of this essay is to review these efforts. First we describe traditional experimentalist views of categorization. Then recent psychological work with proverbs and metaphors is presented, and its implications for these views is discussed.

TRADITIONAL PSYCHOLOGICAL VIEWS OF CATEGORIZATION

Experimentalists have conducted research on concepts and categories for over 100 years, though most intensively since the 1940s. The resulting literature is extensive and cannot be summarized here (but see Bourne, 1966; Bruner, Goodnow, & Austin, 1956; Hunt, 1962; Medin, 1983; Rosch, 1978; and Smith & Medin, 1981, for reviews). What follows provides only the flavor of this research.

According to Smith and Medin (1981), most research on categorization fits into one of three different views – the *Classical, Probabilistic,* and *Exemplar Views.* Each view is fundamentally concerned with the question, What is the likelihood that X will be categorized as Y, where X is some stimulus and Y is a category? By the Classical View, the likelihood is 1.00 if X shares a requisite set of features with Y, and O otherwise. By the Probabilistic View, the likelihood is a function of the extent to which X shares features with Y, where Y is an abstract central tendency of the stimuli that engendered Y. By the Exemplar View, the likelihood is a function of the extent to which X shares features with Y, where Y is a particular remembered instance or set of disjunctively organized instances. This synopsis is elaborated below.

The Classical View

Psychology's earliest theory of categorization can be traced to Aristotle, and hence is known as the Classical View. Proponents (e.g., Bourne, 1966, 1982) claim that categories are summary mental representations that contain sets of *defining features* that are "singly necessary and jointly sufficient" to define the category. They also assume that a concept's defining features are nested in those of its subordinate concept. The defining features of the concept "boat," for example, would be nested in those for "sailboat," all of which would in turn be nested in those for "catamaran."

A typical experiment within this view might be described as follows. The experimenter presents a series of stimuli (e.g., geometric patterns) and the observer responds to each with one of two artificial category names, such as "Dox" and "Zil." The experimenter then provides feedback regarding the correctness of the response. After a brief interval, another stimulus is presented, and so on. This training procedure terminates when the observer demonstrates some specified level of learning. Often, new stimuli are presented during a subsequent transfer test. This paradigm allows variation, such as asking observers to verbalize their hypotheses, or allowing them to select the stimuli, or not giving feedback on every trial, etc. In general, a huge number of task variables (i.e., kinds of responses, temporal factors, kinds of rules that define the concept, etc.) and observer factors have been examined within the framework of this paradigm (see Bourne, 1966).

While studies within the Classical View dominated American laboratory research on categories in the 1940s, 1950s, and much of the 1960s, this is no longer the case. Both logical or, "in principle," as well as empirical factors forced a revision of researcher's beliefs. According to Smith and Medin (1981), there are seven problems that are left unresolved by the Classical View: (a) Disjunctive concepts are excluded, since such concepts need not contain any necessary features, in violation of a key premise. (b) Many categories seem to have unclear cases, whereas the Classical View requires that the features that define the categories be nested completely in a subordinate. (c) Defining features have not been specified and probably never will be specified for a great number of categories. (d) Some category members are often judged more typical than others, and these members are usually learned more easily, reacted to more quickly, and used as reference points more often than other members. However, the Classical View requires either full or equal category membership, or no membership at all, for a stimulus. (e) Typicality values tend to correlate with degree of family resemblance, despite the fact that family resemblance is based on shared, not identical features. (f) Nonnecessary features are frequently used to categorize stimuli (e.g., "flies" for bird). (g) Contrary to the nesting assumption, concepts are sometimes judged more similar to a distant than to an immediate superordinate.

Basically, the Classical View is too logic (set theory) oriented, too Aristotelian at least, and too tied to artificially composed, stimulus-driven categories. Examination of some natural categories (e.g., by Rosch, 1978) quickly revealed most of the inadequacies of the Classical View. The "furniture" category, for example, has unclear cases (e.g., a TV set) and prototypical cases, and there seem to be no defining features, while nonnecessary features are sometimes used to categorize a stimulus. For these sorts of reasons, many, though not all researchers have turned to the Probablistic View (but see Bourne, 1982).

The Probabilistic View

This view actually consists of the featural, dimensional, and holistic (template) approaches to categorization. However, they share three assumptions: (a) Concepts are represented by a summary description that develops through abstraction, and is not necessarily realizable as an instance; (b) the features of a concept are salient, and are likely to occur in instances of the category; and (c) some entity X is categorized as Y iff X contains a critical sum of the weighted features of Y (Smith & Medin, 1981).

Experiments conducted within this framework have exhibited greater methodological variety than classical experiments. Nevertheless, certain paradigms have emerged. In one paradigm, observers first learn to classify stimuli, such as random dot patterns (Posner & Keele, 1968) or schematic faces (Reed, 1972), that have been generated by repeated distortions of an original stimulus, generally referred to as the "prototype." A transfer tasks usually follows in which the observers attempt to classify some of the acquisition stimuli, several new transfer stimuli that are also distortions of the prototypes, and the prototypes themselves. In general, the observers are most accurate at classifying the acquisition stimuli. But they are equally good at classifying the prototypes, even though they have not seen them before. And they are more accurate at both than they are at classifying the new distortions. Posner and his colleagues (e.g., Posner, Goldsmith, & Welton, 1967; Posner & Keele, 1968) have argued that observers learn categories by abstracting information from the exemplars. The prototype, as representative of this information, is easily identified.

Although these results are inconsistent with the Classical View, most Probabilistic theorists nevertheless retain the Classicist's fascination with simple stimuli, artificial categories, features, and the observer's success in identifying stimuli as full members or nonmembers of a particular category. More recently, Rosch (1978) has investigated the structure of naturally occurring categories such as "tool," "furniture," "bird," etc. She discovered that the categories did not conform to strict logical rules, but, rather, were built around prototypes that possess most of the important attributes of the stimuli in the category. According to Rosch, prototypes reflect the actual correlation between the attributes as they occur in the environment. Category members are related on a family resemblance or Wittgensteinian basis, and vary in category status. Moreover, categories occur at different levels, the "basic level" (e.g., "chair" as opposed to "furniture") being particularly important since it conveys more information than higher or lower levels.

Note that several of the problems that besieged the Classical View are not problems at all for the Probabilistic View. Because the summary representation is the central tendency of the category, it may well include features that are neither necessary nor sufficient for defining category membership. Indeed, no defining features exist, though necessary features may. Highly probable or salient features which are not necessary – like "flies" for bird – would be included in the representation. Nor is it problematic that observers do not list a consistent set of features for a category, because no defining features exist. Instead, they list the typical features. The typicality effects that were particularly detrimental to the Classical View are also handled with ease. More typical category members have a greater number of features in common with the representation. The same is true for members that are judged more similar to a distant superordinate than to an immediate superordinate. That is, it is possible to have more features in common with a distant than an immediate superordinate. But the real advantage of the feature approach of the Probabilistic View is its ability to explain ambiguous cases, since natural categories have fuzzy boundaries. In determining the category member-ship of an event, the Probabilistic View makes use of a weighted sum, a totaling up of features that an event shares with a prototype (see Medin, 1983; Smith & Medin, 1981). Events that exceed some criterion are classified according to the prototype. Those that only meet or approach the criterion are ambiguous cases.

Another criticism of the Classical View – failure to deal with functional features – is also a fault of the Probabilistic View. In fact the issue is not limited to functional features or to the Classical or Probabilistic Views. The fundamental is-sue to be addressed by feature theorists is, What constitutes a feature? In Rosch's early work (e.g., Rosch & Mervis, 1975), feature was operationally defined as an-ything an observer listed as characteristic of a category. The lists included mostly perceptual features, but functional features, relational features, and post-hoc fea-tures that are apparent only after an event is categorized (a chair "has a seat"), were also included (Rosch, 1978). The problem is that, if what constitutes a feature is subject to contextual effects or prior knowledge of category member-ship or both, then anything can be a feature. An observer asked to list the features of a chair he or she cannot see will probably include some reference to a seat, be-cause the object is a chair. And he or she may include a reference to its being furni-ture, but probably only if it is contrasted with something like a tree stump. Skeptics are unable to attack feature theories because the concept of feature is to-tally unconstrained. It is also circular, since features necessarily decompose into other features. Features and categories therefore become indistinguishable and the number of necessary primitive concepts increases without bound. Recently, Armstrong, Gleitman, and Gleitman (1983) took issue with feature theories, be-cause they found that even some definitional categories (e.g., odd number) have better members than others, thereby invalidating any argument that typicality ef-fects automatically imply a prototypical category structure.

The Exemplar View

In its strongest form, the Exemplar View does not postulate a summary repre-sentation for categories. Instead, a category is defined by the members or exem-plars that belong to it, and is represented disjunctively by "separate descriptions of some of its exemplars" (Smith & Medin, 1981, p. 144). The more similar the exemplars, the tighter the category. A novel stimulus is classified as a member of a category by assessing its similarity to known exemplars rather than to a proto-type or a set of defining features. Known exemplars that are similar to the to-be-classified exemplar are retrieved for use in the comparison process. Exemplars become category members if they retrieve more known instances of that cate-gory quicker than they retrieve known instances from other categories. Accord-ing to the Exemplar View, the tacit goal of categorization is to maximize within-category similarity while minimizing between-category similarity. Less strict exemplar models (Medin & Schaffer, 1978) allow some summary representation, but maintain that the bulk of the classification process is carried out with reference to more accessible exemplars. Medin (1983) offers a recent overview of the Exemplar View.

Some of the assumptions entailed by the Exemplar View have been tested empirically (Homa, Sterling, & Trepel, 1981; Medin & Schaffer, 1978; Medin & Schwanenflugel, 1981). Medin and Schaffer (1978) argued that, if category membership was assessed with reference to stored exemplars rather than to stored prototypes, then the difficulty of learning that a particular stimulus instantiated a category should increase as the similarity of that instance to instances of other categories increases. This seemed to occur, but there were several deficiencies in the experiments reported – an exceptionally small number of training stimuli were used, 41% of the observers failed to achieve the learning criteria, the categories were totally arbitrary and apparently very confusing, and statistical trends were often treated as significant.

The next section reports research on the structure of categories organized around figurative meanings. As we shall see, the traditional views of categorization cannot address these more abstract, complex, conceptually-driven categories.

EMPIRICAL RESEARCH

Research on Proverb Categories

When proverbs are used in everyday life, it is almost always in a social context in which the proverb performs some speech act, such as to warn, vilify, moralize, etc. Little of a systematic sort is known about these pragmatic aspects, although some ethnographic work has been done (see Mieder & Dundes, 1981). Hence, the experiments described below concentrate on the semantics rather than the pragmatics of proverb categories.

Until 1982, our research with proverbs was not concerned with issues of categorization. Instead, interest focused on issues of semantic memory and synonymy (see Honeck, Voegtle, Dorfmueller, & Hoffman, 1980, for a review), mental representation (see Honeck & Kibler, 1985), and on specific questions about proverb comprehension (e.g., Honeck & Kibler, 1984b). Nevertheless, many of the experiments conducted prior to this time capitalized on observers' abilities to categorize. So they are easily construed as studies of categorization, as well as of figurative language. A brief review of these studies follows (see Honeck, Sugar, & Kibler, 1982, for a more comprehensive treatment).

Old Proverb Research

This research is summarized in Honeck et al. (1980) and Honeck et al. (1982). The gist of it can be conveyed by first introducing the concept of a "proverb family." A proverb family consists of a proverb, verbal or pictorial renditions of the proverb's literal meaning, verbal interpretations of the proverb's figurative meaning, and verbal and/or pictorial instances of this figurative meaning. For example, the family for the proverb *A net with a hole in it won't catch any fish,* might include, *No fish will be caught by a net with a hole in it, A flawed instrument cannot perform its normal function, The missionary who didn't speak their language couldn't convert any of the natives, The quarterback was inebriated and threw wildly to his receivers* – a literal paraphrase, an interpretation, and two instances, respectively, of the proverb.

The glue that holds the family together is not *in* the members themselves, nor in any shared deep structure, propositional structure, or mental imagery. Rather, the glue is a constructed meaning or significance which is most directly and best expressed by the interpretation. However, since the interpretation can be paraphrased in different ways, it is clear that some more abstract, nonverbal mental entity is involved. This schema-like entity is what Honeck (1973) called a "conceptual base" and what Honeck et al. (1980) elaborated into The Conceptual Base Theory of proverb comprehension.

This theory has been confirmed by a number of findings. For example, memory studies indicate that verbal scenarios (3–4 sentence-long instances) can prompt the recall of proverbs (Honeck, Riechmann, & Hoffman, 1975), but that interpretations are the best prompts for recall of other family members (Dorfmueller & Honeck, 1980). The abstract, amodal character of a conceptual base has been convincingly demonstrated by the fact that 7-, 8-, and 9-year-old children can select which of two pictures correctly instantiates a proverb's figurative meaning (Honeck, Sowry, & Voegtle, 1978), and that adult observers can select which of two verbal instances correctly matches a picture of the proverb's literal content (Honeck, Voegtle, & Sowry, 1981).

More recently, Honeck and Kibler (1984b) showed that, if observers rated how well a picture captured the literal content of a proverb, or imaged the literal proverb information, they were unable to distinguish novel positive from novel negative instances of the proverb's figurative meaning. In contrast, observers who processed a four-term analogy which incorporated the subject and the predicate of the proverb along with analogous interpretive information, exhibited above chance ability to make this distinction. Finally, observers who processed both an analogy and an instance for the proverbs, excelled at making this distinction.

The results of these several studies can be explained as follows. Under certain conditions, namely those that lead an observer to *recognize* that the literal meaning of a proverb is inappropriate and that a nonliteral meaning must be sought, the observer *transforms* the literal proverb information and whatever contextual information is relevant. The transformation process often involves analogy formation, which serves as a framework for constructing a *figurative meaning.* This meaning serves as the glue for a complex category whose name is the proverb itself and whose range and kind of *instantiation* is mediated by this meaning. The meaning is the "black hole" of a category universe, since events are assimilated into (and rejected from) the category via the meaning. Events that are assimilated become instances that are similar by virtue of assimilation. Since a large number of events from different sensory modalities can enjoy the same categorical fate, it is clear that the meaning is generative and amodal. As yet, however, the meaning has proven impervious to description in more precise formal terms.

New Proverb Research

As mentioned previously, earlier proverb research did not flow from an interest in categorization. Our recent research has done just that, however. The *Conceptual Base View* of categorization, an outgrowth of the Conceptual Base Theory of proverb comprehension, has served as a framework for this research. Briefly, this view holds that some categories are organized around a conceptual base that serves to relate literally dissimilar events.

An initial experiment clearly demonstrated, contrary to the Classical View, that proverb categories are graded rather than binary, and that category level information in the form of a conceptual base produces the gradedness (Honeck, Kibler, & Sugar, 1985). Each of four groups of observers was asked to rank a set of 10 sentences (i.e., instances) in terms of how well the sentences illustrated the figurative meaning of a proverb (Proverb group); or the meaning of an abstractly worded, excellent interpretation of the proverb (Excellent Interpretation Group); or the meaning of an abstractly worded, poor interpretation of the proverb (Poor Interpretation group); or an unstated general idea that observers were supposed to construct on their own – i.e., no referent sentence was provided (Control group). Each group ranked three different sets of 10 sentences. For example, one set included the proverb, *Bees have honey in their mouths and stingers in their tails,* the excellent interpretation, *Some things that look good on the surface may turn out to be totally bad,* the poor interpretation, *A part of a whole doesn't necessarily fit all contexts or wholes,* and instances such as, *The manipulative son complimented his mother on her new hair style and then asked her if he could borrow the car, The summer raindrops were so heavy they cracked the parched crops,* and *The cookies were delicious and rich in protein,* instances that the Proverb and Excellent Interpretation Groups assigned high, mediocre, and low ranks, respectively.

The results indicated that observers in the Proverb group agreed on the ranks, as did those in the Excellent Interpretation group, and that the two groups' ranks were concordant. Observers in the Poor Interpretation and in the Control groups did not agree on the ranks, nor were their ranks concordant.

Apparently, observers in the Proverb and Excellent Interpretation groups were using quite similar category information to do their rankings. The authors argued that this information was in the form of a conceptual base, and that observers were comparing the *significance* of the events described in the sentences to the conceptual bases, using the degree of the match as a basis for their rankings. Regardless of how the results are explained, however, they are totally inconsistent with the Classical View's requirement that categories be binary. They are also inconsistent with the radical Exemplar View's assumption that instances become instances through contact with similar stored instances. For the present case, the verbal materials were not similar a priori–similarity had to be constructed through interpretation–and for this reason an unelaborated stimulus input could not yield the obtained rankings. In the same vein, no abstracted prototype, in the form of a summary of highly probable attributes, could have produced the results. A prototype, while not necessarily real, contains information of the same kind and on the same level as that "contained" in instances. There are indeed prototypical figurative meanings of proverbs, but that is beside the point.

Using a transfer paradigm, Voegtle (1983) manipulated the composition of proverb families to determine its effect on categorization. During acquisition, a group received families composed of a proverb and an interpretation and an instance of it (Mixed group), or three interpretations that were synonymous (Interpretation group), or three instances drawn from the same semantic domain (Narrow group), or three instances drawn from different semantic domains (Wide group). For example, the narrow group received three instances that involved "business" and shared an underlying message. (Table 1 illustrates the width factor in another experiment.) All groups then received novel positive and negative test sentences that were either interpretations or instances. Observers responded "yes" (it's related in meaning to an acquisition family meaning) or "no." Positive interpretation test sentences most closely approximate their conceptual base, so they should have been detected best. This was confirmed for all but the Narrow group, which performed best on new instances from the same semantic domain. Unexpectedly, the Narrow group performed as well as the Wide group on wide instances–items that shared the meaning but not the domain of the acquisition family.

The fact that abstract interpretations were recognized best contradicts the Probabilistic and Exemplar Views. The interpretations were not prototypes or instances per se. Certainly, an appeal to similarity does not explain the transfer results, because similarity between family members was derived and not due to physical or perceptual features. In general, the three views fail to acknowledge the crucial role of interpretive processes in the learning and use of categories. Just as important, the conceptual bases that the processes produce cannot be equated with "summary information," conceived as an average of instance information. As we said before, a conceptual base contains information of a different order than that "in" the instances of the category.

A lingering question about Voegtle's (1983) results concerns the role of the "width" or variability of the instances in a family. In general, observers in the Narrow group performed as well in transfer as the Wide group. Perhaps Voegtle's observers overcame the overcontextualized learning that could result from narrow experience. Other possibilities are that her narrow categories were actually too wide, or that her observers, since they were in different groups, were less likely to note the difference in category widths than if they had experienced both widths.

Honeck and Kibler (1984a) re-examined the width factor in a within-subjects transfer design. All observers were first exposed to wide and to narrow families during a series of study and paired-associate learning trials. Then they were tested with novel sentences that were either positive or negative instances of the original family meanings and that were from domains that were the same as or different from the original family members. Thus, there were four kinds of test items – positive-sames, positive-differents, negative-sames, and negative-differents. A sample of materials is presented in Table 1. Note that all test items belonged to a particular family, even if they were negative instances. These instances reflected the theme of a family but were inconsistent with it.

The results were almost entirely consistent with the Conceptual Base View. First, the wide condition generated better performance than the narrow condition on all test items except positive-sames, which produced equal performance. Probabilistic and Exemplar Views cannot countenance this result, inasmuch as

TABLE 1
Sample Materials Used by Honeck & Kibler (1984a)

Merbee Family: Acquisition Items[a]
The technician flipped the wrong switches and the rocket couldn't take off.
The shuttle developed a problem in its fuel system and had to return to earth.
After its computer developed a short circuit, the space capsule couldn't take pictures of the craters.
Merbee Family: Transfer Items[a]
Because the astronaut's suit was poorly designed, it couldn't protect him from the high temperatures.
The missionary who didn't speak the natives' language converted no one.
Even though the meteor cracked its windshield, the Enterprise wasn't knocked off course.
The string busted on his guitar but he still played beautifully.

Tussley Family: Acquisition Items
The doctor paid a destitute wino to deliver the illegal drugs and bring back the money.
The professor received the Nobel Prize for the grueling research work she made her graduate students do.
The colonel who sent a platoon on a dangerous fact-finding mission was the only one who was decorated for its success.
Tussley Family: Transfer Items
Realizing that he would get the credit anyway, the second lieutenant sent the private to clear the minefield.
The professional boxer trained the novice to box for the contest, and then claimed the prize money as his manager.
The engineering department made the freshmen take their only required course from the worst teacher.
The rancher hired some hands to put up a fence.

---

[a]Merbee is a narrow family and Tussley is a wide family.
[b]In order, the transfer items for each family are positive–same, positive–different, negative–same and negative–different. In the actual experiment, one more of each kind of transfer item per family was used.

the most *dissimilar* family of instances produced the best performance. Indeed, on the critical positive-different items, the narrow condition yielded chance performance, while the wide condition was at 71% correct. Apparently, more variable, decontextualized experience allowed observers to construct more flexible abstract categories. Homa and Vosburgh (1976), who used random dot stimuli, and Nitsch (cited in Bransford, 1979), who used sentences, have made similar observations.

Many of the preceding results, while consistent with the Conceptual Base View, have not provided direct evidence about the structure of a conceptual base. We already know that a base is nonverbal, nonimagistic, abstract, general, and generative. In general, how is the information in the figurative meaning of a proverb to be construed? Does it have parts or components?

Kibler (1984) has made some inroads on this question. She reasoned that, if a conceptual base has components, then the extent to which an instance was judged as having these components, would be a good indicator of the extent of category membership. She expressed the figurative meaning of several proverbs as sets of components and then generated stories that embodied the components to varying degrees. Some observers rated the extent to which the stories embodied the components. These ratings were converted to ranks such that the more components a story entailed, the better its rank. Other observers ranked the stories associated with a single proverb, in the absence of the explicit components, according to how well they illustrated the proverb's figurative meaning. Observers in these ranking groups consented on the order of the stories, and this order was highly correlated with the ranks derived from the component ratings. Kibler concluded that proverb categories, as one type of figurative category, are organized around miniature theories about the relationships among proverb elements as symbols of complex real world events.

Research on Metaphor

As stated previously, the traditional views of categorization are primarily concerned with the question of the likelihood of X being categorized as Y. These views are not concerned with the anomalous mixing of categories. Indeed, in the predominant Probabilistic View, category level information is inevitably described as a statistical average or weighted sum of stimulus features. This approach is seemingly legitimized, if it is assumed that categorization is stimulus-driven and that a stimulus and a category have characteristics that can be rather easily checked for a match. The question in metaphor, however, is how category X (the topic) can be fashioned into an element of category Y (the vehicle), where Y is a statistically abnormal category for X, and still say something sensible about X. This construal of metaphor implies that theories of metaphor should place greater emphasis on strategies, problem solving, and search for perspective, in short on conceptually driven categorization.

Indeed, a bird's-eye view survey of recent research on metaphor reveals this to be the case. Aware that metaphors show great variation in complexity and kind, investigators have invoked a variety of mechanisms to explain them, including schema-based attribute matching, analogy, and Gestalt physiognomic perception. For example, Ortony and his associates (Ortony, 1979; Ortony, Vondruska, Foss, & Jones, 1984) have promulgated the "salience imbalance hypothesis," which holds that shared attributes that are high salient for the vehicle but low salient for the topic, are transferred to the topic. Ortony et al. (1984) report some evidence supporting this hypothesis. However, Gentner (1980) claims that her "structure-mapping hypothesis" is more valid than the imbalance notion and presents empirical evidence against the notion. She argues that people actually prefer to use complex relational information in comprehending metaphor, and therefore that analogy is used to map information between the topic and vehicle domains. In a counterargument, Ortony et al. (1984) say, for example, that the imbalance notion does not preclude relations as an attribute.

However this controversy is resolved, it is clear that certain issues must be addressed. For example, what is *not* an attribute, and how can attributes and relational information be reliably distinguished? Perhaps more crucial is the question of how attributes can be matched, since they are similar, not identical, as Ortony (1979) notes. Moreover, one can ask whether the imbalance hypothesis explains anything, since mapping of high salient vehicle attributes seem to be an end result, not a cause. Why, if a metaphor embodies this mapping, does it do so, and how does the mapping take place? The structure-mapping hypothesis also seems inadequate. Analogies merely frame information; they are not solutions. One wonders whether there is more to metaphor than attributes and analogy.

Numerous studies suggest there is. Pitts, Smith, and Pollio (1982) found that observers who adopted a Gestalt nonanalytic mental set, then drew abstract lines for a metaphor topic and matched them to one of four pre-designated vehicle categories, produced more novel, more apt metaphoric comparisons than did observers asked to match verbally stated topic and vehicle attributes or to analogize them.

Other investigators have also examined observers' abilities to integrate information arising from different modalities. Marks and Hammela (1982) found, for example, that while adults tend to give consistent synesthetic judgments, children are inconsistent in associating pitch with size, suggesting that this association may be learned while others (e.g., loudness with brightness) may be innate. Similarly, Mills (1983) demonstrated that observers could match abstract cartoons with verbal descriptions, e.g., a triangle crushing a circle is matched with "a car colliding with a pole," or with "a totalitarian regime suppressing free will." We also note Kennedy's (1982; Kennedy & Simpson, in press) claim that, for every figure of speech, there is a "figure of depiction."

The above work on cross-modal integration complements earlier research on: abstract line drawings of proverbs (Kaplan, 1955); the use of abstract line drawings to prompt the recall of metaphors (Verbrugge, 1977); and metaphoric understanding of the surrealistic paintings of Magritte (Johnson & Malgady, 1980). Furthermore, children can: match pictures on a metaphorical basis (Connor & Kogan, 1980), apply dual-function terms (e.g., hard, cold) appropriately to people (Asch & Nerlove, 1960), match such terms with sounds, faces, or colors (Gardner, 1974), analogize parts of the human body to pictures of trees or mountains (Gentner, 1977), and match proverbs with pictures illustrating the figurative meaning of the proverbs (Honeck, Voegtle, & Sowry, 1981).

Finally, Johnson (1983, 1984) has analyzed metaphor interpretations in terms of the level of processing—from simple global to analytic (analogy based) to complex analytic (involving instantiation)—involved in the mapping of vehicle "facets" to topic facets. She found that older observers produced fewer global interpretations, and more complex analytic interpretations. Similarly, Gentner and Stuart (1983) find that "relational metaphors" (e.g., The cloud is like a sponge) increase with age, while "attributive metaphors" (e.g., The cloud is like a marshmallow) do not. Finally, Shantiris (1983) finds that functionally grounded metaphors become more acceptable with age, perceptually grounded metaphors less so, and affectively grounded ones hardly at all.

Metaphor and Categorization

The research just reviewed suggests that many different processes may promote metaphor production and comprehension. None of these processes, whether schema-based attribute matching, analogizing, Gestalt-perception, or cold analytical interpretation, seems very consistent with traditional views of categorization. The topic and vehicle in a metaphor do not share all of their attributes, or even the important or prototypical ones, nor are particular exemplars of the vehicle mapped to particular exemplars of the topic. Perhaps, in some cases, a vehicle prototype, conceived as a Roschian cluster of high salient attributes, is applied to a topic, but unless simple perceptually-based metaphors (e.g., Clouds are marshmallows) are involved, the prototype is not mapped to a topic prototype. Even for such metaphors, attributes may be mapped that have no common literal elements—e.g., the "puffiness" of clouds, which is a seen physiognomic quality, and of marshmallows, which is largely tactual.

The poor fit between traditional views of categorization and metaphor stems from fundamentally different concerns in these arenas. Categorization models are concerned with the likelihood that X will be categorized as Y. In metaphor, the question is not how likely a topic is to be assimilated by a vehicle, but, rather, how a topic can be sensibly construed in the momentary context of a vehicle. Or, stated differently, what can be added to or highlighted about the topic category that is important and insightful, and that would not be revealed by consideration of this category as an abstract prototype in isolation.

The traditional views of categorization therefore seem irrelevant to metaphor.

If someone says *This music is fire crackling through a java sky,* the question is not whether the music is actually fire but what is being communicated about the music when considered from the perspective of a fire. The emphasis is not on truth, logic, and perceptible reality, but on providing a complex emotional-aesthetic–informational package that is probably harder to communicate in more literal terms. Metaphor users know at some level that the topic and vehicle categories are not literally identical or even similar. The categories are chosen *because* they are literally disparate yet communicationally apposite. The user is playfully and intentionally crossing domains that are literally dissimilar by means of a linguistic assertion that would ordinarily signal a truth claim. This is set in motion by the power of language and by the user's desire to utilize whatever cognitive resources are at his or her disposal to capture the significance of an event or situation and communicate it efficiently, even elegantly.

Thus, the traditional views of categorization fail to address metaphor because they are too one-sided in their conceptualization of the role of categories in human thought. Categories are not simply mental compartments that assimilate stimuli because the stimuli happen to be similar enough to the category. Nor are categories merely used to provide stability in perception but rather to think, communicate, be creative, inform action, and so on. The traditional views are concerned with learning at the expense of function. When metaphors are used to juxtapose categories, phenomena occur that are clearly at odds with the philosophy behind the traditional views. Metaphor uses dissimilarity to provoke a search for a perspective. If the perspective is one that yields a similarity between topic and vehicle, it is often not a pre-existing similarity, already bundled up in shared attributes, but, in Max Black's (1962) words, a "created similarity." Metaphor creates a genuine interaction between categories, not a one-sided flow of information from X to Y. The topic, as many have noted, influences the way the vehicle is construed. Traditional views of categorization have failed to address such context effects. And note that it is construal–thought–that is affected, not perception, though perception may ultimately be affected by the thought. Metaphor turns perception on its head. Men do not become wolves, or children butterflies, in the real world. Divorced from the press of the immediate perceptual world, however, the metaphor user can play with categories.

The traditional views of categorization do not address these issues. In large measure, this is because they arose out of Behaviorist philosophy and, in part, because they have not dealt with the problems of language use and understanding. *There are practically no psycholinguistic studies of categorization.* As enlightened Cognitive Behaviorists, theorists working within the three views have emphasized environmental stimuli, or rather their features, and their raw impact on the person. Hence, almost without exception, the three views have concentrated on perceptual categories, often arbitrary ones, though Rosch's (1978) work on natural categories has forced some revisions in the traditional views. And, except for work on strategies and hypothesis testing (e.g., Bruner, Goodnow, & Austin, 1956;

Levine, 1966), the person has been left out of the categorization process. By the Behavorist model, a stimulus is perceived, some features of the stimulus are abstracted, a similarity function is computed between the stimulus and learned stimuli, and, ergo, a classification response takes place. No wonder that an emphasis on dissimilarity, mentally created similarity rather than stimulus-driven similarity, communication and understanding rather than truth value, use rather than learning, thought rather than perception, perspective rather than no perspective, interpretation rather than pattern matching, interaction rather than linear processing, context rather than isolation, and dynamic rather than static mental organization, are all anathema to the traditional views. The proponents of these views will have to grapple with all of the issues that psycholinguistics has faced the last 25 years before the views' generalizability can be taken more seriously.

CONCLUSIONS

Empirical work on proverb categories provides strong evidence that the traditional views of categorization do not address these categories. Empirical work on metaphors has not been linked with these views, but our examination of this link reveals why these areas have "passed like two ships in the night." That the reasons are essentially the same as those that arose in the case of proverb categories is understandable. Proverbs and metaphors perform very similar functions. If proverbs are considered to be complex vehicles, then the utterance of a proverb in relation to some event amounts to a statement of the form, X (the event) is a Y (the proverb), and quite parallel therefore to the common "isa" metaphor formula. Like metaphors, proverbs select out some aspect(s) of an event for comment in the form, often enough, of a speech act. The question is not whether the event is likely to fit in this or that category, but rather, what the proverb says *about* the event. Thus, were the empirical evidence not available, one still might have concluded that proverb categories are not amenable to analysis by the traditional views.

In large measure, these views have built-in assumptions that are very similar to those that characterize what Lakoff and Johnson (1980) call the "myth of objectivism"–i.e., that the world is composed of objects that have properties inherent in the objects, that categories are built on these properties, that meaning is tied to objective truths concerning these properties and their relationships, that similarity consists in sharing these properties, and so on. It is no coincidence, therefore, that Lakoff and Johnson's critique of objectivism in relation to metaphor is quite similar to our critique of the traditional views. We would emphasize that the use of metaphors and proverbs puts categories in action, yet the traditional views have deemphasized function in favor of assimilation. A resurrection of the importance of accommodation would quickly reveal the need to consider interaction of category and event (or category), as well as people's cognitive resources and powers, including intention, perspective, imaginative play, the ability to cognitively re-work and analyze categories, etc. Theories of categorization must eventually incorporate these factors, or be unable to cope with the semantics and pragmatics of more abstract categories.

REFERENCES

Armstrong, S. L., Gleitman, L. R., & Gleitman, H. (1983). What some concepts might not be. *Cognition, 13,* 263–308.
Asch, S. & Nerlove, H., (1960). The development of double function terms in children. In B. Kaplan & S. Wapner (Eds.) *Perspectives in psychological theory.* NY: International Universities Press.
Black, M. (1962). *Models and metaphors.* Ithaca, NY: Cornell University Press.
Bourne, L. E. (1966). *Human conceptual behavior.* Boston: Allyn-Bacon.
Bourne, L. E. (1982). Typicality effects in logically defined categories. *Memory and Cognition, 10,* 3–9.
Bransford, J. D. (1979). *Human cognition: Learning, understanding, and remembering.* Belmont, CA: Wadsworth.
Bruner, J. S., Goodnow, J. J., & Austin, G. A. (1956). *A study of thinking.* NY: Wiley.
Connor, K. & Kogan, N. (1980). Topic-vehicle relations in metaphor: The issue of asymmetry. In R. P. Honeck & R. R. Hoffman (Eds.), *Cognition and figurative language* (pp. 283–310). Hillsdale, NJ: Erlbaum.
Dorfmueller, M. A. & Honeck, R. P. (1980). Centrality and generativity within a linguistic family: Toward a conceptual base theory of groups. *The Psychological Record, 30,* 95–109.
Gardner, H. (1974). Metaphors and modalities: How children project polar adjectives onto diverse domains. *Child Development, 45,* 84–91.
Gentner, D. (1977). Children's performance on a spatial analogies task. *Child Development, 48,* 1034–1039.
Gentner, D. (1980). Studies of metaphor and complex analogies: A structure-mapping theory. Symposium paper presented at the American Psychological Association Symposium on Metaphor as Process, Montreal.
Gentner, D. & Stuart, P. (1983). Metaphor as structure mapping: What develops? Paper presented at the meeting of the Society for Research in Child Development, Detroit.
Goodman, N. (1968). *Languages of art.* Indianapolis: Bobbs-Merrill.
Homa, D., Sterling, S., & Trepel, L. (1981). Limitations of exemplar-based generalization and the abstraction of categorical information. *Journal of Experimental Psychology: Human Learning and Memory, 7,* 418–439.
Homa, D. & Vosburgh, R. (1976). Category breadth and the abstraction of categorical information. *Journal of Experimental Psychology: Human Learning and Memory, 2,* 322–30.
Honeck, R. P. (1973). Interpretive versus structural effects on semantic memory. *Journal of Verbal Learning and Verbal Behavior, 12,* 448–455.
Honeck, R. P., & Kibler, C. (1984a). The conceptual base view of categories: The role of context. Unpublished paper, University of Cincinnati.
Honeck, R. P. & Kibler, C. (1984b). The role of imagery, analogy, and instantiation in proverb comprehension. *Journal of Psycholinguistic Research, 13,* 393–414.
Honeck, R. P., & Kibler, C. (1985). Representation in cognitive psychological theories of figurative language. In R. Dirven & W. Paprotte (Eds.), *The ubiquity of metaphor: Metaphor in thought and language* (pp. 381–424). Amsterdam: John Benjamins.
Honeck, R. P., Kibler, C., & Sugar, J. (1985). The conceptual base view of categorization. *Journal of Psycholinguistic Research, 14,* 155–174.

Honeck, R. P., Riechmann, P., & Hoffman, R. (1975). Semantic memory for metaphor: The conceptual base hypothesis. *Memory and Cognition, 3,* 409–415.

Honeck, R. P., Sowry, B., & Voegtle, K. (1978). Proverbial understanding in a pictorial context. *Child Development, 49,* 327–331.

Honeck, R. P., Sugar, J., & Kibler, C. (1982). Stories, categories, and figurative meaning. *Poetics, 11,* 127–144.

Honeck, R. P., Voegtle, K., Dorfmueller, M. A., & Hoffman, R. R. (1980). Proverbs, meaning, and group structure. In R. P. Honeck & R. R. Hoffman (Eds.), *Cognition and figurative language* (pp. 127–162). Hillsdale, NJ: Erlbaum.

Honeck, R. P., Voegtle, K., & Sowry, B. (1981). Figurative understanding of pictures and sentences. *Journal of Psycholinguistic Research, 10,* 135–153.

Hunt, E. B. (1962). *Concept learning: An information processing problem.* NY: Wiley.

Johnson, J. (1983). A process-structuralist analysis of the development of metaphor comprehension. Symposium paper presented at the meeting of the American Psychological Association, Anaheim, CA.

Johnson, J. (1984). Levels of processing in metaphor comprehension. In Proceedings of the Sixth Annual Conference of the Cognitive Science Society, Boulder, CO., pp. 193–197.

Johnson, M. G., & Malgady, R. G. (1980). Toward a perceptual theory of metaphoric comprehension. In R. P. Honeck & R. R. Hoffman (Eds.), *Cognition and figurative language* (pp. 259–282). Hillsdale, NJ: Erlbaum.

Kaplan, B. (1955). Some psychological methods for the investigation of expressive language. In H. Werner (Ed.), *On expressive language.* Worcester, MA: Clark University Press.

Kennedy, J. M. (1982). Metaphor in pictures. *Perception, 11,* 589–605.

Kennedy, J. M. & Simpson, W. (in press). For each kind of figure of speech there is a pictorial metaphor – a figure of depiction. *Review of Research in Visual Arts Education.*

Kibler, C. (1984). On the structure of conceptual categories. Unpublished dissertation, University of Cincinnati.

Lakoff, G. & Johnson, M. (1980). *Metaphors we live by.* Chicago: University of Chicago Press.

Levine, M. (1966). Hypothesis behavior by humans during discrimination learning. *Journal of Experimental Psychology, 71,* 331–338.

Marks, L. E. & Hammela, R. J. (1982). Children's comprehension of cross-modal metaphors. Unpublished paper, Pierce Foundation Laboratory, New Haven, CT.

Medin, D. L. (1983). Structural principles in categorization. In E. Shepp & T. Tighe (Eds.), *Development of perception and cognition* (pp. 203–229). Hillsdale, NJ: Erlbaum.

Medin, D. L. & Schaffer, M. M. (1978). A context theory of classification learning. *Psychological Review, 85,* 207–238.

Medin, D. L. & Schwanenflugel, P. L. (1981). Linear separability in classification learning. *Journal of Experimental Psychology: Human Learning and Memory, 7,* 355–368.

Mieder, W. & Dundes, A. (1981). *The wisdom of many: Essays on the proverb.* NY: Garland Publishing.

Mills, M. I. (1983). Metaphorical matching of cartoon-strips to descriptions. Symposium paper presented at the American Psychological Association meeting.

Ortony, A. (1979). Beyond literal similarity. *Psychological Review, 86,* 161–180.

Ortony, A., Vondruska, R. J., Foss, M. A., & Jones, L. F. (1984). Salience, similes, and the asymmetry of similarity. Unpublished paper, University of Illinois.

Pitts, M. K., Smith, M. K., & Pollio, H. R. (1982). An evaluation of three different theories of metaphor production through the use of an intentional category mistake procedure. *Journal of Psycholinguistic Research, 11,* 347–368.

Posner, M. I., Goldsmith, R., & Welton, K. E. (1967). Perceived distance and the classification of distorted patterns. *Journal of Experimental Psychology, 73,* 28–38.

Posner, M. I., & Keele, S. W. (1968). On the genesis of abstract ideas. *Journal of Experimental Psychology, 77,* 353–363.

Reed, S. K. (1972). Pattern recognition and categorization. *Cognitive Psychology, 3,* 382–407.

Rosch, F. (1978). Principles of categorization. In E. Rosch & B. B. Lloyd (Eds.), *Cognition and categorization* (pp. 28–48). Hillsdale, NJ: Erlbaum.

Rosch, F. & Mervis, C. B. (1975). Family resemblances: Studies in the internal structure of categories. *Cognitive Psychology, 7,* 573–605.

Scholnick, E. K. (1983). *New trends in conceptual representation: Challenges to Piaget's theory?* Hillsdale, NJ: Erlbaum.

Shantiris, K. (1983). Perception, function, and feeling: Grounds for developmental changes in metaphor evaluation. Symposium paper presented at the American Psychological Association Meeting.

Smith, E. E., & Medin, D. L. (1981). *Categories and concepts.* Cambridge, Mass: Harvard University Press, 1981.

Turbayne, C. (1970). *The myth of metaphor.* Columbia, S.C.: University of South Carolina Press.

Verbrugge, R. R. (1977). Resemblances in language and perception. In R. E. Shaw & J. D. Bransford (Eds.), *Acting, perceiving, and comprehending: Toward an ecological psychology.* Hillsdale, NJ: Erlbaum.

Voegtle, K. (1983). Categorization of figurative concepts. Unpublished doctoral dissertation, University of Cincinnati.

Werner, H. (1940). *Comparative psychology of mental development.* NY: International Universities Press.

Werner, H. & Kaplan, B. (1963). *Symbol formation.* NY: Wiley.

CHAPTER SEVEN

Proverbs, Pragmatics, and the Ecology of Abstract Categories*

Robert R. Hoffman
Adelphi University

Richard P. Honeck
University of Cincinnati

The study of figurative language leads one to ponder all sorts of fascinating language forms, such as metaphors that are about metaphors (*"A metaphor is a goldmine"*). In contrast to such exotic forms, this chapter focuses on a more mundane one, the common proverb, such as *"Don't look a gift horse in the mouth,"* and *"If the shoe fits, wear it."* Previous research (see chapter 6, this volume; see also Honeck, Voegtle, Dorfmueller, & Hoffman, 1980) has focused on uncommon or specially composed proverbs for use in laboratory experiments on semantic memory. The present chapter focuses more on the pragmatics of common proverbs—how many people know, when they use them, what they are used for, etc.

This chapter is organized rather like a research report. First, background research and some basic theoretical notions are introduced. Then, two studies are presented, one on recall and the other on recognition memory. The chapter concludes with a discussion of broader theoretical issues.

*This research was supported by a Postdoctoral Associateship to the first author via grant HD-07151, from the National Institute of Child Health and Human Development to the Center for Research on Human Learning, and by a Summer Faculty Research Grant to the first author from Adelphi University. Requests for reprints should be sent to Robert R. Hoffman, Department of Psychology, Adelphi University, Garden City, NY 11530.

THE NATURE OF COMMON PROVERBS

Many traditional theories of figurative language, and of language in general, focus on creativity, novelty, transformations, and generativity (e.g., Chomsky, 1965; Katz, 1973). While much language is creative, much of it is not. An extreme example would be that of the Nigerians who memorized the Koran without understanding Arabic (Clark & Clark, 1977).

Most actual figurative communication, including common proverbs, is somewhat repetitive or "formulaic." Rather than being creative, formulas are relatively fixed in syntax and content words (Chafe, 1968; Fraser, 1970). That is, certain transformations (e.g., of phrase structure or tense) preserve the nonliteral meaning, while other transformations appear to disrupt it. Many common metaphors are fairly frozen, such as *"We're running out of time," "The words carried great weight,"* and *"The ideas came across well"* (Lakoff & Johnson, 1980, have provided hundreds of examples). Many common idioms are frozen, such as *"fight tooth and nail," "close shave," "lead a dog's life," "get the ball rolling," "flat as a pancake,"* and *"a sight for sore eyes."* None of these is completely frozen, however. For example, *"to pop the question"* can be transformed in a number of ways and yet retain the nonliteral reference to a marriage proposal (e.g., *"the question was popped"*).

In figurative formulas, be they idioms, metaphors, or proverbs, the basic figurative comparison is invariant across exemplars that vary somewhat in specific words or word order. They are not quite creative, and yet are not quite frozen; hence the term "formulaic" (Becker, 1975).

In their estimates of the frequency of occurrence of figurative language in conversations and text, Pollio, Barlow, Fine, & Pollio (1977) reported that idioms and common metaphors outnumbered novel metaphors, by about 20 million per lifetime to 10 million per lifetime. Becker (1975) estimates that the corpus of commonly-known American idioms ranges in the tens of thousands.

The formulaic character of many proverbs shows in the Book of Proverbs of the Bible. Eating is used repeatedly as a symbol for beliefs (e.g., good beliefs or words as *"honey"*), the tongue is used repeatedly as a symbol for words and ideas (i.e., wise, foolish, and evil ones), the whipping rod is used in a number of proverbs as a symbol for the fate of the sacreligious, silver and gold are used as symbols for good ideas or beliefs. Although the following examples of Biblical proverbs and aphorisms may be unfamiliar, they all have a familiar ring: *"A rebuke goes deeper into a man of understanding than 100 blows into a fool," "A word fitly spoken is like apples of gold in pictures of silver,"* and *"A rod is for the back of him who lacks sense."*

Usually, proverbs are stated in the non-past tense. For this reason, they are temporally unrestricted in application. To say, for example, that *"Bees have honey in their mouths and stingers in their tails"* is to make a claim whose (figurative) meaning applies from the indefinite past through the indefinite future. If restated as *"Bees had honey in their mouths and stingers in their tails,"* the claim loses much of its figurative potential. In general, indefiniteness of temporal reference serves notice that a general rather than a particular interpretation is required. The need for a general interpretation is also signalled by indefinite noun phrases, or definite noun phrases that have no particular contextual counterpart (e.g., the four noun phrases in *"The monkey takes the chestnuts out of the fire with the dog's paw"*).

Proverbs are also often signalled by specific grammatical patterns such as conditionals and imperatives, by semantic markers such as the use of paradox and contrast, and by phonic markers such as rhyme, meter, and alliteration (Silverman-Weinreich, 1981). Many proverbs' structures can be described according to a binary theme of topic and comment, as in: "Don't _____ before/without _____," or, "Every _____ is/has a _____." Thus, as a type of figurative language formula, proverbs are often signalled by their syntax. However, proverbs are not restricted to these formulas, since they can be rendered in virtually any sort of linguistic structure.

Another characteristic of figurative language formulas, including proverbs, is that they often have to be explained or taught. Some idioms are good examples (e.g., *"to trip the light fantastic," "to drag a red herring"*), as are some proverbs (*"Silk and velvet put out the fire in the kitchen"*). Often, of course, a formula is not explained, but comprehended on the basis of context or other information. In any event, a person's understanding of a particular form may be incomplete or incorrect. So may their memory for the verbatim form.

In some cultures, proverbs are not only taught but used as teaching devices much more than in mainstream American culture. Members of the Ibo tribe of Africa sometimes seem unable to speak *without* uttering a proverb. Many tribes have the tradition of using proverbs in stories to explain cultural beliefs and histories. The proverbs are specifically taught, and often refer to mother or child: *"The child on its mother's back does not know the way is long," "A boy who tries to wrestle with his father gets blinded by the old man's loin cloth"* (Seitel, 1969).

While reading these examples out of context, it is important to keep in mind that they are used in situations which do *not* include such things as cows or wrestling. How would theories of language comprehension deal with common proverbs and the pragmatics of their use?

ISSUES RAISED BY PROVERBS

In addition to their focus on linguistic (i.e., syntactically based) creativity, traditional theories of language, and figurative language in particular, are *literalist* theories and *listener* theories. That is, they are generally concerned with how listeners go from a novel (possibly nonliteral) input to a paraphrase of the meaning in terms of psychologically basic literal features (for a more detailed analysis of literalist theories, see Hoffman, MacCormac, & Lawler, 1987, and Honeck et al., 1980).

In contrast, consider the case of production: You've warned your friend on a number of occasions about his car's balding tires, and one day he ends up laboring by the side of the road during an important scheduled meeting. When you next see him, you suddenly think of saying, *"A stitch in time saves nine."*

In this sort of situation, the speaker goes from event perception (involving context, world knowledge, and motivational factors) to something akin to the "click of comprehension." He or she is aware of the relation of a known proverb to the events. Sometimes an appropriate proverb can be deliberately chosen for a given situation, but deliberate awareness and connection-making do not seem necessary, especially if the use of proverbs is a part of one's "cognitive style."

The production situation is very different from the interpretation situation on which literalist theories are based, and such theories therefore have problems when they are "turned upside down" and applied to such actual communication situations. Until one knows the proverb, one cannot know which (literal) features it shares or does not share with the (literal interpretation of the) ongoing events. And until one knows the personal and social context, one cannot predict the proverb's pragmatic meaning, and so one cannot use a literal interpretation to explain the proverb's communicative value.

The production situation can be even more complex. Once, in a class on psycholinguistics, one of us asked students to quickly interpret the proverb, *"A stitch in time saves nine,"* to which a student immediately replied, *"An ounce of prevention is worth a pound of cure."* In this situation, both the "right-side up" and "upside-down" versions of the literalist theory would have to be engaged, as is shown in Figure 1.

The stimulus, a proverb, is a literally anomalous sentence. Recognition of the literal anomaly triggers a special inference process that derives the intended figurative meaning in terms of a set of psychologically basic literal features or semantic elements. For the student's response, this literal representation of the proverb's figurative meaning would be matched in some sort of scanning of a long-term memory containing other common proverbs, themselves understood and remembered in terms of literal element readings of their figurative meanings. Once a proverb is found which appears to be a good or best match, it can be used as a response.

The student had not been told to respond to the stimulus proverb with another proverb, and yet the student's response was almost immediate. How could such complex inferential processing occur in so short a time? Certainly, not all theorists in the literalist tradition would advocate the exact model we described above. There are other ways of configuring literalist models for this situation. Our point is that the above sort of analysis does not seem reasonable at all. As we will show, there are theoretical and empirical reasons for leaving literalist views behind (see also Honeck et al., 1980).

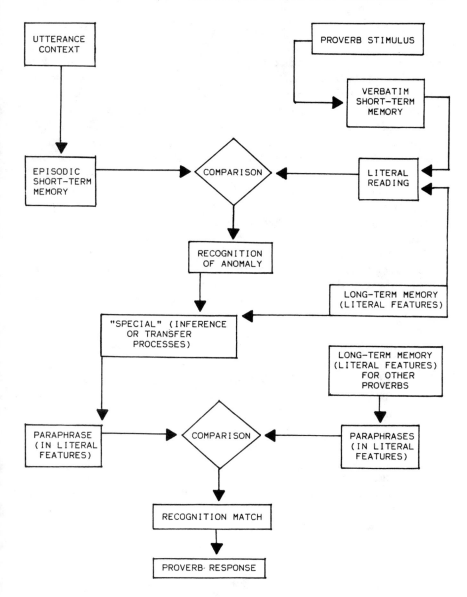

Figure 1

A model for comprehension of novel and common proverbs based on the literalist theoretical point of view. This particular processing sequence is for the interpretation of one
common proverb by another. The model relies on a semantic base of literal features,
comparison processes, long and short-term memories, and a "special" process for
deriving the interpretations of figurative meaning.

Empirical Studies

Research on the comprehension of proverbs, as indexed by latency measurements, has generally involved novel proverbs and has been fraught with problems of variability (e.g., Brewer, Harris, & Brewer, 1974; Staehlin, 1914). Kemper (1981) measured comprehension reaction time for both common and novel proverbs that followed brief paragraph contexts that could refer to either their literal or figurative meaning. Literal use of the proverbs seemed to interfere with comprehension and increase people's reaction time. Similarly, a number of experiments (Gibbs, 1980; Kemper & Estill, 1981; McDonald & Carpenter, 1981; Ortony, Schallert, Reynolds, & Antos, 1978; Swinney & Cutler, 1979) have shown that idioms are comprehended more rapidly than one might expect on the basis of word length. Attempts to get people to take them literally only serve to disrupt the flow of the comprehension process (e.g., the phrase, "*to give a pink slip*" in a paragraph about an actual gift).

The same general finding holds for the comprehension of common metaphor formulas that contain "stock vehicles," such as the comparison of jobs to jails, marriages to refrigerators, roads to snakes, and surgeons to butchers (Gildea & Glucksberg, 1983). It takes longer to judge a sentence to be literally false if it has a readily interpretable nonliteral meaning. Gildea and her colleagues also found that comprehension of metaphors can be influenced by presenting "prime" sentences. For example, a sentence about winters being cold would influence subsequent literal true–false judgments about the metaphor, "*All marriages are like iceboxes*" (Gildea, Glucksberg, & Bookin, 1981). Gildea et al. conclude that if a figurative meaning is available, it will be arrived at. Technically, it is not optional for listeners to initially (and rapidly) comprehend the nonliteral meanings of utterances that include common metaphorical comparisons or stock vehicles.

Apparently, many types of common figurative language formulas are comprehended rapidly. This suggests that they are comprehended and remembered in terms of figurative meaning and concepts, and not in terms of a literal feature transcription, thus obviating the need for the sort of literalist stages described earlier (Hoffman & Kemper, 1987).

The Conceptual Base View of Figurative Meaning

In our past work (Honeck, Riechmann, & Hoffman, 1975; Honeck & Hoffman, 1979; Honeck et al., 1980), we attempted to model the comprehension of novel proverbs without relying on literalist assumptions. We did not assume that context and figurative meanings can be derived or pattern-matched from one another by any process of fusion or transformation. For example, suppose a boy gives his father a watch as a gift, only to wear it himself thereafter. In this context, the proverb "*The cow gives good milk but kicks over the pail*" makes sense, but not because the boy becomes cowlike and the watch becomes milklike.

Early on, it became apparent to us that novel metaphors and novel proverbs are different in important ways. Both metaphors (e.g., *"Juliet in the sun"*) and proverbs (e.g., *"Laws catch flies but let hornets go free"*) can be literally anomalous, even when taken in context, yet proverbs are often both literally and figuratively acceptable (e.g., *"Great weights hang on small wires"*), with the figurative level only partially constrained by the literal level. Proverbs are knowledge-driven, rather than context-driven as novel metaphors are. Proverbs stand out from their context of use in order to comment on it. Clear-case metaphors have explicit topics and vehicles, whereas clear-case proverbs have implicit topics – the whole proverb is the vehicle term, while the topic is an indefinitely large number (i.e., a category) of events. One need not be in the physical presence of a chicken in order to recall and use a proverb that includes the word *"chickens."* Rather, one is in a situation to which a proverb about chickens applies. Thus, the use of proverbs as stimulus materials may be an excellent way of studying the relation between semantic and pragmatic context (Seitel, 1969).

Our early research focused on the cued recall of novel proverbs. Representative materials are presented in Table 1. We were able to show that a statement of the abstract "ground" of a novel proverb would work as a cue for recall of the proverb. We also showed that people can agree on the degree of semantic relatedness of proverbs and their interpretations. Since in these studies the proverbs and their interpretations (the grounds) differed in words, phrase structure, and propositional structure, we conjectured that the comprehension of figurative language

TABLE 1
Representative Materials From the Research on Novel Proverbs

PROVERBS AND THEIR INTERPRETATIONS
From Hoffman and Honeck, (1976), Honeck (1973), and Honeck, Riechmann, and Hoffman (1975).

P: Industry is fortune's right hand and stinginess her left.
I: You must work hard and spend money carefully to get wealthy.
P: There is great force hidden in a sweet command.
I: A little kindness often pursuades better than a rough order.
P: Birth is much but breeding is more.
I: Inhereted genius could not create without a good education.
P: It takes many shovelfuls of earth to bury the truth.
I: It is hard to conceal what is right.

PROVERBS AND SCENARIOS
From Dorfmueller and Honeck (1981), Honeck, Voegtle, and Sowry (1981), and Voegtle (1983).

P: In due time, the fox is brought to the furrier.
S: A jewel thief was successful for a long time. However a detective caught him after ten years. But the detective said that if he had not caught the thief someone else would have.
P: The best pears fall into the pig's mouth.
S: The uncle chose the nephew who only wrote him once in the past ten years ago to go with him on a trip to Europe.

(and possibly much other language) involves an "infinitely" flexible semantic base that is abstract, nonlinguistic, and nonimagistic.

Images versus Abstract Categories

Research in which the image-evoking value of metaphors has been manipulated (Harris, Lahey, & Marsalek, 1980; Johnson & Malgady, 1980; Marschark, Katz, & Paivio, 1983) indicates that such variables as imageability, interpretability, and metaphorical "goodness" are related, as are topic/vehicle similarity and metaphorical goodness. Also, more interpretable metaphors often have vehicles that are more concrete than their topics. So, images are often involved in comprehension, but are they its basis?

Using novel proverbs, Riechmann and Coste (1980) demonstrated that having participants experience the mental (visual) images that are suggested by proverbs' literal meanings may actually interfere with subsequent recognition of the *interpretations* of the proverbs' figurative meaning. Conversely, instructions to comprehend the proverbs' figurative meaning facilitated subsequent recognition of the interpretations. This demonstration confirmed a key assumption of the "conceptual base" hypothesis, that abstract concepts are the foundation for both imaginal and verbal experience.

The next series of experiments explored how recall of novel proverbs could be cued by brief statements of events to which the proverbs could apply. Though comprehension of proverbs may be improved if one is given scenarios from widely different domains (Honeck, Kibler, & Sugar, 1985), the interpretations (statements of the abstract ground) are better recall cues than the instantiations (Dorfmueller & Honeck, 1981; Voegtle, 1983). Also, if given sets of sentences consisting of a novel proverb, a good interpretation of it, and a scenario, the interpretation will tend to be the first to be recalled from a set.

According to the conceptual base hypothesis, instantiations and specific images are a result of comprehension, and sometimes a part of comprehension's referential context, but they are not the *basis* of comprehension (see also Markschark et al., 1983, and Paivio, 1979). A conceptual base is generative. It categorizes an indefinitely large group of instances or events that are literally and referentially distinguishable and yet which, from the perspective of the interpreter, share some sort of featureless family resemblance.

The information from the proverb and its context is not always sufficient to specify a full meaning for that abstract group or category. To this extent at least, the interpreter must add on something that is not directly available. Thus, whenever a listener encounters a novel proverb, the first step is problem recognition. Proverbs usually occur in texts or conversations so as to comment on the context in order to make a special or general point. The literal meaning of the proverb is neither true nor false—it is irrelevant to its context. Since it involves an abrupt shift in subject matter, it seems to violate Grice's (1975) principle of cooperation.

The violation is only apparent, however, since the figurative meaning is appropriate, to be taken as relevant and sincere. As a result of problem recognition, the proverb is taken as an object for "*as if*" play with symbols, concepts, perspectives, events, causes, etc. The listener must understand the relations between terms in the proverb, elements of the narrated or experienced event, and elements of the context or social situation. Concepts and events are compared on whatever levels they *can* be compared. This "transformation" phase results in the formation of a conceptual base (a figurative meaning) which can then be used to recognize or generate further instances or to generate paraphrases.

These phases are not strictly sequential, but partially overlapping cycles involving abstract categories and event perception (Honeck et al., 1980). Unfortunately, very little is known about the psychology of abstract categories, as opposed to single-word concepts and concrete perceptual categories (e.g., dot patterns, schematic drawings of faces, geometrical forms). And while people can often agree on membership in abstract categories (Hampton, 1981), the basis for the agreement is not clear (for discussions of figurative language and traditional views of categorization, see Honeck, Kibler, & Sugar, 1985; and chapter 6, this volume).

The present research is an investigation of people's free recall and recognition of common proverbs. The focus is on how verbatim memory for common proverbs relates to both abstract categories and the perception of events. We wanted the research to provide some answers to the following questions: How do people use proverbs? How many common proverbs do people know? How much variation in the sets of commonly-known proverbs is there among regions of the U.S.?

A STUDY OF FREE RECALL

Participants were 20 introductory psychology students at the Massachusetts State College (largely of Irish and Italian ethnic origins) and 20 introductory psychology students at the University of Minnesota (largely of Scandanavian ethnic origins). Participants were either volunteers or received course credit for their participation.

Data were collected in a small, quiet room equipped with a small table, chairs for the experimenter and the participant, and writing supplies. Each experimental session lasted about 45 minutes.

Participants were instructed to spend 30 minutes recalling from memory all of the common proverbs they might know. The instructions included an example (novel) proverb ("*The best fruit falls into the pig's mouth*") to distinguish proverbs from idioms, famous quotes, and other speech formulas. In a control condition, participants were instructed to recall "sentences you are certain you have heard or seen before," with no mention made of proverbs. Following the free recall session, participants were given a post-experimental questionnaire.

Results and Discussion

The free recall task yielded a corpus of over 600 sentences, many of which were proverbs. The protocols also included a large number of aphorisms (proverb-like literal generalizations, such as *"Early to bed, early to rise, makes a man healthy, wealthy, and wise"*) and some perverbs (perverted proverbs) such as *"The early bird always gets his worm,"* and *"Mind before matter."* All participants recalled between 15 and 25 proverbs, or about one per minute in the free recall task. About one-fourth of the proverbs occurred in more than one participant's protocol, and some were even more frequent (Examples are given in Table 2, under the heading of Target Proverbs).

About 24 percent of the proverbs that were freely recalled in Massachusetts were also freely recalled in Minnesota. Overall, the set of proverbs that were common to the two regions was twice as large as the sets that were not shared. Although a number of the proverbs and aphorisms were clearly tied to one or the other region or ethnic group (e.g., *"As Irish as Pat Murphy's pig"*), most were not.

Participants in the free recall control condition recalled lines of poetry, lines from Shakespeare, Biblical passages or prayers, song lyrics and titles, idiomatic phrases, and cliches. They mostly recalled mundane sentences: *"I am tired,"* *"I love you,"* *"What time is it?"* *"Do you have an extra pen?"* *"What's for supper?"* A few participants recalled sentences from the instructions. Overall, they recalled many times as many sentences as the main group. After some of them wrote page after page of sentences in the 30-minute period, it became apparent that the main limit on their ability to recall sentences was the time limit to the task.

In their post-experimental comments on the task, participants reported that they used strategies to generate proverbs (or, sentences) from memory. *Strategy #1:* Imagining oneself in various situations and trying to think of what proverbs might apply or might come to mind. *Strategy #2:* Thinking of abstract categories in terms of words such as "love" and "death" and using these as cues for the recall of proverbs. *Strategy #3:* Imagining oneself as a family member who uses a lot of proverbs, usually a grandmother or aunt from the "old country." The imagery involves the generation of situations as the participant tries to think of what the relative might say. *Strategy #4:* Using the syntactic structure of one proverb to cue proverbs with similar structure. This strategy showed up in the protocols in the form of series of proverbs. An example is: *"Don't bite off more than you can chew,"* followed by *"Don't count your chickens before they hatch,"* followed by *"Don't put the cart before the horse,"* followed by *"Don't burn your bridges behind you."* *Strategy #5:* Using one proverb as a verbatim or conceptual cue for the recall of other proverbs. This appeared in the protocols in the form of series of proverbs with verbatim or conceptual overlap. An example series is: *"Sticks and stones may break my bones, but names will never hurt me,"* followed by *"Let him who is without sin cast the first stone,"* followed by *"People who live in glass houses shouldn't throw stones."* Another example series is: *"You can't teach an old dog new tricks,"* followed by *"You have to learn to crawl before you can walk."* A third example is: *"Elephants never forget,"* followed by *"Memories are worth the pain of collecting them."*

Usually at the start of the free recall period, four or five proverbs would "come to mind." Next would follow the kinds of concept-based and formula-based series of proverbs exemplified in the strategies described above. All of the participant's protocols demonstrated one or more of the strategies. The first three strategies were the more common ones. Even the participants in the control condition who recalled some proverbs often generated the proverbs as series in their protocols.

In their comments about the task, all the participants indicated that they found the task to be more difficult than they had initially supposed, though the task was really more boring than it was difficult. They often remarked that, while working at the task, they would recall a few proverbs and then "draw a blank." After further thought, another few proverbs would be recalled, followed by yet another blank. As the task went on, the recalls were of more idiosyncratic statements (e.g., quotes from Fritz Perls).

Why should such an apparently simple task be so boring or difficult? The most prevalent strategies involved the imaginal generation of either situations or abstract categories. In the task, the participant is *out* of the sort of situations that usually "bring proverbs to mind" (a number of the participants commented to this effect in the post-experimental questionnaire). As a result, they resorted to using one proverb to suggest another in any way they could – by relying on events, abstract concepts, content words, or syntactical structure.

Participants in the free recall control condition also reported using the strategy of imagining events in order to generate sentences from memory. For example, in one series, *"Hurry up, let's go"* was followed by *"What are you doing tonight?"* which was followed by *"What's on TV?"* There were series in which the sentences referred to a single event, for example, about getting paid, then cashing one's check, then going shopping. The use of the imaginal event strategy accounts for the high frequency of greetings, questions, and commands in the control condition protocols. These sorts of sentences often *begin* or maintain conversations or social interactions, whereas proverbs denote *pauses* or fall near the *ends* of situations, conversations, or stories.

Participants in the main group who reported that they did not like the use of proverbs or clichés tended to yield lower estimates of the number of common proverbs they knew (estimates of about 20–25) than participants who reported that they liked proverbs, whether or not they used them a lot (estimates ranging from 100 to 1,000). Participants who reported that they did not like proverbs tended to be the ones who reported having a close family member who uses proverbs a lot.

A STUDY OF RECOGNITION

Participants were 30 introductory psychological students at the University of Minnesota. They received class credit for their participation.

The corpus of proverbs collected in the free recall study (both Massachusetts and Minnesota) was used in this recognition study. Each proverb selected for use was scored for how often it occurred in the free recall protocols, either low frequency (freely recalled by only one participant) or high frequency (freely recalled by more than one participant). In addition to the proverbs that were selected for use, foil sentences were prepared. These were lines from poetry, Shakespeare, song lyrics, books – exactly the types of sentences provided by the free recall control group. Examples of the target proverbs and the different types of foils are presented in Table 2.

Different groups of participants (each with $N=10$) saw different sets of materials. Each set (N of about 300) included the target proverbs (from the free recall task), the perverbs, and a different type of foil. In this report, we want to focus on the groups shown the literal foils, the proverb foils, and the novel proverb foils.

Data were collected in a small, quiet room equipped with a small table, chairs for the experimenter and participant, and writing materials. Each sentence was printed in large black letters on a three-by-five inch filing card. The participant had to read each sentence out loud and indicate whether it was familiar ("Old"), unfamiliar ("New"), or whether the participant was "Unsure," by placing each card in one of three piles on the table. Following the recognition series was a post-experimental questionnaire, which included a surprise 5-minute period for free recall of the sentences that had just been inspected. Each experimental session lasted about 45 minutes.

TABLE 2
Sentences from the Recognition Study.
For Each Type, the Source and Number of the Sentences is Indicated

---

PROVERB TARGETS (freely recalled in Minnesota) (N = 173)

A rolling stone gathers no moss.
Don't look a gift horse in the mouth.
A watched pot never boils.
One picture can be worth a thousand words.
Too many cooks spoil the broth.
You can't make a silk purse out of a sow's ear.
Don't put the cart before the horse.
Never let the sun set on your anger.
Man does not live by bread alone.

PROVERB FOILS (freely recalled in Massachusetts but not in Minnesota) (= 141)

A man's home is his castle.
A rolling stone gathers no moss.
A journey of a thousand miles begins with one step.

TABLE 2 (Continued)

NOVEL PROVERB FOILS (from proverb dictionaries) (N = 62)

Ashes always fly in the face of whoever throws them.
Eat peas with the king and cherries with the beggar.
Iron may be rubbed so long that it becomes heated.

BIBLICAL PROVERB FOILS (N = 58)

He who spares the rod hates his son.
A wicked man goes about with crooked speech.
Truthful lips endure forever.

PERVERB FOILS (N = 40)

Do unto others before they do unto you.
Today is the last day of the rest of your life.
You can have your cake and eat it too.

SHAKESPEAREAN FOILS (N = 91)

Misery acquaints a man with strange bedfellows.
Parting is such sweet sorrow
Thy head is as full of quarrels as an egg is full of meat.

POEM FOILS (from books of Chinese poetry) (N = 43)

Let things run their course like an unanchored boat.
Lotus flowers will not grow in boiling water.
Pure breeze and bright moon cost not a single penny.

LITERAL FOILS (from novels) (N = 46)

Many people want some change from a continuing pattern of life.
The sun is shining on the dark wood through the window.
As far as I know he didn't learn any occult secrets there.

COMMON QUOTE FOILS (from dictionaries) (N = 29)

Come up and see me sometime.
One small step for man, one giant leap for mankind.
Ask not what your country can do for you, ask what you can do for your country.

Results and Discussion

Of the target proverbs (i.e., the proverbs freely recalled in Minnesota), about 70% were called "Old," especially the high frequency proverbs (93%), irrespective of the type of foils the participants saw. Of the literal foils and novel proverb foils, about 92% were called "New." Of the proverb foils (i.e., proverbs freely recalled in Massachusetts but not in Minnesota), 80% of the low frequency and 93% of the high frequency ones were recognized as "Old."

It can be supposed, then, that most people carry around in their heads *at least* some 300 common proverbs. One might not expect the number to be so large. Nor did the participants themselves: In the post-experimental questionnaire, most of them also underestimated the number of common proverbs that they knew, with estimates having a median of 50 (and a range upper-limit of "thousands"). Furthermore, it was not expected that the sets of recalled and recognized proverbs would be so similar for Minnesota and Massachusetts participants. Proverbs that were freely recalled in Minnesota were not more frequently recognized by Minnesota participants than proverbs that were freely recalled in Massachusetts.

The groups receiving the proverb foils and novel proverb foils were more likely to "catch" the perverbs than the group shown the literal foils. Participants in the literal foil group could decide if a sentence was Old or New simply by reading it to see if it was proverb-like. Hence, they would fail to catch some of the perverbs. Participants in both proverb foil groups had to read each sentence more carefully to decide about its familiarity, and hence they would catch more of the perverbs.

As indicated in their responses on the post-experimental questionnaire, the participants could tell that they were exposed to sentences that fell into different types: "clichés versus totally odd sentences" "clichés and proverbs with sentences that were probably from books."

The post-experimental questionnaire included a 5-minute period for free recall of the sentences just seen. With only a few exceptions, the proverbs that were recalled were high frequency proverbs from the recognition set. Participants recalled an average of about 12 proverbs, about four times the rate for participants in the free recall task. Certainly, this rate would have moderated had the free recall period been extended beyond 5 minutes, yet that was not felt to be necessary in order to demonstrate the cueing effect of the prior recognition task.

As was the case for participants in the free recall study, participants in the recognition task often reported having a family member who uses a lot of proverbs. Although a few of these participants reported that they "hated" the use of proverbs or clichés, most of them recognized more proverbs than subjects who did not report having a family member who uses lots of proverbs.

Participants seemed to fall into distinct groups according to their performance at the recognition task, the types of errors they made, and their responses to the post-experimental questions: *Formulaic Style*: These participants were apparently impulsive and field-dependent. They proceeded quickly through the recognition task and made reading errors. They would read a perverb as it was printed, place it in the "Old" stack, and go on without noticing their error. They were not really recognizing the stimulus, but the formula. In the post-experimental questionnaire, they tended to report having a family member who uses a lot of proverbs. *Quiet Style*: These participants were apparently reflective and somewhat anxious. They proceeded slowly at the recognition task and spoke very softly. They often re-read the proverbs, especially the unfamiliar ones. They used the "Unsure" category more than the other participants. *Hi-verbal Style*: These participants proceeded rapidly through the recognition task and were more likely to find it "fun" or "interesting." They were more likely to "catch" the perverbs and offer the correct version. *Hostile Style*: These participants proceeded rapidly through the recognition task, but inaccurately recognized many perverb foils. They reported in the post-experimental questionnaire that they "hated" proverbs or clichés and that they never used them. Although no independent data corroborate this classification, it seemed to parcel the participants in an unambiguous way.

Looking across the free recall and recognition results, what do they say about the comprehension of abstract categories and events?

CONCLUSIONS

Recognition Without Comprehension

While a main result of the present studies is the demonstration of the size of people's verbatim "storehouse" of common proverbs, the results also reflect memory and comprehension breakdowns and failures. For example, the formulaic-style participants often read a perverb as it was written and went on without noticing their error.

Another form of memory failure occurred when a participant confidently recognized a proverb and yet was confident that what he or she was recognizing was a slightly *different* version, without being able to say exactly what that version was. Participants in both the free recall and recognition tasks often recalled or recognized a perverb or parts of a proverb without being able to recall all of it or its proper form. Sometimes this seemed to occur as a genuine "tip-of-the-tongue" phenomenon. It is known that this phenomenon can be induced by tasks that tap long-term memory without providing much in the way of cues or situational specifics (Brown & McNeill, 1966). So, recognition can occur without being complete or correct in terms of production or possibly even comprehension.

Indeed, comprehension of common proverbs can be anything but quick and effortless. At the United Nations, great pains have been taken to deal with nonliteral expression. Interpreters are instructed to *skip over* proverbs (and metaphors) in the delegates' speeches. Translators find themselves immersed in the learning of common idioms and proverbs (Hoffman, 1983). In an attempt to help the U.N. deal with the problem of proverbs, the diplomat V. deGinzbourg prepared *The external Machiavelli in the U.N.* (1969), which is a compilation of thousands of proverbs across languages and an analysis and comparison of their subtle social and political meanings.

Some of the participants commented in the post-experimental questionnaire that proverbs are used in conversations to induce pauses or to make a point. These reports dovetail with the well-known use of proverbs at the ends of stories, as by the African story-tellers. When aptly used, proverbs can "stretch out" the comprehension process by suggesting new perspectives, feelings, actions, etc. While this is perhaps clearly true of novel proverbs, the present results show that recognition of a common proverb does not guarantee quick, effortless, or correct understanding either. Indeed, this is as expected. Proverbs are, in a sense, complex names for categories whose figurative meanings, while suggested by proverb information, are not determined by it. Proverbs qua proverbs are almost always invoked by complex attitudes and beliefs about the events that transpire in complex social situations. These attitudes and situations need to be around before a proverb is recalled because proverbs are "coded" (remembered) in these terms.

Imagery and Event Perception

Just as the psychology of perception has traditionally taken static forms and retinal images as their starting point, the psychology of cognition has taken static visual form as the paradigm of imagery. However, our research on proverbs, along with some of the research on metaphors (Verbrugge, 1980), shows that images are more tied to event perception and affordances than to the "scanning" of image forms that possess static properties such as "concreteness" and "imagery value." The images that participants experienced in the present study were very dynamic. To paraphrase one participant:

> An image popped into my mind of spilling milk, and the words "Don't cry over" were thought of at about the same instant. The image of a childhood incident came to mind involving high chairs and glasses of milk. At the next instant, Grandmother's voice was heard uttering, "Don't throw the baby out with the bathwater."

As such series of conceptually and associatively related proverbs were recalled, the participants experienced very fluid, multi-modal images of events and situations, often concrete and yet reliant on abstract concepts.

The conceptual base hypothesis began as an attempt to explain how people could make conceptual connections between novel proverbs and their interpretations, connections that appeared to transcend the capabilities of available linguistically motivated psycholinguistic theories. While the comprehension and memory of novel proverbs might appear to be a mundane matter of verbatim memory, the present results substantiate the conceptual base view: Comprehension of common proverbs involves featureless family resemblances, not the mapping of literal features. It involves images and instantiations, but is not based upon them. Rather, it is based on categories of events that are abstractly related and deeply embedded in cultural contexts.

The conceptual base hypothesis is moving from an initial formulation (that meaning is *non*linguistic and *non*imagistic) to a newer formulation (Honeck et al.,

1980) that says something about what meaning *is*: It is through studies of the ecology of figurative language (relying on such concepts as "events" and "affordances") that an understanding of abstract categories will arise.

The Ecology of Abstract Categories

The present results bear directly on ecology in terms of the uses and functions of proverbs – their pragmatics, in other words. The participants in both the recall and recognition studies showed in the post-experimental questions that they understood why proverbs are used in various situations. They mentioned things like: "Proverbs are used to control conversations," "to express morals at the ends of stories," "to make a point forcefully or with humor," "to give advice without being bossy," "to describe feelings," or "to relieve emotional strain."

A more complete list of the functions of proverbs would include: (a) To establish or shift perspectives, (b) to explain events or situations, (c) to admonish (about past actions), (d) to warn (about future consequences of actions), (e) to accuse or attribute, (f) to resolve conflicts (consolation or retribution), (g) to persuade, (h) to speculate, (i) to proclaim (facts, ironies, truths), (j) to alter the speaker–listener relation (e.g., status), and (k) to express the speaker's personality or intentions. There are, no doubt, other functions as well. Of this variety of uses, each is either a reference to the speaker–listener interaction itself or to some narrated or experienced event. Thus, a proverb has at least two contexts – the utterance situation and the literal events described by the proverb itself – and usually three contexts when the utterance reference is not the utterance situation (Seitel, 1969).

Some years ago, the ethnographer Seitel suggested that the types of research methods employed in the present studies could be used to study proverbs on a cross-cultural basis. He proposed experiments using descriptions of situations, in order to cue people's memory for common proverbs and to see if informants would agree on the uses of the proverbs. He also suggested that the memory cues could be systematically manipulated to explore the cognitive processes involved. Seitel regarded proverbs as essentially a social use of metaphor, a part of a larger conversational context. The present research shows that Seitel's ideas about research methods were correct, and that common proverbs can be used in the experimental study of social cognition and the manifestations of culture in cognition.

While it originated in the psychology of perception (e.g., Gibson, 1979), the ecological or contextualist point of view seems to be "catching on" in psychology in general, including cognitive psychology (Hoffman & Nead, 1983; Neisser, 1984). Studies of figurative language which fit the ecological perspective are functional classifications of proverbs (Ojoade, 1983; Oladeji, 1984), research on the figurative language in street slang (Agar, 1975; Taylor & Ortony, 1981), explorations of figurative language in second-language learning (Alam, 1983; Gordon, 1983; Koch, 1982; McDonald & Carpenter, 1981; Narita, 1983; Richter, 1983), and studies of the use of metaphors in politics, business, computer science, sports, education, and other domains of communication (Beck, 1982; Carbonell, 1980; Carroll & Thomas, 1980; Feinstein, 1982; Gentner & Gentner, 1983; Guck, 1981; Hoffman, 1985; Hoffman, Cochran, & Nead, 1987; Kastenbaum 1983; McKay, 1983; Smith & Montgomery, 1982; Weitzenfeld & Klein, 1981). Though only Carroll's work, on metaphor in computer languages, is expressly defined as involving ecological notions, all of the above research focuses on the psychology of figurative language in real-world contexts or tasks. One can expect to see more such work appear in the next few years.

Figurative language has been a topic for philosophical debate for thousands of years. It is only within our lifetime that researchers have begun to conduct programs of laboratory experiments on the comprehension and memory processes involved. Now we see a newer phase of research: Using figurative language as a conceptual tool in our studies of actual communication situations. Such research will no doubt tell us much about event perception and the formation of abstract categories.

REFERENCES

Agar, M. (1975). Cognition and events. In M. Sanchez & B. Blount (Eds.), *Sociocultural dimensions of language*. New York: Academic Press.

Alam, Q. (1983). *Images and metaphors in English written by Indians*. Paper presented at the conference of the Western Humor and Irony Membership, Arizona State University, Tempe, AZ.

Beck, B. (1982). Root metaphor patterns. *Semiotic Inquiry, 2,* 86–97.

Becker, J. (1975). *The phrasal lexicon*. Technical Report, Bolt, Beranek, and Newman, Inc., Cambridge, MA.

Brewer, W., Harris, R., & Brewer, E. (1974). *Comprehension of literal and figurative meaning*. Paper presented at the meeting of the Midwestern Psychological Association.

Brown, R., & McNeill, D. (1966). The "tip-of-the-tongue" phenomenon. *Journal of Verbal Learning and Verbal Behavior, 5,* 325–337.

Carbonell, J. (1980). Metaphor: A key to extensible semantic analysis. *Proceedings of the Association for Computational Linguistics,* Chicago, IL.

Carroll, J., & Thomas, J. (1980). *Metaphor and the cognitive representation of computing systems*. Technical Report, IBM Research Division, Yorktown Heights, NY.

Chafe, W. (1968). Idiomaticity as an anomaly within the Chomskyan paradigm. *Foundations of Language, 4,* 109–127.

Chomsky, N. (1965). *Aspects of the theory of syntax*. Cambridge, MA: The MIT Press.

Clark, H., & Clark, E. (1977). *The psychology of language*. New York: Harcourt-Brace-Jovanovich.

deGinzbourg, V. (1969). *The external Machiavelli in the United Nations*. New York: United Nations Library.

Dorfmueller, M., & Honeck, R. (1981). Centrality and generativity within a linguistic family: Toward a conceptual base theory of groups. *The Psychological Record, 30,* 95–109.

Feinstein, H. (1982). *Effects of attention exercises on the metaphoric interpretation of paintings*. Unpublished manuscript, Department of Art Education, University of Cincinnati, Cincinnati, OH.

Fraser, B. (1970). Idioms within a transformational grammar. *Foundations of Language, 6,* 22–42.

Gentner, D., & Gentner, D. R. (1983) Flowing waters or teeming crowds: Mental models of electricity. In D. Gentner & A. Stevens (Eds.), *Mental models*. Hillsdale, NJ: Erlbaum.

Gibbs, R. (1980). Spilling the beans on understanding and meaning for idioms in conversations. *Memory & Cognition, 8,* 149–156.

Gibson, J. J. (1979). *The ecological approach to visual perception.* Boston, MA: Houghton Mifflin.

Gildea, P., & Glucksberg, S. (1983). On understanding metaphor: The role of context. *Journal of Verbal Learning and Verbal Behavior, 22,* 547–590.

Gildea, P., Glucksberg, S., & Bookin, H. (1981). *Turning bad metaphors into good ones: Liberal activation of figurative meaning.* Paper presented at the meeting of the Eastern Psychological Association.

Gordon, W. (1983). *Translating French-English word play.* Paper presented at the meeting of the Western Humor and Irony Membership, Arizona State University, Tempe, AZ.

Grice, H. (1975). Logic and conversation. In P. Cole, & J. Morgan (Eds.), *Syntax and semantics, Vol. 3: Speech acts.* New York, NY: Seminar Press.

Guck, M. (1981). The contribution of metaphor to analysis of music. *Journal of the Michigan Music Theory Society, 5,* 29–42.

Hampton, J. (1981). An investigation of the nature of abstract concepts. *Memory & Cognition, 9,* 149–156.

Harris, R., Lahey, M., & Marsalek, F. (1980). Metaphors and images: Rating, reporting, and remembering. In R. Honeck & R. Hoffman (Eds.), *Cognition and figurative language.* Hillsdale, NJ: Erlbaum.

Hoffman, R. (1983). *Some implications of metaphor for language translation.* Paper presented at the meeting of the Linguistics Club of the U.N., New York, NY.

Hoffman, R. (1985). Some implications of metaphor for philosophy and psychology of science. In R. Dirven & W. Paprotte (Eds.), *The ubiquity of metaphor.* Amsterdam: John Benjamins.

Hoffman, R., Cochran, E., & Nead, J. (1987). Cognitive metaphors in experimental psychology. In D. Leary (Ed.), *Metaphors in the history of psychology.* Cambridge, England: Cambridge University Press.

Hoffman, R., & Honeck, R. (1976). The bidirectionality of judgments of synonymy. *Journal of Psycholinguistic Research, 5,* 173–183.

Hoffman, R., & Kemper, S. (1987). What could reaction-time studies be telling us about metaphors? *Metaphor and Symbolic Activity, 2,* in press.

Hoffman, R., MacCormac, E., & Lawler, J. (1987). The metaphors of semantics and the semantics of metaphors. Manuscript in preparation, Department of Psychology, Adelphi University.

Hoffman, R., & Nead, J. (1983). General contextualism, ecological science, and cognitive research. *Journal of Mind and Behavior, 4,* 507–560.

Honeck, R. (1973). Interpretive versus structural effects on semantic memory. *Journal of Verbal Learning and Verbal Behavior, 12,* 448–455.

Honeck, R., & Hoffman, R. (1979). Synonymy and anomaly. *Bulletin of the Psychonomic Society, 14,* 37–40.

Honeck, R. P., Kibler, C. T., & Sugar, J. (1985). The conceptual base view of categorization. *Journal of Psycholinguistic Research, 14,* 155–174.

Honeck, R., Riechmann, P., & Hoffman, R. (1975). Semantic memory for metaphor: The conceptual base hypothesis. *Memory & Cognition, 3,* 409–415.

Honeck, R., Voegtle, K., Dorfmueller, M., & Hoffman, R. (1980). Proverbs, meaning and group structure. IN R. Honeck, and R. Hoffman (Eds.), *Cognition and figurative language.* Hillsdale, NJ: Erlbaum.

Honeck, R., Voegtle, K., & Sowry, B. (1981). Figurative understanding of pictures and sentences, *Journal of Psycholinguistic Research, 10,* 153–154.

Johnson, M., & Malgady, R. (1980). Toward a perceptual theory of metaphoric comprehension. In R. Honeck & R. Hoffman (Eds.), *Cognition and figurative language.* Hillsdale, NJ: Erlbaum.

Kastenbaum, R. (1983). *Is neologicalification enough?: The Burrowcrat's search for re-authenticizability.* Paper presented at the conference of the Western Humor and Irony Membership, Arizona State University, Tempe, AZ.

Katz, J. (1973). The realm of meaning. IN G. Miller (Ed.), *Communication, language and meaning.* New York, NY: Basic Books.

Kemper, S. (1981). Comprehension and the interpretation of proverbs. *Journal of Psycholinguistic Research, 10,* 179–198.

Kemper, S., & Estill, R. (1981). *Interpreting idioms.* Paper presented at the annual convention of the American Psychological Association.

Koch, T. (1982). *Idioms in foreign language instruction.* Unpublished manuscript, Gesamtehochschule Kassel, Kassel, F.R. Germany.

Lakoff, G., & Johnson, M. (1980). *Metaphors we live by.* Chicago, IL: University of Chicago Press.

Marschark, M., Katz, A., & Paivio, A. (1983). Dimensions of metaphor. *Journal of Psycholinguistic Research, 12,* 17–40.

McDonald, J., & Carpenter, P. (1981). Simultaneous translations: Idiom interpretation and parsing heuristics. *Journal of Verbal Learning and Verbal Behavior, 20,* 231–247.

McKay, D. (1983). *Metaphoric nonsense in comic periodicals of the Spanish Civil War.* Paper presented at the conference of the Western Humor and Irony Membership. Arizona State University Tempe, AZ.

Narita, K. (1983). *A pitfall of English idioms for Japanese ESL students.* Paper presented at the meeting of the Western Humor and Irony Membership, Arizona State University, Tempe, AZ.

Neisser, U. (1984). Toward an ecologically oriented cognitive psychology. In T. Shlecter & M. Toglia (Eds.), *New directions in cognitive science.* Norwood, NJ: Ablex, Publishing.

Ojoade, O. (1983). *The fool in Nigerian proverbs.* Paper presented at the meeting of the Western Humor and Irony Membership, Arizona State University, Tempe, AZ.

Oladeji, N. (1984). A linguistic and semantic analysis of Yoruba proverbs. In D. Nilsen (Ed.), *Western Humor and Irony Membership yearbook.* Tempe, AZ: Arizona State University Department of English.

Ortony, A., Schallert, D., Reynolds, R., & Antos, S. (1978). Interpreting metaphors and idioms: Some effects of context on comprehension. *Journal of Verbal Learning and Verbal Behavior, 17,* 465–477.

Paivio, A. (1979). Psychological processes in the comprehension of metaphor. In A. Ortony (Ed.), *Metaphor and thought.* Cambridge, England: Cambridge University Press.

Pollio, H., Barlow, J., Fine, H., & Pollio, M. (1977). *Psychology and the poetics of growth.* Hillsdale, NJ: Erlbaum.

Richter, R. (1983). *Idioms and lexical problems in English as a foreign language.* Paper presented at the conference of the Western Humor and Irony Membership, Arizona State University, Tempe, AZ.

Riechmann, P., & Coste, E. (1980). Mental imagery and the comprehension of figurative language: Is there a relationship? In R. Honeck & R. Hoffman (Eds.), *Cognition and figurative language.* Hillsdale, NJ: Erlbaum.

Seitel, P. (1969). Proverbs: A social use of metaphor. *Genre, 2,* 143–161.

Silverman-Weinreich, B. (1981). Towards a structural analysis of Yiddish proverbs. In W. Meider & A. Dundes (Eds.), *The wisdom of many: Essays on the proverb.* New York: Garland Publishing.

Smith, M., & Montgomery, M. (1982). *The semantics of winning and losing.* Unpublished manuscript, Department of Psychology, University of Tennessee, Knoxville, TN.

Staehlin, W. (1914). *Zur Psychologie und Statistik der Metaphern. Archiv für Gesamte Psychologie, 31,* 299–425.

Swinney, D., & Cutler, A. (1979). The access and processing of idiomatic expressions. *Journal of Verbal Learning and Verbal Behavior, 18,* 523–534.

Taylor, M., & Ortony, A. (1981). *Figurative devices in black language: Some socio-psycholinguistic observations.* Technical Report, Center for the Study of Reading, University of Illinois, Urbana, IL.

Verbrugge, R. (1980). Transformations in knowing: A realist view of metaphor. In R. Honeck & R. Hoffman (Eds.), *Cognition and figurative language.* Hillsdale, NJ: Erlbaum.

Voegtle, K. (1983). *Categorization of figurative concepts.* Doctoral dissertation, Department of Psychology, University of Cincinnati, Cincinnati, OH.

Weitzenfeld, J., & Klein, G. (1981). *Comparison-based predictions.* Technical Report, Klein Associates, Inc., Yellow Springs, OH.

CHAPTER EIGHT

Metaphoric Communication and Miscommunication in Schizophrenic and Borderline States *

Richard M. Billow, Jeffrey Rossman, Nona Lewis,
Deberah Goldman, Susan Kraemer, and Patrick Ross

Gordon F. Derner Institute of Advanced Psychological Studies
Adelphi University

She is importunate, indeed distract . . .
Speaks things in doubt,
That carry but half sense: her speech is nothing,
Yet the unshaped use of it doth move
The hearer to collection: they aim at it,
and botch the words up to fit their own thoughts;
Which, as her winks, and nods, and gestures yield them,
Indeed would make one think there might be thought,
Though nothing sure, yet much unhappily.

-Gentleman (describing Ophelia)
in Shakespeare's *Hamlet,*
Prince of Denmark

The puzzle of psychotic language has captivated the interest and eluded the grasp of human experience. Although Ophelia's untimely drowning prevents our discerning whether her psychotic break was a schizophrenic episode, Shakespeare's description reveals his keen insight into the dynamics of psychosis:

---

*Portions of this paper were presented in R. M. Billow (chair), Metaphoric Communication and Miscommunication in Schizophrenic and Borderline States, symposium at the 92nd Annual meeting of the American Psychological Association, Toronto, Canada, August 1984.

O! this is the poison of deep grief; it springs
All from her father's death . . .
When sorrows come, they come not single spies,
But in battalions . . .
Poor Ophelia
Divided from herself and her fair judgment,
Without the which we are pictures, or mere beasts.

-King Claudius, in *Hamlet,*
Prince of Denmark

Shakespeare views Ophelia's psychotic language and behavior as a reaction ("poison") to overwhelming emotional pain ("deep grief"). He infers a morbid splitting process ("divided from himself") which results in the de-animated concretization ("pictures") and primitivization ("mere beasts") of experience. Shakespeare anticipated the contemporary conception of schizophrenia as a splitting of the ego which results in schizoid flattening of affective experience, as well as in the primitivization of thoughts and feelings.

Such a theory of psychotic thought and language disturbance as a reaction to unbearable psychic pain (anxiety) is one that has received wide currency among psychoanalytic writers, amongst others, and upon which our research partially is based.

One of the most striking aspects of schizophrenic language is its handling and mishandling of metaphor. Numerous writers have commented on the schizophrenic's overconcreteness, or literalness, in which the metaphorical utterances of others are responded to as if they were literal communications (Arieti, 1955; Bateson, Jackson, Haley, & Weakland, 1956; Searles, 1965). Searles (1965, p. 564) cites an example of a young man who replied to Searles' commenting, "You can't have your cake and eat it too," by angrily stating, "I don't want to eat any cake in this hospital! *You* can eat cake here, if you want to; I don't want to eat any cake here." Searles points out how the patient's concrete interpretation of the figure of speech enabled him to avoid the meaning of the original comment.

In contrast to this concreteness is the highly symbolic, apparently metaphorical speech produced by many schizophrenic individuals. While such communication may be impressive and compelling because of its elaborate imagery and word play, it is often incomprehensible to the listener. For example, Bleuler (1950, p. 52) reported one example of a female patient who said, "As a child I was already an apartment." Many writers assert that the full meaning of such apparently metaphorical communication is veiled from the speaker, as well as from the listener. Bateson et al. (1956) uses the term "unlabelled metaphor" to convey the idea that the schizophrenic is unaware of the figurative quality of his or her own words. Arieti (1955, p. 213) also believes that the figures created by schizophrenics tend to be pseudo-metaphors, claiming that "tightness to the denotation prevents the schizophrenic from using figurative or metaphorical language, contrary to what it may seem at first impression." Jung poignantly expressed this distinction to James Joyce when the latter argued against Jung's opinion that the author's daughter was mentally ill. In response to Joyce's claim that "Her speech is exactly the same as my writing," Jung replied, "Yes, but you dive. She falls."

Although the latest version of the American Psychiatric Association's Diagnostic Statistical Manual lists metaphoric speech as a prodromal or residual symptom of schizophrenia, to our knowledge there has been no published empirical study (other than those using proverb interpretation tasks) supporting or refuting this pervasive clinical assumption which accompanies the other assumption, which is that schizophrenics are ametaphoric, or overly concrete.

The studies from which we report preliminary findings, emanating from the Adelphi Metaphor Laboratory, represent the first testing of the assumptions. Separate research programs are cuurrently being carried out using entirely different types of metaphoric stimuli, testing both hospitalized and outpatient schizophrenic and borderline adults, hospitalized nonpsychiatric adults, borderline children, and control populations of normal children and adults.

Although the methods and populations differ, each research program addresses the underlying question: What is the nature of the metaphoric deficit, if any, in psychopathological states? Our hypotheses are informed by psychoanalytic thinking: (a) that such deficits would be distinct from overall intellectual deficits and would relate to conflict and to personality variables; (b) that a motivational element would exist, being to avoid psychic reality and attendant emotional pain; (c) that a defensive element would exist, i.e., miscommunication and obfuscation may be served by metaphor as well as by deviant metaphor; and (d) that what is discovered in the laboratory would have application for psychoanalytically oriented diagnosis and treatment.

In this chapter, we will present data from two programs of research, one involving adults, the other involving children.

PROGRAM 1:
METAPHORIC AND EGO
FUNCTIONING IN PSYCHOPATHOLOGICAL ADULTS

In this large investigation, which to date has involved the testing of over two hundred hospitalized individuals, three preliminary reports have emerged. Rossman (1985) studied the cognitive interrelationships involving metaphor comprehension, Goldman (1984) studied cognitive interrelationships involving metaphoric production, and Lewis (1983) studied such interrelationships as they related to measures of personality functioning derived from the Rorschach.

A. Metaphor Comprehension in Schizophrenic and Borderline States: Preliminary Findings

Two types of metaphor representing differing levels of abstraction (similarity versus proportional operations) were presented to hospitalized schizophrenic and "borderline" patients, and to hospitalized medical controls. Proverbs were also administered, along with a 144 item-structured psychiatric diagnostic interview, and cognitive tasks derived from the Wechsler Adult Intelligence Scale (WAIS) (Wechsler, 1955).

The comprehension of proverbs, in contrast to metaphor, has been subject to considerable empirical research with psychopathological populations (Gorham, 1956; Hertler & Chapman, 1978; Kilburg & Siegel, 1973). Since Benjamin (1974) first introduced proverb interpretation in a study of schizophrenic thinking, the task has been considered as a measure of abstracting ability, and continues to be frequently used in mental status examinations. We sought to understand whether metaphor comprehension represented a different type of task than proverb comprehension. Proverbs, in contrast to metaphors, require social comprehension skills as well as developmentally advanced stages of abstract thinking, i.e., Piagetian formal operations (Billow, 1975), which make them not a pure task of metaphoric thinking.

Because of the hypothetical relationship between anxiety and disturbance in metaphor performance, high affect-arousing and neutral affect-arousing metaphors and proverbs were presented to separate subject populations. Much cognitive research has explored the effect of anxiety and affect-arousing stimuli on schizophrenic thinking. Chapman and Chapman (1973) estimate that about two-thirds of the studies have revealed a schizophrenic deficit in response to affect arousal.

Most of the high affect stimuli pertained to painful aspects of human experience, such as conflictual feelings towards parents anger, fear, rejection, emotional deprivation, dangerous impulses, violence, and death. The low affect stimuli portrayed pleasant or neutral images that usually involved inanimate objects, animals, and natural phenomena, rather than people. Examples of figurative stimuli appear in Table 1.

We sought to explore whether differences in metaphor comprehension existed among the three diagnostic subject groups; and further, whether such possible differences were related to the affectual as well as cognitive nature of the stimuli. We hypothesized (a) that schizophrenics would show the greatest difficulty in comprehension of figurative language, (b) that this difficulty would be most apparent when affect arousing stimuli were presented, and (c) that any figuration comprehension decrement could be shown to be distinct from a generalized cognitive deficit.

No specific hypotheses were made concerning the borderline group, which was included for several reasons. There is currently much controversy over what

TABLE 1
Examples of Stimuli

	Similarity Metaphors
Low Affect:	Sunlit lakes are jewels on the landscape.
	A happy bird is a flute with feathers.
High Affect:	My mother is a fire in my memory.
	Father's death was a knife in my heart.

	Proportional Metaphors
Low Affect:	A television is a window on the world.
	A night's sleep is recharging for your battery.
High Affect:	A starving man is a car without gas.
	An overprotective parent is a smothering blanket.

	Proverbs
Low Affect:	The Mona Lisa was not painted in an hour.
	Too many tailors ruin the suit.
High Affect:	One man's meat is another man's poison.
	Many kiss the hand they wish to cut off.

constitutes the borderline clinical entity as well as over its defining characteristics (Gunderson & Singer, 1975; Grinker, Werble, & Drye, 1968; Kernberg, 1967; Kohut, 1971). It was our expectation that our findings could elucidate possible cognitive deficits in this patient group in need of much empirical research. Borderline subjects also served as a nonpsychotic but hospitalized psychiatric control group. The second control group consisted of hospitalized major medical patients with no diagnosable major psychiatric illness.

We will report on data obtained from 30 schizophrenics, 24 borderlines, and 28 medical control subjects. The patients were hospitalized either at a county medical center or at a Veterans Administration hospital. All subjects were native English-speaking males between the ages of 20 and 55. The average age was 35. To minimize effects of prolonged medication and hospitalization, as well as to assess the schizophrenics during their acute phases, testing was administered during the patients' first ten days in the hospital, as soon after admission as possible.

i. The Relationship of Metaphor Comprehension to Proverb Comprehension

Our findings suggest that, for schizophrenics, metaphor and proverb comprehension are quite different tasks, particularly when assessed for correctness of response. We base this conclusion on the virtual lack of correlation between each of our metaphor tasks and the proverb task. In this regard, the schizophrenics differed sharply from the borderline and nonpsychiatric patients. With the nonschizophrenics, the substantial correlations between proportional metaphor and proverbs surpassed those reached between the two metaphor tasks.

When the responses to the figurative tasks were assessed on the basis of deviant verbalizations, (excessively literal or bizarrely autistic) irrespective of correctness, a slightly different picture emerged. The tendency for a subject to reject responding, to be literal or to be autistic on one metaphor task very moderately related to the same tendency on the other metaphor task, and on the proverb task. Even here, the large number of significant correlations between metaphor tasks and the proverbs rarely reached .40. Hence, it would seem that prior research conclusions with schizophrenic subjects using proverb stimuli should not be generalized to make statements about metaphoric thinking.

ii. Diagnostic Differences

When intellectual factors are held constant, both by restricting and matching the I.Q. scores in the range of each diagnostic category, and by partialling out remaining intellectual variance (on accuracy scores), striking differences appear between the schizophrenics and the two nonpsychotic groups. We are not considering here the effects of emotional context. The schizophrenics respond less accurately than borderlines and medicals on each metaphor task as well as on the proverb task. In addition, they were more likely than either group to give at least one autistic-bizarre response and at least one literal response. The borderlines were significantly less accurate than medicals and significantly more accurate than schizophrenics on the metaphor tasks. Their performance was otherwise indistinguishable from medical controls. (All diagnostic effects were at the $p < .01$ level of significance or better.)

In interpreting the above as well as the following findings, two nosological questions must remain open. We did not compare the schizophrenics to another group of psychotically impaired individuals. The markedly different performance of the schizophrenics in response to metaphor stimuli may be characteristic of psychosis per se, and not specific to schizophrenia. Further, schizophrenic patients themselves differ on many dimensions, including those of premorbid intellectual functioning and current level of disorganization. By attempting to match schizophrenics on intellectual functioning to our control groups, we eliminated the more floridly disturbed individuals. These are the particularly challenging individuals, who have stimulated the clinical literature on language and thought disturbance in schizophrenia (e.g., Searles, 1965). Such issues of motivation to avoid metaphoric meaning are specifically addressed to the more seriously thought disordered psychotic subjects. In our larger study, we are investigating schizophrenics across the full range of mental and personality functioning.

The other nosological issue concerns our borderline population. We must emphasize that we have studied a particular type of patient, one ill enough to be hospitalized, but one who, to be included in our study, did not show schizophrenic symptomatology. A structural diagnosis (see Kernberg, 1967) of these patients is being carried out presently, using inferences from the Rorschach concerning ego boundaries, object relations, reality testing and ego strength. Preliminary data which we report on below indicate that such dimensions are indeed cogent when considering metaphoric functioning and deviance.

iii. The Effect of Emotional Context

Metaphor appearing in a high anxiety context had a particularly disruptive influence on the schizophrenics. In fact, the three diagnostic groups do not differ in accuracy of interpretation in the low affect condition. Thus, in the combined high affect (similarity and proportional) metaphor treatment, schizophrenic accuracy was approximately 40%, while the accuracy of the medicals was 73%, and the accuracy of the borderlines 71%. In the low affect condition, the schizophrenics reached a 63% accuracy on the combined metaphors, as compared to the 72% accuracy of the medicals and the 63% accuracy of the borderlines.

The anxiety-reactive performance of schizophrenics regarding interpretation inaccuracy on metaphor may be contrasted to their performance on proverb interpretation. The schizophrenics were significantly less accurate in proverb interpretation than were other subjects, a finding which did not vary according to the affect level of stimuli.

Regarding deviant verbalizations, whereas the schizophrenics were more likely than other subjects to be autistic, this effect was significantly more pronounced in the emotionally charged metaphoric context. Of our schizophrenic subjects, 87% emitted an autistic response to one or both sets of metaphoric stimuli in the high affect condition, while only 40% were autistic in response to the low affect conditions. For comparison purposes, the incidence of autistism was 14% of medicals in the high affect treatment, and 29% in the low affect treatment. For borderlines, the figures were, respectively, 25% and 14%.

The pattern of findings concerning literal responses is similar. The schizophrenic subjects who were significantly more literal in their responses to metaphor than their nonpsychotic peers also showed a significant further decrement in the high affect metaphor contexts. Forty percent of the schizophrenics gave one or more literal interpretations to the low affect metaphors, while 87% supplied literal interpretations in the high affect conditions. The medicals, in contrast, had a 29% incidence of literalness in each metaphor condition, while the borderlines had, respectively, 17% and 8% in the low and high affect conditions.

Varying the emotional content of our proverbs did not differentially affect deviant verbalizations.

iv. The Effect of Cognitive Structure on Emotional Context

We found two contextual factors relating to schizophrenic deficit in metaphorical thinking: cognitive complexity and the above mentioned effect of affectual stimulation. The schizophrenics had the most difficulty with our high affect proportional metaphors, in terms of accuracy, autism, and literalness. The high affect similarity metaphors also lowered schizophrenic performance, but to a much smaller degree. Whereas the schizophrenics interpreted correctly more proportional metaphors than similarity metaphors in the low affect condition, their performance in the high affect conditions was sharply reversed. The proportional metaphors, cognitively more complex but not more difficult than our similarity metaphors, became exceptionally troublesome in a high anxiety context.

We may ask why the same dual factor effect did not occur with the analogically complex proverbs. Our explanation is that proverbs, unlike our metaphors, most often may be interpreted in a manner removed from their specific semantic context. While both the metaphors and proverbs appeared in a high affectual context, the respective interpretations of the two types of stimuli usually differed markedly on the dimension of emotionality. For example, an appropriate interpretation of our metaphor, "An overprotective parent is a smothering blanket," had to deal with the theme of a life-threatening parent. But an interpretation of our proverb, "Too many doctors kill the patient," could have been easily placed in a neutralized context, as in, "It's not good to ask for too many opinions about something." The life-threatening theme is thereby transformed, removing context and patient from the anxiety dimension.

In the high affect context, the subject has two tasks: to control his anxiety arousal and to think abstractly. Freud (1911) made the point that abstraction, i.e., thought itself, may be a mode of appropriately controlling anxiety, but also that thought may arouse and extend anxiety. We are suggesting that, regarding proverbs, thinking abstractly may provide a way of controlling anxiety. The two tasks of anxiety control and abstraction may be carried out simultaneously. There is no added incentive in the high anxiety proverb context to avoid meaning by becoming especially inaccurate, autistic, or literal.

Metaphor comprehension, in contrast to proverb comprehension, stimulates and extends the personal, sensuous, and emotional arousal provided initially by the content of the metaphor. Interpretation may make anxiety more meaningful and, thereby, possibly more painful. The subject is not offered an opportunity to fully neutralize anxiety-arousing contents by thinking abstractly, as he is with proverbs. However, less advanced abstract thinking is required in interpreting similarity metaphors than in interpreting proportional metaphors (Billow, 1975). For this reason, the schizophrenic may have greater opportunity to mentally organize himself in the face of anxiety. He or she would have less of a need to disorganize by inaccurate, autistic, and/or literal responding.

That is, the two tasks of controlling anxiety and thinking abstractly are uneven in the two types of metaphor tasks. Both types require the same energy in anxiety mastery, but similarity metaphors call for less energy expended on abstraction than do proportional metaphors. For this reason, disturbed subjects may have an easier time with high affect similarity metaphors than with high affect proportional metaphors, as our data suggests.

v. Relationship Among Miscomprehension, Verbal, Deviance, and Clinical Decision Making

For all diagnostic groups, the relationship between the inaccuracy of a response and the likelihood of a deviant mode of responding, i.e., bizarre, or literal, was most often statistically highly significant. Such correlations, however, rarely accounted for more than 20% of variance. Similarly, the relationships of verbal deviance between and within figurative tasks were powerful statistically, but moderate numerically. According to our data, it makes little sense to call an individual "concrete," "literal," or "ametaphoric," if we mean by these terms a characteristic tendency which extends across figurative comprehension (or production) tasks, or across inaccurate and deviant modes of responding. Too much individual variability remains to infer a single ability or disability tapped by our tasks.

At the same time, the highly robust patterns of correlations point to several cognitive and cognitive-personality factors related to metaphoric responsivity. We are currently factor analyzing data from a much larger subject and data pool, and believe that we have findings of heuristic utility.

We may ask, from a clinical perspective, the diagnostic significances of the most typical qualitative response of a subpopulation. We may ask also about the diagnostic significance of an occasional inaccurate, autistic, literal, or omitted (rejection) response to metaphor.

Although the model incidence across subjects for autistic responses was zero, the mean incidence of autism varied considerably both between subject and between treatment groups. We found that 20% of the schizophrenic responses to high affect metaphors contained an autistic verbalization, whereas only 8% of schizophrenics' responses contained autism in the low affect treatment. In contrast to the schizophrenics' performance, the incidence of autism in either treatment condition remained 2% or less with borderline and nonpsychiatric patient responses.

Can subject diagnosis be predicted on the basis of metaphoric inaccuracy or deviance? All subjects interpreted accurately as well as inaccurately figurative stimuli (metaphor and proverbs). The differences amongst the three groups in terms of correctness, although highly significant, do not in themselves lead to confident predictions. The best indicator was the incidence of autism in response to high affect metaphor, since almost all schizophrenics became autistic at least once in the 16 items, while only very few medical or borderline subjects answered in this deviant manner. Whereas the absence of autism does not rule out schizophrenia, the occurrence of this deviant response to high affect metaphoric stimuli is more typical of this clinical entity, at least within our subpopulation and in terms of our stimuli. We found this to be true also when high affect leads were given to schizophrenics to produce metaphor, not merely to interpret metaphor (see below).

We found proverb responses to be less sensitive to psychopathology than high affect metaphor. Thus, the incidence of autism was approximately twice as frequent by schizophrenics in response to high affect proportional metaphor than in response to high affect proverbs (23% vs. 12%).

We are left with the question of the generalizability of our conclusions to situations of psychotherapy and of the diagnostic interview.

The zero modal incidence of items to which an interpretation was rejected, coupled with the very low mean number of items rejected, indicates that our subjects were quite cooperative and motivated. This was indeed the impression received by our interviewer teams, who found most of the subjects interested and friendly. (We tended to lose subject participation later on in our lengthy testing procedure, either during the Rorschach or psychiatric interview.) It is possible that the more grossly negativistic or decompensation-prone individuals actually self-selected themselves out of the investigation by declining to participate.

In real-life clinical settings, such factors become central as negative transference, distrust and uncooperativeness, and patient rather than experimenter-induced anxiety and resultant regression and/or decompensation. We are currently carrying out analyses of patient verbalizations in response to our psychiatric interview. The patients were given open-ended, highly personal questions to respond to spontaneously. Differences among groups on dimensions of metaphor responsivity and deviance should closely reflect the vicissitudes of the clinical communicative field. The use and misuse of metaphoric language by our subjects in the field setting is being compared to their performance regarding metaphor comprehension and productivity under controlled laboratory conditions.

B. Metaphor Production in Schizophrenic and Borderline States: Preliminary Findings

The basic design of our metaphor comprehension study was repeated, presenting a task in which metaphor had to be created by our subjects, rather than merely comprehended. The task consisted of eight sentence stems which the subject was asked to complete by creating two different metaphors for each one. Subjects were given a sample stem with several good metaphorical completions as a model for the task. Each stem is composed of an adjective, noun, and the verb "is" or "are," (e.g., "The starry night is_____.)" An example of a completed metaphor stem which is both correctly abstract and creative is, "A strong conscience is *a cage around a tiger.*" In order to examine the effect of affective stimuli on spontaneous production, half of each group of subjects were given high-affect stems (e.g., "A furious mother_____)," while the other half were given low-affect stems (e.g., "A sunset_____.)"

We will report on data derived from 40 schizophrenics, 40 borderline, and 40 hospitalized, nonpsychiatric medical control patients.

i. Diagnostic Differences

The schizophrenics responded less accurately (P < .01) on the production tasks, just as they did on the figurative tasks presented for comprehension. The borderlines were as accurate as the medical subjects in metaphor production, in contrast to their lower accuracy level in metaphor comprehension. The schizophrenics were significantly (P < .01) more autistic than the other two populations; there were no significant differences on the dimension of literalness.

Subjects from each diagnostic group who were given the high affect stems produced responses which were significantly better (more accurate) than those given the low affect stimuli, opposite to our predictions and opposite to what we found with metaphor comprehension. In the high affect condition of the metaphor production task, the accuracy of the schizophrenic subjects was 69%, as compared to an almost 100% accuracy rate for both the medical and borderline subjects. In the low affect condition of this task, schizophrenics had a 62% accuracy rate, as compared to an 85% accuracy rate for the medicals and an 82% accuracy for the borderlines.

The better metaphor production performance of subjects in the high affect condition can be understood in several ways. An examination of the metaphor stems suggests that there may be differences inherent in the stimuli which produce differential response sets. Although an attempt was made to match the stimuli on difficulty level, the high affect stimuli, by the nature of their content, may be more evocative and therefore more eliciting of a response. The high affect metaphor stems dealt with thematic content including violence, interpersonal conflict, and bodily harm. The low affect stems were more commonplace and perhaps less stimulating of creative responsiveness. They dealt with inanimate objects, animals, and natural phenomena (e.g., snowflakes, starry nights).

Another explanation of subjects' better symbolic functioning involves the adaptive level of anxiety that the high effect stimuli appeared to activate. Sublimatory defenses appeared to have been mobilized by these metaphor stems, enabling subjects to symbolize in the face of anxiety. Perhaps the moderate level of anxiety worked to heighten creativity in the less disturbed subjects, producing better responses than when no anxiety was present.

The above finding was particularly noteworthy for the schizophrenics, whose better performance on the high affect stimuli appeared especially uncharacteristic. A closer look, however, revealed how the schizophrenics handled what we described in the previous section as dual tasks of both thinking abstractly and controlling anxiety. As a group, the schizophrenics were more accurate in their responses to the high affect stems than they were to the low affect stems, but they were also more autistic (see Figure 1). They became both more correct and more incorrect (very autistic), representing the deeper split in their personality when compared to other groups. One might speculate that their autism was partially defensive. It allowed them necessary distance from material that was too

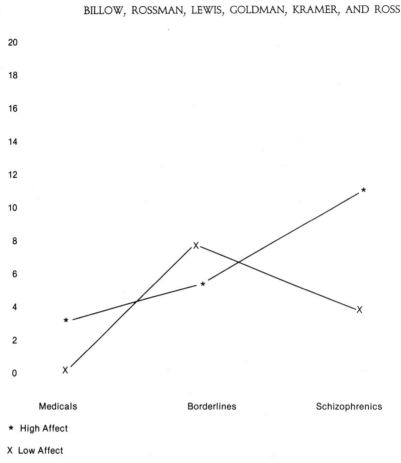

FIGURE 1
Metaphor Production
Mean Number of Autistic Responses
Hign and Low Affect

affect-arousing and potentially disorganizing. We came to a similar conclusion when considering the responses of our deeply disturbed children.

ii. Metaphor Responsivity in the Disturbed Adult Patient.

In psychoanalytic psychotherapy both patient and therapist must be capable of appreciating the presence of a metaphoric aspect to their relationship, and of tolerating and exploring it. Some of the difficulty that very disturbed patients have in therapy may be a function of impaired abilities to use language metaphorically, and to appreciate that some aspects of their relationships with their psychotherapists are metaphoric (transferential).

When we studied the metaphoric responsivity of different diagnostic groups in terms of their comprehension of, and ability to, produce metaphor in neutral and in heightened affectual contexts, some striking correlations with the theoretical literature were found, as well as some important divergencies. When borderlines were asked to produce metaphors, their total performance was as correct as normal subjects. However, individual responses were sometimes as bizarre (autistic) as those produced by schizophrenics (see Figure 1). Such bizarre utterances – which did not differ significantly from schizophrenics in total number (but did differ from nonpsychiatrics) – suggest difficulties in differentiating between private and public, fantasy and reality, communication and autism. As the literature suggests, borderlines can appear as normal or neurotic, as evidenced by their appropriately abstract metaphor responses, but they also have characterological disturbances which sometimes make them seem more similar to schizophrenics, as evidenced by the bizarre quality of a significant number of responses, particularly in the low affect condition.

The emphasis theorists have given to the borderline's tendency to regress only in highly affect-arousing situations was not supported by this study. When the borderlines were asked to produce metaphors to affect-arousing ambiguous leads, they were no less accurate, and in effect they were less bizarre than they were when presented with low anxiety leads. When schizophrenics were presented with the affectively charged stems, they were significantly more bizarre than they were in the low affect condition.

The results also have implications for psychotherapy. They may be interpreted as supported the efficacy of insight-oriented psychotherapy with borderline and schizophrenic patients. Although these patients reveal some difficulty with figurative communication, they can also be metaphorically responsive. Therefore deeper interpretive work appears to be appropriate with nonpsychotic borderline patients, and with some schizophrenic patients, particularly when the clinican is aware of the disorganizing effects of anxiety. As we mentioned in the previous section, even the most disturbed of our schizophrenic subjects were able to comprehend metaphor, although at a lower accuracy level (under anxiety conditions) than their less disturbed peers. Such conclusions hold when our patients had to produce as well as interpret metaphors.

C. Metaphor Comprehension and Personality Variables

We hypothesized that symbolic capacities are related to the establishment and maintenance of a firm sense of self. Metaphor requires a temporary merging of disparate semantic elements at a deeply personal level. Psychoanalysis assumes that, at such a level of self-experience, early body feelings and fantasies are unconsciously aroused. Poorly integrated individuals lack adequate boundaries between self and other, between feeling and thought, and between fantasy and reality. We hypothesized that such individuals would find the semantic merging and subsequent separation involved in metaphor comprehension threatening and difficult, particularly when the symbolic content is affect arousing, expressing painful conscious as well as partially unconscious conflictual experience. We expected that our most disturbed subjects, the schizophrenics, would show the strongest relationship between poor self-integration and disturbance in symbolic capacity.

The Rorschach inkblot test was used to draw inferences about personality integration. In producing a response to the Rorschach test, the subject projects something of his or her own experience of himself or herself (i.e., his or her personality) into his or her perception of the inkblot. Since the inkblot stimuli are themselves relatively unarticulated, it is thought that individuals with poorly differentiated self-boundaries have difficulty with the task, and display this difficulty by making certain types of deviant responses. In *contamination, fabulized combination, incongruous combination, external-internal*, and *fluid* responses, for example, spatial elements are combined, often fused, into a perceptual gestalt that violates natural boundaries. In *contamination* responses, two discrete percepts are fused into one, such as a "batfish." When the boundary disturbance is not so great as to cause fusion, inappropriate combinations result, as in "man with wings" (an *incongruous combination*), or "two ants playing with a ball" (*fabulized combination*), or "a magician; you can see the inside of his brain" (an *external-internal* response). In a *fluid* response, no stable inkblot percept is achieved, because the subject's boundaries are in flux.

A composite scale of Ego Boundary Disturbance (EBD) was created by adding the number of different types of deviant scores a subject produced. This Rorschach scale was correlated with scores on linguistic tasks.

We indeed found a strong relationship between ego boundary integrity and correctness of metaphor and proverb comprehension. There were highly significant negative correlations across all subjects between the measure of EBD and all three linguistic measures, as Table 2 shows. As expected, this relationship was stronger in the schizophrenic subgroup than in the other two subgroups. In fact, the covariance between the Rorschach and linguistic measures among all subjects

TABLE 2
Relationship Between Ego Boundary Disturbance and Correct Interpretation of Metaphors and Proverbs[a]

	All Subjects	Schizophrenics	Borderlines	Medicals
Similarity Metaphor	−.44**	−.43*	−.39	−.18
Proportional Metaphor	−.38**	−.41*	−.09	−.17
Proverbs	−.32*	−.30	.09	−.29

[a]Pearson product-moment correlations
*P < .05
**P < .01

appeared to be accounted for almost entirely by the schizophrenics. Our data also show that the relationship between disturbance in symbolic capacity and self-boundaries is not due merely to pervasive deterioration in cognitive functioning in the schizophrenic subjects, since the correlations between metaphor comprehension and EBD remained even after the influence of IQ was partialled out.

A second major finding was that disturbances in ego boundaries were accompanied by specific deficiencies and deviances in symbolization, as manifested by autistic and literal interpretations of metaphors and proverbs. This is illustrated by the correlations in Table 3. Deviant interpretations of the verbal stimuli were highly significantly correlated with EBD. In the schizophrenic subgroup, these correlations were of a greater magnitude, and were highly significant in spite of the smaller sample size.

Another major finding concerned the impact of anxiety on the symbolic process. As can bee seen in Table 4, the relationships between EBD and the verbal symbolization measures were magnified in situations of anxiety, that is, among subjects given affect-arousing rather than neutral verbal stimuli. It appears that poorly integrated individuals are less able promptly and effectively to contain the anxiety and resolve the conflict that may be aroused by a symbolic task than are individuals with intact ego boundaries. In other words, quality of ego boundaries becomes a particularly important factor in ability to interpret metaphor when these verbal stimuli themselves invoke anxiety.

Already disrupted ego boundaries, as exist in schizophrenia, render the impaired subject particularly vulnerable to the potentially disruptive impact of metaphors. Further, the themes of the high affect metaphors especially may renew

TABLE 3
Relationship Between Ego Boundary Disturbance and Verbal Deviance on Metaphors and Proverbs[a]

	All Subjects	Schizophrenics	Borderlines	Medicals
		Autism		
Sim Met	.46**	.60**	.23	.04
Prop Met	.34**	.44**	−.12	−.01
Proverbs	.38**	.47**	.15	−.06
		Literalness		
Sim Met	.24*	.54**	−.12	.07
Prop Met	.35**	.66**	.14	−.07
Proverbs	.14	.27	−.30	−.07

[a]Spearman rank order correlations
*$P < .05$
**$P < .01$

TABLE 4

Comparison of Correlations: Ego Boundary Disturbance and Low
Versus High Affect Arousing Figurative Stimuli – All Subjects

	Low Affect	High Affect
Correctness[a]		
Similarity metaphor-EBD	−.34*	−.53**
Proportional metaphor-EBD	−.26	−.51**
Proverbs-EBD	−.34*	−.30
Autism[b]		
Similarity metaphor-EBD	.33*	.61**
Proportional metaphor-EBD	.17	.47**
Proverbs-EBD	.40*	.36*
Literalness[b]		
Similarity metaphor-EBD	.06	.40*
Proportional metaphor-EBD	.35*	.36*
Proverbs-EBD	15	.14

[a]Pearson product-moment correlations
[b]Spearman rank order correlations
 *P   .05
**P   .01

unresolved infantile fears and conflicts which are implicated in the development
of disturbed ego boundaries (Mahler, 1968; Mahler, Pine, & Bergman, 1975).

PROGRAM 2:
IDIOMATIC LANGUAGE IN PSYCHOPATHOLOGICAL CHILDREN

We (see Boxerman-Kraemer, 1984) extended the exploration of metaphoric
communication and miscommunication to two age groups of normal and emotionally disturbed children, 5 to 6 1/2 years, and 7 to 8 1/2 years, of age. While it
has been suggested that metaphoric communications be used as a compromise interpretive technique in the pschotherapeutic treatment of borderline and schizophrenic children (Ekstein, 1966), there had been no empirical examination of the
response of these children to figurative language. Clinical anecdotes in fact suggest that the seriously disturbed child often has a highly idiosyncratic and emotionally alarming response to common figures of speech. Rosenfeld and Sprince
(1963) recount the example of an 8-year-old boy whom, upon hearing the an-
nouncement that school would "break up" for the holidays, became terribly
afraid the school might explode or be destroyed.

Such responses may not seem terribly surprising when one considers that figurative language is by nature ambiguous, often emotionally charged and highly
aggressivized, frequently cast in the imagery of the body and its functions. Consider, for example, such potentially charged, but common, idioms as "my heart is

breaking," "she really hit the ceiling," or "it's raining cats and dogs." We hypothesized that the response of the disturbed child to such figurative expressions would likely reflect, not simply the forms of thought possible at his or her specific developmental level, but also, would likely be shaped by the various affective realities confronting him or her internally and as stimulated by this emotionally powerful language. We speculated also that the child's response to metaphor would be colored further by the various defenses he or she typically employs to deal with conflicts in psychological growth.

Common idiomatic expressions set as the "punch-line" within four-line vignettes were presented to two age groups of 33 normal and 33 severely borderline children of at least average range intelligence. The borderline subjects represented a loose diagnostic grouping of nonmedicated children treated as outpatients in the psychiatric clinic of a New York City hospital. Children diagnosed as "schizoid disorder of childhood" or "impulse/conduct disorder," or who presented a symptom picture consonant with the range of borderline conditions of childhood as outlined by Pine (1974), were included as subjects. All children shared certain developmental failures or aberrations in ego function and object relationships, with the majority presenting problems with impulse control, especially in the management of aggression. This group of children was much more disturbed than the adult group which was labelled "borderline" in the work reported on above. The matched control group was drawn from students at a private school in New York City, representing a broad mixture of socio-economic backgrounds, of diverse ethnic origin.

The 12 idiom items presented to the children were of four types, varying both in degree of emotional arousal and in their inclusion or noninclusion of body imagery, in order to determine the impact of affect and anxiety on idiom comprehension. For example, "have you lost your tongue?" was an emotionally arousing, body idiom, whereas "let's put our heads together" was a low affect, body idiom. Non-body idioms included such emotionally arousing items as "it disappeared into thin air," and low affect phrases as "let's keep the ball rolling." After hearing each vignette, each child was engaged in a brief open-ended clinical inquiry to facilitate exploration of the child's production of thought and fantasy. An open-ended dialogue was chosen both to encourage spontaneity and in order to replicate more closely what goes on in therapeutic interviews.

The children's interpretations of the idioms were scored quantitatively for accuracy and abstractness, similarly to our scoring procedures of metaphors administered to adults. The qualitative scores were somewhat more elaborate in this study, however. Inaccurate responses included both errors relating to developing cognitive abilities (such as magical, animistic, or literal thinking) and those reflective of psychopathology, such as responses characterized by peculiar, fantastic elaborations or bizarre associations. A second series of qualitative ratings captured salient features of the children's attitudes, behaviors, and defensive strategies manifested during the production of both correct and incorrect responses.

Analyses of the quantitative scores revealed clear developmental trends in both the borderline and control groups, with accuracy of interpretation increasing proportionally with age. The borderline children proved far less adept at producing the conventional meanings of the idioms, with the older borderlines lagging behind even the young normal subjects. The performance of the borderline group was extremely erratic, with frequent fluctuations between high and low level responses, and rapid departures from cogent interpretations to idiosyncratic fantasy.

The borderline children's deficits in metaphorical understanding became even more exaggerated when idioms were presented to them in the emotional context of body related themes or affectively charged imagery (Figures 2 and 3). The accuracy level of the young normals was also diminished, although less markedly, in the face of emotional arousal, confirming observations of developmental theorists who have emphasized how typically young children are unable to make full use of cognitive and linguistic abilities – particularly newly achieved levels of thought or skill – in emotional circumstances, and in moments of extreme stress or ambiguity.

The kinds of misinterpretations offered by the borderlines and controls differed greatly. Where failures in comprehension amongst the control groups represented immaturities in abstract thinking related to developing cognitive abilities and to the phenomenological-linguistic orientations of young children, the responses of the borderline children frequently reflected deviations in thought and reality orientation. These distortions emerged even in instances where their responses sufficiently captured the meaning of the figurative expressions. The borderline child's production of vivid, highly aggressivized fantasy and personalized associations in response to the idioms was unique and pronounced. For example in a story about a missing baseball glove which just "disappeared into thin air," 8-year-old Leo explained: "it just ripped to pieces, someone ripped it to pieces, til you can't see it no more, it just went up to God; if it's just like a body and he's dead, it went to God, it has wings too." This tendency to endow even the more neutral imagery so consistently with aggressive intent was such that, at times, it seemed the only evident affective reality for these children was their anxiety about the consequences of their own or others' aggressive impulses.

In the most extreme instances, the borderline children demonstrated a total unwillingness to symbolize even in the form of fantasy, with the idiom image becoming a concrete piece of experience whose presence was actual, immediate, and undisguised. Thus, 6-year-old Arthur responded to the idiom "that burns me up!" by burying his face in his hands and exclaiming: "All I have to do is get out of here before the fire comes!" Notably, the numbers of aggressive intrusions and fabulized elaborations produced by the borderline children escalated significantly in the presence of anxiety generated by affect laden idiom imagery and by body content.

Many of the answers of the borderline children revealed disturbances of affect, defense, and internalized object relations. In contrast to the controls, borderline

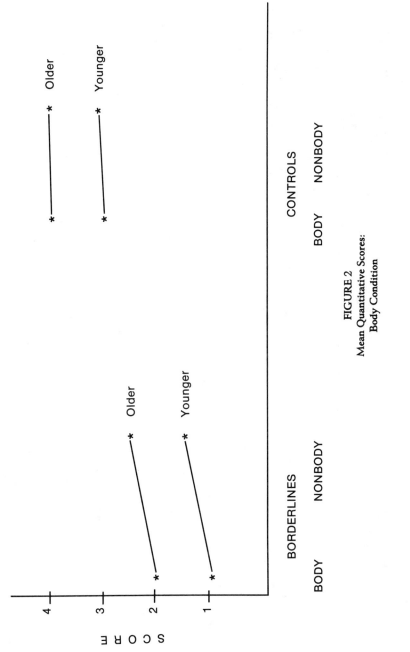

FIGURE 2
Mean Quantitative Scores:
Body Condition

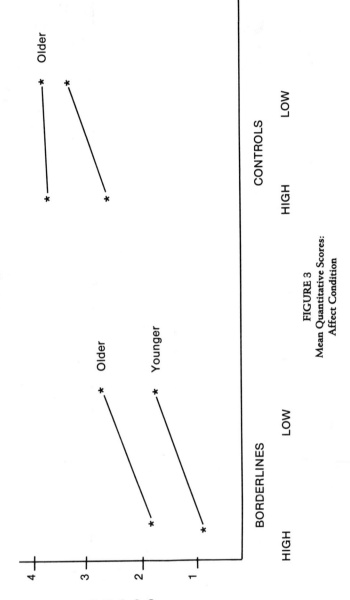

FIGURE 3
Mean Quantitative Scores:
Affect Condition

children demonstrated powerful emotional reactions to many of the idioms, and employed a variety of primitive defensive strategies in an apparent effort to manage the enormous anxiety generated by the idiom imagery. For example, where the young controls tended to respond to even the high affect idioms with humor and curiosity, fancifulness and enjoyment, the borderline child's response was often one of catastrophic panic ("He cried his eyes out? Oh, my GOD! how did that happen?"), followed by desperate efforts to dismiss the idiom through insistent denial and negation ("No way! your eyes can't pop out from crying") or through rejection ("Oh, my God! Don't read that one!" or "This is crazy, it's all crazy! If I told you that one, you'd run out of here screaming!"). Efforts at avoidance and obfuscation often took extreme form, with the borderline children plunging into exaggeratedly "crazy" talk and behavior (Cain, 1964).

The borderline child's vulnerability to emotionally arousing body imagery appears to be linked to his or her inordinate preoccupation with aggressive fantasy and with possibilities of body injury (Chethik, 1960), and to the faulty separation which exists for him or her between fantasy and reality (Kernberg, 1983), the ego boundary disturbances we investigated with adult subjects. Both of these appear to limit his or her ability to maintain sufficient safe distance from primitive feelings and fantasies in order to convert them into thoughts or symbols. The unique defensive strategies utilized by borderline children suggest, then, that their many "unshaped" fabulized responses might be understood not merely as "nothing," i.e., as the regressive discharges of an overwhelmed and overstimulated ego. The intense responses seemed at times to represent a deliberate flight away from reality into an idiosyncratic fantasy world in which pain became pathologically symbolized. Again, Shakespeare's description of Ophelia is particularly apt. These very disturbed children would "botch the words to fit their own thoughts." As in our studies with adults, such language often could be interpreted by the sensitive clinician as expressive of an aspect of the subject's particular existential predicament.

In other studies in progress, we are finding that disturbed individuals have preferences for interpreting or misinterpreting metaphoric meaning, and that these preferences are partially dependent on the nature of the emotional disorder, and partially dependent on the emotional context of the metaphor. We are also studying the relationship between the spontaneous "botches"–the deviant metaphors–created by our disturbed subjects, their appropriate expressive language, and several personality variables, including ego boundary disturbances. Such findings will be presented in subsequent reports.

REFERENCES

Arieti, S. (1955). *Interpretation of schizophrenia.* New York: Robt. Brunner.
Bateson, G., Jackson, D. D., Haley, J., & Weakland, J. (1956). Toward a Theory of Schizophrenia. *Behavioral Science, 1,* 251–264.

Benjamin, J. J. (1974). A method for distinguishing and evaluating formal thinking disorders in schizophrenia. In J. S. Kasanin (Ed.), *Language and Thought in Schizophrenia*. Berkeley and Los Angeles: University of California Press.

Billow, R. M. (1975). A cognitive development study of metaphor comprehension. *Developmental Psychology, 11*, 415–423.

Billow, R. M. (1977). Metaphor: A review of the psychological literature. *Psychological Bulletin, 84*, 1, 81–92.

Bleuler, G. (1950). *Dementia praecox, or the group of schizophrenia,* (Trans. by J. Zinkin). New York: International University Press. (Originally published 1911.)

Boxerman-Kraemer, S. (1984). *The comprehension of idiomatic expressions by normal and borderline children: A developmental study.* Unpublished doctoral dissertation. Institute of Advanced Psychological Studies, Adelphi University.

Cain, A. (1964). On the meaning of *"playing crazy"* in borderline children. *Psychiatry, 27*, 278–289.

Chethik, M. (1980). The borderline child. In J. Noshpitz (Ed.), *Basic handbook of child psychiatry,* (Vol. 2). New York: Basic Books.

Chapman, L. J., & Chapman, J. P. (1973). *Disordered thought in schizophrenia.* Englewood Cliffs, NJ: Prentice-Hall.

Ekstein, R. (1966). Interpretation within the metaphor. In R. Ekstein, *Children of time and space, of action and impulse.* New York: Appleton-Century Crofts.

Freud, S. (1950). Formulations regarding the two principles in Mental Functioning. In *Collected papers* (Vol. IV, pp. 13–21). London: Hogarth. (Originally published 1911).

Goldman, D. A. (1984). *A comparative study of metaphoric processes in borderline, schizophrenic and normal adults.* Unpublished doctoral dissertation, IAPS, Adelphi University.

Gorham, D. R. (1956). A proverbs test for clinical and experimental use. *Psychological Reports, 2*, 1–12.

Grinker, R., Werble, B., & Drye, R. D. (1968). *The borderline syndrome.* New York: Basic Books.

Gunderson, J. G., & Singer, M. T. (1975). Defining borderline patients. An overview. *American Journal of Psychiatry, 132*, 1–10.

Hertler, C., & Chapman, J. (1978). A scoring manual for literalness in proverb interpretation. *Journal of Consulting and Clinical Psychology, 46*, 551–555.

Kernberg, O. F. (1967). Borderline personality organization. *Journal of the American Psychoanalytic Association, 15*, 641–685.

Kernberg, O. F. (1975). *Borderline Conditions and Pathological Narcissism.* New York: Jason Aronson.

Kernberg, P. (1983). Borderline conditions: Childhood and adolescent aspects. In K. Robson (Ed.), *The borderline child: Approach to etiology, diagnosis and treatment.* New York: McGraw Hill.

Kilburg, R. R., & Siegel, A. W. (1973). Formal operations in reactive and process schizophrenics. *Journal of Consulting and Clinical Psychology, 40*, 371–376.

Kohut, H. (1971). *The analysis of the self.* New York: International Universities Press.

Lewis, N. (1983). *Ego boundaries and comprehension of metaphor in schizophrenia: A study of symbolic processes.* Unpublished doctoral dissertation, IAPS, Adelphi University.

Mahler, M. (1968). *On Human symbiosis and the vicissitudes of individuation.* New York: IUP.

Mahler, M., Pine, F., & Bergman, A. (1975). *The psychological birth of the human infant.* New York: Basic Books.

Pine, F. (1974). On the concept "borderline" in children: A clinical essay. *The psychoanalytic Study of the Child, 29*, 341–368.

Rosenfeld, S. K., & Sprince, M. P. (1963). An attempt to formulate the meaning of the concept "borderline." *The Psychoanalytic Study of the child, 18*, 603–635.

Rossman, J. (1985). *Metaphoric comprehension in schizophrenia.* Unpublished doctoral dissertation, IAPS, Adelphi University.

Searles, H. (1965). The differentiation between concrete and metaphorical thinking in the recovering schizophrenic patient. In *Collected papers on schizophrenia and related subjects.* New York: International Universities Press.

Wechsler, D. (1955). *WAIS Manual.* New York: The Psychological Corporation.

CHAPTER NINE

Transitional Metaphors and the Political Psychology of Identity Maintenance

Aaron David Gresson III

School of Social Welfare
Rockefeller College of Public Affairs and Policy
State University of New York at Albany

In a heterogeneous reality we can only expect heterogeneous solutions, though we can expect as well that some will have greater success or appear more compelling or persuasive to people than others. (Platt, 1984, p. 111)

The human project has always included, among its diverse tasks, the control and containment of the individual and collective imagination, particularly the fears and anxieties concurrent with daily life. Religion and myth traditionally served as core "curatives" for such human passions. More contemporary and complex societies do not have precisely the same "curatives," although the needs for such persists; and the means of containment and control do seem to follow steps similar to religious mythologizing (Becker, 1974). The shift from simple to complex social systems, while retaining some continuities in need, task, and function, has generated an increased awareness of and, at times, weariness with regards to human differences, or heterogeneity.

Heterogeneous societies – those having diverse groups with divergent, often contradictory interests, values, and beliefs – are particularly challenging for the societal leaders with regard to the management of fears and anxieties around *identity*: Who am I? What are my reference groups and obligations to them? Who wants me? Whom do I want? Such are the questions dominating the so-called "identity society." And it is in such a social space that identity-related fears and anxieties emerge as special concerns and that the society embarks on a series of "nation-building" projects (Fishman, 1972a, b). Language, particularly of an integrative sort, becomes critical to these projects of identity maintenance and shifting. Coalitional rhetoric and ideology abound herein; and metaphors and "condensation symbols" are being frequently created and debunked (Graber, 1976).

This chapter identifies a particular type of metaphor as most critical to such periods of social change: the Transitional Metaphor. This type of metaphor is concerned with the fears and anxieties accompanying change, loss, and separation, whether due to growth, development, or termination (death). In this chapter, I first define the transitional metaphor and delineate some of its forms and functions generally, and especially in "transitional society." Next, I provide an empirical illustration of how one transitional metaphor, "the rainbow," emerged and played itself out in the context of ethnopolitics. Here I seek to show how diverse parts of the social system, namely the mass media, politicians, and various interest group leaders, employed the notion in a "transitional" fashion. In this section, I also seek to illustrate some aspects of metaphoric transformation, especially its developmental dynamics. Finally, the chapter explores some of the implications of this discussion of transitional metaphors. Here, I focus on implications associated with intra-psychic, intersubjective, and macro-systemic dimensions of metaphoric transformation.

TRANSITIONAL SOCIETY AND ITS LANGUAGE

Linguistic scholars (Fishman, 1972a, b) have commented frequently on the language shifts and metaphorical switchings accompanying the transition from simple to more complex societies. Within such an observational context, emphasis has generally been upon the societal, cultural, and psychological forces making for language maintenance or change. These discussions, moreover, have typically proceeded from a view of a dominant versus a subordinate language group, with the latter rushing ambivalently toward the former. Under such conditions, society per se is viewed as "transitional." However, recent concern for the so-called "global political economic" crisis has prompted an enlarged sense of the "transitional." Here the stress is on the impact of certain sociocultural changes for the average person's psychological well-being and adaptation; and it is argued among some (Bell, 1978; Faber, 1979; Lasch, 1984) that man generally finds himself anxious, confused, and struggling for a sense of integratedness and integrity similar to more primitive versions of homo sapiens.

This orientation has provided us with a new set of concepts: "psychological man," "protean man," "generative man," "one-two-many dimensioned man," "narcissistic society," and "minimal self." These ideas aim at conveying this enlarged "transitional" character of man. But the enlarged sense of transitional society implies more. "Transitional" has come to refer more recently to the inner psychological processes regulating anxiety due to separation, loss, change, etc. (Faber, 1979; Winnicott, 1953). Within this meaning context, the contemporary adult's predicament has been likened to the infant and young child's:

the whole issue of "civilization's malaise" – including its *economic* malaise – must be approached from a direction which focuses closely upon the ordeals of infancy and early childhood, an approach which recognizes and explores the ambivalence and the anxiety of the early period, the splitting of the primal internalizations or "objects," and the extent to which that pre-oedipal anxiety persists into...[adolescence and adulthood], causing a *transitional* dilemma. (Faber, 1979, p. 40)

The idea of "transition" referred to by Faber differs markedly from that familiar to most students of language continuity and change. Faber is here drawing upon the work of Winnicott (1953, p. 7) who first systematically discussed the infant's use of cooing/babbling, blanket, or teddy, etc., as a means of dealing with the discovery and management of the anxiety due to separation from mother, being a separate self and relating to others:

I have introduced the terms "transitional object" and "transitional phenomena" for designation of the intermediate area of experience, between the thumb [sucking] and the teddy bear, between the oral eroticism and true object-relationship, between primary creative activity and projection of what has already introjected, between primary unawareness of indebtedness and the acknowledgement of indebtedness ("Say: ta!").

Clinicians (Applegate, 1984) have used Winnicott's formulations to identify many nontypical objects and situations as transitional: adolescence, drugs and alcohol, marriage, mourning, cars, etc. In each instance, the reasoning is that crises of separation and loss promote anxiety around one's identity and place within the world; that this anxiety motivates one to defend oneself from psychic disintegration; and that one symbolically attaches to things which console one as one lives between the spaces of a bygone connectedness and an as yet unrealized reconnection: "The symbol, accordingly, is a link to the parent, and the development of symbolic mentation in man serves to only a biological purpose but a defensive purpose as well" (Faber, 1979, p. 39).

In this chapter, I identify certain bodies of thought, specifically ideology and its rhetorics and metaphors, as capable of aiding the above stated *transitional task*. Transitional metaphors, then, are to be seen as a part of both the scholarly and popular vocabulary of a society-in-transition: that is, one which is separating itself from old ways of seeing, being, and doing, and on its way to alternative forms. Thus defined, transitional metaphors are a perennial part of social change and continuity; and they possess qualities associated with both stasis and development.

Transitional Metaphors

Traditional societies, seeking to manage the uncertainties of life and contain the accompanying anxieties by playing out prescribed roles, rely upon myths, ritual symbols and other mechanisms. Modern societies, especially pluralistic ones, also rely upon such mechanisms to explain, predict, and control the anxieties accompanying sociocultural change. Transitional metaphors pertain to both sources of anxiety: those deriving from the experience of life per se (i.e., death, hunger, intimacy, betrayal, etc.) and those which accompany modernity: ethnopolitics, global political economics, the possibility of nuclear holocaust, and planetary chemical pollution.

As here defined, the transitional metaphor is a word or expression which recapitulates the primal awareness of the "loss of the womb" (the secure, warm oneness with universe and mother) and the efforts to grasp this separation in a cognitive-emotional manner. This formulation gives rise to a wide variety of expressions. For example, some pertain to being "in between:"

(1) Between the Devil and the deep blue sea
(2) Between a rock and a hard place

Others transcend this "place" by hinting at both the primal loss and the anticipation of some degree of recovery. Here, for instance, is a lyric from a contemporary Negro Spiritual:

Mother and Father have gone on . . .
Sister still living in sin. . . .

These illustrations reflect the "transitional mode of awareness" (Faber, 1979). Winnicott (1953) noted that "transitional objects" were connected to imagination and other cognitive functions through the infant's evolving capacity for symbolization. *Symbolization enables the individual to move toward an inner, self-soothing capacity: an abstracted replacement of the security of mother, family, social group, etc.* The "transitional mode of awareness" pertains to a collective rather than individual sense of circumstances and attempt to manage such. Consider, for instance, an auto bumper sticker slogan currently in vogue:

Prevent the Nuclear Winter
Support the Nuclear Freeze

Other, more traditional notions include:

(1) Take it easy
(2) Be cool, man
(3) Hang in there, baby

These expressions are intended to be soothing, comforting supports. They are in sharp contrast with "nuclear freeze" type metaphors, which emphasize the creation of a technology capable of cosmic annihilation. Yet both types are concerned with "transitional anxiety." Another form of such metaphors are those emphasizing life span shifts or changes:

(1) The child is father to the man
(2) Out of the mouth of babes
(3) Once a man and twice a child

Paradox, or the balancing of contradiction, is critical to such metaphorical forms. The idea is not merely to enlarge meaning through the illumination of related-ness between two or more events or phenomena; rather, the goal is "the preserva-tion of those *internal, psychological boundaries* which control the anxiety that persist-ently arises from the presence" (Faber, 1979, p. 40) of good and bad, being and nothingness, within each of us. Thus, we might generate notions such as "The Devil's Disciple," or "God's Demon Seed," to depict this duality of identity.

The identification of what is "good" and "bad" self, desirable and undesirable, is not always easily known. For the mature adult, choosing from among conflict-ive identities has been often difficult but possible; for the young child, such choos-ing can be psychologically impossible and result in "splitting" people, particularly parents, into all good and all bad representations. Of course, when one is forced to make such an inaccurate assessment, one's own self-image is affected (Blanck & Blanck, 1979; Mackey, 1984). Societies which encourage the creation of negative and positive stereotypes (i.e., Jew, Black, homosexual, etc.) are especially contrib-utory to such "splitting" behavior; hence the idea of self-hating Jews, Blacks, etc. (Gresson, 1982). Some transitional metaphors seek to deal with the anxieties and related cognitive-affective experiences associated with the management of what Goffman (1963) has called "spoiled identity." For example, the recent rise of the expression "Brown People" to reflect pride in black–white parentage is suggest-ive of a desire to downplay both the traditional insistence that mulattoes are Black and the rejection of one's biological connection to the racist overlord. An-other, more complex illustration is the following title to a volume on Black women (Smith, Scott, & Hall, 1982):

All the women are white; all the blacks are men,
But some of Us are Brave

In this instance, Black female behavioral scientists are attempting to emphasize that they are *neither men nor White*; and that this is a very significant distinction. Like mulattoes, Black women have been historically identified with "Blackness." But their experiences of self, particularly vis á vis Black men and white women (Hooks, 1981) have led them to want and need to clarify a "separate reality" in which two critical aspects of self are emphasized equally. "Some of Us are Brave" expresses the context of this renegotiated identity by alluding to the perceived historical failure/betrayal by both Black men as sexists and White women as racists. "Bravery is Black woman" becomes a transitional metaphor in its self-soothing capacity. Thus a Black female administrator recently declared:

> I have felt the pangs of guilt evoked by those who would lead me to believe that to protect myself and promote my general welfare is to let my people down. I am now beginning to see how it is possible to let my people down by *failing* to protect myself and my interests and to seek fulfillment of my own needs. Indeed, in modern organizations, racism and sexism dictate that I AM MY PEOPLE. I AM BLACK. I AM WOMAN. (Dumas, 1980, p. 214)

In this latter case, we are given a clue to the (a) psychohistorical and (b) renegotiative aspects of transitional metaphors. Though related, these differ; the first pertains to the contingencies which led to the formulation of the idea that Blacks ought to behave in a certain manner if racial loyalty is to remain intact; the second relates to the experiences dictating the need and desire for a change, a reformulation of what is a "good" self-representation. In the present illustration, the cognitive-transformational character of transitional metaphors is reflected within the *remembrance* and *recreation* of identity, the *dwelling within* and *reintegration of* the past and present. (It might be noted in passing that it is perhaps significant that some artists who seek to facilitate this shift refer to themselves as *mediums*, like Alice Walker, and *mystics*, like Julius Lester [1982].) I think that these terms are a kind of metacommunication about the metaphorizing process being experienced and validated by the artist.) The above cited case parallels, moreover, the psychoanalytically described move from birth to selfhood (Mahler, Pine, & Bergman, 1975) by reflecting the psychological processes of differentiation, practicing, and individuation (reintegration). Cognition obtains throughout this "journey": primarily through the symbolic use of ideas and concepts which chart the journey and seek to insure a safe, albeit rough, passage. Once again we may turn to a "Brown People" type metaphor/lyric from the 1970s:

> If white is Right,
> And black is Beautiful, What can Brown Be?

In such metaphoric expressions we see both a developmental and a perennial quality. The shifting meanings and valuations of identity are perennial, in that people seem forever bent on using problematic comparisons. The neo-Freudian, Wilhelm Reich, illustrated this in what he designated the "emotional plague" of nations:

> In World War I "the Italians" were the friends and allies of the Americans. In 1942, during World War II, they were arch enemies, and in 1943, friends again. In World War I, 1914, "the Italians" were the arch enemies of "the Germans," "hereditary enemies" from way back, as it were. In World War II, 1940, "the Italians" and "the Germans" were "blood brothers," again on grounds of "heredity." (1971, p. 206)

Clearly, the political use of symbols such as depicted above can be hard on the populace if they do not find ways of ignoring them (Fishman, 1972a, b). Because they intuitively understand the politics of coalition-building, people seem able to retain an inner stability. They do so, moreover, by retaining a basic disassociation from the "other." Thus, the popular traditional notion that the "only good Indian is a dead Indian." The easy substitution for "Indian" of "Jew" or "Negro" reflects the cognitive substitution of a transitional metaphor, one, in this case, aimed at protecting against the anxiety of implied "oneness" with a "natural enemy."

The idiosyncratic, developmental quality of transitional metaphors does not exclude the operation of cognitive substitution or vacillation around competitive identities. It does, however, suggest the peculiar and significant impact of cultural creations such as modern technology upon the psyche, individual and collective. Mass media and communication are illustrative here. Indeed, it is possible to show how the perennial and developmental qualities of transitional metaphors interrelate. In so doing, it is possible to more graphically describe the dynamic nature of transitional metaphors, including their responsiveness to mass communications media. While much recent scholarship connecting language, social change, and complex groups has been carried out (Giles, 1977; Husband, 1979), it has not yielded sufficient descriptions of the core properties and processes. The following section will present an empirical illustration of the various aspects of transitional metaphors as novel metaphors. In this way, it will be possible to extend the growing literature on the interplay of mass media functioning and ethnopolitical activity, particularly around identity maintenance through the management of transitional anxiety.

TRANSITIONAL METAPHORS AND THE MEDIA: THE CASE OF THE "RAINBOW" METAPHOR

Each nation that enters the cycle of modernization must at some point break through in three fields: political and social reform, language, and journalism.
(Passin, 1968, p. 443)

and in the sky there's a rainbow and all of the colors are black, it's not that the colors aren't there: it's just imagination they lack. Everything's the same back in my little town.   (Paul Simon, "My Little Town")

Over the past decade, scholars (Gregg, 1971; Gresson, 1978) have increasingly considered the ego functions of rhetorical communication. This consideration of the use of language arose partially out of the observation that some rhetorical forms, particularly so-called "protest rhetoric," seemed to lack the properties—logic, conciliation-orientation, etc.—typically ascribed to rhetoric. In this context I offered (Gresson, 1978) the proposition that such rhetoric has often a dual, intra-inter group focus. The preceeding discussion of transitional metaphors follows in this tradition of argument: such metaphors seem to speak to both intrapsychic (conscious and unconscious) and intersubjective needs, conditions, and intentions. In order to further clarify the above argument, this section will examine a recent historical event, one characterized by, among other things, an incipient root or core transitional metaphor: the "Rainbow Coalition." This analysis will proceed with the aid of Haskell's (1986) psychological theory of metaphoric transformation and Husband's (1979) empirical study of the social psychological processes mediating social structural events.

Haskell (in press) has offered a general theory of metaphor which emphasizes its cognitive basis and dynamic developmental nature:

> It will be suggested here that the *fundamental cognitive operation of the various phenomena labeled "metaphor"* is the transformation of invariance. Further this operation is not primarily a linguistic one, but is essentially a psychological one. . . . In brief the theory suggests that these transformation of invariance are generated from a *Cognitive-Sensory Matrix* where a pre-verbal "logic", constituted by sensory-motor-affective constitutients are structurally ordered by *Cognitive-Sensory Schemata.* The latter is both sensuous and abstract, and performs a mediation function between inner constraints (perhaps neurophysiological) and external stimuli. Both the matrix and the schema operate on a non-conscious level. Transformations of invariances among the schemata are carried out by an Analogic Transform function or operation. Analogic Transforms are what reduce the multiplicity of incoming data to categories, sets, groups, and other equivalent relations, using such media as sound, structure, form, and on the level of language, meaning.
>
> The theory presented is a *Developmental* one, where ontogenetically early cognitions are constituted by the relative fusion of the sensory-motor-affective constitutients with the referent and the symbolic vehicle; developmentally later cognitions are constituted by their relative distance or detachment from earlier sensory-affective origins. Synthetic, "live" or "vivid" metaphors, generated by analogic transforms, are earlier on the developmental continuum than are "dead" "metaphors"; the invariant transforms of mathematics are still later on the developmental continuum, though theoretically remain linked in some degree to their origins.

Because of the seminal and comprehensive nature of Haskell's theory, I have quoted from it extensively. Much of it cannot be discussed in the present context, however; and I will confine explication to his identification of the essential cognitive-affective aspect of metaphor and the developmental continuum, which is itself describable in terms of the degree of emotional or existential connectedness. Haskell, like a few other scholars, has seen that metaphors often refer to feelings and the senses, and that the neglect of such in metaphor theorizing is due to confusion:

> Phenomenologically emotion should be distinguished from feeling. According to Ricoeur (1979) emotion is a first order experience. Presumably it is "non-cognitive",

it is what we usually think of when we think of irrational or at least a-rational, a strictly physiological event. *Feeling* on the other hand, according to Ricoeur, is a second order *"intentional* structure." (p. 154). Feeling as opposed to emotion, then, is not merely an inner-bodily state but an interiorized cognitive structure, an imaginative, schematizing, synthetic operation. (p. 26)

Transitional metaphors come to mind easily with regard to this formulation of the cognitive-affective basis of metaphor, for anxiety is a core physiological state (emotion) which motivates an "intentional" defense (metaphor). But an even more critical connection is implied in the above formulation: self-identity and the development of more or less stable "ego boundaries" evolve from linking up intrapsychic experience (including states, moods, etc.) to externally meaningful others, ideas, events, etc. Winnicott (1953) posited imagination, a cognitive function or capacity, as a *maturational requisite* to verbalized (abstract) formulations which could stabilize, quiet, or soothe the anxieties of genesis (i.e., aloneness, separation, fear, etc.). Feeling, as such, is a sought of first-level, socially-mediated cognitive capacity or creation; it is a springboard to higher level ego functions, and serves to both stimulate and mediate them. For example, consider the earlier discussion of mulattoes and "Brown" metaphors: here, feelings and anxieties about racism and color-consciousness (including color and caste preferences) have given rise to a metaphor which is both euphemistic ("brown" rather than "mulatto") and sensuous-synthetic. Both the cognitive-affective and developmental aspects of metaphorizing may be illustrated by this passage from a very recent and historically significant study of mulattoes in the United States. Seemingly trying to soothe the attributed anxieties of those who fear interracial intimacy, Williamson (1980, p. 192; emphasis added) writes:

> Negroes are not going to choose to marry whites in any great numbers, *and the internal mixture within the Negro world is going to continue to refine the "browness" of Negro people.* More important, American Negroes are in the process of synthesizing a new culture that is neither African nor European, neither white nor black, but rather both. The people are brown and so too is the culture.

These are powerful lines. They are, too, fantastic for they seem sensitive to neither the psychohistory of White racism (Kovel, 1971) nor to the political economic realities which structurally dominate the lives of the masses of "colored people." What the passage does show, nonetheless, is how a complex of feelings, shaped and defined by historical fact, can evolve over time, stimulating in the process a variety of ideologically based and metaphorically expressed cognitions. In the present case, the development has proceeded from "Negroness" to "Blackness" to "Browness". *Synthesis* and *integration* are implied in this developmental process and is alluded to in the above-cited instance. The notion of the "rainbow" is a metaphor which seems to translate, intuitively and subconsciously, at the very least, the above-cited passage into a "transitional" metaphor: this occurs at

the most elemental level: *"The internal mixture of the Negro world."* From this perspective, the *rainbow* is viewed as referring to intra-psychic, Black concerns. But metaphors, particularly transitional metaphors, are dialectical. They do not evolve to a
static, fixed meaning. Rather, they are bounced back and forth among meaning
contexts and "bought into" by different people according to a variety of heterogeneous motives and interests (Platt, 1984). More will be said regarding the heterogeneity factor in the next section, when we take up implications of transitional
metaphors for the theory of psychological transformations. But this issue of plu-
rality or difference does serve as a convenient preface to mass media functioning
and ethnopolitical activity. The focus is two-fold: (a) how do people of different
orientations view the "same event," and (b) how does the media impact of this
process?

Husband (1979), building on the theoretical work of Tajfel (1974), sees "social
identity" as the core concept necessary to a fuller understanding of how individuals and social groups (including the mass media) relate to each other. "It is
the dynamic relationships between social categorization, social identity, social
comparison and psychological distinctiveness which forms the creative core"
(Husband, 1979, p. 179) for understanding both how an individual will negotiate
his or her relationship to the in- and out-group, and how the out-group, in turn,
will seek to define itself in relation to him or her. The concepts used by Tajfel and
Husband enabled the latter to conclude, regarding his empirical study of press
coverage of race relations in Britain during the 1960s, that the press, in alliance
with the politicians, operate with certain preconceptualizations which must be
followed through in order to be intelligible to the masses; that such formulations
of the news is biased toward the elite; and "that the potentially autonomous psychological dynamic of identity maintenance can no longer be left out of any mass
media functioning within situations of intergroup contact" (1979, p. 191).

Husband found that the press "created" news which fitted the preconception
and needs of the "power elite." This was achieved partially by permitting certain
politicans to dominate news coverage. It was also facilitated by reporting certain
kinds of images of the "power elite" and the people it protected. For example, the
Britons are felt to have a self-image as ultra-civilized and "fair," forever seeking to
promote justice and harmonious relations. This self-image, however, is a precari-
ous one, forever threatened by facts to the contrary. When faced with something
like widespread racial discrimination within its own borders (physical and psychical), it reacted by defining "the other" as "outsider," "uncivilized," and "immi-
grant." Husband's study showed that the politicians and media both clung to this
self–other differentiation and partially unified White Britons through this ploy.

In his study, Husband implicitly points to two kinds of "transitional anxiety";
one inheres in the problematic way Britons have historically identified-defined
themselves, and the other relates to the fact that the designation of "immigrants
= blacks" as a means of cohesion-building is increasingly dangerous, since nearly
40% of Britain's Blacks are native born. Husband also points to one way in which

"transitional anxiety" was managed by two parts of the social system: the politician and the news media. But Husband does not give us an understanding of how people, with all of their differences, coalesce around the notion "immigrants are Blacks." He does not, accordingly, overcome what Platt (1984) and others have come to call the "heterogeneity" problem. He does, nonetheless, point us to a study of the media as an aid in understanding the emergence, structuring, and operation of "transitional metaphors" as described in this chapter. The media's treatment of the "rainbow" metaphor will help illustrate the salient processes under consideration.

The Rainbow: An Empirical Illustration

Content analysis of news media is now a popular and accepted way of approaching *what* people are "cued" to know as well as *how* they are instructed (Graber, 1984; Husband, 1979). This section reports my examination and evaluation of three major newspaper coverages of the so-called "Rainbow Coalition" aspect of the 1984 Presidential Campaign. The news papers examined were the *New York Times*, the *Los Angeles Times*, and the *Washington Post*. The period of coverage was May 1983 to July 1984. Identification of pertinent articles was aided with the Index to National News Papers. Based on the conceptual clues provided by Haskell (1986) and Husband (1979), the news papers were analyzed for and will be discussed in terms of: (a) the Cognitive-Affective Basis of the Metaphor, and (b) The Developmental Process of the Metaphor.

The Rainbow as Cognitive-Affective Metaphor

The notion "Rainbow Coalition" is held to have emerged out of the 1982 Chicago mayoral election. Later it was used in the Boston mayoral election. The widespread popularity of the notion came with its inculcation into the ideology and rhetoric of Jesse Jackson's Presidential campaign. Jesse Jackson's own usage of the term in his campaign may be held as the definitive statement insofar as the in-group is concerned:

> Jesse Jackson credited a "rainbow coalition of blacks, Latinos, Asians, gays, Puerto Ricans and Native Americans all coming together this time around" for his strong third place showing in Tuesday's New York Primary. (*Los Angeles Times*, April 4, 1984, p. 12)

The media's perception of this "metaphor's" salience will be considered in the next section. Here we need note only the essential fact that this coalitional grouping contains both those traditionally identified as "minorities" and some others considered "oppressed," *and* that the news media do not offer coverage which might help clarify the terrain or psychological climate preceeding the metaphor's emergence. It is, however, both possible and useful to identify these forces, since the transitional metaphor is defined partially in terms of the presence of "transitional anxiety." Perhaps the most graphic illustration of this precondition is the title of a volume written by an upwardly Mobile black male professional, Harold Byrd (1978): Can't Plead Black Anymore.* Bayard Rustin, the well-known Black leader of the 1970s, recently echoed this theme in *The Atlantic* magazine: "The plight of blacks belongs within the context of the plight of all America's poor: black, Hispanic, and white. The agenda of blacks today must be part and parcel of an agenda for all Americans" (1984, p. 122). The concrete conditions binding Blacks to other socioeconomically oppressed groups are not new, nor is the assertion made by Rustin – after all, it is a basic tenet of American Communism! But this is a significant renewed stance on the part of mainstream Black rhetors.

This stance reflects, I believe, a general sense of a changing political economic climate in the United States and elsewhere. It is a stance, moreover, which differs markedly from that of the 1960s which decried preceived efforts of women and others to identify with "Blackness" (Gresson, 1978). The present period is one, in fact, in which blacks have increasingly challenged each other's integrity and racial commitment, often claiming intra-racial betrayal (Gresson, 1982). It is a time when much revolutionary rhetoric has failed, as has, in the eyes of many, the movement itself. Thus, "Black is Beautiful" is a "dying metaphor." And in the wake of so much "death" emerges a new theme: "If White is right, and Black is beautiful, when is Brown's turn . . . ?"

Such is the psychological climate underpinning the "rainbow" metaphor, for it is now seen that those other than Blacks may have to share in the thrust towards a more viable and new revolutionary ideology.* The emergence of "Black Conservatives" and "Black Republicans" point in an inverse manner to such a shift; and we see that those from outside the Black grouping may also recall and revive the revolutionary past. For example, a recent issue of the *Gay Community News*, out of Boston, Massachusetts, provided the following editorial tribute to Black History Month:

> Our Movement's roots are intertwined with the movements for Black Civil Rights and Black Power, movements which carved out the contexts, the language, the emotional, legal and strategic footprints for lesbians and gay men to follow in. And

---

*It is significant, moreover, to note that the chief action signaling this type of thinking during the Jackson campaign was when a Black news reporter published Jackson's apparent "ethnic slur" against Jews. This event not only created a new wrinkle in the campaign, but clouded the integrity of the notion "rainbow." It also gave an added dimension to Byrd's declaration, since the reporter in question disavowed "racial betrayal" in the name of "loyalty to the news reading public."

*As we shall see in a forthcoming section, the seeds for the present focus on the "rainbow" were certainly evident as far back as the late 1960s. Malcolm X (1970, p. 7), moving toward universalism and the presence of a *colored majority*, wrote: "looking beyond the white man...you see the nations of the earth that are black, brown, red and yellow, who used to be down, now getting up. And you see them, you find that you look more like them than you look like Sam (the white man)."

when Black women in those movements spoke up against sexism, raised issues of power, sex, and gender, they in a sense shot the first shots of the women's and the subsequent gay/lesbian liberation struggles. (February 16, 1985, p. 6)

Passages such as the above are *integrative,* signalling, insofar as coalition rhetoric and transitional metaphors are concerned, a move toward successful ideology-making (Platt, 1980, 1984). Beyond integration, there are other, essentially symbolic qualities of such metaphorizing. For example, the "rainbow" reflects as a sort of root metaphor for social reintegration and personal resolution of (radical) diversity and transformation. Consider the following popular modifications of the original usage:

(1) The Unisex Rainbow Salon
(2) The Rainbow Video Corporation
(3) Rainbow Cablevision Service

These usages reflect a combining of the "rainbow" on diverse dimensions with products associated with this particular period in history: Unisexuality, for example, is contextually associated with the recent ideology of androgyny, with an emphasis on the renegotiation of sex roles and the idea of sex role itself. Both "women under men" and "gays under straights" are metaphors stressing the felt oppression of women and homosexuals. Women Rights and Gay Rights, like "Black Rights," point to the identity link being fostered through the idea of a "rainbow" coalition, even though significant differences are involved in the overall process. Perhaps the single, compelling connector is "Rainbow = Liberation." It is in similar context of liberation that personalized video technology is associated with the "rainbow"; here, however, home video has become associated with liberalized viewing rights ("Adult"/Sex channels) and a *heterogeneous* list of viewing options.

In both cases, moreover, there is a reference to *time.* There are evident the *remembrance* and *renegotiation* features essential to this type of metaphorizing. There is an implied reference to the more traditional division of the sexes and its transformation; and there are likewise implied the "freezing of time" available with the VHF system, on the one hand, and the "expansion of space" with the aid of satellites and cable reception, on the other. We are not directly able to infer what motivations or inner meanings these usages hold for the creators or their audiences. Still, these usages succeeded the emergence of the acknowledged "parent" event (The 1982 Chicago mayoral election), and are significantly connected to the cultural events for which the "rainbow" is a symbolic equivalent.

The "rainbow" comes to represent, affectively, the possibility of fulfillment, expansion, self-gratification, and a merging with the material rewards of an affluent, dominant society: The pot of "Gold" at the end of the Rainbow. It is possible to pursue such an affective, anxiety-reducing, meaning-shift because there are perceived "cognitive alternatives" (Giles, Bourhis, & Taylor, 1977). People know that certain traditional moral codes and constraints have been lifted; they can pursue the "tabooed" legitimately. Weinstein and Platt (1969) have described this complex acting-out as "the wish to be free." Such cognitive-affective interest, however, carries its own frustrations and anxieties. The desire to renegotiate the terms and features of inclusiveness generate counter-metaphorizing processes. This occurs within various elements of society which do not find the sought-for changes desirable. The media are among such elements, particularly where radical shifts, such as race relatedness, are concerned. A closer look at the media handling of the "rainbow" metaphor is illustrative.

The Rainbow as Developmental Metaphor.

In her important volume on news reporting and processing, Graber (1984, p. 66) noted, regarding the *Chicago Tribune's* coverage of the 1976 Presidential Campaign: "While the quantity of coverage was ample, the quality of the mix of information provided was open to question on several counts. These related to the adequacy of information, especially during the primaries, the appropriateness of patterns of topics, and the depth and slant of the coverage." Graber is here speaking of the *cueing* issue, the biasing of perspective by manipulation of the material and its presentation. As such, cueing is not an idiosyncratic event, unique to a particular newspaper. It is an intricate aspect of media communication. It was this that Husband (1979) found the British press guilty of: misrepresentation of the prejudice and racism underpinning the British race riots of the 1960s.

With respect to the emergence of transitional metaphors, the cueing process is an aid to understanding the way in which such metaphors are framed and negotiated by certain segments of the population. *In particular, we are provided a limited but critical view of the unfolding of a metaphor in its cognitive and affective meanings as the press apprehended and presented it,* albeit from a biased perspective. We may begin with an indication of the press's contextualizing of the emergence of the "rainbow" metaphor. Table 1 presents a representative sampling of the pattern of topics covered.

We might begin by noting that the news media carried very few articles on the "rainbow" or on its positive goals. On the contrary, most of the articles were negative, or more precisely, *oriented to contain the threat of an uncontrolled identity shift among the population.* The articles represented here may be identified as cueing five dominant themes:

1. The "rainbow" as unreal
2. The "rainbow" as anxiety producing
3. The "rainbow" as a failure
4. The "rainbow" as dishonest
5. The system as cooperative/tolerant

The first two articles, using the words "charismatic" and "students votes," seem to cue the reader for the fantastic quality of the metaphor. Interestingly, and

TABLE 1
Representative Newspaper Coverage Titles of the "Rainbow Coalition"

Source	Date	Title
Wash Post	6/31/83	Jesse Jackson: His Charismatic Crusade for the Voters at the end of the Rainbow Coalition
NY Times	2/18/84	Jackson Pitch Wins Students But Not Votes
NY Times	3/10/84	The Rainbow Coalition's Hazy Future
LA Times	4/4/84	Rainbow Coalition Cited by Jackson for Strong Finish
LA Times	5/8/84	Jackson's Rainbow Called Fake by White
NY Post	5/3/84	Jackson Victory in D.C. Shows Vote Polarized (Failure of Whites to Join Rainbow Coalition)
Wash Post	6/29/84	Why Does Jackson Get Rained On?
NY Times	7/11/84	Jewish Leaders expressed criticism
NY Times	7/10/84	Black Democrats in a Poll prefer Mondale to Jackson as Nominee

perhaps unintentionally, the articles imply the critical difference between Jackson and the other candidates, and the progressive quality of the "rainbow" metaphor, by associating him with morality, innocence (naiveté), and similar properties. Other articles, incidentally, make similar associations. By inference, we see that the "transitional metaphor" goes to the core of the problem of "cultural failure" (Platt, 1984). The media, however, rarely addressed this dimension.

If anxiety generates the emergence of "transitional metaphors," such metaphors can, also, promote parallel, *new* anxiety by pointing to cultural solutions other than the traditionally valued ones, even though these have led to the initial anxiety (Tomkins, 1964). The third newspaper title, identifying the coalition as having a "hazy future," calls forth ambiguity and with it, anxiety. Shortly thereafter, following the media's own chronology, the "rainbow" is accused of concrete failures. But we see in these particular articles the media's own duplicity: For example, consider the title: "Jackson's 'Rainbow' called fake by white." This article's title implies a white indictment of the "rainbow" per se. However, the article revealed that an individual White woman, *who was a member of the coalition*, was angry at a particular Black Jackson organizing unit. It was felt that the Ohio vanguard – not Jackson or the Coalition – were playing power politics. *The woman did not call the coalition "fake."* The media did!

The hint of racial divisiveness implied in these articles seemed gradually to gain concrete shape within both society and subsequent coverages. Racial disharmony was a central theme in articles four, five and six. The "failure" of the coalition was emphasized by stressing that Blacks, not Whites, were supporting Jackson:

> While Jackson made much of the fact that it was "a rainbow coalition" that provided a sizable vote, it was black New Yorkers with turnouts as high as 90% in some areas, who gave Jackson the bulk of his support. (*Los Angeles Times,* April 4, 1984, p. 12)

> Jesse L. Jackson's overwhelming Democratic primary victory here Tuesday was a celebration of black political power in the District of Columbia, but it further underscored Jackson's inability to attract white supporters to his "rainbow coalition." (*Washington Post,* May 3, 1984, p. A1)

For Husband (1979) and Graber (1984), the above passages are illustrative of cueing. But from a perspective which emphasizes metaphoric development, such cueing helps to clarify the "transitional" nature of the rainbow metaphor. This is so because of the dual function of the metaphor: it says something to the in-group (*itself heterogeneous*) and to the out-group. To the in-group, the message is that the anxieties of going beyond the grouping are possible and effective; to the out-group, there is a need to ensure that the majority grouping is not made unduly anxious regarding its "social identity" (Husband, 1979). This latter function leads to cueing, which may be here called "counter-metaphorization." By this I mean that the limits of the metaphor are drawn graphically by indicating the points of "breakdown," contraindication, etc. The articles cited above aid this action by attempting to destroy the inner integrity of the "rainbow" metaphor. Stressing its "failure" to attract Whites *and* Jackson's "abandonment" by certain Jewish groups was intended to eliminate a part of the "rainbow:"

> Irving M. Levine, spokesman for the American Jewish Committee, said of all candidates: "There ought to be enormous caution by all candidates that they do nothing to inflame ethnic, racial and religious tensions." (*New York Times,* July 11, 1984, p. A17)
>
> Maybe it would have been smart for Jackson to have repudiated Farrakhan early on. For while it seems clear that such a repudiation would have gained him little or no additional electoral support, *it might have calmed a few of the editorialists who have raged against him.* (*Washington Post,* June 29, 1984, p. A19)

The above passages illustrate cueing *and* "counter-metaphorization." The *Post* passage, unwittingly perhaps, admits the media's cognitive-affective investment in the process: "The editorialists' rage" could not have been quieted by Jackson's actions, any more than the Black reporter who exposed Jackson's ethnic slur could be dissuaded by appeals to "racial loyalty." Interestingly, both the White editorialists and the Black reporter were conveying messages which clarify the "rainbow" as transitional metaphor. The White editorialists were provided an event, reported by the Black newspaper man, which enabled them to concretize the doubts earlier reported with regards to the "rainbow" coalition: it had already been called fake by the press; now there was "real" evidence to this effect. With regard to the anxiety around the implied "identity shift," the editorialists were saying essentially that things remained "secure," "intact," and "unaltered." In this case, Jews and Blacks, traditional "natural allies" according to coalition rhetoric, and obvious parts of the "rainbow," are at odds. This is not a new state of affairs; it has a long established history (Gresson, 1982). *Reenactment of this history serves, however, to remind doubters (and possible pursuers of the "rainbow") of the real state of affairs.* A sort of "self-fulfilling prophecy" is thus stated and staged. Indeed, one columnist wrote, "Blacks and Jews need a real dialogue...nostalgia can't sustain the alliance" (*Los Angeles Times,* April 12, 1984, Sec. II, p. 7). His insight, however, was anticlimatic.

The above described dynamic constitutes an "out-group" dimension. Its affective salience is perhaps best captured in one news title which is a clear "counter-metaphorization": "Why does Jackson Get Rained On?" But the answer to this query, rhetorical though it be, points to intraracial disharmony. After all, the Black reporter and Minister Farrakhan are the identified "enemies within," excluding Jackson himself. They are the reasons, ostensibly, for his experienced "downpour." And it is this complex of real and imputed intraracial discord which enables the media to move to persuade the Blacks – those preliminary voters who had supported Jackson and enabled him to identify a "rainbow coalition" – that their own efforts had been symbolic gestures not to be confused with the hard-minded pragmatism for which Blacks are known. This media effort was power-fully demonstrated by the *New York Times* in an article entitled "Black Democrats in a Poll Prefer Mondale to Jackson as Nominee." In this article and several companion pieces, the *Times* seems to be putting the *finalized meaning* to the "counter-metaphorization" process:

> Although three-quarters of the blacks who voted in the Democratic Presidential primaries this year voted for the Rev. Jessie Jackson, black Democrats prefer Walter F. Mondale. . . . Politicians interviewed by The Times said the poll findings meant that blacks were putting pragmatism ahead of pride. (*New York Times,* July 10, 1984, p. 1)

The press has now succeeded in conveying a message to the "in-group" which presumably comes from the "in-group" itself. That message, and certainly Black conservatives and men such as Philadelphia's Mayor Goode reinforced it by their actions, translated as the "rainbow = Black pride." It does not even cognitively represent Black people. Yet, and here is the interesting irony and paradox, one which is only perhaps understood in terms of the political psychology of race in America, *the rainbow is a metaphor for Black people.* Moreover, it is a "transitional metaphor," for ultimately it spoke to their collective cognitive capacity to see beyond the pragmatics of class, color, religion, etc., to act in a dramatic ritualistic display. And what was left, affectively, for Blacks was aid in dealing with the "transitional anxieties" accompanying the shift in social climate which we symbolically designate as "Reaganism." Perhaps no more telling evidence for the preceeding analysis of the media and its dynamic relationship to the "rainbow" as "transitional metaphor" can be offered than the following passage. This passage is taken from the *Bay State Banner,* Black Boston's newspaper. The speaker, Lamond Goodwin, national director of the Rainbow Coalition, is here addressing a group of Black politicians at a Harvard University-sponsored conference on Black Politics:

> "Blacks are the most partisan voters in the country, with the majority voting for the Democrats since 1932. The only groups that supported Mondale were blacks, Jews, Orientals, and Hispanics," said Goodwin, who declared that support from such quarters was the truest evidence of the existence of a Rainbow Coalition.
>   He concluded that many blacks voted against Reagan and that rising numbers would dealign from the Democratic Party in the future. Goodwin believes that many of the first time black voters came to the party through the efforts of Rev. Jesse Jackson and that many of these people have been "psychologically alienated" by the perception that the party has treated Jackson unfairly. (April 25, 1985, p. 17)

The unaddressed contradictions accompanying these diverse "readings" of the "rainbow" point to the metaphoric meanings beyond coalition per se. They suggest that the principle of balance is central to the metaphorizing process: attend to the population's anxieties but do not permit too radical a shift. It is also clear from the present discussion that both passions and previous psychohistorical biases are stimulated by the emergence of certain transitional metaphors. Table 2 illustrates this by some of the metacommunications surrounding the "rainbow" metaphor. We cannot tell from the present level of analysis what individuals would say regarding the cognitive-affective validity of such a metaphor. But clearly the metaphor's psychological role is not necessarily parallel to the larger social systems' uses of it.

What this all suggests is that the symbolic aspect of the transitional metaphor constitutes a partial threat by symbolizing the possibility of an identity shift which is not only largely mythical but psychopolitically problematic. Analysis of the articles, while saying little regarding the social psychological processes mediating intra- and extrapsychic productions, has pointed us to the structure of thought implicated in them. We will conclude our discussion with a brief consideration of some of the implications for further inquiry.

TABLE 2
Metacommunications and the Counter-Metaphorization Process: The Rainbow Case

Source	Date	Title
NY Times	1/29/84	Thomas Szasz on "Clergyman/President"
Wash Post	2/18/84	Editorial: Mr. Jackson's Choice of Words
NY Times	1/23/83	A rightful place for Semantic Symbols
LA Times	4/12/84	Blacks and Jews need a real dialogue
LA Times	3/20/84	Jackson Complaining Media are Ignoring his Triumps
LA Times	1/29/84	Media/rivals handle Jackson with kid gloves
LA Times	1/6/84	Jackson seeks moral tone in Campaign by replacing politicians with ministers
NY Times	2/8/84	Jackson, in role apart, stresses Third World Approach to Foreign Policy

TRANSITIONAL METAPHORS IN PSYCHOSOCIAL CONTEXT: TOWARD A HEURISTIC MODEL

The "rainbow" metaphor may be treated as relational rhetoric; it is focused on the definition and negotiation of relationship among potential coalitions. The "rainbow" is also here defined as a transitional metaphor, one concerned with the psychosocial management of anxieties due to perceived angers. As such, the "rainbow" has helped us to apprehend the dynamics of relational rhetoric in three interrelated contexts: *intrapsychic, intersubjective,* and *macrosystemic.* This exercise of defining and examining transitional metaphors in relational context, moreover, has reinforced and gone beyond more traditional analyses by focusing on both certain (a) primodal/psychohistorical proclivities of the actors, and (b) on their "cognitive dialectics." Following from a somewhat enlarged psychoanalytic tradition (Blanck & Blanck, 1979; Mackey, 1984; Kovel, 1971), the primodal domain pertains to the givenness of a human condition in which anxiety, however defined, underpins the particular modes of ego development and adaptation, yielding a cultural matrix which is intricately, albeit unconsciously, linked to basic survival concerns, and maintained in a delicate, permanent balance.

"Cognitive dialectics" is one way of describing this interplay of cognition, affect, and history; and while typically associated with dialectical psychology (Buss, 1979; Riegel, 1979), it is equally as relevant to metaphor as a cognitive product capable of societal manipulation (Giles, Bourhis, & Taylor, 1977; Haskell, 1984). More concretely, here I have in mind the "rainbow's" impact on various actors: the news media, politicians, and populace; presumably, each of these segments of society became involved *personally* with the negotiation of meaning with respect to the metaphor. What we are confronted with in all novel metaphors is metaphoric comprehension. Yet such a matter is itself related not only to native intelligence and cultural background but also to the particular status of a given culture and to the diverse interests and concerns of the populace generally (Platt, 1984). Transitional metaphors, derived from personally compelling encounters with generalized others, as well as significant others, is therefore submerged within an individualized singular and plural conceptual and emotional tension whose developing salience is dependent upon ongoing meaning-messages.

The preceding discussion of transitional metaphors, taken against this backdrop, points us toward a consideration of Haskell's (1984, p. 30) contention that "metaphorical type productions have cognitive implications." In the remaining pages, I will briefly sketch in some of these possibilities.

The Intra-Psychic Dimension of Transitional Metaphors

Symbols rather than metaphors have been associated with strong emotional appeal and intrapsychic stimulation (Bartel, 1984; Foss, 1949). For example, the so-called "condensation symbol," has been criticized (Graber, 1976, pp. 307–8) for "oversimplifying or blurring complex situations . . . by arousing emotions and bypassing reason, or by calming needed anxiety and anger." The transitional metaphor is held to fulfill precisely this "irrational" aspect of the individual yet it is equally felt to be a cognitively based production. What we are here presented with is the need to conceptually allow for the intricate link between symbol and metaphor at a cognitive-affective rather than linguistic level. Using the "rainbow" example, we might begin to deal with two distinct though related psychical issues. First, following research on "novel metaphors" (Fraser, 1977), we might begin to pursue the matter of what properties of the individual are related to taking a particular stance with regards to a metaphoric expression. Some of the critics of the "rainbow," for example, seemed to have accepted its symbolic function; others seemed to have been more persuaded by its metaphoric function. Clearly, the two functions need not be mutually exclusive, but where they are experienced as a developmental progression by the same person, what cognitive-affective shifts occur within the person? Were anger and fear at an untenable "fusion" unique to those who called it a fake? Did only the racial integrationists find it suggestive of a new societal change whose day was long overdue? Or did people have mixed anger and hope with regards to the expression?

Second, what degree of felt "cognitive alternative" (Giles, Bourhis, & Taylor, 1977) or cognitive validity underpin the different emotional responses to the metaphor? At least one of the architects of the "rainbow" suggested that early supporters of the coalition (i.e., Black Democrats) might leave the Party (and by inference the coalition) because of a perceived shift in its "cognitive persuasiveness." Of course, it is perhaps evident, once again, that cognition seemed to be held as the reason both for Blacks preferring Mondale over Jackson (recall the *New York Times* Poll) and later (according to the *Banner* article) disliking the party's treatment of him.

It is the cognitive aspect of individual responses to the metaphor which propels Haskell's argument for metaphoric development itself paralleling the individual's "varying degrees of competency and sensitivity" with respect to metaphoric comprehension (1986, p. 54). It is equally as true, I believe, that the intrapsychic cogitations with regards to the metaphoric expression allow the individuals to *claim for themselves and their feelings* an intersubjective validity.

The Intersubjective Dimension of Transitional Metaphors

Earlier, I quoted a passage from the *Gay Community News* where it was suggested Black women's liberation concerns were closer to homosexual liberation issues than the Civil Rights/Black Power Movements per se: "And when Black women . . . spoke up against sexism, raised issues of power, sex, and gender, they in a sense shot the first shots of the women's and the subsequent gay/lesbian liberation struggles."

The above argument, coming some 15 years after the famous expressions "Woman as Nigger" and "Student as Nigger," seems to speak to the developmental cognitive dialectics of radical revolutionary rhetoric. From a so-called condensation symbol, the historic association with Black liberation efforts by women and others has evolved into a more or less sophisticated ideological relatedness. To be a part of a "rainbow" is quite different than being a "nigger equivalent." It is also more cognitively persuasive and capable of interpersonal negotiation. What is here being suggested is that the transitional metaphor, unlike condensation symbols, does not offend, even when found to be "fake." Thus, it is interesting to note that the "rainbow" metaphor has not generated anything like the intersubjective anger the "Woman as Nigger" expression did (Gresson, 1978). The words of one of the expression's critics are perhaps sufficient to make the point: "I just don't agree . . . with the idea inherent in . . . 'woman as nigger' . . . The analogy breaks down too quickly" (Psychology Today, 1970, pp. 79–80).

In this case, the swiftness with which the analogy breaks down is not to be understood so much in terms of cognitive associationism as much as cognitive-emotionalism. And it is this capacity of the transitional metaphor to sustain a positive cognitive-emotional connection, despite contradictions, which is relevant. Another, premier example may help complete this point. During the great Black–Jewish conflict of the late 1960s and early 1970s, one Jewish spokesman declared:

> I have sometimes wondered whether my attitudes to the Black-Jewish confrontations was ultimately not entirely dependent upon the facts. I am reminded of the trite: "I have made up my mind! Don't bother me with the facts!" . . . I have made up my mind that black and Jew have a community of American interest which vastly overrides black anti-Semitism and Jewish Racism. I have chosen to stress those "facts" which corroborate my made-up mind. (Miller, 1972, p. 113)

The operative word here is *choice*. But it is more; it is choice which can be sustained by tradition, myth, ritual, etc. And this is precisely what Blacks and Jews have had in addition to some very real and significant communions. Because of this psychohistory, moreover, the *Los Angeles Times* piece by Dreyfus on the need for a "real dialogue" among Blacks and Jews seemed somewhat anticlimatic, even though it developed some important "facts." The "rainbow" could not be effectively compromised for the "believers" because it was sustained, not by *nostalgia,* but by *the need for nostalgia.* The "rainbow" fulfilled this need over against the "facts" *and* diminished to a degree the long held myth of Black–Jewish "natural affinity."

It is suggested, then, that *beliefs as need and choice as defense are aspects of the transitional metaphor which may bear some relation to other properties felt to characterize metaphoric comprehension, and might be meaningfully considered in future inquiries.*

The Macro-Systemic Dimension of Transitional Metaphors

Clearly, the intrapsychic and interpersonal aspects of the "rainbow" are inter-connected with each other and with the society generally. But the heterogeneous nature of society itself influences the heterogeneous manner in which the meta-phor is apprehended. And the ensuing dynamic propels the development or met-aphoric transformation which characterizes it. By seeing that metaphors are not only processed intrapsychically and privately, but intersubjectively as context-related metaphorizing occurs, we see that so-called "novel metaphors" may have a novel *counter-metaphorization* aspect. For example, in the previous section we saw how the symbolic qualities ascribed to the "rainbow" as transitional metaphor, constituted a mosaic of anxiety-identity related themes. These themes, however, did not only concern Black–Black, Black–White, and past–present relational ten-sions, but also societal level issues. This is why the mass media was so clearly "implicated" in the negotiation of the meaning of the "rainbow" for the mass au-dience. Jackson's accusation of the media and the media's denial of wrong-doing (Table 2) are illustrative of this dialectic.

Haskell's emphasis on the life-span of the metaphor – from "novel" to "hot" to "dead" – suggests development over relatively long periods of time. Here I em-phasize the short-term development stimulated by "cognitive dialectics." In so doing, *we see how the transitional metaphor evolves into a root metaphor by revealing a socie-tal level concern with fear and anxiety and need to reintegrate divergent forces within the society.* What this implies is that some metaphors may not so much "die" as change into symbols; and where such metaphors are of a "transitional" sort, they reintegrate into forms with social significance but *without* the same anxiety-producing im-pact. For example, a circular recently released in Boston by a group (one of several around the country) of professional, human service workers, is offered as an illus-tration of the framing of the reintegration aspect of the root metaphor, the "rainbow."

> Emotional problems are fundamentally rooted in the political, social and economic conditions of our times – in rising poverty and unemployment; escalating racism, sexism, anti-Semitism and anti-gay attitudes and practices; and in rapidly decreasing opportunities for people, especially poor and working people, *people of color*, and women to "make it" in society. (Statement of Purpose, Association for the Develop-ment of Social Therapy, 1985; emphasis added)

The emergence of associations of not altogether compatible categories is reflect-ive of the "rainbow's" influence at the *reintegrated*, macro-systemic level. In this illustration the "rainbow" has come to be the "historical" glue, so to speak, legitimizing the juxtaposing of several social problems.

It is probably because of the persuasiveness of the "transitional metaphor" at the macro-systemic level that some of the media writers (Table 2) themselves sent metacommunications, such as the *Post's* editorial on "Mr. Jackson's Choice of Words" (February 18, 1984) and the *New York Times'* piece "A rightful place for Semantic Symbols" (July 7, 1983). The implicit message is that such metaphors may be experienced as self-soothing and anxiety-reducing for some, and be anything but consoling for others.

CONCLUSION

Transitional metaphors have been shown to constitute a dynamic sequential process, one aimed at managing the fear and anxiety of loss and separation. They speak to personally or existentially felt needs but in a collective manner. This is due to their emergence in a complex, multi-leveled situation. Three dimensions were hypothesized to describe these multiple levels.

The rainbow coalition was used to illustrate the transitional metaphor. Analysis of this particular transitional metaphor helped identify some of the properties and processes characterizing such metaphors. In particular, the discussion of transitional metaphors and the "rainbow" helped suggest how metaphors operate as cognitive-emotional creations and how such creations are dialectically developed. This development seeks to occur in a manner where the end result is resolution of the metaphor into certain symbolic and substantive functions.

REFERENCES

Applegate, J. S. (1984). Transitional phenomena in adolescence: Tools for negotiating the second individuation, *Clinical Social Work Journal,* 12(3), 233–243.

Bartel, R. (1984). *Metaphors and symbols: Forays into language.* Urbana, IL: National Council of Teachers of English.

Becker, E. (1974). *The denial of death.* New York: Vintage.

Bell, D. (1978). *The cultural contradictions of capitalism.* New York: Basic.

Blanck, G., & Blanck, R. (1979). *Ego psychology II.* New York: Columbia University Press.

Buss, A. R. (1979). *A dialectical psychology.* New York: Wiley.

Byrd, H. E. (1978). *Can't plead black anymore.* Los Angeles: Author.

Dumas, R. G. (1980). Dilemmas of black females in leadership. In L. Rodgers-Rose (Ed.), *The black woman.* Beverly Hills, CA: Sage.

Faber, M. D. (1979). The metaphors of Marx: A Literary-Psychological View of *Das Kapital. Psychocultural Review, 3,* 39–58.

Fishman, J. A. (1972a). *The sociology of language.* Rowley, MA: Newbury House.

Fishman, J. A. (1972b). *Language in sociocultural change.* Palo Alto, CA: Stanford University Press.

Foss, M. (1949). *Symbol and metaphor in human experience.* Princeton, NJ: University Press.

Fraser, B. (1977). *The interpretation of novel metaphors: A reply to Pavio.* Paper presented at the Metathought Conference, University of Illinois, September 26–27.

Giles, H. (Ed.). (1977). *Language, ethnicity and intergroup relations,* New York: Academic.

Giles, H., Bourhis, R. Y., & Taylor, D. M. (1977). Towards a theory of language in ethnic group relations. In H. Giles (Ed.), *Language, ethnicity and intergroup relations.* New York: Academic Press.

Goffman, E. (1963). *Stigma*. Englewood Cliffs, NJ: Prentice-Hall.

Graber, D. A. (1976). *Verbal behavior and politics*. Urbana, IL: University of Illinois Press.

Graber, D. A. (1984). *Processing the news: How people tame the information tide*. New York: Longman.

Gregg, R. B. (1971). The ego-function of the rhetoric of protest. *Philosophy and Rhetoric, 4,* 71–91.

Gresson, A. D. (1977). Minority epistemology and the rhetoric of creation. *Philosophy and Rhetoric, 10* 244–262.

Gresson, A. D. (1978). Phenomenology and the rhetoric of identification – A neglected dimension of coalition communication inquiry. *Communication Quarterly, 26,* 14–23.

Gresson, A. D. (1982). *The dialectics of betrayal.: Sacrifice, violation and the oppressed*. Norwood, NJ: Ablex.

Haskell, R. E. (1986). *Social cognition, language and the non-conscious expression of racial ideology. Imagination, Cognition & Personality, 6* (1), 75–97.

Haskell, R. E. (1987). Deep cognition: A psychological theory of the origin and development of the tropological transformation function. *Metaphor and Symbolic Activity, 2.*

Hooks, B. (1981). *Ain't I a woman: Black women and feminism*. Boston: South End Press.

Husband, C. (1979). Social Identity and the Language of Race Relations. In H. Giles & B. Saint-Jacques (Eds.), *Language and ethnic relations*. New York: Pergamon Press.

Kovel, J. (1971). *White racism: A psychohistory*. New York: Vintage.

Lasch, C. (1984). *The minimal self: Psychic survival in troubled times*. New York: W. W. Norton & Co.

Lester, J. (1982). The black writer. *The New England Journal of Black Studies, 2,* 82–85.

Mackey, R. A. (1984). *Ego psychology and clinical practice,* New York: Gardner Press.

Mahler, M. S., Pine, F., & Bergman, A. (1975). *The psychological birth of the human infant: Symbiosis and individuation*. New York: Basic Books.

Malcolm X. (1970). *On Afro-American history*. New York: Pathfinder Press.

Miller, Rabbi A. W. (1972). Black anti-semitism and Jewish racism. In *Black Anti-Semitism and Jewish Racism*. New York: Schocken.

Passin, H. (1968). Writer and journalist in the transitional society. In J. A. Fishman, C. A. Ferguson, & J. D. Gupta (Eds.), *Language problems of developing nations*. New York: Wiley.

Platt, G. M. (1980). Thoughts on a theory of collective action: Language, affect, and ideology in revolution. In M. Albin (Ed.), *New directions in psychohistory; The Adelphi papers in honor of Erik H. Erikson* (pp. 69–94). Lexington Books.

Platt, G. M. (1984). Conditions for collective action: Material and cultural influences. In M. Lewis & J. Miller (Eds.), *Social problems and public policy, Vol. III,* Greenwich, Ct: JAI Press.

Riegel, K. F. (1979). *Foundations of a dialectical psychology*. New York: Academic Press.

Reich, W. (1971). *The mass psychology of Fascism*. New York: Farrar Strauss and Girous.

Ricoeur, P. (1979). The Metaphorical process as cognition, imagination and feeling. In S. Sacks (Ed.), *On Metaphor* (pp. 141–157). Chicago: University Press.

Rustin, B. (1984). Are blacks better off today? *The Atlantic,* (October) pp. 121–123.

Tajfel, H. (1974). Social identity and intergroup behavior. *Social Science Information, 13,* 69–93.

Tomkins, S. (1964). *Affect, imagery, consciousness*. New York: Springer.

Smith, B., Scott, P. B., & Hall, B. (Eds.). (1982). *All of the women are white; all of the blacks are men; but some of us are brave*. New London, CT: Feminist Press.

Weinstein, F., & Platt, G. (1969). *The wish to be free, society, psyche, and value change*. Berkeley, CA: University of California Press.

Williams, G. (1979). Language group allegiance and ethnic interactions. In H. Giles & B. Saint-Jacques (Eds.), *Language and ethnic relations*. New York: Pergamon Press.

Williamson, J. (1980). *New people: Miscegenation and Mulattoes in the United States*. New York: The Free Press.

Winnicott, D. (1953). Transitional objects and transitional phenomena: A study of the first not-me possession. *International Journal of Psychoanalysis, 34,* 1–25.

CHAPTER TEN

Foucault and Language: Unthought Metaphors

Irene E. Harvey
Philosophy Department
Pennsylvania State University

INTRODUCTION: ARCHAEOLOGY AND THE UNTHOUGHT – A METAPHOR OF THEORY

Foucault does not have a theory of metaphor. He does, however, use one. It is this usage, within his strategy of archaeological analysis, which we shall attempt to describe here, and in turn we shall go on to thematize at least a portion of what is left unthematized by Foucault himself.

Foucault's notion of archaeology, as discourse analysis, involves a number of features which include the following: (a) it is concerned with discourses as such, not what they represent or refer to; (b) it is not in search of connecting links between discourse, not aiming towards continuity or systems but specificity; (c) it is in search of a "set of rules" (Foucault, 1982) which are presupposed in the usage of a particular discourses but which are not explicit; (d) it is not organized around totalities such as "books," "*oeuvres*" (identified by the name of an author as a *complete* set of writings,) etc., and is not concerned with origins of such totalities in the psychological or sociological sense, but rather with their institutional and political conditions of possibility; (e) it is not a return to the intention of the speaker or author, and is not concerned essentially with meaning but rather with a level of *exteriority* (which includes an elusive aspect of the discourse which is both more and less than what was intended) of the discourse and attempts a "regulated transformation of what has already been written" (Foucault, 1982). Archaeological analysis is thus not within the traditional guidelines of a history of ideas, not a hermeneutical project, and even less a deconstructive one.

Instead, Foucault aims to analyse *epoques* in "history" which, although discontinuous in relation to other such epoques (and hence identifiable from within), entail a certain systematicity and obey particular and stable organizing principles.

With respect to our issue at hand – language – Foucault has analysed (archaeologically) the predominant discursive practices in western thought from the 16th century to the present (Foucault, 1973). In so doing he has located four such epoques – each discontinuous with the others – and these will be analysed here.

In order to fix the boundaries of his epochal determinations, he has instantiated the dominant metaphors of the age as their representatives. For the 16th century, we have the metaphor of the Book; for the 17th and 18th centuries, we have that of the Table; for the 19th century, we have Roots; and for the 20th century ("our age") we have that of the unthought. We propose the following analysis: first, to consider *what* Foucault's claims are for each age, concerning in particular their respective understandings of language (its role, function, meaning, weaknesses, and strengths); and second, to consider the *way* he makes such claims. It will not be his specific metaphors which we will be concerned with in the second section, but the "dominant metaphor of the age" which allow him to isolate epoques, draw lines of discontinuity between such ages, and to organize as a system – interlocking and reciprocally supporting – that same epoque. It is not that Foucault has rejected all the tools of a traditional history of ideas (i.e., continuity, progression, historicity, etc.), but rather that he *isolates* epoques in which these same "forms" can be found. The role of metaphor here will be shown to be nothing less than an example of what Derrida (1982) has shown metaphor to be able to do in general and in principle. Namely, to implicitly, unthematically (at the level of the unthought) organize, ground, orient, and structure a discourse which it seems to only decoratively inhabit or be attached to in an external or extrinsic manner. This is not the place to analyse in full Derrida's theory of metaphor (as a metaphor of theory within the Western tradition of philosophy), but we will point in the direction of an interlacing of Derrida's thought with Foucault's – or a deconstruction of Foucault – precisely via the focus of the unthought in Foucault and, more specifically, via his *unthought metaphors*.

A. METAPHORS OF THE AGE –
FOUCAULT'S ARCHAEOLOGY OF LANGUAGE

Foucault's archaeology of language focusses on the way language was understood from within various different epoques of European history. He is not concerned with developing a theory of language at the philosophical or essential level. Rather, his object of study changes radically from one age to another and is essentially connected to what Dilthey (Rickman, 1976) called *Weltanschauung* or general world view (picture) held to be valid for that age. Thus it is clear that the truth value of these interpretations or understandings is not what is at issue for an archaeological analysis. *That* language was understood in a particular way, and *what* that way was, is instead the focus here. In addition, Foucault does not attempt to draw parallels between these ages or epoques but rather instantiate their differences in a radical way. He does not, therefore, build bridges or seek common grounds between the said epoques. History and hence historicity is radically discontinuous, for Foucault, and it is this that his analyses attempt to document at the archaeological level–or the level of discursive practices which, on the one hand, entail theories, understandings, and interpretations of the world, yet, on the other, are not representatives or representations of anything but themselves. This paradox will be addressed as we proceed via the specific determinations accorded to language in the epoques mentioned above; namely, the age of the Book, of the Table, of Roots, and our own–that of the unthought.

(a) The Age of the Book

Foucault claims that language was understood in the 16th Century from within a world view dominated by the metaphor of the Book. Nature, the world, space and time, and man's connection to all of this, including God, were understood on this basis. For example, he says: (1973, p. 27)

> the space inhabited by immediate resemblances becomes like a vast *open book*; it bristles with written signs; every page is seen to be filled with strange figures that intertwine and in some places repeat themselves. All that remains is to decipher them.

The structure of this book-like world entailed four types of resemblance which in turn play the role of synthesizing, uniting, harmonizing, and gathering the world together as one text. These types of resemblance include: (a) *conventientia*–signifying a spatial adjacency; the things in the world are linked via their proximity and chain-like connection to all other things; resemblance based on adjacency; (b) *accumulatio*–things are linked at a distance and have no need of physical contact or proximity, i.e., reflection in a mirror; things scattered across the universe communicate with each other via imitation; (c) *analogy*–a combination of the first two, including a notion of proportion; resemblances by relations; man is the centre of this level; (d) *sympathies*–resemblances that traverse the greatest distances in an instant; principle of mobility and connectedness; dominant characteristic is that of assimilation of all parts into a unified whole or system; hence, this includes the other three forms (Foucault, 1973). With these four systems of resemblance, then, the 16th century, Foucault argues, was able to articulate its world as essentially connected or internally connected; as a system of order with organizing principles; as nonprogressive and stable; and as based on a fundamental principle of identity which, although scattered, dispersed, and differentiated in appearance, was at base nonetheless a unity and a whole.

Language was understood at this time as assisting in the world's representation and communication of itself to itself, and hence it was considered essentially to have the same structure as the world. Language could signify and represent, be understood or deciphered, because the world itself signified, represented, was understood, and could be deciphered. Thus there is no fundamental break or distance between language and the world at this time. Rather, language can operate as it does—as a form of representation—only because it is *internally* related to the world. As Foucault claims (1973, p. 31):

> the value of *language* lay in the fact that it was a *sign of things*. There is no difference between the visible marks that God has stamped upon the surface of the earth, so that we may know its inner secrets, and the legible words that the scriptures, or the sages of Antiquity, have set down in the books preserved for us by tradition. The relation to these texts is of the *same nature* as the relation to things.

Thus, language is understood as an exact parallel to the world, and to Nature, and it is on this basis that it is seen to be essentially referential and structured via representation. Because the world is, however, not transparent to us, in its essence (that is, we do not know it immediately and its "secrets" are not immediately transparent to us), language also has the characteristic of an initial opacity. On the one hand, it represents what is and is invisible, unformative, and external in the process, yet on the other, it holds within itself the secrets and truths of the world. The fact is, however, that the world is essentially knowable, decipherable, understandable, and meaningful. In turn, so is language for the 16th century world view. Although "an opaque and mysterious thing, closed in upon itself, a fragmented mass, language is not an arbitrary system; it has been set down in the world and forms a part of it both because things themselves hide and manifest their own enigmas like language and because words offer themselves to man as things to be deciphered" (Foucault, 1973).

It is therefore the case that language was considered to be, on the one hand, one *thing* among others at this time, yet also a privileged thing that could represent all other things. We shall address this paradox as it erupts in full form in the 17th and 18th centuries, or the Classical Age.

For the 16th century, it is already clear that language entails a number of paradoxes. But these paradoxes (of hiding and revealing, being opaque yet transparent, etc.) are not located specifically within language. They also characterize nature and the world as a whole—as ordained and ordered by God. God is the *author*, scriptor, of this world, and hence it is written in divine language. Man's language is but a bad copy but nonetheless ordained by God. The root or ground of resemblance is the text, the Book, in which aspects are but pages, words are but things, and signatures are but authors. All is a mystery, yet all can be deciphered within the book. Its covers, limits, boundaries presuppose such closure, totality, unity, and completeness. This is at least Foucault's reading of the 16th century at the archaeological level. Let us return finally to this "great metaphor of the book" which opens and closes on the 16th century for him (1973, p. 34; emphasis added):

The *great metaphor of the book* that one opens, that one pours over and reads in order to know nature, is merely the reverse and visible side of another transference, and a much deeper one, which *forces language to reside in the world*, among the plants, the herbs, the stones, and the animals. Language partakes in the world-wide dissemination of similitudes and signatures. It must therefore be studied itself as a *thing in nature*.

(b) The Age of the Table

In the 17th and 18th centuries, "the profound kinship of language with the world . . . was dissolved" (Foucault, 1973). There is thus a rupture which occurs between the 16th century and the 17th century for Foucault, which in turn results in a profound rupture between language and the world. The understanding of the world as a network of resemblances, each representing and supporting the others, has gone. We have instead the age of the Table; the mathesis universalis, the taxonomia of the sciences, and the development of "artificial," symbolic languages. "Table" here is thus the symbol of a world turned mathematical, searching for precision, exactitude, and "complete enumeration." It is now a world where wholeness, in the 16th century organic sense, has been transformed into completeness, exhaustiveness, and formal totality. A world where all the possibilities could be formulated in advance – mathematically. In this "age of the Table," language "has withdrawn from the midst of beings themselves and has entered a period of transparency and neutrality" (Foucault, 1973). We shall proceed to show, from Foucault's archaeological standpoint, the general world view which made such a transformation of the meaning of language necessary.

The detachment of language from the world established a new order for knowing and a new relation between language and knowledge. Nature was no longer the guideline for what was to be known, but became more of a raw material to be worked over, a mysterious veil which had to be pierced through with the tools of science. Within this context, the *name* takes on more importance than ever before since it begins to have a constitutive and organizing function rather than a mimetic one. As Foucault says (1973, pp. 117–118):

> it is the *Name* that organizes all Classical discourse; to speak or write . . . is to make one's way towards *the sovereign act of* nomination, to move, through language, towards the place where things and words are conjoined in their common essence, and which makes it possible to give them a name.

Further:

> The *name* is the end [*telos*] of all discourse.

Thus, names continue to be made possible (as correct names, or true names) via an internal and essential connection between words and things – their true and common essence – but the priority for ordering and organizing the world is now given to knowledge itself rather than nature.

There is in turn a theory of *signs* generated in the 17th century which is anachronistically similar to that developed by Saussurian linguistics. A sign (and hence a word, or language in general) is what it is by virtue of its relation and embeddedness in a sign *system*. It receives its "signifying function" from that system not from its essential though hidden relation to "what it signifies or represents." As Foucault says (1973, p. 59):

> From now on . . . it is *within knowledge* itself that the sign is to perform its signifying function; it is from knowledge that it will borrow its certainty or its probability.

The essential role of the sign is thus not representative but relational, and that within its own proper system. It is a short step from this and the privilege given to naming and, hence, taxonomia (which overtakes the sciences as its goal) to the setting up of *tables* which will entail completeness and closure for the system of knowledge.

Since science now becomes concerned with an *exhaustive* enumeration of the world, locating all that is, fixing the boundaries of each object and their relations to all other objects (of nature or man), and since there is no longer an organic link between *knowledge* and the world, *tables* become essential tools and frameworks for knowing. Not only was "the centre of knowledge in the 17th and 18th C. the table," but further:

> The sciences always carry within themselves the project . . . of an *exhaustive ordering of the world*; they are always directed, too, towards the discovery of *simple elements* and their *progressive combination*; and at their centre they form a *table* on which knowledge is displayed in a system contemporary with itself. (Foucault, 1973, p. 74; emphasis added)

With the table as the central metaphor for this age, Foucault sums up the mathematical desire of the age as well. Calculation, formalization, and systematization now characterize the sciences, and in a radically new way. The development of sign systems that essentially differ from that which they represent also has an effect on the meaning of language and increasingly allows artificial languages to become the model for understanding natural languages. Algebra and scientific, univocal terminology now are seen as superior to the unscientific, less rigorous, equivocal, ambiguous, natural languages. In turn, language is distinguished from sign systems in general and indeed threatened by them.

> It was the sign system that gave rise simultaneously to the search for origins and to calculability; to the constitution of *tables* that would fix the possible compositions, and to the restitution of a genesis as the basis of the simplest elements; it was the sign system that linked all knowledge to a language, and sought to replace all lan-

guages with a system of articicial symbols and operations of a logical order. (Foucault, 1973, p. 63)

Thus, the demand for exactitude, precision, and mathematical order begins to spread over all fields of knowing at this time.

This is also the age where similitude becomes the occasion for error. The senses now deceive us, as Descartes (1968) amply illustrated, and hence the reliance on artificial, epistemological, and scientific bases is realized and completed. One can now no longer trust one's experience in the world, and the world itself no longer offers itself as an interconnected, organic whole or text, and Nature no longer gives us signs. "We give the laws to Nature," as Kant (1965) told us at this time. Indeed, between Descartes and Kant we have the dominant philosophic representatives of the age.

In this context, referentiality is no longer the guarantee of truth, but rather systematicity, closure, completeness – the most significant of the ideas of Pure Reason, for Kant. Language then functions, as interwoven with knowledge and radically dissimilar to nature, immediately nonetheless. Although natural language is devalued on the one hand (in comparison to artificial and more precise languages), it is, on the other hand, the immediate locale of what is known. The name function and the tabling of names is only possible via language. In fact, language and knowledge are so intertwined that a theory of knowledge in the 17th and 18th centuries automatically includes language as its bearer. This did not lead, and could not, Foucault insists, to a theory of signification or of language at the philosophic level. Language is still essentially transparent, that is to say, invisible. There is a precise fit between what is known and what can be said. Thus, epistemological concerns hold *a fortiori* for language; or, to put it another, more modern, way, the signifier is always reduced (made invisible) in favor of the signified. This is not to return to the referent, however, but rather to stay at the level of ideality, at once the essence of nature and the goal of language to represent to us. This is the ultimate function of a sign at this time, but it is not seen as such. That is, the signifying function, although evidently constitutive (for us looking back), was considered in the 17th and 18th centuries to be simply a means to an end. As Foucault says (1973, p. 65):

> This universal extension of the sign within the field of representation precludes even the possibility of a theory of signification. Signification cannot constitute a problem . . . it is not even visible.

We shall see that the leap from the end of the 18th century to the 19th, or from the age of the Table to that of Roots, is also a transformation of the transparency of language into its opacity and formative powers. In short, language will become a problem, an object for study, and it will be shown to have its own proper laws of functioning and organization.

(c) The Age of Roots

Near the end of the 18th century, Foucault (1973) tells us, "thought detaches itself from the squares it inhabited before," "that table is about to be destroyed
while knowledge takes up residence in a new space–a discontinuity" (p. 217).
One of the great paradoxes of the 19th century, age of Roots, was the discovery
of *history*, which entailed a search for origins, a tracing back to *roots*, an analysis of
the laws of history and so forth, and, on the other hand, a radical dislocation of
language from its formerly representative function and even from its essential
connectedness to knowledge, occurs. Language has been cut loose from its tie to
the Logos, and "literature" (Foucault, 1973) is born at this time. With this new-
found freedom, language becomes opaque, an object to be studied, on the one
hand, and transformative, formational, and the locus of man's freedom, on the
other. It expresses the *will* now, for the first time, and hence is connected to the
political and the psychological. In addition, the search for origins now turns to
"great hidden forces" (Foucault, 1973) beneath the surface of things, hidden laws
which make what is manifest manifest. Language can mean or signify because it
obeys its own laws, not because it is directly – internally or externally – related to
things. As Foucault says (1973, p. 281):

> If the word is able to figure in a discourse in which it will mean something, it will no
> longer be by virtue of some immediate discursivity that it is thought to possess in it-
> self, and by right of birth but because...*the word...obeys a certain number of strict laws*
> which regulate...all the other elements of the same language; so that the word is no
> longer attached to a representation except in so far as it is previously a part of the
> grammatical organization by means of which the language defines and guarantees
> its own coherence.

The tendencies of the 17th and 18th centuries are fulfilled in certain respects in
the 19th, since the tables of formalization of languages can be situated within
their very structure, not in their relations to the world or to knowledge as such. In
turn, texts become more and more opaque and the conditions of the possibility of
their objective, reliable and certain meanings, become questionable and indeed
problems. At this time, theories of hermeneutics dominate, philology is in full
bloom, and exegesis becomes a flourishing practice. Since language exhibits nothing directly or immediately any more, not even, or especially not, its own laws of
functioning, its very capacity for such concealment is now studied and examined.
Thus, linguistics is fully developed at this time and new theories concerning the
origin and development, indeed evolution, of languages, arise.

The other side of the linguistically opaque coin entails the speaking/writing
subject. Language, although it is no longer essentially connected to the world, is
in an inverse relationship even *more* connected to the *one* using it. The author or
speaker, as origin of one's speech – in this age of roots – thus becomes a central fo-

cus in this epoque's understanding of language and its potency. What language expresses is the *will* of the subject. What a text expresses is the intention of its author. This psychological origin is, however, displaced the instant that it is recognized. If language is always collective, that is, the language of a people, then what can be said in it is always in terms of that collective. Indeed, this is the age when *Weltanschauung* philosophy is born as well. Thus, the will represented and expressed by a particular usage of language is the will of the people for whom that language is their medium. As Foucault (1973) says:

> Language makes visible the fundamental will that keeps a whole people alive and gives it the power to speak a language belonging solely to itself.

Further:

> Language is neither an instrument nor a product – but a ceaseless activity – an energeia. In any language, the speaker...is the people. (p. 290)

It is a short step from this to the connection of language with the political. Rather than specifically epistemological concerns, language is linked to man's collective capacity to express himself, and in turn to his freedom (Foucault, 1973). Indeed, freedom of speech, freedom of assembly, freedom of the press are newly born at this time, we should recall. Thus, language is a link to one's past, one's traditions, heritage, a link to the present contemporaneity of a community, and a link to the future freedom which language itself seems to promise. Language becomes a framework that is, on the one hand, flexible and fitted with potentialities, yet, on the other, carries within it the secrets of the past as the memory of the culture it brings living expression to. The paradox here, as Hegel expressed it, is that freedom becomes understood as the "recognition of constraint." Thus, History must be related to history, the future possibilities to a remote and forgotten past; and the guarantee of certitude in this matter will be (as it was in the 17th and 18th centuries) *closure*. Foucault (1973) situates the philosophies of the 19th century in the gap between *History* and *history*, or between the telos and the archè as both were discovered and expressed in this age of roots:

> philosophy was to reside in the gap between history and History, between events and the Origin, between evolution and the first rending open of the source, between oblivion and the Return. It will be a Metaphysics only in so far as it is Memory. (p. 219)

Thus, language is the center of man's existence in the 19th century. It is man's link to his own historicity, his finitude, and yet his collective immortality. It is his link to knowledge of the world – as man's historic world – and also equally his link to falsity. Only in language, as Hegel (1977) also explained, can something be true or false. Thus, the literacy, fictive, and imaginative uses of language become more and more recognized as language turning in on itself; language playing with itself, using its own laws of production, internal coherence and internal transformation, etymology, etc. to extend itself in *its own ways*. Language thus begins to have "a life of its own" in the 19th century, on the one hand, as the "expression of a people" (and not a single individual), but, on the other hand, as the pure expression of itself, as the expression of its ownmost possibilities. It is this latter trait which will take on a force of its own in the 20th century. For Foucault (1973), it is in turn Mallarmé whose play with language playing with itself will become the paradigm for our age of the *unthought*. As he says, for Mallarme, "it is nothingness that is speaking." (p. 305).

(d) The Age of the Unthought

If the 19th Century discovered history, roots, and man, it was and still is the task of the 20th century to be concerned with the unthought, the unreflected, those "experiences constantly eluding themselves," the *shadows* of history, roots and man. The question now, Foucault (1973) claims, is: "How can man think what he does not think, inhabit as though by a mute occupation something that eludes him?" (p. 323). Not only are we concerned with the "unthought" dimension, but its realization as a problem in a dramatic way de-centers our previous notions of the subject, of consciousness, of the will, of community, of nature, of history, and ultimately of "man." In this sense, our age is concerned not only with the end of humanism, as Heidegger formulated it, but also perhaps more radically with the end of "man." This "unthought" dimension certainly has its origins in the 19th century recognition of the loss of origins, the simultaneous search for and loss of roots for what is, the shifting ground of historicity upon which all knowledge is built. But the shift that occurs in the 20th century establishes the unthought as that unreflected, and for some unreflectable, ground which orders, governs, organizes what is thought "behind the back," as it were, of the thinker. As Foucault (1973) says, the modern cogito "is concerned to grant the highest value, the greatest dimension, to the *distance* that both separates and links thought-conscious-of-itself and whatever, within thought, is rooted in non-thought" (p. 324). Thus, the space between consciousness and the non-conscious, the reflected and the unreflected, becomes the 20th century focus of investigation, according to Foucault.

With respect to language, we have the subject (as a conscious cogito) *overtaken* by the linguistic. The subject is now not only situated in a language of the community and *its* way of seeing the world or *Weltanschauung*, not only situated in a language whose grammar may or may not be known explicitly by the user, and not only situated in a language which the subject most evidently did not create but inherited fully formed, but also is situated *only* in language and by virtue of language. One's very thought, speech, expression, and all signifying functions are now seen as conditioned, organized and pre-scripted by the linguistic. "Man" becomes a function within a play of signifiers, as Lacan (1977) pointed out by saying that "the subject is a signifier for another signifier" (p. 30). In short, man seems in his most wakeful reflection and self-conscious moments to be ever more fully asleep than in his prereflective, lived through, idle chatter of the lifeworld. As Foucault says (1973, p. 323):

> How can man be the subject of a language that for thousands of years has been formed without him, a language whose organization escapes him, whose meaning sleeps in an almost invincible sleep in the words he momentarily activates by means of discourse and within which he is obliged, from the very outset, to lodge his speech and thought.

The dilemma of modernity is thus, for Foucault, a struggle with the unthought by thought trying to think itself. The problem is, the very tools he uses for the project keep him securely within the unthought, and, as the unthought, it is invisible to man. The question is, as effaced or as invisible, the unthought is simply "not there." Yet we now have cognizance of this fact and of the slippage between *intention* in the act by a subject, and the *manifestation* of the "intention" as other or something else than what was intended. In short, we now have evidence for the space between the thought and the unthought. Yet we also only ever have this evidence "after the fact," as Merleau-Ponty and indeed Hegel (1977) before him (in the 19th century) were quick to point out. The question for our age, then, is no longer a tracing back to origins, although it is not dissimilar in some respects, but an uncovering within what is manifest, clear, distinct, thought, and reflected that which escaped thought, analysis, etc. the first time around. As Foucault says, this is no longer a question of truth but a question of Being, of ontology. We are no longer concerned, as Kant was, with the conditions of the possibility of understanding and knowledge, but rather with the conditions of the possibility of a primary *misunderstanding* or a primary and perhaps primordial *unthought* dimension to human existence.

As the dominant metaphor of our age, the unthought still remains to be thought in a more radical way, we suggest. Foucault's own analysis, as we have traced it to this point, itself partakes of this modern structure. Archaeology itself is certainly concerned primarily with the unthought aspects of the "past," of historical epochs whose frameworks of understanding and analysis, although explicitly used by that age in question, could only be invisible *as* frameworks while they were used and in place. Just as today, if Foucault is correct, the "unthought" as *our* problem is not considered an historically, discursively produced phenomenon, but rather an essential problem for epistemology in general, ontology in general, and inquiry in general. It is, in short, our truth. In the same way, for the age of the Book, the Book was the paradigm of truth; for the age of the Table, the Table played the same role, and, mutatis mutandis, for the age of Roots. Each age, as Foucault has shown, takes it upon itself to reinterpret all former ages according to its own dominant metaphor, and, in this sense, Foucault is an example of himself.

We wish now to suggest some problems with this format of analysis – the usage of paradigms based on "dominant metaphors" (which sometimes go explicitly by that name for Foucault, and at other times do not but are implied nonetheless) – and to consider the *unthought* within Foucault's own position. As we mentioned at the outset, Foucault will be shown to *use* a theory of metaphor, or perhaps more accurately to be *used* by a theory of metaphor which he himself never explicitly thematizes, proposes, or articulates. We should qualify what follows in several ways, however. First, this is not a criticism of Foucault's argument with respect to his descriptions as far as they go of each of the epoques outlined above. Second, this is not a deconstruction of Foucault from a Derridean point of view, although our format and style is not unlike such a project. Thirdly, and finally, this is not a psychoanalytic approach to Foucault, not in search of an *unconscious* dimension of his thought that would be his alone. Rather, we hope to show that: (a) history is not really as discontinuous, as Foucault would like to make it; (b) the metaphors play an organizing role in Foucault's analysis, and one that is questionable with respect to epistemological considerations; (c) the overlaps from one age, epoque, to another cannot be understood from within Foucault's framework; and (d) each epoque is not really so homogeneous or systematically organized as Foucault's analysis seems to indicate. We shall, in what follows, only briefly point towards an archaeology of archaeology, therefore, and suggest a direction for further analysis.

B. THE UNTHOUGHT STRUCTURE
OF METAPHOR IN FOUCAULT'S ANALYSIS

The structure of metaphor which animates Foucault's analysis of the 16th to the 20th centuries will be shown to entail the following: (a) a principle of identification or identity of an age, the circumscription of boundaries of inside/outside; (b) a claim to the discontinuity and lack of common ground between one age and another, as between one metaphor and another; (c) the establishment of an internal systematicity for each age, such that each appears homogeneous within its own particular boundaries. We shall examine each of the effects as they in turn represent a theory of metaphor, unarticulated and unthematized (unthought) by Foucault himself but not articulated as such. It was Derrida who first pointed out that metaphors are never innocent. Metaphor animates the discourse of metaphysics (and all Western discourses are essentially metaphysical for him) in such a way that it *appears* to be an epiphenomenon, to be merely decorative, to be merely externally related to that discourse, yet it in fact is *essential* and thus internally related. Indeed, metaphorics (or systems of metaphors) organize, orient, demarcate, structure, and limit metaphysical or theoretical discourses, Derrida claims (1982). We thus aim here, on the one hand, to, articulate the unthought in Foucault, and on the other, to put Derrida's theory of metaphorics to the test.

(a) A Principle of Identification

As we have shown, Foucault articulates the differences between each epoque (from the 16th to the 20th centuries) with respect to the dominant metaphors of each age. For the 16th century, the age of the Book, and the 17th and 18th centuries, the age of the Table, he does this explicitly. For the 19th century, the age of Roots, and for the 20th century, the age of the Unthought, he does this more indirectly but nonetheless powerfully, we suggest. As a principle of identification and/or identity of the age or epoque in question, the dominant metaphor takes on the function of a name, or more precisely, a proper name. The metaphor becomes a circumscription of the proper/property/propriety of an age. For the 16th century, the appropriating metaphor was that of the Book. This, on the one hand, established a radical break between the 16th century epoque and the 17th/18th century on the basis of the radical break between Books and Tables. One indeed usually sets books *upon* tables in order to be read. In turn one could generate an implicit Hegelian/Kantian theory of history lurking behind Foucault's metaphors (For instance, this position implies Hegel with respect to a building of one historical stage upon another without destroying the latter, and Foucault is Kantian with respect to the *identity* of the subject/author of the book as the ground of its (supposed) unity.) The conditions of the possibility of the age of the Book are revealed in the 17th/18th centuries with respect to the great metaphor of the Table (in all its senses). The point here, however, is that Foucault insists that the relation between epoques is essentially one of quantum leaps or radical breaks. It is no accident, we suggest, that Books, Tables, Roots, and the Unthought themselves as concepts, metaphors, names, circumscribed and circumscribable areas of our world, *do not* essentially, that is internally, overlap. Why did Foucault not choose the following four metaphors: Books, Pages Bibliographies, and the Blank Spaces (between the lines)? In some sense, these four metaphors could have equally well satisfied the qualities Foucault wanted to illustrate (he says) by the four metaphors he chose. The issue here is, of course, that our choice would establish *internal* relations between the epoques, thereby creating the possibility of reading history as continuous and internally connected. Each age would be distinctive but not a radically distinct epoque. History would not entail quantum leaps, as it indeed does for Foucault. Our question is, why and on what basis does Foucault make this claim?

(b) The Homogeneity of an Age

There is not only a principle of differentiation established by metaphors but also one of *internal coherence* for each particular epoque. As long as an age is characterized in general under the sign of one "dominant metaphor," its homogeneity is established, its systematicity guaranteed, and its internal/external relations of radical otherness are sustained. The 16th century, as the Age of the Book, itself becomes a Book of an age. It is as though each event, each theory, philosophy, and each development, are but individual pages which go together to make up one unified narration – a Book. We do not have Books in the 16th century, but one Book; all the world is a Book, all the world is unified, and all that Foucault finds in the 16th century contributes its part to such a framework. There are no internal differences cited which would not contribute to such a narrative, such an encyclopedic unity, but rather all becomes a representative of the general structure of representation which *typifies* the epoque – the Book. What happens to the dissidents of the age? What happens to the remnants of the past or previous ages? What becomes of those who are not *typical* of that Age? They become quite necessarily invisible. They are not a part of the "dominant" trends; the dominant metaphor of the age has excluded them, and a priori at that. Far from representing the age, the dominant metaphor defines the age. It organizes the centre of an age around which all "significant" events turn. The metaphor of the age thus becomes an eidos, a concept, an essence which in turn allows all the particular examples or manifestations of that "metaphor" to be appearances or signs for that same essence. The obvious Platonic structure exhibited here within Foucault's unthought theory of metaphor is, however, not our concern for the moment. We shall return to this, however.

(c) The Blind Spots Established by Metaphors

The dominant metaphors of the ages entail a structuring of *visibility* and *invisibility*, as well as a privileging of some events as typical and rejecting of other events as atypical. What lights up in Foucault's analysis are examples of his dominant metaphors. One might well assert that the examples were first and the metaphor simply *re*presents them after the fact. However, according to all good theories of hermeneutics, we now know that thought and understanding never begin in a vacuum, never successfully perform the epochè, and never fully clear the decks to begin an "objective" analysis. Rather, the foreconceptions, preunderstandings, unthematized yet orienting structures, inhabit an analysis to begin with. Indeed, what is *found* by an analysis tends to be the realization, manifestation, of those foreconceptions. What this means is that the metaphors in Foucault's depiction of epochal history do not simply arrive on the scene after the fact. Rather, they prefigure what will become visible or invisible, significant or insignificant, dominant or subordinate, representative or not, for that particular age. Not only organizing the internal coherence of an age, they eliminate all incoherences. They indeed make invisible (by means suggested above in terms of privileging, etc.) those features of an age which do not obey the *law* – do not fit the structure, and/or do not represent the same thing. This is not intentional bad faith on Foucault's part, but rather a more general phenomenon, as we shall see.

Let us suggest some alternatives to Foucault's history of the West and his epochal/metaphorical determinations, in order to further reinforce the theory of metaphorics which has been obliquely pointed towards above. First, consider Plato. All of the ages Foucault has articulated partake of Platonic structures. The age of the Book, as the age of representation, where the order of the world and that of knowledge and language cohere, is certainly also described in Plato's Laws (1961) and many of his dialogues. Aristotle (1941) too claimed that language functions at all because it is a faithful representation of that which it represents. Speech is a copy of thought, and writing a copy of speech. This copy-ability (*iterability*) is what allows language to function at all, for Aristotle. How could Foucault account for the fact that what he calls the Age of the Book—the 16th century—also can be found in the Age of the Greeks, specifically, that of Plato and Aristotle. Foucault's metaphorics *preclude* this possibility. Not only is history discontinuous for Foucault and thus unable to entail any common ground (of any significance); it cannot contain *overlaps* either, from one age to another. This contaminates the metaphors. Books are not Tables, which are not Roots, which are not the Unthought, and so forth.

Concerning the internal unity of an age, we have already suggested why this may indeed not be a fruitful framework, at least with respect to epistemological considerations; however, there is no doubt that an age can be typified, systematized, and organized around one central metaphor—Foucault has indeed succeeded—but the question is, what has been *lost* in such a procedure? Why the demand for an organizing center, a concept of an age? What does this desire for unity, coherence, systematicity, and order entail—contrary to Foucault's own claims?

Finally, with respect to the radical differentiations set up by Foucault's metaphorics, we suggest that the "ages" do overlap, not only on the basis of a common tradition (i.e., Plato and Aristotle), and not only via some contamination which would account for the transitions from one epoch to another (radically different) one, but also in a *nonsystematic* way. For instance, the *unthought* could also be seen to characterize Kant's entire project (1950) for the three Critiques. (It is, for Foucault, however, the metaphor of our 20th century age.) The conditions of the possibility of what is actual, given, manifest, are indeed the *unthought* but thinkable sides of those same characterizations. In addition, we might call Foucault's own style of analysis a *typical 19th century* style—being concerned with the historicity of things, the *roots*, the origins, and the loss of the same. Would these overlaps make Kant, for instance, truly or in fact (despite his actual historical location) a 20th century thinker? Would Foucault truly be a 19th century man? If we move in this direction, which clearly, by implication, Foucault's analysis obliges us to do, then we have certainly lost any sense of history whatsoever. If we do not collapse history in fact into history in principle, then we must address the epochal issue as a whole. Of what benefit and for what purpose/reasons or ends is the epochal-metaphorical chopping up of history set up? What role do his hidden metaphorics play in setting up a number of traps in Foucault's analysis which he seems to be unaware of or blinded by? Clearly, metaphor is not innocent, is not a-epistemological, and is not to be taken for granted, ignored, or addressed lightly as a frill for one's discourse. Metaphorics, as Derrida has claimed specifically, using Aristotle as the good example, does indeed ground theoretical analysis, and effaces itself in the process.

What must still be analysed is *how* the effacement occurs, and why metaphor necessarily inhabits theoretical discourse. It is not suggested, however, by us or by Derrida that one should or could simply exorcise metaphors from one's discourse. Rather, one must take into account après coup, perhaps, the fact that metaphorics surreptitiously usurps the orientation of one's analysis, surreptitiously inserts itself into the discourse, and in turn surreptitiously contaminates any supposed purity or objectivity of the analysis. Further investigations of this fact have yet to be accomplished, but it is clear that the case of Foucault is not isolated or a simple exception. What kind of rule this investigation and that of the metaphorics of Aristotle constitute, however, is yet to be clarified fully.

REFERENCES

Aristotle, (1941). *The basic works of Aristotle.* New York: Random House.

Derrida, J. (1982). *Margins of philosophy.* (A. Bass, Trans.) Chicago: University of Chicago Press.

Descartes, R. (1968). *The meditations.* (F. E. Sutcliffe, Trans.) Harmondsworth, England: Penguin Books.

Foucault, M. (1973). *The order of things.* New York: Vintage Books.

Foucault, M. (1982). *The archaeology of knowledge.* (A. M. Sheridan, Trans.) New York: Pantheon.

Hegel, G. W. F. (1977). *The phenomenology of spirit.* (A. V. Miller, Trans.) Oxford: Clarendon Press.

Kant, I. (1950). *Prolegomena to any future metaphysics.* (L. W. Beck, Trans.) New York: Bobbs-Merrill.

Kant, I. (1965). *The critique of pure reason.* (N. K. Smith, Trans.) New York: St. Martin's Press.

Lacan, J. (1977). *The four fundamental concepts of psychoanalysis.* (A. Sheridan, Trans.) Harmondsworth, England: Penguin Books.

Plato (1961). *Plato–collected dialogues.* Princeton, NJ: Princeton University Press.

Rickman, H. P. (1976). *W. Dilthey–selected writings.* (H. P. Rickman, Trans.) London: Cambridge University Press.

PART III

Nonconscious Metaphor

CHAPTER ELEVEN

Metaphor as Mitsein: Therapeutic Possibilities in Figurative Speaking

John E. Shell, Howard R. Pollio, and Michael K. Smith
The University of Tennessee, Knoxville

Metaphor has become an increasingly important area of study because it provides insight into how people invest speaking with lively meaning. Understood as creative act, metaphor draws on ordinary vocabulary while making something new of it. A novel meaning is disclosed and relationships within the dialogue are furthered. This meaning may be explicated after the fact, but does not easily survive paraphrase or translation. It includes the hearer who understands it as a unique event within the dialogue at that point. It is more than an intellectual act and more than a reference to some ordinary object in reality – perhaps playful, perhaps profound, metaphor discloses new possibilities of speaking and of being together.

METAPHOR AND CONTEMPORARY LINGUISTICS

The creative aspect of metaphor has only been reluctantly studied by linguists who traditionally have wanted to discount it. In a nonmetaphoric world of discourse, language is assumed to be well organized and highly structured with clear, enumerable rules. Each word is assumed to have a meaning fixed by prior usage and to remain a stable element of the lexicon. Each word also is assumed to refer to some thought or object of reality, and logical rules are provided to determine their permissible patterns of combination (Katz, 1972). The linguistic approach to language (and speaking) likewise posits syntactic rules that are precise, universal, and eternal (Chomsky, 1957). In addition, speakers and hearers are thought to share such rules and to evaluate utterances and understandings against them. Errors are seen as due to lapses in speaking, nonsensical combinations, or to a lack of knowledge of relevant rules. In some cases, an utterance may be syntactically correct but semantically anomalous, e.g. "Colorless green ideas sleep furiously." In no case, however, should it be possible for deviant sentences to slip through the logical net of language and come out semantically meaningful.

Are these logical models of words, sentences, and meanings accurate? In testing speaker knowledge of logical sentence categories, Steinberg (1979) asked college age speakers to code sentences into the linguistic categories of synthetic, analytic, or contradictory. If a sentence could not be fit into one or the other of these categories, the student was to code the sentence as anomalous. When the category of metaphor was introduced into the task, many so called anomalous sentences were found not to be quite so anomalous and were coded as metaphoric (Pollio & Smith, 1979). Under the stress of these and other earlier data (Pollio & Burns, 1977), semantic feature models became more sophisticated and complex (e.g., Sternberg, Tourangeau, & Nigro, 1979).

Despite this change, almost all linguistic (or psycholinguistic) approaches to metaphor still implicitly assume that speaking is a utilitarian process whose primary function is to convey information about some putatively objective reality. Literal meaning as lexical reference is primary; hence, metaphor can only be treated as an artful but subsidiary embellishment. If necessary, metaphor can be accounted for in terms of analogies both within and between semantic fields and/or semantic features. Such models endeavor to rescue lexical purity at a level of abstraction far away from the seemingly unpredictable combinations of language regularly produced by speaking people.

We do not, however, usually live our linguistic lives in terms of utilitarian purposes or in situations of linguistic disarray. Rather, there is a structure to human speaking that is both historical and emergent and it is this double structure to speaking that needs to be understood. While a conversation is constrained by cultural and linguistic factors, it is also an opening up of possibility. This must be the case, for every conversation is a part of our existence and indeed constitutes it at that moment. To some abstract theory, a statement may appear anomalous — within conversation it is almost never without meaning or sense. The issue is not truth as correspondence between signifier and thing, or grammaticality or even politeness. Every statement is an element of some conversation that has a present, a history, and a future. It is a manifestation of the possibilities of two people being together. It is a segment of their lives which they are sharing at that moment, and the question becomes not one of truth but one of how much and how well they share it.

METAPHOR IN PSYCHOTHERAPY

Psychoanalysis traditionally has thought of language in much the same way as linguistics, although with its own unique concepts of logic, history, and determinism. The manifest utterance was thought to express a latent meaning, determined by the patient's mix of impulses and defenses. Freud himself did not address the question of metaphor directly; Anderson (1964), however, did survey classical analytic sources and found an insistence throughout on paraphrasing metaphor into rational exposition, with intellectual understanding the goal. In this literature, metaphor was included among the *Fehlleistungen,* a slipping through of instinctual impulses, however disguised and displaced. As such, metaphor had to be worked through into secondary process like every other similar bit of material. Primary process, in which some A is asserted be some B, was to be decoded into sequential and realistic statements, thereby rendering unconscious meanings conscious. Metaphor was to be harnessed by the reality principle.

Sharpe (1940) stated the classical Freudian position, that metaphor is an expression of conflict between instinct and inhibition analogous to a neurotic symptom. Given this understanding, the proper treatment was to translate metaphor from its encoded, symptomatic form into a direct reference to hidden impulses. Voth (1970) suggested that analytic work could be furthered by explicitly focusing on metaphor and recommended that analysts request associations to elements of the metaphor, just as to a dream, for the condensation and displacement that characterize dreams also govern metaphor. Ekstein and Caruth (1966), taking a slightly different approach, suggested *not* translating the metaphor into literal language in order to facilitate communication with severely disturbed patients. This temporary strategem was designed to avoid the inundation that threatened if primary process material were addressed directly. For Ekstein and Caruth, metaphors are allowed for the time being to keep their function of hiding what is really going on.

Arlow (1979), making a break with this traditional view, went so far as to suggest that "psychoanalysis is essentially a metaphorical enterprise." Patient and analyst may communicate through metaphor and this is a necessary process rather than an unfortunate hindrance. Despite this change in perspective, metaphor remains an error that requires understanding in terms external to it. Metaphor is an unconscious analogy for which the missing term must be supplied by theoretical understanding. The goal of treatment remains a literal – i.e., a biological – redescription of the impulse(s) in order to arrive at an historical reconstruction and/or insight.

Other studies have dealt with the empirical issue of metaphor in therapy. Barlow (1973), for example, began by distinguishing between frozen figures, which are quite similar to ordinary vocabulary items, and novel metaphors, which "do the work" (Pollio & Barlow, 1975). In one particular session of Gestalt therapy, the patient's novel figures were found to correlate moderately well with utterances judged to reflect patient insight. Two patterns of relationship were found: in one, there was a co-occurrence of novel figurative language and insight; in the other, bursts of novel metaphor alternated with literal statements expressing insight.

These results were considered only suggestive, since Gestalt therapy makes explicit use of figurative techniques, thereby generating an unusually high rate of metaphor. Examining sessions from a long-term psychoanalytic therapy, Barlow (1973) found that regions judged to contain insight were either highly metaphoric or strictly literal. The metaphoric ones affirmed a relation between past and present experience, or stated a general case. The literal ones either stood alone or explicated a prior metaphoric statement. Barlow contends this pattern is not only the key to understanding the relationship of literal to figurative language, but to the process of psychotherapy more generally. Novel metaphors juxtapose diverse elements of a patient's life. They portray them in a form rich with implication, which is then worked out through the process of "literalizing" the metaphor. A productive metaphor will occur again and again as different implications and applications are worked out in "a continuous, dynamic process" (Pollio, Barlow, Fine, & Pollio, 1977). What the patient gains from therapy is not just a particular insight into one aspect of his or her life, but the capacity to use this process further "to maintain contact with his experience of himself and others".

Amira (1982) reasoned that successful therapies should show higher rates of novel metaphor than unsuccessful ones. To this end, he compared cases with elaborate measures of total outcome (Strupp & Hadley, 1977) and found no significant difference in figurative output between successful and unsuccessful cases; this finding led him to question Barlow's analysis. He suggested looking to the qualities of both kinds of figurative language and their multiple uses. To this end, he extracted examples of figures – both novel and frozen – that were "fraught with clinical significance," alluding to a "certain vibrant quality." His response to the empirical problem was to include both novel and frozen figures in his analysis. This undoubtedly added to the problem, making it even harder to discern significant patterns, not to mention burying "vibrant" qualities even deeper. Not only may frozen figures be felt to be important; not all novel figures need be quite so important, and a theoretical rationale now seems required for making finer distinctions among figures which takes the dialogue of therapy into account.

METAPHOR AND HUMAN DIALOGUE

Dialogue is created through the shared participation of two people. Its structure is not only that of reference to some external reality, but to the creation of a reality in which participants situate themselves. Dialogue proceeds by revealing the stance of the participants toward one another and includes more than cognitive/linguistic elements. In its most significant form, it can become intensely private because the usual social constraints and assumptions, the naive realism of mundane conversation, are discarded. An outside observer may have trouble understanding what is said, for the participants have developed a shared language. It has its own history and its own indeterminate future. Such private language must be metaphoric, for it bursts the bonds of public, lexical meanings. Dialogue is not only a process of communicating meaning but of creating it.

It is easier to work with molecular statements about something than with the whole of a dialogue. In the former case logical structure and meaning can be checked for veracity, statements can be compared to what they refer, and meaning as shared reference would seem accessible to all. Metaphor in this sense can be reduced to analogy, which then may be exhaustively paraphrased into literal language and its lexical meaning rescued. It is far harder to adopt a conceptual set for dialogue, for in this case there is no extralinguistic *thing* to which it refers. Dialogue can be checked only against itself. This requires a method different from positivistic analysis. It requires the method of disciplined "subjectivity" known as phenomenology.

"Phenomenology" is a term coined for the study of how things appear. It is one strand in the philosophical debate about essence and ontology and, as such, offers an alternative to naive realism, which posits that things are "out there," objective and separate. This Cartesian dichotomy creates the problem of how subject and object can possibly interact. Phenomenology avoids the problems entirely by making no presupposition about reality: The object and the consciousness of it are identical. Whatever is "out there" reveals itself only in intentional human activity, and consciousness is always consciousness of something (Pollio, 1982).

The specific version of phenomenology to be applied to the case of human dialogue is borrowed largely from Heidegger (1927/1979). This approach assumes that meaning is not hidden behind confusing "outward" manifestations; appearance and the consciousness of it are already a meaningful unit. Reflective consciousness and the presumption of an independent, third-person observer are special cases of human activity, not fundamental ones against which all others are to be measured. Everything occurs in the context of subject and object together, what Heidegger called Being-in-the-world. The hyphens, which can be so daunting, merely emphasized that the words are not to be understood as separate and that events are co-constituted by self-and-world. Mind and body, similarly, are not two-fold. Human being cannot be understood as physiological or cognitive processes in isolation; they too occur in the context of human existence. Freedom and situated choice replace cause and effect, for they reveal themselves in the possible activities of Being-in-the-world. There is no arbitrariness or relativism in this position but an awareness of possibilities in a self-world created from the past and aimed toward a future.

Other people inhabit the human world and are themselves active centers of a personal self-world. They are prominent constituents of our context and problematic because they too are free. Following Buber, we can say that one aspect of Being-with-another that both accepts and intends the freedom of the other is dialogue. Dialogue is an achievement beyond utilitarian words: it is a sharing in which personal self-worlds merge. Utterances which may be anomalous when taken out of context do not impede dialogue, nor is it necessary to seek hidden meanings, for by furthering the dialogue, such utterances reveal their meaning. In the world of dialogue, metaphors create the world.

Black (1962) has argued that a metaphor cannot be replaced by some set of literal statements, for it involves a system of mutual influence and modification by both terms of the figures. This interaction alters the original system or context of both. Metaphor has a "power to present, in a distinctive and irreplaceable way, insight into how things are" (Black, 1979, p. 21). It reveals both elements of the metaphor in a new light. To say "The man is a wolf," is not just to assert he has some properties of a wolf—it is meant to create a structural correspondence. A new set of associations is created in which the man seems more wolf-like and the wolf more man-like. This capacity to say something other than simple references to the "facts" of reality yields the possibility of created meanings.

Ricoeur (1977) criticized Black for discussing metaphor at the level of the word. The man both *is* a wolf and *is not* a wolf. The copula is at issue, thereby creating an ontological and not a semantic problem. Ricoeur further suggests that the relationship is more like that between the concrete and the abstract, that is, a matter of interpretation. In denotative language the word stands for one thing. In poetic language there is "a certain fusion between meaning or sense and the sense" (p. 290). The referential function of the word recedes before the actuality of the dialogue.

Ricoeur (1981) appropriates Black's view of metaphor while seeking to go beyond it. He acknowledges metaphor as a local event, constrained by semantic factors, but points to it as embedded in the broader context of discourse. Following Austin, Ricoeur contends that a decisive aspect of discourse is that it is an illocutionary act: "What is said of the subject is one thing; what I 'do' *in* saying it is another" (p. 168). Discourse has a content—something to which it refers—but it also reveals the world of the speaker or writer. Reference is not only to extra-linguistic reality, but to its own existence. It predicates what it means as well as *that* it means.

Within this analysis, Ricoeur (1981) concentrates on written texts because he feels that it is where the problem of interpretation is greatest. He writes of "the power of a work to project a world of its own and to set in motion the hermeneutical circle, which encompasses in its spiral both the apprehension of projected worlds and the advance of self-understanding in the presence of these new worlds" (p. 171). The text is fixed, allowing successive readings. Its meaning appears alienated because the event of creation and the event of understanding are now separate. The aim of hermeneutics is for the reader to enter the world proposed by the text. The text reveals a world, but this world comes to be shared by the reader in a specific act of understanding. Through this act, the world of the text and the world of the reader merge.

While this may be true of texts and more ordinary conversations, it does not apply to therapeutic dialogue, which is about something *and* which reveals how the patient has come to be situated in the world and tries to make sense of it. The meanings the patient finds in it, or has been unable to find, constitute the structure of the patient's life – what in clinical literature is discussed under topics such as character style, transference, and resistance. These are not events or concepts that can be pointed to easily, yet they are central to the therapeutic endeavor. It will be argued later that hermeneutic methods can be applied productively in this situation. The point here however, is that Ricoeur's analysis need not be confined to written texts. The distinction between text and understanding which Ricoeur finds in discourse also holds between utterance and interpretation in therapeutic dialogue.

Ricoeur argues that metaphor can be understood only in terms of discourse and can be thought of as a miniature discourse. Metaphor takes the form of a proposition which lays claim to meaning, but at the same time clashes semantic sets. As a proposition, it is anomalous; as an event in dialogue, it is meaningful. It is an interpersonal event, disclosing the being of that speaker at that moment with that listener. The participants in the dialogue reveal their stances toward the world, toward each other, and toward themselves; each utterance is presented for interpretation and invites a furthering response. The participants can understand only if this complex situation is taken into account. More than discrete bits of information, a dialogue is "an architecture of themes and purposes" (Ricoeur, 1981, p. 175). Each utterance contributes to and depends on the unfolding progress. Semantic understanding can be complete, accurate, and exhaustive: participating in dialogue – and the world it proposes – is always provisional, tentative, and open.

The meaning of dialogue is not hidden behind the words but disclosed through them. As reference to some object, it can be decoded; as event, it is an invitation to interpret. Successive efforts to understand and further the dialogue are a dialectical process toward the broadest possible understanding of an event that opens up possibilities. By talking about things, the speaker reveals his or her world. The patient's values and intentions emerge from what is said and how it is said. What he or she does not say is also important. The range of dialogue may be broad or narrow. Statements have a truth value that can be checked, as well as an immediacy in revealing mood, attitude, and existence. What the patient says about things invites the listener to share his or her world and to see it as he or she does. As code for objects, the dialogue refers; as disclosure, it is an event "waiting for fresh interpretations which decide its meaning" (Ricoeur, 1981, p. 208).

MEANING AND INTERPRETATION IN PSYCHOTHERAPY

This way of describing metaphor permits a new approach to the question of meaning and interpretation in psychotherapy. This approach, however, requires an initial excursion through what, in the philosophical literature, is usually called phenomenological hermeneutics. To begin, consider the following situation: A person comes to a therapist presenting a problem with life. The intent is treatment, that is, a change positive to the person's value system. What is presented and how is a manifestation of that person's life. So, too, are the expectations of the therapist. Before we hear the complaint, we already know something about this individual – the fact of coming for help is an example of the patient's way of handling a current problem.

One patient wants a nerve pill, another a rescuer, a third an explanation. The adolescent, dragged in by parents or police, wants to be left alone by this new authority figure. Each human being always has a situation and there is always something to be taken care of in it. Both the task and the manner of attending to it are fundamental to living, not something added on to an otherwise well-functioning logical process. Something the patient cares about has become a problem; it offers resistance to his or her smooth functioning. The issues that arise and are brought to the therapist are aspects of the self-world in which the patient lives and whose tasks are lived out. Seeking help in the first place is an aspect of this world. If we could follow the patient around for awhile, we undoubtedly would see other things that stand out for him or her (and some that do not) and how he or she handles them.

Phenomenology, as the word is used in psychiatry, means the description by the patient of his or her problem. Typically, it is felt to be inadequate. Phenomenology, as the word is used here, is a method of describing what the problem is, how it is experienced, and what it means for the patient. It implies an insistence that how and what the patient is, is continually being displayed. His or her being is not a collection of attributes, instincts, and defenses, nor a vague theoretical idea like a set of logical features defining a word. Discarding preconceptions about *what* he or she is, we are left with the incontrovertible fact that he or she *is*. Human being has a structure through which it manifests itself.

Already in this last sentence we can see a difficulty: Being does not *have* a structure, it *is* that structure. It is not other than its manifestations. Heidegger summarized, "*Das 'Wesen' des Daseins liegt in seiner Existenz*" (1927/1979, p. 42). Taking the words in their everyday sense, this sentence could be translated, "The 'essence' of existence lies in its existence". It is better if we leave *Dasein* standing, like most translators, since it is both an everday word compounded of the words da and sein – being there – and the center of Heidegger's thought: "The 'essence' of *Dassein* lies in its existence." Since existence is *eksistere*, how a thing stands out, and *essence* a form of the Latin "to be," it may be instructive to retranslate Heidegger as follows: "The 'being' of that Being-There is as it appears." Even this still leaves us with that little word *is*.

We are a bit further along, for Being is now situated in a particular there, at some particular time. These are not attributes, like color or size, or even spatial location; rather, they are fundamental modes of being. They are the recognition that Being is always situated. Being in time means that Being has a history and a future; it arises and passes away. In time and space it has its limits; the self-world of being has a horizon. Beyond the horizon, Being *is* no more; hence the possibility of nonbeing is another fundamental mode of Being, and one which makes going on being fundamentally problematic. Being is not just this or that; what it is, is one possibility among many. The situatedness of Being has limits, but within these limits there are always possibilities.

Patients who come to therapy wish something about their situation were different. They imagine a different possibility and want help in arranging it. How they imagine this help, their expectations of the therapist and the treatment, is the transference. They initiate a project with the therapist to gain what they want. Initially, they want to *have* some attribute, which will not change the structure of their world, just improve it. If they continue beyond symptom relief, who they *are* – their history and future – becomes the issue. Possibilities emerge which had not been evident before. The therapist's theoretical orientation provides a framework for understanding the problem in a broader context of possibilities excluded by the patient. There is, at least implicitly, an understanding of human being in it.

Freud's achievement was an exploration of human being and doing. He defined psychoanalysis not only as a method of treatment, but also as an area of study that would "gradually yield a new scientific discipline" (1923/1940, p. 211). Bettelheim (1983) argues that Freud intended a human, and not a natural, science; an approach to "man's soul." Despite Bettelheim's analysis, much of Freud's theorizing was based on the positivistic axiom that there was a firm foundation to psychoanalysis in physiology (e.g., 1900/1942, 1915/1946). From this perspective, the problems patients bring to therapy had to do with impulses and their mental representation. What the psychoanalyst was to bring to bear on this situation was a greater knowledge of these impulses and of the person's defenses against them. The interpretation by the psychoanalyst of hidden meanings led to insight for the patient and relief from conflict. As originally formulated, insight was an addition.

Freud's understanding of hidden meanings, and his theoretical formulations of them, were so powerful that they have come to be codified and fixed. This created the problem that the meaning of symbols and dreams and symptoms could be located in a domain separate from that of the person; that is, in a theory which was granted priority over the person. Just as the theory of semantic features imposed by linguistics limits its capacity to deal with situated human speaking, a theory of psychodynamics based on biology restricts itself to a particular view of the meaning of patient utterances. In the psychoanalytic hour, such utterances are usually presumed to refer to other things. The patient's way of relating to the analyst is a re-enactment of infantile modes that have remained active but hidden in adult life. The analyst has access to the theory, which explains what the patient is "really" talking about, and he or she "imparts this information to the patient" (Fenichel, 1945, p. 25). This presumes that the analyst knows a prior sort of truth and that skill in interpretation has to do only with timing, that is, how much of the hidden material a patient will be able to deal with at any particular moment.

Freud (1937/1950) likened psychoanalysis to archaeology, unearthing fragments of an earlier time. Throughout his career he insisted the goal of psychoanalytic treatment was to make these unconscious fragments conscious. Spence (1982) has recently suggested an alternative to Freud's simile. Rather than digging up buried facts, patient and therapist construct a "narrative truth" that makes sense to both of them. It focuses on contemporary meaning, not on historical veracity. Spence's intent is to reduce the analyst's reliance on authoritative theory and its epistemological and ontological assumptions. This shift away from positivism leaves Spence feeling that there is no firm foundation for therapy and that "the impossible profession becomes even more so" (p. 294).

Giving up naive realism, as Spence suggests, does not necessarily mean lapsing into despair at any certainty of truth or seeking an Archimedean platform in religion or metaphysics. "Psychic reality" is relative only if some absolute reality is assumed. Taken as self-world, it can be known as it is. In seeking a fundamental ontology, Heidegger concluded there is certainly a world in which human being finds itself. His complete philosophy, in fact, may be seen as an attempt to describe the structure of that world. His description of human being in human terms avoids the language of energy and mechanism borrowed from early physics. It strives to reveal the individual in his or her situation and how he or she unreflectedly experiences and acts in it. It does not deny the importance of the body or of psychosexual development, but recasts them as co-constituents of the situation, not as objective facts.

Such a redescription puts human being at the center of our concerns and makes questions of value and meaning central. A new and rigorous discipline of man's soul becomes possible in which ethics are crucial; that is, how the individual structures the world of others. They are there and must be dealt in ways that cannot be described in terms of a modulated discharge of sexual energy. The touchstone for Heidegger is to be found neither in religion nor in physics, but in the concrete, everyday reality of the individual and his or her projects. Heidegger's method of approaching the problem of reality provides a valuable correction to the dangers of an inchoate relativism.

THERAPEUTIC DIALOGUE:
A HEIDEGGERIAN PERSPECTIVE

Heidegger's exploitation of the resources of the German (and occasionally Greek) language is perhaps the major reason he is so difficult to approach. No philosopher has relied so heavily on the manipulation of ordinary words to illuminate his thinking. This strategy had its origin in the topic Heidegger chose to deal with: the everyday person in the everyday world. In a waggish mood, we might say he was just answering the question, "How *are* you?" The ponderous English translations of his work lose both its everyday quality and the sense of how terms are related etymologically. For example, the central term *eigen,* meaniing one's own, is translated generally as "authentic." Now the origin of the English in the Greek *authentike* is precisely what Heidegger is after, since it means "one who does a thing himself." In modern English usage, however, authentic has come to mean real, reliable, genuine; quite a different meaning. Heidegger builds on the initial root to include the words *ereignen,* to happen, *aneignen,* to acquire. In English, his thesis that something that happens or is acquired is what one does oneself may seem paradoxical or obscure, not playfully profound as originally intended. When *aneignen* is translated "to appropriate," with its origin in the Latin *proprium,* one's own, the implication is maintained.

Dasein is thrown into a world which it must appropriate to its own projects. Human being is these projects, and the tools used for them by which it creates a self-world. This self-world reveals itself through meaningful human activity; as a matter of fact, it *is* that activity. The desk, pen, and paper which are taken up in the project of writing; the physiology necessary for sitting in the chair and holding the pen; the history that led up to being educated and wanting to write; the culture that raises questions and makes universities available to answer them: These possibilities actualize themselves in their usefulness toward the project of writing a paper on metaphor.

The world in which Dasein finds itself is a world filled with other people. Being in this world, therefore, is also a being with others, a *Mitsein*. This, too, is not an accidental attribute. The world in which Dasein makes its way is one of language and culture. Activity here reveals itself as possible ways of being with others and as the meaning of our relatedness. Fundamentally isolated, we live in a *Mitsein* through shared activity and meaning. This sharing is the construction of a self-world in which another person is protected and fostered in his or her own existence. It makes room for birth, growth and death as they are. *Mitsein* makes existence useful and satisfying and, in so doing, overcomes the possibility that the world will be experienced as *unheimlich,* un-home-like, strange, awful (Heidegger, 1954). The situation of *Mitsein* requires constant effort and is never achieved once and for all. Utter isolation is always a possibility, and with it the annihilation of being.

Human being also is its future possibility, its concerns and its projects. The most intimate, unconditional, and unavoidable possibility is death. Just as being is not exhausted as a concept by biology, so death is not simply biological cessation. It is the brute possibility of not being and utter isolation. To banish it to the future is to deny that the possibility exists now – certain but not yet set. Death is not something extra, "something stuck on," that one can think about now and then. All one's past accomplishments and future projects reveal themselves against the possibility of nonbeing. Finding oneself in this situation is *Angst*, for death is the ultimate possibility of being.

Angst often appears as anxiety, but more typically its death-like possibility is denied. There is a deliberate lack of concern about death, a refusal to consider that such a possibility exists and colors our projects. Death is held at a distance by abstraction; it is not *my* death, just death the concept. Human being falls away from its world to create a sham in which we need not face the possibility of loss of the world. Human being seeks to e free of anxiety by denying that old projects and relationships have an end.

Heidegger terms this mode of being, which is dedicated to an avoidance of possibility, *das Man*. This is an indefinite pronoun, as in *"Man sagt . . . "* ("One says . . . " or more loosely—and accurately—"it is common knowledge that . . . "). Such a project is average, undistinguished. By leveling out choice, it avoids individual involvement and responsibility, and aims at avoiding anxiety and loss. Its projects and designs are also not unique. It is not "one's own"; it is not *eigen*. *Das Man* lives entirely in public and accepts the world-view of the public. There is nothing private (or one's own) that might be shared with another, for the risk of misunderstanding or of realizing one's isolation is too great. Novelty is sought not for the purpose of establishing new relatedness, but for the purposes of distraction and entertainment. By accepting and relying on modes of relating, fixed by past history, *das Man* avoids *Angst* and thereby is certain of his or her relationships.

This inauthenticity is prior to and necessary for becoming able to appropriate through one's own activity. It is just one, very common, way in which choice and responsibility are relegated to the world. Old ways of being with others are maintained and structure new relationships with old meanings and purposes. Future possibilities are limited by what went before. One's own activity is obscured by what are experienced as external demands. There seems to be a mechanical necessity, before which one can only be passive. Forms of relationship are set and lived out as if other possibilities did not exist. They persist as "facts," for if one discovers other ways of relating, the possibility of not-being-related arises. The strategy of *das Man* is to prevent this possibility.

Initially a patient comes to a therapist seeking a solution that is already formulated, although perhaps not well articulated. In talking about the presenting problem the patient reveals the structure of his or her self-world through the choice of form and content. The therapist probes both form and content, reflecting on the dialogue as relationship. The therapist tries to see through the particulars of the patient's report to understand why the problem is presented at this time, in this manner. The patient's "architecture of themes and purposes" has brought up the problem and the prior attempts at resolving it. The therapist involves the patient in a dialogue that reveals the place of the problem in the patient's self-world. The therapist checks what is happening against his or her theory and experience, in order to understand it in a broader context, especially when things are awry.

In therapy discrepancies in how patient and therapist understand the everydayness of life is revealed. The patient sees something as necessary; the therapist sees other possibilities. The horizon of the world in which the patient is free to choose is constricted. Something in that world functions with mechanical necessity and the patient is at its mercy. Of that the patient is sure. It is the patient's particular version of *das Man*, restricting the possibilities of the situation. The restriction is also revealed in the necessity of a particular form of relatedness, i.e., the transference. The patient is alienated from the fuller humanity of the therapist, unable to see other possible ways of being with him or her. The future can only be a continuation of the past; choice and responsibility are relegated to external factors. They are experienced as fact, not possibility.

The actualization of a possibility makes it a fact. Carrying out our projects makes them real, even those which seem only necessary. The appearance of necessity is how they reveal themselves to us and how we are unable to see through their constituents to other possibilities. They are *das Man*. "Interpretation within the transference" works by reducing facticity. New possibilities of the therapeutic situation are opened up. There are historical facts, one's personal history, which comprise the structure of our self-world. They include a complex pattern of parental interaction which laid the foundation of how we are. That pattern cannot be changed now, but neither must it continue. The therapist's interpretation educates and elaborates the ways in which this pattern is transferred to new situations, thereby limiting possibilities. He or she suggests other meanings, other possibilities.

The patient takes the pattern as fact. Things must be so. The therapist does not participate in this *das Man*. He or she brings a different frame of reference and experiential world to bear on the situation. Their *Mitsein* has become incongruent and problematic. An alienation appears between them. The patient's "architecture of themes and purposes" seems strange to the therapist. As something outside his or her self-world, it is not automatically understood and requires attention. Since it is not immediately understood, and outside the pale of the general culture, it appears opaque, something more mechanical than willed. This distance permits and requires a certain objectification. The law-like abstractions of psychoanalytic theory provide such explanatory statements. They are part of the analyst's personal history, his or her Dasein, through which such phenomena emerge. His or her tentative, probabilistic interpretations necessitate (and permit) a shared understanding and a shared language. The dialogue moves forward as both participants seek to understand mutual intentions. As these intentions become transparent in the developing interaction, they cease to be alien or to function mechanically. The patient evaluates and finds meaning in his or her intentions. The old mechanical pattern is dissolved through allowing other possibilities into his or her world. The old necessity becomes a constituent of his or her own world where he or she is now a central driving force.

The reconciliation of hermeneutic phenomenology and psychoanalysis occurs in the process of interpretation. Conceived as methods, not as bodies of knowledge or theory, they are clearly commensurate. The orthodox Freudian position, that the analyst's interpretation of the patient's statements is confirmed by observing further statements, provokes the accusation that psychoanalytic theory involves a self-satisfying cycle. Without some referential "reality," it can make no claim to truth in any ordinary sense of the term.

This situation also applies to the so-called hermeneutic circle, where the problem is not how to get out of it, but how to enter and understand it properly. As such, hermeneutic analysis is an elaboration of the notion that understanding does not take place in a vacuum. New data are disclosed in the light of previous experience; interpretation becomes a process of disclosure. Hermeneutic interpretation is not an attempt to reduce a pattern to its elements, nor to translate it into other terms. It seeks to disclose the meaning of what is at hand, so as to make further events possible. It adds nothing and subtracts nothing. Through interpretation, the data become transparent and their range of possible (authentic) meanings increases. It should be obvious that this is not a convergent procedure yielding a "correct" answer. Rather than narrowing to a final result, the hermeneutic circle opens to include more and more of a being-in-the-world that is the matter at hand. The range of the pattern that is the person increases; its horizon expands to include more known and not-known areas of the field of patient and therapist. Their *Mitsein* acquires new possibilities.

METAPHOR AS MITSEIN

Therapeutic metaphor is created within a human situation, the *Mitsein* of patient and therapist. The patient discloses his or her stance toward the world, the listener, and himself or herself, presenting the metaphoric utterance for interpretation and inviting a further response. The "meaning" of the metaphor is how it contributes to the ongoing dialogue. Within fixed lexical meanings, it is the creation of something new. Any reduction to words and phrases exhausts itself in past history and/or utilitarian communication. The dialogue is created as we go, out of the matter provided by the facts of our history and a future as yet unset. The dialogue can be the appropriation of old meanings and purposes into a new style of being. The therapeutic task of the dialogue is not to explicate past history, but to free the patient from its concreteness.

Metaphor is an instance of future oriented dialogue. It is not the exchange of information about something or some idea; it is part of a world we are in the process of constructing. The proper unit of analysis is not a linguistic sign and its referent exchanged between two separate, biological organisms, but rather what they make of the situation. There is not here a process of deciphering, but of interpreting. The therapist construes possible meanings and seeks to validate them. The understanding of a particular utterance is checked against the dialogue – not seeking one true reading, but a match with multiple interpretations and intentions. Dialogue is the creation of a lived world with another, a being-together, a *Mitsein*. It is holistic in considering the participants and their context in intentions and purposes.

Striking metaphors occur within the context of therapeutic dialogue that serve to reveal and describe fundamental aspects of the patient's self-world. They are an invitation to the therapist to share in a most private and vulnerable experience. Such an invitation indicates that the history of the dialogue to that point has been good enough, that the therapist's presence is not an event to be warded off or simply coped with. Ordinary conversational norms are cleared away, so that the patient can now establish meaningful contact with another person. Such metaphors are not difficult to understand. They have an immediacy and simplicity that make them directly accessible, if the therapist is able to lay aside the need for ordinary meaning.

The process of explicating radical metaphors is neither one of decoding something strange, nor one of translating something esoteric into literal language. It occurs in applying the implicit model motivating the metaphor to concrete situations and in clarifying how these are structured like the model. As therapy proceeds, matters become simpler and simpler, for the model becomes clarified. What had been complicated by a density of external factors becomes transparent as the activity of the self in structuring its world; it is this activity that is shared with the therapist.

Long term therapy involves two people who establish a relationship with the avowed purpose of making some change in the life of one of them. The patient comes with certain ideas about what would be better. What emerges over time is that the relationship must change and that the patient's original hopes must be superseded. The therapist also does not stay the same, untouched and unmoved by the dialogue. The therapist has no privileged access to an objective reality, just the reality of his or her own self-world. Countertransference is not an error, but the themes and purposes the therapist brings to the session. The intention of patient and therapist becomes one of developing a capacity for relationship that will actualize the greatest possibility. It is a dialogue, the end to which is not foreseeable. Occasionally, therapist and patient may talk about their relationship; then their dialogue becomes the content of their dialogue. Even when they are not talking about their relationship, the relationship reveals itself. The patient's attitudes, values, and assumptions structure what he or she chooses to talk about and how it is done. An intellectual understanding is not by itself therapeutic. Therapy is a living world created by the participation of two people whose metaphoric activity is fundamental to it.

Within psychoanalytic literature, there are occasional instances of this view. For example, Shengold (1981) suggests that metaphor is a first step in the process of insight. As such, it provides the link between sensory intensity and sober reflection. It is the means by which earliest memories can be evoked containing "primal metphorical links" between body-ego and representations of an external world. Following Winnicott, he calls such experiences transitional phenomena – phenomena that relate the interior to the exterior world. Like transitional objects, they are not wholly invented nor merely found. They are invested with an intensity that can dispel "the defensive wrapping around the patient's emotions" (p. 301). This in turn leads to convictions about one's self and one's experience of prior times.

Discovering this intensity is not a cognitive process. The old analytic notion of learning about one's history is only a partial description. It is necessary, for, as Ricoeur says, "The hermeneutic of self-understanding takes the detour of causal explanation" (1981, p. 264). This detour leads to a "working through," which involves the re-establishment of a common ground for dialogue. Some of the patient's themes and purposes are not accessible to reflection. They are disavowed, repressed, split off, for there was a time when they could not be own as one's own (eigen). There was something that could not happen (ereignen) with the Mitsein shared with another. Such "unconscious" meanings are experienced as if they were external causes. Operating like natural laws, there seemed to be no other possibility to the patient.

Balint (1968) defines regression as the need for a particular form of relationship. The dialogue of regressive therapy is a search for a particular form of past relatedness within the limitations of what is now possible. What Winnicott refers to as "primary maternal preoccupation" is expected, even though the time for such relationship has passed. It is an old project which was not completed, and thus is carried forward into a time when the possibility of completion is ever more remote and unlikely. Regressive therapy gives such a relationship a chance of sorts. The patient's need for such a relationship is acknowledged in all seriousness, but any fulfillment would be a sham, for it is not now literally possible. There is a tension between old needs and future possibilities that structures the dialogue.

The experience of these old desires has a mythic power, through which the therapeutic situation is the old relationship. This experience prevents the terrifying loss of all relatedness while affirming the possibility of a different sort of relationship in the future. If the dialogue is to proceed, it must be seen that the current situation is not the old one. The patient may complain that people from whom he or she has sought help, such as doctors, lawyers, and teachers – perhaps even therapists – have always been disappointing. To the patient, this is simply the way the world works. Such helpers are disappointing. The therapist will be primed with this history and its meaning when the patient begins structuring their relationship in this way. Interpretation refers to the patient's history; when the patient is able to see it as a consequence of his or her own unfulfilled desires, it will set the stage for insight. Interpretation restores the tension between is and is *not*. Therapy proceeds insofar as the patient is able to experience both the old disappointment and a new relationship with the therapist.

Metaphor is a dialogic device that creates tension between past and future, between fact and possibility, between identity and differences. In this light, psychoanalysis is indeed "essentially a metaphorical enterprise." Interpretation does not resolve the tension, but carries it forward. The mythic comes into contact with the possibilities of being with another person. The relationship is enlivened by the mythic, and acquires a liveliness that is different from a discussion of day-to-day problems. The consulting room becomes a *Tummelplatz*, a place to romp (Freud, 1946/1914) and the participants playmates. There are scuffles, disruptions, and unmet demands, but also mutual devotion. The business of being together becomes easy, and the novelty of that which is encapsulated in metaphor becomes shared language.

The process of opening up and clearing away, this "working through," is the necessary event in time. It will have a content, involving old events and relationships, but this knowledge is a means and not an end. The patient presents aspects of a self-world that have been alienated and now function as necessity. The therapist brings a different understanding to bear, and together they arrive at a new meaningfulness. Because the patient is now related to the therapist, becoming disconnected does not threaten and old projects can be given up. The patient acquires an ability to deal with situations as possibilities, not as concrete, oppressive realities. The constraints of what is of concern, and how to take care of it, are reduced. The self-world becomes transparent and the events of this world become more useful and more human.

The metaphors "which do the work" may be seen as instances of a future oriented, interpersonal process, whose vital quality is not located in individual words or phrases, but in on-going dialogue. We should expect a small number of "radical" metaphors (perhaps only one) to organize and serve as the focus for long periods of therapy. Such metaphors are elusive as an object of study, for the unit of analysis must become the entire therapy itself. Future empirical work will have to take this into account. Radical metaphors will be novel, but not always as judged by observers outside the dialogue. Their novelty lies in the possibility of expanding and developing their meaning as dialogue proceeds. They are radical in that they concern the self's most intimate and powerful projects, giving expression to wide areas of significant experience and sharing these with another person. The dialogue expands through the possibilities created both by being with another person and by that unique agency of language known as metaphor.

REFERENCES

Amira, S. A. (1982). Figurative language and metaphor in successful and unsuccessful psychotherapy (Doctoral dissertation, Vanderbilt University, 1982). *Dissertation Abstracts International, 43,* 1244B.

Anderson, C. C. (1964). The psychology of metaphor. *Journal of Genetic Psychology, 105,* 53–73.

Arlow, J. A. (1979). Metaphor and the psychoanalytic situation. *Psychoanalytic Quarterly, 48,* 363–385.

Balint, M. (1968). *The basic fault: Therapeutic aspects of regression.* London: Tavistock.

Barlow, J. M., Jr. (1973). Metaphor and insight in psychotherapy. (Doctoral dissertation, University of Tennessee, Knoxville, 1973). *Dissertation Abstracts International, 34,* 1268B.

Bettelheim, B. (1983). *Freud and man's soul.* New York: Knopf.

Black, M. (1962). *Models and metaphors: Studies in language and philosophy.* Ithaca, NY: Cornell University Press.

Black, M. (1979). More about metaphor. In A. Ortony (Ed.), *Metaphor and thought* (pp. 19–45). Cambridge, England: Cambridge University Press.

Chomsky, N. (1957). *Syntactic structures.* The Hague. The Netherlands: Mouton.

Ekstein, R., & Caruth, E. (1966). Interpretation within the metaphor: Further considerations. In R. Ekstein (Ed.), *Children of time and space, of action and impulse: Clinical studies on the psychoanalytic treatment of severely disturbed children.* New York: Appleton-Century-Crofts.

Fenichel, O. (1945). *The psychoanalytic theory of neurosis.* New York: Norton.

Freud, S (1942). *Die Traumdeutung* [The interpretation of dreams]. In *Gesammelte Werke* [Collected works] (Vol. ⅔). London: Imago. (Original work published 1900)

Freud, S. (1946). Erinnern, Wiederholen, Durcharbeiten [Remembering, repeating, working through]. In *Gesammelte Werke* [Collected works] (Vol. 10, pp. 126–233). London: Imago. (Original work published 1914)

Freud, S. (1946). Triebe und Triebeschicksale [Instincts and their vicissitudes]. In *Gesammelte Werke* [Collected works] (Vol. 10, pp. 210–233). London: Imago. (original work published 1915)

Freud, S. (1940). "Psychoanalyse" ["Psychoanalysis"]. In *Gesammelte Werke* [Collected works] (Vol. 13, pp. 211–233). London: Imago. (Original work published 1923)

Freud, S. (1950). Konstruktion in der Analyse [Construction in analysis]. In *Gesammelte Werke* [Collected works] (Vol. 16, pp. 41–57). London: Imago. (Original work published 1937)

Heidegger, M. (1979). *Sein und Zeit* [Being and time]. Tubingen, Germany: Niemeyer. (Original work published 1927)

Heidegger, M. (1954). Bauen Wohnen Denken [Building Dwelling Thinking]. In *Vortrage und Aufsatze: Teil II* [Lectures and essays: Part II]. Pfullingen, Germany: Neske.

Katz, J. J. (1972). *Semantic theory.* New York: Harper and Row.

Ortony, A. (Ed.). (1979). *Metaphor and thought.* Cambridge, England: Cambridge University Press.

Pollio, H. R. (1982). *Behavior and existence: An introduction to empirical humanistic psychology.* Monterey, CA: Brooks/Cole.

Pollio, H. R., & Barlow, J. M. (1975). A behavioral analysis of figurative language in psychotherapy: One session in a single case study. *Language and Speech, 18,* 236–254.

Pollio, H. R., Barlow, J. M., Fine, H. J., & Pollio, M. (1977). *Psychology and the poetics of growth: Figurative language in psychology, psychotherapy, and education.* Hillsdale, NJ: Erlbaum.

Pollio, H. R., & Burns, B. C. (1977). The anomaly of anomaly. *Journal of Psycholinguistic Research, 6,* 247–260.

Pollio, H. R., & Smith, M. K. (1979). Sense and nonsense in thinking about anomaly and metaphor. *Bulletin of the Psychonomic Society, 13,* 323–326.

Ricoeur, P. (1977). *The rule of metaphor: Multi-disciplinary studies of the creation of meaning in language* (R. Czerny, Trans.). Toronto: University of Toronto Press.

Ricoeur, P. (1981). *Hermeneutics and the human sciences: Essays on language, action, and interpretation* (J. B. Thompson, Ed. and Trans.). Cambridge, England: Cambridge University Press.

Sharpe, E. F. (1940). Psychophysiological problems revealed in language: An examination of metaphor. *International Journal of Psychoanalysis, 21,* 201–213.

Shengold, L. (1981). Insight as metaphor. *Psychoanalytic Study of the Child, 36,* 289–306.

Spence, D. P. (1982). *Narrative truth and historical truth: Meaning and interpretation in psychoanalysis.* New York: Norton.

Steinberg, D. D. (1979). Analycity, amphigory, and semantic interpretation of sentences. *Journal of Verbal Learning and Verbal Behavior, 9,* 37–51.

Sternberg, R. J., Tourangeau, R., & Nigro, G. (1979). Metaphor, induction and social policy: The convergence of macroscopic and microscopic views. In A. Ortony (Ed.), *Metaphor and thought.* Cambridge, England: Cambridge University Press.

Strupp, H. H., & Hadley, S. W. (1977). A tripartite model of mental health and therapeutic outcomes: With special reference to negative effects in psychotherapy. *American Psychologist, 32,* 187–196.

Voth, H. M. (1970). The analysis of metaphor. *Journal of the American Psychoanalytic Association, 18,* 599–621.

CHAPTER TWELVE

Metaphor and Historical Consciousness: Organicism and Mechanism in the Study of Social Change

Richard Harvey Brown

"Man" as a biological entity preceded "humans" as cultural being. The chief difference between biological being and being human is the capacity to construct meaning through language. Scientific knowledge is one such system of meaning and, like religion, art, kinship, fashion, or law, it too is constructed through language. And language is through and through metaphoric. Tropes are not merely a stylistic adornment of plain speech or scientific discourse. In addition to this illustrative or ornamental function, tropes are the symbolic materials of discourse itself.

Every human group has some notion of its origins, nature, and destiny, usually expressed through rite, myth, and theological doctrine. For modern societies, these questions tend to be cast in secular, often scientific, language. In particular, the study of our origins as a people is articulated in what is called historiography or historical science, as well as related discourses such as archaeology, paleology, or historical sociology.

My contention is this essay is that such discourse is metaphorical. Following Gambattista Vico (1972), Kenneth Burke (1959, 1969), and Hayden White (1973, 1978a, 1978b), I suggest that historical (or any other symbolic construction) is ineliminably mediated by root metaphors through which we make experience (or the "historical record") comprehensible or, more strongly, through which we *have* experience of history. Historical consciousness, in sum, is metaphoric.

In developing this position I first establish the cognitive status of metaphor. To say that the natural or human sciences are metaphoric is not to devalue their cognitive power, but rather to reveal their basis in language. Understanding science as metaphoric undercuts the claims of positive science to be an absolutely privileged discourse, but at the same time it provides grounds for the relative privilege of discourses in their own domains by showing how these domains are themselves construed linguistically.

Given the cognitive status of metaphor, I then show how historical science construes its domain mainly either as an organism or as a machine. Though long standing controversies have made the study of social change a maze of changing theories, two well-tread paths have been marked in this labyrinth: functional evolutionism and experimental empiricism. The evolutionists take their cues from Aristotle and conceive of change as slow, orderly, continuous, and teleological. Societies are viewed as social organisms whose internal developments follow the pattern dictated by an immanent nature. Endogenous and historical changes harmonize to produce progressive movement and entelechy. In contrast, the empiricists, asserting that any theory of change must derive from a close empirical investigation of the thing changing, oppose any a priori assumptions about the nature, direction, form, rate, and outcome of change, and reject what they deem to be metaphorical models. Yet they too invoke a metaphor – the world as a machine – for their redescription from the organismic model.

THE COGNITIVE STATUS OF METAPHORS

The question of the cognitive status of metaphors tends to appear whenever philosophers discuss the fundamental questions of similarity, identity, and difference. This is not only because metaphors are employed in every realm of knowledge; it is also because metaphors are our principal instruments for integrating diverse phenomena and viewpoints without destroying their differences.

Despite its apparent centrality, however, until modern times metaphor was not acknowledged to have an explicitly cognitive function. Aristotle, for example, divided the uses of speech into three categories: logic, poetic, and rhetoric. Given this division – and the assumption behind it that language plays no part in creating that which it describes – metaphor may be used to illustrate a point or sway a crowd or as an ornament of poetic style. Yet, as he put it, "All such arts are fanciful and meant to charm the hearer. Nobody uses fine language when teaching geometry" (Aristotle, 1967, Rhetoric, III, p. 1404a). This view of metaphor prevailed for many centuries. Indeed, under the joint influence of plain-speaking Protestants and early positive scientists, the function of metaphor – along with "fine language" in general – was further demoted.

Beginning with Vico, however, this traditional view has been challenged by philosophers such as Nietzsche (1960), Coleridge (1956), Croce (1955), and Goodman (1970). Instead of seeing metaphor as an embroidery of the facts, such thinkers viewed it as a way of *experiencing* facts, and by making them objects of experience, giving life or reality to them. In their view, poetic imagination stretches the mind *and* reality, the word *and* the thing, through metaphor. By revealing the concrete physiognomy of the experienced world, metaphor was thought to historically or logically precede the concretized meanings of literal or scientific discourse. Still, by stressing the emotional and precognitive nature of poetic revelation, the romantics reinforced the traditional dichotomy between metaphor and scientific thought. Moreover, by so energetically distancing themselves from scientists, they placed themselves in the company of schizophrenics, aphasiacs, and children whose utterances, by the romantics' own criteria, could not be distinguished from poetic metaphor (Wheelright, 1962, 1968).

Another view of metaphor is the cognitive aesthetic (Brown, 1977) or more commonly, the tension theory. Borrowing the romantics' insight that creative thought is metaphoric, this view extends the idea of metaphor as a logic of discovery to include science as well as art. Moreover, it distinguishes creative activity in both these fields from the normal science or art that goes on in each. Such a theory has profound implications for the philosophy of science and for logic of method in the human studies, for it suggests that both the deductive and the inductive models of scientific explanation be reformulated by the view that formal representations—whether in science or in art—be understood as a metaphoric redescription (or creation) of the domain of the explanandum (see Berggren, 1962, 1963; Black, 1962; Brooks, 1965; Haskell, 1968; Hesse, 1970; McCloskey, 1964; MacCormac, 1976; Ricoeur, 1972; Schon, 1963; and Turbayne, 1962).

Metaphor is just as vital to natural science as it is to poetry. In science, however, the referents are of very special sorts: the analogy is between a purely formal (ideally, mathematical) theory or model, and some empirically visualizable phenomenon (ideally, observable through controlled and calibrated methods). But even this difference fades when we speak of the "root metaphors" or paradigms of science. For here metaphors serve to define the boundaries of a given domain of discourse, and to set limits for subtheories that can with consistency be extrapolated within it. For example, Aristotle's paradigm of motion was rest, a balance between force and resistance, whereas for Galileo uniform motion was just as natural as rest. But for Newton, a body's motion was to be taken for granted only when it moved at uniform speed in a Euclidean straight line, free from all forces,including its own weight. Consequently, given their different foundational assumptions about the nature of motion, Newton had to introduce the theory of gravity to explain why, in the absence of resistance, an imaginary ship would not sail off into space along a Euclidean straight line. But, on the basis of different root metaphors, "Galileo would have considered the circular motion of such a ship around the earth entirely natural and self-explanatory, while Aristotle would have denounced the entire idea" (Berggren, 1963, p. 461; Toulmin, 1961, p. 79).

Historical sociology, like science and the arts, also must re-present its world with metaphors. Social and historical scientists, however, have not understood scientific theorizing to be metaphoric and, hence, they generally have felt compelled to choose between a literalistic, reductive scientific positivism on the one hand, or a vaporized conception of creative intuition on the other. Yet, as I have tried to show, this forced choice is based on erroneous assumptions about the natures of scientific and artistic knowledge. The choice for historians and sociologists is not between scientific rigor as against poetic insight. The choice is rather between more or less fruitful metaphors, and between using metaphors or being their victims.

All this is especially true of root metaphors—those sets of assumptions, usually implicit, about what sorts of things make up the world, how they act, how they hang together and, usually by implication, how they may be known. As such, root metaphors constitute the ultimate presuppositions or frame of reference for discourse on the world or on any domain within it. Thomas Kuhn (1970) used the term "paradigm" to describe such ultimate frames and to distinguish between the normal science that is conducted within them and the scientific revolutions by which they are changed. Max Black (1962) spoke of "conceptual archetypes" in a similar connection (p. 241); Paul Diesing (1971) used the term "implicit ontology" (p. 124). Other closely related concepts include "*weltanschauung*" (Dilthey, 1962), "*habitus mentalis*" (Panofsky, 1955), "*eidos*" (Bateson, 1941), "philosophy" or "world view" (Krasnow & Merikallio, 1964), "dominant ontology" (Feibleman, 1956), "myth" (Bruyn, 1966), "domain assumptions" (Gouldner, 1970), "controlling assumptions" (Randall & Haines, 1946), "institutional epistemology" (McHugh, 1970), and "metaphysics" (Douglas, 1971; Burtt, 1954).

Root metaphors differ from models or illustrative metaphors in two ways. First, they are characteristically below the level of conscious awareness. If ordinary speech is made of frozen metaphors, root metaphors are akin to frozen models—they are a kind of submerged or implicit model underlying the writer's thought (Black, 1962). Unlike models, however, root metaphors are comprehensive. They are, in a sense, the implicit metamodels in terms of which narrower range models are couched. We might say that root metaphors describe worlds, whereas models describe the contents of those worlds. Because of this, root metaphors can only be iconic: For their users, they *are* the world and contain everything in it; hence they cannot be analogically compared to anything else.

Two such metaphors in the study of history are the organism and the machine, as expressed respectively by two principal schools of historical sociology—evolutionary functionalism and experimental empricism.

HISTORY AS ORGANISM:
FUNCTIONIST EVOLUTIONISM AND THE EMPIRICIST CRITQUE

"The world," according to evolutionists, "embraces in its constitution all that it is destined to experience actively or passively from its beginning right on to its end; it resembles a human being, all of whose capacities are wrapped up in the

embryo before birth" (Seneca, 1910, sec. 29). "The education of the human race
. . . has advanced, like that of an individual, through certain epochs or, as it were,
ages, so that it might gradually rise from earthly to heavenly things, and from the
visible to the invisible" (St. Augustine, 1881). "Our science therefore comes to describe at the same time an ideal eternal history traversed in time by the history of
every nation in its rise, development, maturity, decline, and fall" (Vico, 1972).
"New, higher relations of production never appear before the material conditions
of their existence have matured in the womb of the old society" (Marx, 1946).
Cultures are organisms, and world history is their collective biography. Every Culture passes through the age phases of the individual man. Each has its childhood,
youth, manhood, and old age" (Spengler, 1928). "The thesis [of evolutionists, ac-
cordingly] is that the savage state in some measure represents an early condition
of mankind, out of which the higher culture has gradually developed or evolved,
by processes still in regular operation as of old" (Tylor, 1878, pp. 3–4).

On these assumptions, it follows that "Everytime we undertake to explain
something human, taken at a given moment in history – be it a religious belief, a
moral precept, a legal principle, an aesthetic style, or an economic system – it is
necessary to go back to its most primitive and simple form, to try to account for
the characterization by which it was marked at that time, and then to show how
it developed and became complicated little by little, and how it became that
which it is at the moment in question" (Durkheim, 1965). Thus, "If one goes
back to a primitive society, one finds the beginnings of the evolution of what we
call institutions. Now these institutions are, after all, the habits of individuals . . .
handed down from one generation to another. And we can study the growth of
these habits as we can study the growth and behavior of an animal" (Mead, 1956,
p. 23). "An evolutionary universal, then, is a complex of structures and associated
processes the development of which increases the long-run adaptive capacity of
living systems in a given class. This criterion is derived from the famous principle
of natural selection" (Parsons, 1966). Similarly, "a world system . . . has the characteristics of an organism, in that it has a life-span . . . , that life within it is largely
self-contained, and that the dynamics of development . . . .through stages . . . are
largely internal" (Wallerstein, 1974, pp. 5–7, 353–4).

Through spanning many centuries and ideological points of view, these
statements express the same basic notion that society is, or is like, an organism.
This organic image of society is deeply rooted in Western consciousness. Indeed,
so widespread is the biological metaphor that scholars often fail to recognize it as
the central presupposition of their own social thought. In the dominant,
functionalist, version of evolutionism, society is compared to an individual biological entity. However, in social Darwinist and Marxian conflict theories, the
comparison is not to the single organism but to the biological species; here the imagery is one of competition between individuals or classes, and survival or dominance of the stronger. To define the essential features of the biological metaphor,
however, it will be useful to examine its original Aristotelian formulation, where
it is presented didactically and explicitly. Indeed, the evolutionary and the

homeostatic aspects of functionalist theory seem to be a congeries only because their root in organismic thought is not specified. Once it is made explicit, as in the writings of Aristotle, then these two different aspects of functionalism can be seen as alternative elaborations of the same biological metaphor. In this procedure I will be using an evolutionary approach to the history of ideas in order to prepare for a critique of the idea of evolutionism itself.

Aristotle could see two poles in previous Greek speculation: change, becoming, or cause was stressed by Ionian nature philosophers such as Thales and Anximander; permanence, being, or form was central for Plato. Aristotle unified these notions in his concept of form *as* cause. The material cause of the atomists is incapable of explaining the *why* of becoming, he said, for it lacks that which the concept of becoming itself makes intelligible – the unity of the thing that it welds into a whole. Those who see reality only in form, however, cannot explain how this reality came to be, and so treat the form as eternal and everything else as illusion, and hence tell us nothing of the world. Thus for Aristotle genuine wholeness must be the product of becoming, but at the same time it cannot be the mere mechanical aggregation of parts. Instead, a true whole (that is, a universal species or class, or any society, period, or unit of scientific analysis), emerges only where all parts are dominated by a single purpose and strive to realized it.

> Natural things are exactly those things which do move continuously, in virtue of the principle inherent in themselves, towards a determined goal; and the final development which results from any one such principle is not identical for any two species, nor yet is it any random result; but in each there is always a tendency towards an identical result if nothing interferes. (Aristotle, 1967, *Physics,* II, p. viii)

Aristotle also asserted that if "natural things are exactly those things which things which do move continuously," then "unnatural" things must be those which do not. The natural and the unnatural are thereby distinguished by the criterion of regularity of occurrence and, indeed, Aristotle insisted that this distinction be made *before* a scientific investigation of a thing could be undertaken:

> It is obvious why there is no science of [the unnatural or accidental] for all science is of that which is always or for the most part, but the accidental is in neither of these two classes. (Aristotle, 1967, *Metaphysics,* XI, p. viii)

This way of thinking was then applied to politics and society. Men and women unite "because of natural instinct to leave behind one of their own kind, and of the desire for self-sufficiency." From this self-generated union comes families, clans, *gens* and *phrates,* which unite to form villages and city-states. The city-states is thus the end of a natural, regular teleological evolution. It is a species, a good, the fulfillment of man's nature as a political animal (Aristotle, 1967, *Politics,* I, p. ii). Not all peoples have reached this state of self-realization, it is true. But Aristotle's theory is concerned with the "natural" process of development, not with "accidents" or "monstrosities." Not all acorns become oaks. In each particular case this depends on local conditions of soil, climate, and so on. It is for just this reason that to understand oaks or anything else as a general class or species, science must focus on their ideal development, that is, what they become "if nothing interferes." Thus there are some things that simply are not suited for scientific investigation (specific historical events, for example), and even with proper scientific subjects (such as the *polis*), any occurrence that cannot be associated with the unfolding of that thing's telic potential must be treated as an "accident" and excluded from scientific study.

We now may sum up the main components of the biological metaphor as it derives from Aristotle:

- Natural things, the proper subjects for science, are those that change according to the law of their nature or telos, as opposed to those that happen by chance, which is outside the realm of science.
- Even in the development of natural things, there can occur accidental events; these also lie outside the scientific study of that thing.
- Change is natural, regular, continuous, purposive, directional, necessary, and self generated. *Naturae non facit saltum*: nature does not make leaps.
- Differences between examples of the same natural class of things can be explained in terms of their being in different phases of the same evolutionary pattern. That is, the more "primitive" examples have either started later or have been arrested in their development by some impediment. Hence, contemporary "primitive" societies reveal what contemporary "advanced" societies were like at an earlier stage of growth.

Students of historical sociology and the history of ideas have shown this biological metaphor to be a fundamental assumption underlying the vast majority of Western social thought. Boas (1896) and Maitland (1911) in the late nineteenth century, Teggart (1916, 1939, 1941) and Hodgen (1936, 1952, 1964) in the early twentieth, and Robert Nisbet (1969) and Kenneth Bock (1956, 1963, 1978) today, all have been critics of those thinkers—from Plato to Parsons—who have made use of the organic metaphor. Their experimental empiricist critique is as follows: The dualism between "natural processes" and "accidents" has led to the search for causes or processes of change outside of specific historical events. By naming the subject matter "natural" before investigating it, "laws of development" are invoked to determine which aspects of the phenomenon should properly be considered part of its development, and which, being "accidents," should not. This has led to the habits of dismissing inconvenient data as irrelevant and of using the assumption of biological growth as a classification system for those data that happen to fit. Rather than seeking regularities by comparing discrete things or events, Aristotelian laws of development are established a priori. They are not demonstrated inductively from data; instead, they become the principle for selecting the very data they presume to explain. This is a tautology in the formal sense, in that the thing to be explained (society) and the thing that is supposed to explain it (society's coming to be) are both known by the same indicator (the "nature" of society). Hence, though the "Aristotelian fallacy" resonates well with the teleological method of common sense, it is unacceptable as modern empirical science. By contaminating their independent and dependent variables, the evolutionists have rendered their theses untestable.

Why are these issues important today? Have not the procedures of Aristotelian evolutionists like Comte and Spencer been "thoroughly discredited," as Howard Becker (1940) put it, and hence may they not "be dismissed without further ado?" (p. 525). Could it not be said that even "by 1920 evolutionism in the social sciences was completely defunct?" (Murdock, 1949, p. xiii). The answer to these questions, say empiricists such as Teggart, Bock, or Nisbet, is a resounding No. Indeed, they suggest that much social thought continues to commit the same Australian primitive to American modern (see Nisbet, 1969, p. 263).

In Parsons' theory of historical change, then, certain characteristic functions are seen as inherent in the "nature" of society, that is, as part of its essential defini-Greek and Christian scholars, and of the eighteenth century "moderns" and nineteenth century champions of progress, Parsons suggests that "human society" has generally passed through the stages of "primitive, intermediate, and modern." This is not merely a logical taxonomy, any more than it was for Spencer and Comte. On the contrary, the logical series is identified with "socio-cultural evolution" that, "like organic evolution, has proceeded by variation and differentiation from simple to progressively more complex forms." This is to be a universal history of "total society," the key explanatory concept in which is the "evolutionary universal . . . a criterion derived from the famous principle of natural selection." The particular histories of specific peoples are, by implication, either to be ignored or slotted into the logico-temporal scale of development from Australian primitive to American modern (see Nisbet, 1969, p. 263).

In Parsons's theory of historical change, then, certain characteristic functions are seen as inherent in the "nature" of society, that is, as part of its essential definition as a class. Hence these functions tend to be elevated to a status ontologically superior to that of the specific actions within specific societies that they are intended to explain. The a priori assumption about the nature and evolution or homeostasis of society or system is used as the principle for selecting data to support this assumption, and should exceptions be found to the "natural" development or stability, these can be dismissed as "mutations," "accidents" or "chance historical events," rather than being examined as possible disproofs of the posited order. Given such an approach, the task becomes that of finding those characteristics from which a posited state of equilibrium or change can be deduced. The "findings," as Kenneth Bock (1963) put it, are "then presented as an analytic statement of what *must* happen rather than a merely empirical generalization of what *did* happen" (p. 236).

Having criticized the evolutionists, empiricists then advanced an approach of their own (and tried sometimes to demonstrate it, as in Teggert's (1939) *Rome and China* or Hodgen's (1964) *Early Anthropology*). This mode of explanation assumes that change occurs when a critical event takes place outside the thing to be explained. Such an event may come from another society (e.g., trade with China changed the Roman Empire). Within a single, hermetic society, however (e.g., Japan in the eighteenth century), the event will be found in one institutional area that causes change in another. Thus, in asserting a commitment to experimentalist methods of controlled comparative observation and verification, the empiricists reject the functionalist assumptions of telic rationality in social order, and of "functions" that explain institutional or social systemic "evolution." Instead, they insist that all explanatory concepts be operationalized so as to refer to specific historical events, that all events to be explained be included in the analysis, and that all concepts and events be described in logical and temporal sequence. When events occur outside the predicted sequences, rather than dismissing them as "deviant cases" or "accidents," instead the investigator must accept them as falsifying evidence, and either abandon or modify her original hypothesis (see Bock, 1963, p. 237; Gellner, 1965).

HISTORY AS MECHANISM:
EXPERIMENTAL EMPIRICISM AND ITS LIMITS

The first great crack in the organic metaphor came in the sixteenth and seventeenth centuries with the work of Galileo, Newton, Bacon, and Descartes. Life went out of nature. Physical imagery began to replace that of the organism. Nature, and soon history, man, and society, were seen as a machine. One of the first explicit transfers of mechanical thinking to the human realm is found in Hobbes' *Leviathan* (1957):

> For seeing life is but a motion of limbs, the beginning whereof is in some principal part within; why may we not say, that all *automata* (engines that move by springs and wheels as doth a watch) have artificial life? For what is the *heart* but a spring; and the *nerves,* but so many strings; and the *joints*, but so many wheels, giving motion to the whole body, such as was intended by the artificer. (p. 5)

This tradition was continued in philosophical radicalism, which Bentham defined "as nothing but an attempt to apply the principles of Newton to the affairs of politics and morals" (quoted by Matson, 1966, p. 18). Such ideas were so widespread that they even found expression in the works of such dialectical thinkers as Marx and Freud. Invoking the model of physics, Marx (1946) claimed to represent "the economic law of motion of modern society" as a natural law (pp. 16–17). Equally striking is Freud's (1954) early "Project for a Scientific Psychology," the goal of which was "to furnish us with a psychology which shall be a natural science . . . to present psychical processes as quantitatively determined states of specifiable material particles and so to make them plain and void of contradiction" (p. 355). Whereas neo-Marxists and neo-Freudians have revised these early mechanistic metaphors, they persist with little change in the forms of orthodox Marxism, statistical sociology and behaviorist psychology.

The metaphor of mechanism eventually penetrated into the study of history, which in the nineteenth century had still been closer to literature than to science. Peter Gay (1974, p. 210) expressed this shift in his comments on "style" in historical scholarship:

> This pressure toward objectivity is realistic because the objects of the historian's inquiry are precisely that, objects, out there in a real and single past. Historical controversy in no way compromises their ontological integrity. The tree in the woods of the past fell in only one way, no matter how fragmentary or contradictory the reports of its fall, no matter whether there are historians, one historian, or several contentious historians in its future to record and debate it. (p. 210)

Historical sociologists are even more forceful in seeking to assimilate historical understanding to causal analysis on the model of mechanics. "The most important phase of historical work," said Weber (1949), "namely, establishment of the causal regress, attains validity only when in the event of challenge it is able to pass the test of the use of the category of objective possibility, which entails the isolation and generalization of the causal individual components." (p. 176). The "ultimate objective" of such an approach, declared Theda Skocpol (1979) "is, of course, the actual illumination of causal regularities across sets of historical cases" (p. 39). A similar position is asserted by Perry Anderson (1974):

> The premise of this work is that there is no plumb-line between necessity and contingency in historical explanation . . . . There is merely that which is known—established by historical research—and that which is not known: the latter may be either the mechanism of single events or the laws of motion of whole structures. Both are equally amenable, in principle, to adequate knowledge of their causality . . . [to] rational and controllable theory in the domain of history. (p. 8)

This conception of history—as a nomothetic theoretical enterprise seeking causal laws explaining objective facts—is legitimated by contemporary positivist philosophy. The mechanistic metaphor at the root of this approach is defended by logicians' analysis of the Aristotelian tautology, by Hempel's (1945, 1959) discussion of covering laws, and by Ryle's (1954) demonstration that, to be a cause, a thing must be an event and not a process of a law. Other philosophic developments, however—namely those related to structuralism and phenomenology but also including critical and pragmatic philosophy of science—have encouraged criticism of the mechanists' formulation. The focus of such criticism is on the questions, What is an event? What is our unit of study and how can we know it?

Common to all the empiricists is the belief that a properly conducted science of history requires the controlled comparative analysis of observable events. Yet a principal problem of this position, a problem that few of its practitioners have acknowledged, is the assumption that events and their inter-relationships are unambiguously available for inspection. This central weakness invites a critical examination of the term "event." Once skepticism arises about the warrant for ordering various happenings under the concept "event," then the entire method of logic and the empiricists is called into question.

A central aspect of the problem of conceptualizing the event is that of establishing boundaries. In what sense does an event refer to a phenomenon bounded in space and in time? Positivistic historians typically have treated events as if they were equally and mutually available to all who examine "the historical record." But how is this historical record to be interpreted, or even known to be an "historical record" in the first place? How can happenings be properly conceptionalized as "events"? When does an event begin, and where does it end?

In addition to these difficulties in delineating events out of historical happenings, there is a further paradox in the experimental empiricist position: the assumption that *explanations* of events are constituted of "If X, then Y" statements, "causes" preceding "effects." That is, one set of events is explained as having been caused by another, prior, set of events insofar as both sets of events are instances of a more universal "covering law." Hence, questions arise concerning the nature of causal relationship. What we see then is the potential for a two pronged attack on empirisist historicism. One prong pierces the assumption of an accessible fact world what can be unproblematically conceptualized as events. The other punctuates the assumption that these events can be accounted for by machine-like causal relations.

This attack is as follows: The naturalistic fact-world is not in itself a finding of science; instead it is a presupposition or assertion about the nature of Being in general. As such, it is a metaphysical proposition and, hence, its cognitive authority depends on its philosophic justification. It is true that positive science gives procedures for deducing logical relations between concepts (the "events"). Yet, as the logical positivists themselves discovered, these procedures offer no help in knowing the relationship between the conceptual categories and the "contents" to which they were purported to refer (the "happenings"). Moreover, because this approach is based in the metaphor of the machine, it entirely omits intentionality, which for many scholars is central to historical action and historicist explanation.

The usual method by which empiricists deal with such difficulties is to describe the so-called logic-meaningful nature both of the events themselves and of their causal relationships. Yet, to the extent that empiricists invoke or presuppose the logico-meaningful form of accounting, they themselves are guilty of the very use of mentalisms and tautologies of which they have accused evolutionists. This difficulty appears to be ineliminable, if only because of the logical and practical impossibility of either a science of the total event or an apodictic basis for defining which aspects of events are relevant. As Simmel (1977) said, "A science of the total event is not only impossible for reasons of unmanageable quantity. It is also impossible because it would lack a *point of view* or *problematic*. Such a problematic is necessary in order to produce a construct that would satisfy our criteria for knowledge. A science of the total event would lack the category that is necessary for the identification and coherence of the elements of the event" (p. 82). This suggests that the telos for organizing happenings into events must be the cognitive purpose of historical scholars. Such cognitive purposes are implicit in the root metaphors through which they craft their accounts.

ROOT METAPHORS AND HISTORICAL FIGURATION

It should be clear that my purpose in undressing the organismic and mechanistic metaphors is not to embarrass metaphoric thinking but to reveal the figurative aspect of historical science. And once it is understood that these *are* metaphors, their relative adequacy in light of other metaphors may be more clearly seen. Mechanism is a good place from which to see the tautological nature of much biologistic thinking. Conversely, the biological metaphor is more able to deal with immanent factors, intentionality, and systems transformations than is mechanism. Similarly, features peculiar to both these metaphors can be limned by light from other metaphoric perspectives.

Such a critical self-consciousness is illustrated by George Kubler's (1962) reflections on appropriate root metaphors for the history of art:

> The biological model was not the most appropriate one for a history of things. Perhaps a system of metaphors drawn from physical science would have clothed the situation of art more adequately…, especially if we are dealing in art with the transmission of some kind of energy; with impulses, generating centers and relay-points; with increments and losses in transit; with resistances and transformers in the circuit. In short, the language of electrodynamics might have suited us better than the language of botany; and Michael Faraday might have been a better mentor than Linnaeus for the study of material culture. (p. 9)

Numerous philosophers have argued that such ordering schema are a prerequisite to any rational thought or, indeed to the making sense of perception itself (Kant, 1949; Hoffman & Honeck, 1981; *Journal of Mind and Behavior*, 1982). In this sense, root metaphors are frameworks for interpreting meaning within which sensa become facts, facts become concepts, and concepts become discourse. This metaphoric basis of thought was discerned by Nietzsche (1960), and it was noted again by Morris Abrams (1953):

Any area for investigation, so long as it lacks prior concepts to give it structure and express terminology with which it can be managed, appears to the inquiring mind inchoate – either a blank, or an elusive and tantalizing confusion. Our usual recourse is, more or less deliberately, to cast about for objects which offer parallels to dimly sensed aspects of the new situation, to use the better known to elucidate the less known, to discuss the intangible in terms of the tangible. (p. 31)

In *World Hypotheses,* Stephan Pepper (1942) suggested how the formation of root metaphors might take place:

The method in principle seems to be this: A man desiring to understand the world looks about for a clue to its comprehension. He pitches upon some area of common-sense fact and tries if he cannot understand other areas in terms of this one. The original area becomes then his basic analogy or root metaphor. He describes as best he can the characteristics of his area, or, if you will, discriminates its structure. A list of its structural characteristics becomes his basic concepts of explanation and description. (p. 91)

For example, the *organicist* approach reconstructs and integrates selected elements of its field into components of a synthetic process. Actions or events are "explained" to the extent that they can be ordered around some common telos that defines the nature and purpose of each particular element. The logic here involves the establishment of a hierarchy of reality or meaning organized around a superordinate telos. The evolutionary approach in historical science is an instance of such organist thinking in that it posits – evolutionists would say "discovers" – a "stage" of "development" that has been or will be arrived at in or by history. This schema is then used to determine what will be considered a part of "History" and what will be its significance. It is in terms of the evolutionary whole, in other words, that the historical parts are constituted and comprehended.

By contrast, the metaphysics of the *mechanism* is clearly expressed in early modern philosophy of science: It is reductive, naturalistic, and nominalistic. Analysis rather than synthesis, reduction to primary elements rather than elevation to a transcedent telos, is its style. It is as though the organistic view had been turned on its head; in place of the parts being instances of the whole, as the parts of the body take their essence from their function in a larger system, the whole is seen as an instance of the parts, much as a machine exists as such because of the aggregative causal actions of the elements within it.

Modern linguistics at least since Jakobson, and perhaps since Vico two hundred years before, subsumes prose discourse and poetic texts under a general theory of figuration. Through stylistic analysis, we come to see familiar prosaic dimensions of poetic texts as well as the poetic dimensions of prosaic expressions. This confluence of poetry and prose also allows us to link more generally the languages of art and the languages of science. Both artistic as well as scientific inquiry require some protocol of discourse in terms of which their experiments become meaningful. Because they are themselves linguistic creations, however no such protocol can claim with consistency an absolute hegemony over the others. This catholicity rejects the claim that there is a single correct version of what happened in history or how or why. Instead, we become aware that there are a number of possible correct views, though each may be differently encoded. It is not a question of one approach best corresponding to the basic facts of history, since each approach to historical science defines differently what are to be taken as basic facts. We do not ask whether Durer or whether Degas represents the human nude more correctly. Instead we see them – along with the science of anatomy – as different systems of notation (see Gombrich, 1960). Should not the same be true of different modes of historical figuration?

Root metaphors are linguistic orientations that provide a notational system in which certain kinds of data, and not others, appear as evidence. Organicists, for example, focus on those facts that can be orchestrated into some given *process* of development. Mechanists orient themselves toward the kinds of events that can be made to stand for general causal *laws*. In either case, however, an analysis of root metaphors suggests that the cognitively responsible relationship to our modes of inquiry is neither absolute dogmatism nor absolute skepticism, since each of these attitudes seems to free us from the obligations either to provide an intellectual warrant for our thought modes or to accept moral responsibility for the practical interests that, as rhetorical constructs, they may serve. Instead, our negative dialectic can yield an attitude of stoic cosmopolitanism. Such a stance requires that the author appreciate the limits of her chosen mode of discourse, respect the etiquette that it implies, and not imperialistically extend it beyond its proper application. In abandoning absolutist claims made in the name of any particular root metaphor, such cosmopolitanism also celebrates our capacity to define who we are and what we might become.

REFERENCES

Abrams, M. (1953). *The mirror and the lamp.* New York: Oxford University Press.

Anderson, P. (1974). *Lineages of the absolutist state.* London: N.L.B.

Aristotle, (1967). *Works* (W. D. Ross, Ed.), London: Oxford University Press.

Bateson, G. (1941). Experiments in thinking about observed ethnological material, *Philosophy of Science.*

Becker, H. (1940). Historical sociology. In H. Barnes & H. Becker, (Eds.), *Contemporary social theory.* New York: Appleton-Century.

Berggren, D. (1962). The use and abuse of metaphor. *Review of Metaphysics, 16*(2), 237–258.

Berggren, D. (1963). The use and abuse of metaphor. *Review of Metaphysics, 16*(3), 450–472.

Black, M. (1962). *Models and metaphors: Studies in language and philosophy.* Ithaca, NY: Cornell University Press.

Boas, F. (1896). The limitations of the comparative method in anthropology. *Science, 4,* 901–903.

Bock, K. (1956). *The acceptance of histories. Toward a perspective for social science.* Berkeley, CA: University of California Press.

Bock, K. (1963). Evolution, function, and change. *American Sociological Review, 28*, 229–237.

Bock, K. (1978). Theories of progress, development, evolution. In T. Bottomore & R. Nisbet (Eds.), *A history of sociological analysis* (pp. 39–79). New York: Basic Books.

Brooks, C. (1965). Metaphor, paradox, and stereotype. *British Journal of Aesthetics, 5,*(4), 315–318.

Brown, R. H. (1977). *A poetic for sociology. Toward a logic of discovery for the human sciences.* New York and London: Cambridge University Press.

Bruyn, S. (1966). *The human perspective in sociology.* Englewood Cliffs, NJ: Prentice-Hall.

Burke, K. (1959). *Attitudes toward history.* Boston: Beacon.

Burke, K. (1969), *Grammar of motives.* Berkeley, CA: University of California Press.

Burtt, E. A. (1954). *The metaphysical foundations of modern science.* Garden City, NY: Doubleday.

Coleridge, S. T. (1956). *Biographica literaria* (G. Watson, Ed.), New York: Everyman's Library.

Croce, B. (1955). *Aesthetic as science of expression and general linguistic.* New York: Noonday.

Diesing, P. (1971). *Patterns of discovery in the social sciences.* Chicago: Aldine.

Dilthey, W. (1962). *Pattern and meaning in history* (H. P. Rickman, Ed.), New York: Harper and Row.

Douglas, J. (1971). The theory of subjectivity in sociology. Mimeo., Department of Sociology, University of California at San Diego.

Durkheim, E. (1965). *The elementary forms of religious life.* New York: Free Press.

Feibleman, J. K. (1956). *The institutions of society.* London: Allen and Unwin.

Freud, S. (1954). Project for a scientific psychology. *Complete works.* Vol. 1. London: Hogarth.

Gay, P. (1974). *Style in history.* London: Jonathan Cape.

Gellner, E. (1965). *Thought and change.* Chicago: University of Chicago Press.

Gombrich, E. H. (1960). *Art and illusion.* New York: Pantheon.

Goodman, N. (1970). *The structure of appearance.* Cambridge, MA: Harvard University Press.

Gouldner, A. (1970). *The coming crisis in western sociology.* New York: Basic Books.

Haskell, R. E. (1968). Anatomy of anology: A new look. *Journal of Humanistic Psychology, 8*(2).

Hempel, C. (1945). The logic and functional analysis. In L. Gross, (Ed.), *A symposium on sociological theory.* (pp. 271–307). Evanston, IL.: Row Peterson.

Hempel, C. (1959). The function of general laws in history. In P. Gardiner (Ed.), *Theories of history.* Glencoe, IL: Free Press.

Hesse, M. B. (1970). The explanatory function of metaphor. In Y. Bar-Hillel (Ed.), *Logic, methodology, and philosophy of science.* Amsterdam: North Holland.

Hobbes, T. (1957). *Leviathan.* Oxford: Basil Blackwell.

Hodgen, M. T. (1936). *The doctrine of survivals.* London: Allerson & Co.

Hodgen, M. T. (1952). *Change and history.* Viking Fund, Publications in Anthropology #18.

Hodgen, M. T. (1964). *Early anthropology in the 16th and 17th centuries.* Philadelphia: University of Pennsylvania Press.

Hoffman, R. R., & Honeck, R. P. (1981). *Cognition and figurative language.* Hillsdale, NJ: Erlbaum.

Journal of Mind and Behavior (1982). Special issue. *The Pepper papers.* (Vols. 3 and 4).

Kant, I. (1949). *The philosophy of Kant.* (C. J. Friedrich, Ed.), New York: Modern Library.

Krasnow, H. S., & Merikallio, R. A. (1964). The past, present, and future of general simulation languages. *Management Science, 2*(2), 236–267.

Kubler, G. (1962). *The shape of time: Remarks on the history of things.* New Haven: Yale University Press.

Kuhn, T. S. (1970). *The structure of scientific revolutions.* Chicago: University of Chicago Press.

MacCormac, E. R. (1976). *Metaphor and myth in science and religion.* Durham, NC: Duke University Press.

Maitland, W. (1911). The body politic. In H. A. L. Fisher (Ed.), *The collected letters of William Maitland.* London: Cambridge University Press.

Marx, K. (1946). *Capital.* New York: Everyman's Library.

Matson, F. (1966). *The broken image. Man, science and society.* Garden City, NY: Doubleday.

McCloskey, M. A. (1964). Metaphors. *Mind, 73,*(290), 215–233.

McHugh, P. (1970). On the failure of positivism. In J. D. Douglas (Ed.), *Understanding everyday life, Toward a reconstruction of sociological knowledge* (pp. 324–330). Chicago: Aldine.

Mead, G. H. (1956). The problem of society. In *The social psychology of George Herbert Mead* (pp. 17–42). A. Strauss (Ed.), Chicago: University of Chicago Press.

Murdock, G. P. (1949). *Social structure.* New York: MacMillan.

Nietzsche, F. (1960). Uber Wahrheit und Luge im aussermoralischen Sinn (On truth and lie in an extra-moral sense) (Vol. 3). In K. Schlechta (Ed.), *Werke in drei Banden.* Munich: Carl Hanser Verlag.

Nisbet, R. (1969). *Social change and history. Aspects of the western theory of development.* New York: Oxford University Press.

Panofsky, E. (1955). *Meaning in the visual arts.* Garden City, NY: Doubleday.

Parsons, T. (1964). A functional theory of change. In A. Etzioni & E. Etzioni (Eds.), *Social change: Sources, patterns, and consequences* (pp. 87ff). New York: Basic Books.

Parsons, T. (1966). *Societies: Evolutionary and comparative perspectives.* Englewood Cliffs, NJ: Prentice-Hall.

Pepper, S. (1942). *World hypotheses.* Berkeley, CA: University of California Press.

Randall, J. H., Jr., & Haines, G. (1946). Controlling assumptions in the practice of American historians. *Theory and practice in historical study: A report of the committee on historiography,* Bulletin 54. New York: Social Science Research Council.

Ricoeur, P. (1972). La metaphore et le probleme central de l'hermeneutique. *Revue philosophique de Louvain* (4th series), *10*(5), 93–112.

Ryle, G. (1954). *Dilemmas.* London and New York: Cambridge University Press.

Schon, D. A. (1963). *The displacement of concepts.* Also published as *Invention and the evolution of ideas.* London: Tavistock Publications.

Seneca, L. A., (1910). *Quaestiones Naturales.* J. Clark (Ed.), London: Macmillan.

Simmel, G. (1977). *The problems of the philosophy of history. An epistemological essay.* (G. Oakes, trans.). New York: Free Press.

Skocpol, T. (1979). *States and social revolutions.* Cambridge, England: Cambridge University Press.

Spengler, O. (1928). *The decline of the West.* (Vol. 1). New York: Alfred A. Knopf.

St. Augustine. (1881). *The city of god.* (M. Dodd, trans.) New York: Hafner Pub. Co.

Teggart, F. J. (1916). *Prolegomena to history.* Berkeley, CA: University of California Press.

Teggart, F. J. (1939). *Rome and China: A study of correlation in historical events.* Berkeley, CA: University of California Press.

Teggart, F. J. (1941). *Theory and process of history.* Berkeley, CA: University of California Press.

Tylor, E. B. (1878). *Researches into the early history of mankind and the development of civilization.* New York.

Toulmin, S. (1961). *Foresight and understanding: An enquiry into the aims of science.* Bloomington, IN: University of Indiana Press.

Turbayne, C. M. (1962). *The myth of metaphor.* New Haven: Yale Univesrity Press.

Vico, G. (1972). *The new science of Giambattista Vico* (T. Bergin & M. Fisch, trans.). Ithaca, NY: Cornell University Press.

Wallerstein, I. (1974). *The modern world-system. Capitalist agriculture and the origins of the world economy in the sixteenth century.* New York: Academic Press.

Weber, M. (1949). *The methodology of the social sciences* (E. A. Shils & H. Finch, trans. and eds.). Glencoe, IL: Free Press.

Wheelright, P. E. (1962). *Metaphor and reality.* Bloomington, IN: University of Indiana Press.

Wheelright, P. E. (1968). *The burning fountain: A study in the language of symbolism.* Bloomington, IN: Indiana University Press.

White, H. (1973). *Metahistory. The historical imagination in nineteenth-century Europe.* Baltimore, MD: Johns Hopkins University Press.

White, H. (1978a). The historical text as literary artifact. In R. H. Canary & H. Kozicki (Eds.), *The writing of history. Literary form and historical undersatnding* (pp. 41–62). Madison, WI: University of Wisconsin Press.

White, H. (1978b). *Topics of discourse. Essays in cultural criticisms.* Baltimore, MD: Johns Hopkins University Press.

CHAPTER THIRTEEN

Structural Metaphor and Cognition

Robert E. Haskell
University of New England

I shall not open this chapter by defining what I call structural metaphor, because in the end it will define itself. Suffice it to say for now that this type of metaphor has always been used by speakers and writers, sometimes consciously, at other times not so consciously. Those schooled in the forms of literary style are, to one degree or another, aware of structural metaphor; most readers fail to perceive it. It has been vaguely known by various labels, such as mimesis and dramatistic expression, largely because in so far as it has been known, it has neither been generally understood nor specifically identified as a metaphoric process. In this chapter, I would like to define it by offering two examples of structural metaphor (and semantaphor) and to suggest its cognitive function and implications. The first example I will use is an essay by the psychoanalyst and structuralist Jacques Lacan (1966), the second, an essay by the critic and poet Archibald MacLeish (1964). I will then present evidence of the cognitive significance of the use of structural metaphor.

"PSYCHO"-LINGUISTICS

Jacques Lacan is a French psychoanalyst not widely known by American readers until recently. Lacan reinterprets Freud's writings, especially Freud's concept of the unconscious. For Lacan, the unconscious is structured like a language. It is the study of language, then, that Lacan sees as a kind of "royal road" into the unconscious. To read Lacan is laborious and difficult. Much of it seems purposely obscure and oblique. But there seems to be a method to his style. What I would like to suggest here is that Lacan's style is based on his ideas about the unconscious and the function of language. Lacan seems to put the "psycho-" back into psycholinguistics.

The Lacanian Way-In

As many have commented, much of Lacan's writing appears to be either bad translations, or the work of someone who is simply unable to write clearly. But this is not the case. Lacan opens his article "The Insistance of the Letter in the Unconscious," in a sense, by closing the reader out. He says he is going to tighten the article up ". . . *in order to leave the reader no other way out than the way in.*"

What are we to make of this? First of all, Lacan in-forms the reader in the beginning of his essay that ". . . *this will not be a written work.*" (p. 102; emphasis added). He says that the article stands half way between the written and the spoken word; it is in-deed "speech" written down.

Here is a return to the oral tradition of ancient rhetoric, to a block of time before the press of the Gutenberg revolution; it is a return to a type of conception regarding language and mind that is prior to the Aristotelian "rationalized" or "intelligible" Idea; it is a return to the Word, to the plenum of an inner linguistic space.

In this respect, Lacan refers to and speaks of language in a manner similar to Cassirer (1946), Gadamer (1975), Ricoeur (1970), Snell (1960), and Vico (1948). For these philosophers of Language, like Lacan, the seat of language and words spring from a fluid "psychological" source. For Cassirer, language and myth spring from an inner metaphorical thought process; for Gadamer, from an inner process of "linguisticality"; for Lacan, in part, from what he calls "Desire."

To the descendents of Aristotle and Decartes was bequeathed a disembodied notion of language. Lacan resurrects an ancient body of thought buried in an oral tradition. Lacan reminds the Word of its origins. He objects to a positivist view of language where only lip service is given to the Word. To Lacan, the static notated words of the positivist merely lie on the surface of meaning. Still, how is one to "get in" to the inner movement of the Lacanian Word?

The "Lacanian Bar"

Now familiar is the Lacanian $\frac{S}{s}$ where the signifier (= S) over the signified (= s) is divided by the line (= _____) here called the "Lacanian Bar." The Bar represents the *transformational* process of (a) metaphor to metonymy, (b) of unconscious to conscious, (c) of the "letter" into the word, (d) of speech into language. Normal writing is accomplished by the notated word, the "S" above The Bar. "Speech" is closer to being below The Bar, as are dreams, and is thus notated by the lower case "s". Lacan's writing, being on or below The Bar, is similar to dream speech. The "way in" to Lacan's writing, then, is to descend below The Bar, for the text in question, it will be recalled, is written half way between the written and spoken word.

Now this "way in" attempts to force the reader below The Bar. Lacan's article makes use of footnotes to assist the reader. Ironically, however, they are written in normal discursive style, i.e., above "the bar", so to speak, while this "above the bar" writing style is purposefully obscure, i.e., "below the bar." Thus Lacan's "s" is actually upper case in his footnotes, whereas his "S" is in fact lower case in his text. He thus brings nonconscious meanings to the surface. Lacan writes in "speech." Accordingly, like music, (a metaphor, it might be noted, that he uses periodically) it should be listened to, not visually read. In a manner of speaking, then, Lacan is a speech writer. Quite literally, to Lacan all written words are mere "figures of speech," rhetorical tropes expelled from The Bar.

Inside Lacanian Psycholinguistics

In an excellent article by Holloway (1977), the author, in the title, asks "*What Does Lacan Mean?*" I would like to suggest, however, that the question should be: "*How Does Lacan Mean?*" The answer cannot be derived from formulating the question in terms of *What*. *How* Lacan means is achieved by *watching what he does*. Lacan practices *what* he preaches, and *how*.

Section I of Lacan's article is quite novel in style from the other two sections. It more closely approximates "speech." It reads like a Gertrude Stein piece, quite ungrammatical from a writing point of view. Beyond this, Lacan turns his ideas into concrete structures like the surface of mobius example he is so fond of using: He turns the infinite surface of metaphor into the edge of Logic (metonymy). Here we see what Lacan calls the "Double Twist" of Metaphor. In writing on and below The Bar, Lacan subtly inserts a subliteral critique of traditional psychoanalysts' lack of understanding of the Word.

Ideas that exist above The Bar are not only generated and shaped but anticipated by below the Bar metaphorical-like structures and associative networks. Lacan readies his reader for his upcoming thesis by an explicitly stated example, by using a diagram of "his-and-her" restroom doors, thereby subliterally suggesting the anality of psychoanalysts' understanding of words as things, with anality, presumably itself being a metaphor of containment, the retaining of meaning, the constriction of semantic movement. Lacan's "above the bar" text is ostensibly literal, but it is spotted with "below the bar" subliteral theses throughout his essay. Psychoanalysts' reading of language, says Lacan, is "*buttressed by many sticky fingers*" (p. 103). Subsequent to the explicit statement of his restroom-doors diagram, he subliterally predicates words and phrases which literally belong to above The Bar subjects but in fact they are subliteral or metaphorical references.

He speaks of *low blows* that are *not immaterial*. He says "From what *shining center* the signifier *goes forth* to reflect its light *into the shadow* . . . This signifier will now carry a purely *animal* dissension meant for the usual *oblivion* of *Natural mists*. . . ." Perhaps even more subliterally: "It begins to *sound* like the *history* . . . come *hissing out below*." (p. 109) Now toilet training "metaphors" continue: "a meaning all the more *oppressive in that* it is all *the more content* to make us *wait for it*" (p. 111) (i.e., content makes us wait, unlike the *praxis* structure Lacan is *doing*.) Further on we find: *"adds nothing* to the *trashcan* style in which currently by the use of . . . ready made mental *jetsam,* one *excuses* oneself" (p. 136) [all emphases added]. These embedded "figures" are covered over in the text by the more literal context to which they belong.

For the more literal minded, these little gems, these micro-metaphors, reflect the smearing of feces, breaking wind, butts (i.e., asses), feces dropping into the toilet. They are all consistent with Lacan's explicit and literal graphic example of restroom doors. In addition, they are the subliteral charging of psychoanalysts with being anal, which is consistent with his explicit charge that they do not know what they are doing. Further, in Section II, Lacan says that psychoanalysts think that "intellectualization is the word – execrable." (p. 132). It is no accident that this word is a close approximation to "excretion," especially when Lacan juxtaposes it to "spit" (metonymic meaning). Moreover, Lacan says that "its disciples like to *wallow in it.*" (p. 107) (anal expulsive). More Anality: "I shall never . . . it is content to make us wait for it" (Anal retentive). Toilet training runs deep.

Lacan is doing what he is talking about: He is engaging in semantaphor. Semantaphor, as we have seen, is the subliteral and metaphorical use of "associated" *words* that are homogeneous with the object of discussion. Hence, the ostensible words that Lacan intersperses, like "hissing out below," "low blows," "excuse oneself," all congruent with his thesis of anality. He is linking, connecting linear metonymy (= S) to the metaphorical (= s) levels of meaning and sound; he auditions here in the text, all the while talking of the sliding back and forth across The Bar of the signifier and signified, that is, of notated meaning and the reference to its inner experience.

Again Lacan is doing-what-he-is-talking-about. Each section of his paper is a recycling of this practice, but on a new level. Lacan demonstrates the invalidity of traditional dichotomies of poetry/prose, metonymy/metaphor, analogue/digital, and logic/rhetoric. All the same, the demonstration is only a facsimile, for such concretion remains "only" a metaphor as the Bar *"can reveal only the structure of a signifier in the transfer"* (p. 109). That is, while unconscious meaning can cross the Bar into consciousness, it is thereby altered. We see transformations of it but not its pure character; hence the transfer effect. The whole article – as in-deed most of this writing – virtually resonates with such examples, as given above, from below The Bar. Lacan's semantaphors insert themselves in those interstitial spaces left by literality and logic. *This network of mini-metaphors of associated meanings constitute what I shall call semantaphors, while his doing what he is talking about, I refer to as structural metaphor.*

If one is ready to hear, one can find his or her "way in" to the "text." Lacan does offer "the way in." He says, or so it sounds, that language frequently functions "to say something quite other than what it says" (p. 113). This is the "signifier effect." In other words, normal discursive language always reflects meanings and associations from "below the bar"; it has attached to it unconscious meanings and associations. The signifier, the spoken word, always points to and has attached to it unconscious structures of meaning. Further the unconscious, which, for Lacan, is structured like a language, functions in large part onomatopoetically, as homogeneous with its subject.

Lacan's so-called "literary style" is, in a word, his "psycho-"linguistics. There is a method to his madness:

> "I have only to plant my tree in a *location*: climb the tree, *indeed* illuminate it by *playing on it* the light of *descriptive context* . . . and if I know the truth let it be heard, in spite of all the between-the-lines censures by the only signifier *I know how to create* with my *acrobatics among the branches of the tree, tantalizing to the point of burlesque,* or *sensible* only *to the experienced eye,* according to *whether I wish to be heard by the mob or the few."*
> (p. 113; emphasis added)

This *praxis* style, this doing what he is talking about is what I have termed structural metaphor, that is, where the structure of talk simultaneously fulfills the verbal promise of the content as it is being spoken. While it would require a tome to trace the underground meanings encased in the above quote, suffice it to say here that its encrypted meaning demonstrates the "way in."

The reader who wishes to understand the signifier effect on a structural and semantic level must watch what Lacan does with temporal notations. Just as the psychoanalytic concept of the unconscious is considered to have no sense of time, of past and present, Lacan uses the temporal and spatial references "now," "this," "here," to in-form the reader, who is sensitive to below-the-bar and unconscious meaning, that "now" in the text means, "now." Frequently, these temporal and spatial references are structural metaphors en-forming the reader what Lacan is actually doing in his text; they are cues telling the reader that he is *doing* what he is talking *about.*

Section II of Lacan's paper is written essentially "above the bar" in a more rational, literal, and linear fashion than the other two sections, and it is now concerned with normal communication. *It is an assent to consensus.*

What is one to make of such writing? It seems clear that Lacan knows what he is doing, not only from his proclamation in the text, but from the fact that Lacan was well versed in the literary symbolist genre, and in the Structuralist thought of Levi-Strauss (see Wilden, 1968). Through the use of such semantaphors and structural metaphor, Lacan creates a written form directed to the unconscious, which he says is structured like a language. Lacan is in fact engaging in what has been termed by Barthes (1974) as structuralist discourse, the aim of which "is to make itself entirely homogeneous with its object" (p. 416).

The Lacanian puns and play on words are common in the structuralist literature. And they are misunderstood by rational-literal readers. Levi-Strauss, the father of structural anthropology, in analyzing primitive myths frequently uses puns and play on words. A critic, Edmund Leach (1974) accuses him of "intellectual gymnastics" (p. 27). But, similarly to Lacan, Levi-Strauss tries to do in his writing what he is writing about, for a tenet of structuralist thought is that there are nonconscious structures of cognition and that cognition is sensitive to such structures, and indeed constructs its meaning on the basis of them. As Levi-Strauss (1961) says of his own work, "Whatever unity might be claimed for it will appear hidden in the recesses of the text, and perhaps even beyond it. In the best of circumstances that unity will only be worked out in the readers mind" (p. 38). Semantaphor and structural metaphor, then, are not only rhetorical devices but are natural functions of thought.

James Joyce was a master of semantaphors (see Litz, 1972). But one finds them in everyday speech. Often, in everyday speech or writing, they can be found. In the writing or speaking of a person discussing say, "nakedness," the word "overbearing" (= bare-ing), or the phrase "has a bearing" (= bare-ing) will be used. More often than not, these are not conscious puns. Semantaphors are essentially "normalized" slips of the tongue, the latter being a special case of a more general cognitive process. Semantaphorical relations are akin to the pun. They are a special case of structural metaphor.

STRUCTURE AND METAPHOR

MacLeish and the Structure of Meaning

A more masterful example of structural metaphor is to be found in the writing of the poet Archibald MacLeish (1964). Not being well informed about the field of literary criticism, I do not know how many others are aware of what MacLeish does, how he constructs his writing. But surely experts in that field are generally aware of what I am calling his use of structural metaphor, more generally known as "mimesis." While reading MacLeish's critique of a sonnet, I had the strange feeling that something was going on other than a single critique. I could not perceive it, however, until I read it over about five times: *he was doing in the very structure of his own written critique what he was saying about the sonnet.*

In critiquing a sonnet about a swan, MacLeish says "there is a swan who enters the sonnet in the fifth line and who dominates it thereafter" (p. 32). If one counts what MacLeish, I assume, means by "lines," the reader will find MacLeish's word "swan" in his fifth line of writing in two respects. The first "line" is broken into four clauses, then we have the next sentence which constitutes the *fifth* "line" as it is one unbroken sentence, and this is in-deed where the "swan" enters his own writing: (1) "To begin with," (2) "we can argue that there is," (3) "if not a structure of meaning," (4) "at least a subject of meaning." (5) "There is a *swan* who enters the sonnet in the fifth line and who dominates it thereafter." The second way the "swan" enters in the "fifth line" of Macleish's writing is by counting the lines on the page that constitute the actual lines of the paragraph. If one does so, one finds the word "swan" at the beginning of the fifth paragraph-line.

Further, MacLeish makes use of more subtle structural metaphor. In critiquing the white swan of the sonnet he says, "one begins to conceive this swan frozen into the white ice and the black mire at the pond's edge" (p. 32). This is a structural metaphor of the actual printed page, of the white frozen page upon which the black print is imposed. Thus the meaning of the swan is not to be found in the printed words but in those spaces between them, i.e., structurally: In-deed the "swan" at the beginning of MacLeish's fifth line is at the pond's (read: page's) edge.

In literally writing about the sonnet, MacLeish is writing metaphorically about what he is doing. Like Lacan, MacLeish plays with time and space, making simultaneous the literal and the figurative, which in part are two levels of literal meaning. When he tells of "these" words, "this" swan "here" whose literal referent is the sonnet he is critiquing, he is also referencing the "this" ice, the "here" of the white page of his own writing. It is a masterful use of structural metaphor. The entire essay is constructed in this way. MacLeish (p. 22) is a master of structural metaphor and semantaphor. In describing the structure of a poem, he says, "Here are eight sentences . . . ," meaning the poem he is writing about. In fact MacLeish himself uses eight sentences and when he writes about the poem having what he calls nineteen "lines," he too constructs nineteen lines. When he writes about the sounds that the poem "make in the mouth," it is clear that ones mouth is involved, just as it is to one's hearing when he writes about the sounds the words make *"in the ear"* when they are spoken.

Here is the difference between the oral and written tradition made concrete. In writing about the "double structure" of words as sound and as meaning, he says, *"No,* I *know no* poems in which the double structure of sounds as words and sounds as meaning . . . " (p. 93, emphasis added), he engages in the double structure of sound in the "No, I *know no* . . . " and even more subtly in the reference to the difference of the sound and meaning of the first "no," the second "know," and the third "no," by the double structure of the phrase "words as sounds (plus) and words as meaning." Is this simply intellectual gymnastics? I think not, as we shall see.

Structural Metaphor and Meaning

It is obvious that Lacan and MacLeish (and in the short passage by Levi-Strauss which was quoted above) both consciously construct in their writing the kind of structural metaphors just outlined. What is more, these authors and others like Levi-Strauss make very little attempt to in-form the reader what it is they are doing. What in-forming they do is somewhat encrypted, or structural. It will be recalled, for example, that both Lacan and MacLeish subliminally inform by constant repetition of such sentences as "here" are eight sentences, or "this" structure, all of which are embedded into the literal meaning of their writing. Lacan says he is going to "leave the reader no other way out than the way in." And Levi-Strauss tells us that the unity of his writing will be "hidden in the recesses of the text . . .

and will only be worked out in the readers mind." The question is, why be so cryptic and why write in a manner that is homogenous with the subject matter? Is it simply the esoterism of an eccentric psychoanalyst and anthropologist, and the overactive literary imagination of a reknowned poet? I think not. Part of the answer is epistemological, the other part communicational, both directly related to metaphor and cognition.

First, Lacan, Levi-Strauss, and MacLeish are well acquainted with Symbolist poetic theory (see Boon, 1972) and therefore both believe that the mind or cognitive process is tied closely to nonconscious linguistic processes, and that the deep structure of cognition is poetic in nature. Further, they believe that there is an "inner speech" process that is quite different from rational-logical language production, and that the latter is founded upon this poetic inner speech (see Cassirer, 1955a; Edie, 1976; Merleau-Ponty, 1964; Vico, 1948; Werner & Kaplan, 1963, for discussions of inner speech). Thus what they are doing, as indeed Lacan states, is to render their writing as close to inner speech as possible.

The second reason they write in this manner, at least for MacLeish, is that this style of writing ostensibly affects communication. Presumably, a structural metaphoric style adds meaning. As MacLeish asks of the poem he is writing about, but which in fact is a double reference to the structure of his own writing (outlined above), "Is there a relationship between *this* structure and the capacity of the poem to mean?" (p. 22; emphasis added). All of this makes good "poetic" theory, but is it true that cognitive processes actually function in this manner? The traditional answer by cognitive psychologists, on those rare occasions when they entertain the possibility of poets and writers having something significant to say to cognitive psychology, has been that such theory is simply the figment of the literary imagination and simply a stylistic device. This is the same attitude cognitive psychology has held about metaphor. If the symbolist and structuralist theory is valid, then there should be evidence for it outside of literary data, evidence both for its existence and for its effect on communication.

I would now like to suggest three lines of research that are in support of the cognitive significance of structural metaphor. The first line is from my own linguistic research, the second from cognitive psychology, the third from clinical data.

COGNITION AND STRUCTURAL METAPHOR

In my own research into the linguistic structure of individual and group conversations, I discovered quite by another route the very "psycho-" linguistics Lacan and MacLeish demonstrate in their writing, only occurring naturally in conversation. For instance, when a group of people are talking about a literal topic, say two authority figures such as policemen, the elements of that topic are often structurally metaphorical to the actual situation in the group discussion. In the actual group, there will be two people dominating the interaction, who are being "metaphorically" discussed, none of the discussants are, of course, aware of what they subliterally *mean*. This type of communication I have elsewhere termed "subliteral," or "analogic." (Haskell, 1978, 1981, 1983, 1984b).

Moreover, when the subliteral meaning of the structural metaphor becomes cognitively salient, it is demonstrated by linguistic temporal and spatial shifts: The linguistic structure changes from "those" policemen to "these" "here" policemen. In other words, the decreasing cognitive "distance" between the literal meaning of the topic and the metaphoric or subliminal meaning is reflected in the shifts of language use. Occasionally, as the cognitive distance decreases even more, the group may quite abruptly switch the topic of conversation and begin to talk to the two dominant members which were being previously discussed metaphorically, but still not aware of the connection. Even more rarely, the "distance" between the metaphorical and literal topic break down and a member may recognize with surprise the metaphoric connection, and comment on its "coincidence." In Lacanian terms, the signified has crossed over the bar–into the discourse of the signifier. The "transfer effect."

More along the lines of MacLeish's demonstration of what I am calling structural metaphor, I have found that often a discussion about specific numbers used in a literal topic will be structurally metaphorical to the actual structural composition of the group. These numbers will be associated with shifts from "that" to "this' and from "there" to "here" and "now," again indicating the cognitive connection between the literal topic and the actual situation. As I have suggested elsewhere, in structural metaphoric conversation (Haskell, 1983) the traditional distinction between literal and metaphorical is obliterated. It is in fact a "rational poetics."

If structural metaphor is a communication device to increase meaning, why do the authors not inform the reader directly? One answer is that it is also a strategy to cognitively manipulate the reader nonconsciously. Another answer is that it would not be effective if consciously perceived. Once again, is the first of these answers simply the result of an overactive and creative literary imagination? And is the second based on the psychoanalytic assumption of the unconscious, or is it possible that communicating "structurally" does influence the reader nonconsciously? This form of structural communication is frequently used in television commercials, sometimes quite obviously, sometimes quite subtly.

Evidence for Structural Metaphor

There is evidence in cognitive research that relates directly to (a) that structural metaphoric communication does influence cognitive response, and (b) that, if its recipient was aware of it, it would be ineffective. There are two areas in psychology that bear on these issues. They are the study of so-called subliminal perception or discrimination without awareness, (Dixon, 1981) and hypnosis research (Bowers & Meichenbaum, 1984; Hilgard, 1977; Haskell, 1984a).

Dixon's volumes are an encyclopedic and detailed review of the perception of *stimuli below the level of conscious awareness,* clearly demonstrating that such stimuli influences thoughts and behaviors. This holds true for both auditory and visually displayed stimuli. For example, in one experiment (Dixon, 1981), a neutral picture of human face was shown to two groups of subjects. One group had the word "Happy" subliminally superimposed on the picture. The second group had the word "Sad" superimposed. The group that was subjected to the subliminal stimulus "Happy" tended to evaluate the neutral face as happy, and the group that was subjected to the subliminal stimulus "Sad" tended to evaluate the neutral face as "sad." What is more the closer the stimulus is to conscious awareness, the less effective it is in eliciting a response. As Dixon points out, subliminal stimuli seem to act as posthypnotic suggestions, where a person, after the hypnotic session, is not aware of why he or she is responding in a particular way. What I am suggesting here is that structural metaphor could conceivably function subliminally and influence the reader's perceptions and meaning of the text. This does seem strongly implied by writers such as Lacan and MacLeish, but since this phenomenon has not been widely recognized, cognitive data have not been brought to bear on the phenomenon.

A further set of data that can be used to explain how structural metaphoric communication works are the neurological findings from what has come to be known as split brain research. We know that the two cerebral hemispheres appear to function, in general, quite differently (Sperry, 1968; Springer & Deutsche, 1981). The left hemisphere is more attuned to logical, rational, analytical data, while the right hemisphere is more attuned to metaphorical, spatial type data. The two are connected by a structure called the corpus callosum, which appears to be the main link informing each hemisphere, by transferring information processed in one to the other. When the corpus callosum is severed, each hemisphere is largely separate from the other. By and large, it is the left hemisphere that possesses language ability, and, hence, it is the input of data to this hemisphere of which we are consciously aware. Split brain patients, however, cannot speak about and are not generally aware of information processed only in their right hemispheres. Presumably it is the right hemisphere that is partly involved in subliminal perception. That is, data not consciously processed by the left hemisphere evidently may be stored in the right hemisphere, but for various reasons does not cross the corpus callosum.

It has been suggested (Galin, 1974) that much of what we call "unconscious" may be information confined to the right hemisphere, and that, without language, we have no means to be aware of it. The information nevertheless influences cognition and behavior. One split brain patient was shown the picture of a nude body to the right hemisphere. The patient giggled but had no awareness of why the giggling. In short, the information was being registered on a certain neurological level, but it did not reach what we ordinarily call consciousness. Subliminal stimuli do effect behavior and meaning. It seems reasonable to hypothesize that semantaphoric and structural metaphor, which are not consciously perceived, would also effect behavior and meaning.

It is quite reasonable, at least theoretically, that the praxis structure, the structural metaphor that MacLeish builds into the printed page, functions as nonconsciously perceived stimuli by the reader. The question is, by what subliminal cognitive process would such a mechanism work, and is there research that would support such a notion? I think the answer is to be found in the cognitive research on figure–ground relationship and subliminal perception. In other words, the literal printed page is the "figure" and MacLeish's structurally metaphoric form built in to the literal page of print is the "ground."

When MacLeish, then, is talking about the eight sentences of the poem he is analyzing, it is the "figure"; when at the same time he builds eight sentences into his own writing, it is the "ground." The reader may be subliterally cued by his use of the temporarily ambiguous "this" or "here," which have double referents, i.e., (a) the poem's eight sentences, and (b) the eight sentences of MacLeish. Thus the structural metaphor functions as an embedded figure-ground relationship. Consider the following research.

Replicating the earlier work of what has become known as the Poetzl effect (Poetzl, 1917; see Dixon, 1981), Fisher and Paul (1959) and Eagle, Wolitzky, and Klein (1966) presented subjects with pictures with embedded figures in them before subjects went to sleep. Subjects had no direct awareness of the embedded figures, but only of the main picture. The interesting results were that subjects tended to have dreams that contained directly or indirectly the embedded figures in the pictures, not the main subject matter of the picture. It is the very structure of the embedded figure, including the "empty space" around a figure (i.e., the ground) that helps to define what is meaningfully perceived. Translated, this means that subjects nonconsciously perceived the "ground" of the picture, which cognitively registered on some meaningful level. Dixon (1981) suggests that the normal figure-ground distinction does not seem to hold under subliminal conditions. Thus, using the MacLeish example, when the attention of a reader is focused on a page, the reader is in effect in an "altered state of consciousness" similar to a hypnotic (i.e., focused state of concentration) state, and sensitive to subliminal stimuli. In this state, the reader's normal perception of figure-ground relations may not hold, therefore rendering "ground" as much a meaningful stimulus as the "figure." All structural metaphor may function in a similar manner. So far, all of the above research that I have alluded to is fairly well controlled experimental laboratory data.

From the clinical work (and from naturalistically controlled experiments) of the renowned psychiatrist Milton Erickson (Erickson, Rossi, & Rossi, 1976) who pioneered novel hypnotic and therapeutic strategies that I have termed the "new hypnosis" (Haskell, 1981), come strategies relating directly to metaphor, and more specifically to structural metaphor, as well as to the subliminal use and effect of metaphors. For some reason Erickson's work on metaphor has not been recognized by metaphor researchers, or by those in subliminal perception research.

The first type of structural metaphor used by Erickson to communicate subliminally, and it might be mentioned apparently quite successfully from a therapeutic point of view, is the use of stories that *structurally* correspond to a patient's problem. The patient, of course, is not aware that the story structurally matches his or her problem. To the patient (just as in my group mentioned above), the story is simply a literal one. To a child having bedwetting problems, Erickson explained the workings of the muscles which open and close the iris of the eye, an explanation which Erickson constructs to be isomorphic to the workings of the opening and closing of the sphincter muscle that controls urination. The child ceases bedwetting (see also Gordon, 1978). A further method that Erickson uses is what he terms an "interspersal" method, where he utilizes embedded sentences or messages within a sentence. For example, in a therapeutic communication to a patient about constant ringing in the patient's ear, Erickson may say, "I once knew a person who had constant pain, and I said to them when *you* focus *your* attention elsewhere, *you* will find that *you can not notice your problem*" [emphasis added]. By playing on the double meaning of the word "you" and by a change in voice tone, Erickson is embedding a message to the patient, so the patient is not aware of it.

Another form of structural metaphor, deriving from Erickson's work, is what is called "mirroring" a patient's body posture and movements (see Grindler & Bandler, 1981). Mirroring is structurally matching a patient's "body language," as it has been more popularly called. When a patient crosses his or her left leg, the therapist does too; if the patient puts his or her right hand on his or her chin, the therapist does too, and so on. This appears to be a very powerful method of establishing communicational rapport. I have used both types of structural metaphors in my work and research, and have found them to be quite effective. But more rigorous and controlled research needs to be conducted.

Structural metaphor, then, is a subliteral action mode that is equivalent or isomorphic to the content or thought being expressed. This praxis mode can be semantic where a writer uses words that have associated meaning; it can be phonetic where the sound of the words used are equivalent to the literal content as in puns; it can be structured in that the form or style or structure of what is being written or spoken about. In short, it is isomorphic to the given content of the interaction. Structural metaphor is thus a form of meta-communication. What makes it "metaphoric" is its invariance, its equivalence-relationship to the subject matter.

I would like to suggest that, like Lacan, MacLeish, and other structuralists and symbolist poets and philosophers before me, this mode of communication is not, in its origin, a consciously constructed mode, but rather is an inherent function of cognition. Giambattista Vico (see Chapter 4, this volume) was the first to understand its "poetic" origins. Plato used it in his *Phaedrus,* in the sense that he actively engaged in what he was talking about (see Cornford, 1957). Plato, of course, came from an oral tradition, before the time of widespread written, abstracted literacy. Perhaps the ancients knew something we moderns only glimpse, and of which cognitive psychology knows nothing.

The communication of "ideas" via action is, according to Piaget's developmental cognitive psychology, what he calls a pre-operational mode of cognition, which is prior to the child's ability to engage in logical operations. Perhaps structural metaphoric communication is a higher order equivalent of pre-operational thought. The place where it is frequently found is in the imagery of dreaming. Dream processes are action modes, not primarily an abstract linguistic mode (see Haskell, 1986). What Lacan and MacLeish, the symbolist poets, and Vico have done is to tap into this mode.

In conclusion, structural metaphor is a mode of communication where the form or structure of a message is isomorphic with the content of the message. While Lacan and MacLeish use structural metaphor as a stylistic device, just as semantic metaphor itself has been used as a stylistic device, it is nevertheless a fundamental cognitive operation which occurs naturally, as was indicated by my group language data. It functions cognitively in a subliminal mode and is apprehended as figure-ground, and as embedded-figures are perceived. Augmenting cues to the existence of structural metaphor are by the use of the ambiguous and atemporal "this" and "here" reference.

From a cognitive point of view, the question is, why does structural metaphoric cognition exist? Here we are on even more speculative ground. Perhaps structural metaphor points to a series of cross modal invariant neurological structures such as those Marks and Bornstein suggest for some sensory metaphors (see Chapter 3, this volume). These cross modal invariancies may also cognitively function as abstract storage structures which store and retrieve information on the basis of isomorphic configurations. Thus when MacLeish, for example, writes about the sounds "made in the mouth" or "in the ear," the actual muscles in the mouth when the phrase is said (out loud or subvocally) are isomorphic to the content, and may in fact function as a sensory motor cue and/or reinforcer of the concept being written about. It is known that the more sense modalities that are involved in learning, the more easily learning occurs.

It should be relatively easy to design experiments to see if structural metaphoric writing or speech has the effect that Lacan, MacLeish, and others of a structuralist orientation theorize it does.

In any event, if what I am calling structural metaphor, and the relationships I have drawn here, are valid, then the structuralists' perspective and cognitive psychology need to engage in constructive research, taking structural metaphoric cognition very seriously. The implications of the findings here, for linguists, cognitive psychologists, and for those working with groups are significant. While language production is obviously and by definition an oral mode, it is most often analyzed as "written" text. This approach reflects our contemporary epistemology of Aristotelism and Cartesian rational, clear, and distinct cognition. We need to cognitively study modes like poetry, dreams, and myths. For it is these modes that may tell us a great deal about the structure of the cognitive processes of which we are currently unaware.

Dreams and myths also seem to exhibit structural metaphor. (See Cassirer, 1955; Kuper, 1979; Heynick, 1981; Levi-Strauss, 1963). Further research into these areas may move the study of symbolism out of the realm of the mysterious and into the clearer realm of cognitive science. And rather than less respect for the workings of the mind, the brain, whatever one wishes to call it, we will stand more in awe of its functioning.

Finally what has been termed "symbolic" may turn out to be a normal cognitive function of multiple levels of neurological processing that do not reach conscious awareness but which nevertheless influence the conscious meaning of a concept or object.

REFERENCES

Barthes, R. (1974). Sciences versus literature. In M. Lane (Ed.), *Introduction to structuralism*. New York: Harper.

Boon, J. (1972). *From symbolism to structuralism*. New York: Harper Torchbooks.

Bowers, K., & Meichenbaum, D. (Eds.). (1984). *The unconscious reconsidered*. New York: Wiley-Interscience.

Cassirer, E. (1946). *Language and myth*. New York: Dover.

Cassirer, E. (1955a). *The philosophy of symbolic forms: Vol. I. Language*. New Haven: Yale University Press.

Cassirer, E. (1955b). *The philosophy of symbolic forms: Vol. II. Mythical thought*. New Haven: Yale University Press.

Cornford, F. (1957). *Plato's theory of knowledge*. New York: Bobbs-Merrill.

Dixon, N. F. (1981). *Pre-conscious processing*. New York: Wiley.

Eagle, M., Wolitzky, D. L., & Klein, G. S. (1966). Imagery: Effect of a concealed figure in a stimulus. *Science, 151*, 837–839.

Edie, J. (1976). *Speaking and meaning: The phenomenology of language*, Bloomington, IN: Indiana Univ. Press.

Erickson, M., Rossi, E. L., & Rossi, S. I. (1976). *Hypnotic realities: the induction of clinical hypnosis and forms of indirect suggestion*. New York: Irvington.

Fisher, C., & Paul, I. H. (1959). The effects of subliminal visual stimulation on imagery of dreams: A validation study. *Journal of the American Psychoanalytic Association, 7*, 35–83.

Gadamer, H. G. (1975). *Truth and method*, New York: Seabury Press.

Galin, D. (1974). Implications for psychiatry of left and right cerebral specialization. *Arch. Gen. Psychiatry, 31*, 572–582.

Gordon, D. (1978). *Therapeutic metaphors*. Cupertino, CA: Meta.

Grindler, J., & Bandler, R. (1981). *Transformations: Neuro-linguistic programming of the structure of hypnosis*. Moab, UT: Real People Press.

Haskell, R. E. (1978). An analogic model of small group behavior. *International Journal of Group Psychotherapy, 27*, 27–54.

Haskell, R. E. (1981). On the "new hypnosis" of Milton H. Erickson, M.D. *Interfaces: Linguistics, Psychology and Health Therapeutics, 15,* 1–5.

Haskell, R. E. (1983). Cognitive structure and transformation: An empirical model of the psycholinguistic function of numbers in discourse. *Small Group Behavior, 14,* 419–443.

Haskell, R. E. (1984a, November). *Hypnosis and cognitive psychology.* Paper presented at the American Society of Clinical Hypnosis Conference, San Francisco, CA.

Haskell, R. E. (1984b). Empirical structures of mind: Cognition, linguistics, and transformation. *The Journal of Mind and Behavior, 5,* 29–48.

Haskell, R. E. (1986). Logical structure and the cognitive psychology of dreaming. In Haskell, R. E. (Ed.), *Cognition and dream research* (special double issue of the Journal of Mind and Behavior). New York: Institute of Mind Behavior.

Heynick, F. (1981). Linguistic aspects of Freud's dream model. *International Review of Psycho-analysis, 8,* 299–314.

Hilgard, E. R. (1977). *Divided consciousness: Multiple controls in human thought and action.* New York: Wiley Interscience.

Holloway, R. (1977). The unconscious is structured like a language: What does Lacan mean? *Interfaces: Linguistics, Psychology and Health Therapeutics, 7,* 15–21.

Kuper, A. (1979). A structural approach to dreams. *Man, 14,* 645–662.

Lacan, J. (1966). The insistence of the letter in the unconscious. In J. Ehrmann, (Ed.), *Structuralism.* Garden City, NY: Doubleday Anchor Books.

Leach, E. (1974). *Claude Levi-Strauss.* New York: Viking Press.

Levi-Strauss, C. (1961). Overture to le cru et le cuit. In J. Ehrmann (Ed.), *Structuralism.* Garden City, NY: Doubleday Anchor Books.

Levi-Strauss, C. (1963). *Structural anthropology.* New York: Basic Books.

Litz, A. W. (1972). *James Joyce.* Princeton, NJ: Hippocrene Books.

MacLeish, A. (1964). *Poetry and experience.* Baltimore, MD: Penguin Books.

Merleau-Ponty, M. (1964). *Signs.* Evanston, IL: Northwestern University Press.

Poetzl, O. (1960). The relationship between experimentally induced dream images and indirect vision. *Psychological Issues* (Monograph No. 7), *2,* 41– 120. (Originally published 1917)

Ricoeur, P. (1970). *Freud and philosophy: An essay on interpretation.* New Haven, CT: Yale University Press.

Snell, B. (1960). *The discovery of the mind: The Greek origins of European thought.* New York: Harper Books.

Sperry, R. W. (1968). Hemisphere disconnection and unity in conscious awareness. *American Psychologist, 23,* 723–733.

Springer, S. P., & Deutsch, G. (1981). *Left brain, right brain.* San Francisco: W. H. Freeman.

Vico, G. (1948). *The new science* (T. G. Bergin & M. H. Fisch, trans.). Ithaca, NY: Cornell University Press.

Werner, H., & Kaplan, B. (1963). *Symbol formation: An organismic developmental approach to language and the expression of thought.* New York: Wiley.

Wilden, A. (1968). *The language of the self.* Baltimore, MD: Johns Hopkins University Press.

CHAPTER FOURTEEN

A Phenomenology of Metaphor: A Praxis Study into Metaphor and Its Cognitive Movement through Semantic Space

Robert E. Haskell
University of New England

TO SPEAK, PERCHANCE TO PLAY AND WORK

Despite a recent shift in focus, the literature on metaphor is still largely confined to a description of its use as a literary symbolism device with which to merely ornament rational thinking. In fact, most scientists and many philosophers think that they have escaped the prism barbs of the semiotics of metaphorical thought. But they wear its sign on their backs. Indeed, it is these signs that determine the direction of their dialectical, rhetorical, and symbolic movement in cognitive space.

From a logical point of view, this study may be seen as irrational, for it will be written almost entirely *in metaphor* (as the term is ordinarily and not so ordinarily defined). It is therefore a *praxis* metaphorical study into the meaning of metaphor and its cognitive movement through semantic space, where a host of metaphors will be used to serve its meaning. Praxis creates a sort of linguistic ideogram, where thought by way of language paints pictures of itself. It is not narcissistic, but rather a healthy self-respect. The Chinese language in this regard is healthier than our own. The Chinese have a penchant for metaphor. The structure of their language demands it. The ideogram, after all, is a picture, not an abstract "letter." The ideogram *resembles* what it represents. The ideogram, then, is a sort of mental map. Thus does the Chinese language thereby transform its people into a whole nation of cognitive cartographers.

It is any wonder that they have been mapping the topography of inner and outer space for so many thousands of years? Their language makes them natural phenomenologists of metaphor. Perhaps this is why the West finds the Chinese mind so enigmatic.

Metaphor is structurally a part of the Chinese language and thoughtways, whereas Western logicians see metaphor as an impurity in logical discourse. But metaphor shall shake the logician awake, for sleeping logic has lost its definitive shape; it no longer conforms to the intricate contours of existence. So metaphor must shake logic awake for fit again's sake. In fact, metaphor is all we have for Being and Time to dig at the hide of meaning lying deep within the cockles of Man.

In keeping with this view, what is to follow then is a *praxis* study into the phenomenological meaning of metaphor. As such, *it contains its own goal, reflects its own image, and projects its own structure. It is constituted of itself and conditions its own definition; it makes an example of itself. As gestures are the mime of thought, so is praxis the onomatopeia of style.*

REFLECTION AND PHENOMENOLOGY

Man has always had a brain. He has not always been aware of it. Within the space of geologic time that Man has inhabited the earth, he has only been able to detach himself, self-reflexively, from his sensory being within the relatively recent past. Until he acquired the faculty of reflection and put names to psychological processes, bodily motion and mind were undifferentiated. The muscles of thought remained untutored.

According to one scholar, the necessary conceptual processes and terms required for detached self-reflexion were not evident until about the time of Homer.[1] Prior to that time, Man could not get out of his own head. Since that time, however, we have all been out of our minds.

Is this not generally what phenomenology is about? Whatever the answer, it is specifically what this study is about. It is an attempt to re-establish contact with "living thought,"[2] thoughts that once more move with the rhythm of our being; to turn cacaphonous logic into a symphony of existence, and to stop our tongues from stammering out the staccato of rhetorical alienation.

The phenomenological process in which this study is engaged is, as far as possible, a *praxis* description of metaphor. And since inner meaning structures can only be reproduced in facsimile, phenomenology becomes inevitably and eternally welded to metaphor. Thus, the tenor of this study is phenomenological, the vehicle metaphorical. Metaphors are the eidetics of Being.

Hence, this study is an expedition into the hinterlands of thought: its mission is to inquire into the origination of concept formation. It is an exploratory journey into the very source of conceptual meaning itself. Unfortunately, we can't go home again, only to a similar place. At best we are phenomenological archaeologists, digging into the ancient ruins of a past existence. The most that can be expected is a reconstruction, a facsimile (i.e., simile-fact).

The phenomenologist, then, becomes a Doctor of Meaning, a specialist in the internal medicine of the mind. The major tool is metaphor. Metaphor, then, is to phenomenology what the x-ray is to medicine. Formal logic, by comparison, is but a dull scalpel that hacks its way through the flesh of rhetorical discourse.

Indeed, to Wesstern logicians, metaphor has been viewed as a kind of counterthink; indeed, a sort of counterfeit thought, not reflecting the consensual countenance of Reason. Even the smallest glance at the history of logic unfolds a view of metaphor that logicians still haggle over. The spirit of the critique is that, in the evolution of reason, logic transcends metaphor as a valid form of thought. What is more, the essence of the thesis is that the dialectic of metaphor is the very antithesis of pure reason. This is why logicians usually recant their use of metaphor. This study will attempt a synthesis of these two phenomena of thought and suggest that these giants of philosophical reasoning belong together.

Phenomenology and metaphor go together as a natural pair, not only because metaphor is all we have to describe inner experience, but also because what we now call abstract thought has its origins in metaphor. The experience of "thinking" and "intellectual comprehension" is a metaphorical derivative of primary sensory processes. The literal terms we now use were once "metaphors" of sensory processes.[3] Metaphors are extensions of our sensory being.

Mythic metaphor lies at the foundations of language and logic. This underworld, however, appears to have no precise network of rules. Metaphors are seemingly ad hoc, capricious, and can be selected almost at random; they are ostensibly irrational, whereas language and logic are rule dominated. If this is the case, thought becomes problematic in the extreme, for how it is that irrationality gives birth to rationality? The answer is that the physics of thought, like physics itself, awaits the rules of transformation (or is it Laplace for whom they wait) rationally linking (but not through probability equations) the micro world of quantum mechanics to the macro world of Newtonian lawfulness. The physical state of thought reflects the state of physics: metaphorical processes are the indeterminate micro universe underlying the macro universe of language and logic. For the most part, all that can be said (at this point) is that somehow randomness turns into reason.

Because language and logic evolve from metaphor, they necessarily reflect their origins. Language and Logic thus constitute a sort of bubble chamber wherein can be observed the traces of our "subatomic" sensory experience; they are our springboard, from which we can dive into our phenomenal selves to recover the subterranean basis of cognitive and semantic movement.

Accordingly, a phenomenology not based on a consciousness of its metaphorical origins, as well as its current expressions, becomes simply a kind of philosophers' psychoanalysis, where deep meaning structures become a sort of intellectual Id, giving rise to eidetic images of ego to be elaborated further into formalized rules of logic, the superego of rational beings.

Living reason requires both logic and metaphor (though both, as we will have occasion to see, ultimately collapse into unity); they are two sides of one being. Living reason is a mobius strip where the surface of metaphor turns into the edge of logic; they are the core and the periphery of the infinitely closed space of meaning. The landscape of living thought is non-Euclidean and cybernetic; logic and metaphor turn into and upon each other, a sort of curved syntactic semantic space where the one hand of cognition applauds its own samsara.

The topology of metaphorical thought is mythically convoluted, whereas logic is topographically Euclidean and irons out the curved space of metaphor. Only logic can be square. And much of phenomenology, despite claims to the contrary, is straight. A metaphorical orientation raises living thought to its apex, where, unlike logic, it does not miss the point of existence. Phenomenologically, humans *construct* their reality, and by self-reflexion are free to choose among multiple rhetorical worlds. Metaphorical reality is also an integral reality creating a multilevel matrix of meaning, leading to a phenomenology of semantic, syntactic, and cognitive structures. Absolute reality, the "thing-in-itself," is crucified on the acrostics of metaphor. A metaphorical reality twinkles with a universe of perspectives which smiles at the traditional logician with a galaxy of Cheshire-grins.

Though metaphor is not confined to words, as it also finds expression in the various arts, the medium through which it will be expressed in this study is language. It is, nevertheless, a sort of a painting with words. However, while verbal images and conclusions may be drawn on this canvas of meaning, all that can be expected here is a mere brush with the truth.

METAPHOR AND CLASSIFICATION:
HOW A THOUGHT GETS A NAME

Our everyday speech is replete with metaphor, some more obvious than others. For instance, "feeling high," "feeling down," "the 'advancement' of science," "the fruit of one's labors," "to sow the seeds of distrust," "drowned in sorrow," "a flight of fantasy," "call to mind." We say that our emotions "get carried away," we have a "flash of insight," or an "unpolished personality"; we call a person "cranky" or an "old crab"; behaviors are "calculated," we "gain respect," time "passes," "flies," and "marches on"; we have a "twinge of remorse."

More importantly, other unrecognized metaphorical forms carry what might be called "cues" to their existence "such as" "for example," "it's a kind of," "a sort of," "reminds one of," "it's a . . . ," "as it were," "it's like," "it's the same as," "for instance." Still less obvious ones are words themselves, as the study of philology reveals: all words are "faded" and "dead" metaphors of petrified meaning.

According to the current doctrine of Webster's unabridged dictionary, that veritable catechism of linguistic meaning, metaphor is "the likening of one thing to another; comparing one thing to another; to speak of one thing as if it were another." Though nothing could be less clear regarding the ontology of metaphor, the dictionary nevertheless is a beginning, a sort of cultural primer to the dead metaphysics of language.

There is nothing in Webster's definition that would lead one to believe that metaphor has anything to do whatsoever with the original creation of meaning. Instead of a root function, it leaves the reader with an impression that metaphor is but a secondary branch of meaning that essentially compares what already exists. There is, however, a more primitive level of comparison leading to linguistic growth.

Webster, along with most of humanity, has been historically mislead by grammarians about the nature of metaphor. To grammarians, metaphor is constituted, obviously enough, by rules of grammar. For example, the simile "you are *like* a frog," is trivially transformed into a metaphor by dropping the "like." Certainly this is just a form of linguistic prestidigitation, for the "like" would in any case be assumed, so nothing has been added to discourse.

This type of definition, though it does distinguish "simile" from "metaphor," is a distinction without a meaningful difference. Moreover, what it distinguishes is merely what itself creates. It does not get to the essentially epistemological problem of metaphor: how shall a thing be called?

Metaphor and Reality

The meaning of metaphorical truth lies in its epistemology. On the one hand, if reality is accepted as a cognitive given, then metaphor is reduced to the status of a figure of speech where ontic categories are described in terms of one another as a mere linguistic game. On the other hand, if reality is considered not a perceivable given, then ontic categories do not exist, in which case the status of a metaphor is raised to a necessary, relational epistemological tool.

In the latter view, all perceptions are constructed, and therefore all classification and naming is "figurative." In the former view, reality is given and therefore "literal." The gallery on the pro, or figurative side is mainly filled with those from the literary "sciences," and a number of philosophers who are concerned with aesthetics. The gallery on the con, or "literal," side of the argument is composed mostly of laymen and many positivist-type scientists and philosophers. The tempo of this debate has been steadily increasing. And so the beat goes on.

The present study will attempt to begin a *praxis* synthesis. Contrary to a positivist position, this study does not begin from the premise (despite the positivist claim that they have no premise), that the "facts speak for themselves." As can be seen in the literature of the psychology of perception, "facts" are not given but are constructed from inner psychic structures.[4] To perceive, therefore, is to project; it is to "throw" oneself integrally into a fact, to become part of it.

The "perceptual" world is in Heraclitean flux, but, due to the nature of our visual system, it is rendered stable.[5] *Since nothing ever occurs in exactly the same way, all so-called "recurrences" are but analogous (metaphorical) events.*[6] Throughout evolution, our nervous system evolved to abstract out of events their *similar* (i.e., metaphorical) characteristics. Survival would obviously depend upon such a trait. Our nervous system, then, reduces this flux to "constant images."[7] Perception is an approximation to reality; it is a facsimile (i.e., something similar to a fact). From this point of view, all reality is (literally) metaphorically figurative.

As to the second problem of metaphor, the naming process, an understanding of classification is necessary, for it is within these winding corridors in which all concepts are contained that the very shape of thought emerges.

Classification

So compulsive are we, that all must have a name. Sometimes, we have many names for the same thing; at other times, we have the same name for many different things. We not only have names for concrete objects like Trees, Dogs, Cats, Bats, and Fleas, but even for things which are not even "there," like the Equator.

One general model (metaphor) to describe the classification process is a "network" scheme, a vast system of multi-leveled matrices of inter-connecting nodes, each node being a concept.[8] According to this scheme, each "plane" has two kinds of nodes, Type nodes and Token nodes; the former are primary concepts, the latter secondary. A Type node will have many Token nodes associated with it. Some Token nodes function individually as subcategories of the primary nodes; others collectively function as contextual relations. There is no predetermined hierarchy of super classes, so every node is potentially the "patriarch" of its own separate hierarchy. To retrieve information, a search rule is required. Concepts, then belong to a network of other concepts; and they are classified by their *similarities.*[9] The concept "triumph," for example, is connected to (a) the Arc de Triomphe, (b) the motorcycle, (c) a conquest, and (d) the number "three"; to "dog," we can associate (a) the canine, (b) a frankfurter (a kind of sausage, not the German City), and (c) an ugly man or woman.

Thus, a word has a rossetting orbit of meaning caused by the relative positions of other nodes in a given universe of discourse, just as the perturbative orbit of the planet Mercury is erratic due to the relative distance of other planets in its universe as it travels its course around the sun. Hence, to understand a word, one must draw or chart its astrological position, as it were, within the cognitive semantic space through which it moves.

It is the search rule, based upon similarity relations, which calls in meaning. A rule sets in motion a "scanning" of the networks for relations by matching the structural elements of each node. When sufficient similarities have been accumulated, classification has occurred.[10] The sum of the "sort" is the limit of the category. The "patriarchial concept" is created by its own relations.

Whether "two things" are considered the "same" depends on whether the rule calls for emphasizing the similarities or the differences between "two" objects or concepts. If similarities are emphasized, "two" become "one"; if differences are emphasized, the "two" remain "two" (or what was once "one" gets divided into two).[11]

This classification process is manifested in the structure of the evolutionary theory of species. The naturalist classifies species according to a rule of similarity along a specific dimension of anatomy or biology. The naturalist "scans" and "matches" a plethora of characteristics and creates a species (a category). This process continues on higher levels to genus, phyla, etc. It is a harmonic of a basic definitional frequency.

Every sentence is an eclectic complex of multiple planes of meaning which resolves into a single plane of meaning by reconstructing itself. Metaphor lies coiled within the interstitial convolutions of every set of categories. The metaphor is a connection amid the chaos of conceptual debris; it is being amid consensual nothingness.

The network is a veritable garden of consensual meaning where metaphor is regarded as a weed. But a "weed" is simply a plant which has no relevance for the gardner; it is not inherent in the "thing," just as a poison is any substance taken in too large a quantity in too short a period of time.

The process of reconstituting continues at yet higher levels. What were considered "weeds" or "debris" now become a problem of wedding accepted but separate categories. It is a problem of conceptual husbandry, where divorce procedures are in play before the consummation. Cries of miscegenation for banding together unlike beings are heard; accusations of adding apples and oranges are voiced. The potential fruit of this union is refused. The whole affair is soundly repealed.

To say that something absolutely does not belong in a certain category is to transform "rule" into "law"; it is epistemological dogmatism.[12] For instance, does "nutrition" apply only to animals and thereby make plant nutrition a "mere" metaphor or analogy? Or does it include both? Most specialists concerned with classification and information retrieval would maintain the latter view. But at the same time, plant *vitamins are not* classified as "vitamins" but are called *auxins*.[13]

What is this protruberance in the body of "nutrition" – half belonging and half hanging out? Is "nutrition" only a "kind of" analogy? Is it a historical hesitation, an ambivalence toward making a definitional decision? Not really. The growth of concepts is a shifting process, a coming together and a coming apart, depending on the rules of a "relevant" similarity which changes periodically. An analogy at one period becomes "the same thing" at another. The concept of nutrition is in a transition period of growth.

A similar, though of course a somewhat different, example is the mathematical function of exponential increase which *can* be applied to the growth of populations, to the multiplication of bacteria, to egg production, and to the growth of knowledge as indicated by the increasing number of books and journals. Since none of these "examples" will have the "same" exponential magnitude, is it applied to these events "by analogy," or does this function indicate "one process" which is reflected in each of these domains? Evidently, the latter is considered to be true, as this mathematical function as it applies to phenomena is called the exponential "law."

It was only made a "law," however, by classifying its applications not as simply analogic but as belonging to the same "class" of events. This is a cardinal epistemological point for a theory of metaphor: *All metaphors, by changing the rule which creates a given set of categories in the first place, become not metaphors but "different instances" of the "same phenomena."*[14]

As in the social world, so too in the conceptual world: phenomena are married to each other by ministering a rule, the difference being that what the rule joins together, any man can put asunder. For one person's metaphor is another's reality.

To create categories then, a search rule scans the networks for invariants; they are then grouped under one rubric. Sub-level invariants create relations between concepts. When the relations fail to be traversed, they fade; the main category loses its continuity, its context. It becomes dead meatphor, an empty abstraction; a collection of them becomes *definition*, the bureaucrat in the institution of reason. The dictionary then becomes a mere tour guide taking us through a veritable pharmacopoeia of medicinal meaning; it is a taxonomy, a mere *Gray's Anatomy* of living reason. Naming seeks refuge in portmanteau.

On the fringes of definitions, then, are clustered conceptual debris, residues of consensual ontic categories, waiting to reach a critical semantic mass, like so many anomalies clustered around a theory (theories are, after all, but concepts writ large).

Again the relationship is a problem of abstraction, of whether one concentrates on similarities or differences. If one thinks the differences are significant, then apples and oranges; if similarities are seen as significant, then they bear fruit. Without similarity there is no continuity, only contingency.

Mixed metaphor, then, depends on one's perspective (the rule). In effect, every sentence is a mixed metaphor of analogic construction, but faded meaning transforms it into digital data. Metaphor carves classification, and therefore meaning, out of contingency; the abstracted word-concept merely stamps its impress upon it. Compared to meatphor, "words" are simply notational systems for thought, and if mixed metaphor is cacaphonous reasoning, allegory is symphonic thought.

Metaphor

Metaphor is habitually used by all, but recognized by few, each person having a different name for it. In fact, we all mainline metaphor, and are addicted to only ostensibly different substances. In any event, to go "cold turkey" is at best a strain on our body of meaning.

Each discipline has its own view of metaphor. It acts as a chameleon taking on the protective coloration of its surroundings, an amoeba con-forming to what it ingests.

To the grammarian, as previously mentioned, metaphor is a mere "figure of speech" indicated by rules of usage. To the philosopher, metaphor is called "eternal recurrence," "induction," "likeness," "synonymity," and "universals." But since phenomena occur only once, and each "fact" is different, they are both instances of metaphorical reasoning.[15] To the scientist, metaphor is analogy, whose structural aspects have been gleaned; or it is the "model," a metaphor abstracted from its context; it is a metaphor in the nude.

To the biologist, metaphor is analogy, functional relationships of similarity (i.e., gills = lungs), and homology, structural relations of similarity (i.e., wings = arms). To the mathematician, metaphor is isomorphic relations, identical structural correspondence. For the psychologist, it is (stimulus) generalization, a stimulus being extended to "similar" stimuli; transposition, an object acting equivalent to another by reason of its relative position in an ordered sequence; constancy phenomena, rendering invariant perceptual variation; it is abstraction and the transfer of learning.[16] To this writer, metaphor is all these and more. The allegory is an extended and systematic sequence of metaphors. A metaphor is an elliptical or ramified simile; and, as analogy is unfolded metaphor, so is the metaphor an elliptical allegory.

While all of the above terms are unique in that they have different characteristics, i.e., structural, functional, extended, proportion, elliptical, etc., they are similar in that all contain within themselves, either manifestly or latently, transformation of invariance. *They are therefore, if one wishes, different species of the genus metaphor.[17] Instances of metaphor extend from images with specific content to abstract ratios of proportionality, as in mathematical or geometrical progression.*

But there is more: to the dancer, bodily expression is nonverbal metaphor. Indeed, extending this notion, our very behaviors are metaphors pointing backward to an inner state of being, where every muscle movement is a functional and elliptical simile transposing itself into strings of behaviors and generalizing into allegories of activity, constantly recurring in repetitive patterns attempting to induce isomorphic behavioral icons of meaning, to transfer an inner feeling to an outer behavior, but resulting in only a syntactical score in a dance for life.

But it is only a model of meaning, for behavior is only proportional to the ratiocination of inner meaning. Coordinated ongoing activity, then, becomes a living symphony. Thus, the choreographer is to dance what the conductor and composer are to music. Similarly, so is metaphor to behavior, for metaphor taps its baton in orchestration of our behavioral rhetoric. As the structures of metaphor lie deeply coiled within the networks of classification, its functioning lies within the intentional patterns of cognitive rhetorical and semantic meaning.

Metaphor is the prism through which meaning is refracted. Metaphor is not a simple figure of speech, stuttering out a kind of reality—it is eloquent and thoughtful oratory, expounding rhetorically on the very reality of reason; it is a psycho-epistemological process reflecting the very function of the nervous system.[18] Metaphor is reality itself traveling incognito.

The Sound of Metaphor

Words are metaphors, nodal points, reaching into the multi-leveled networks of meaning. To play meaningfully with words is not a simple minded matter; it is to create realities. Yet, while it is not child's play at its deeper levels, for adults it can be pun. The pun is the sound of metaphor.

Linguists are aware of the antithetical meanings of ancient and primal words. In the oldest languages, opposites such as strong/weak, light/dark, above/below, etc., were expressed by the same root word, a binary meaning. As thought and language evolved, these constructed, primitive nodes were extended. The action of metaphor (in its generic sense) allows words and roots to move freely over the whole field of language.[19] This was the first detente in the war of meaning.

Nodes of meaning are spaned by metaphors of sound and imagery; they are the audio-visual aids of understanding. Puns are the sounds of meaning that Levy a contrapunctual melody to the Straussian waltz of thought itself.

Accordingly, a word is a double eutendre creating exogamous relations, the linguistic manifestation of the incest taboo whereby relations extend themselves. To be a pun already assumes a family of meaning. Any given pun, then, is a reciprocal relation of a nuclear configuration. It, nevertheless, is extensively related to distant relations. Though the pun is a kin to avuncular metaphor, it is frequently rejected because of its antinomies pointing to objectionable filial origins.

The pun, therefore, is basic to language and thought; it is a micro-metaphor operating in the sounds beneath the barren reefs of language. In the vast undersea islets of coral networks, it creates sounding in order that meaning does not come aground.[20]

A metaphor is a sort of macro-pun as, indeed, a macro-metaphor is a universe of discourse. It should not be mistaken for conceptual pretidigitation, nor for verbal slight-of-tongue, for the pun is a sound concept.

LANGUAGE, LOGIC, AND METAPHOR

Structure

"Inquiry presupposes language." Both lead to meaning; for it is only through language that we gain the answers to the questions posed by inquiry. Flowing from the questions are answers that bear the mark of the language used. Language is the copula between the subject-question and the predicate-answer; it is at once the tenor and the vehicle of meaning. In this sense, language talks to itself, for the rest of the universe is mute; it is indeed a strange kind of tool that manufactures itself. Language, then, is epistemologically primary.

It has now been demonstrated, and is a commonly accepted proposition by some, that our "literal" language is but a repository of faded metaphor; that "concrete" words in reality are dead metaphors embalmed by time; that novel metaphorical meanings become ironed into cliche by the starch of common usage. Words therefore are but mere fossils of extinct species of meaning. Language thus functions as much as a museum as a library of current works.

Phenomenologically, meaning has more than its consensual coverings suggest. In effect, linguistic nuances, our current fashion shows of metaphorical style, are but long-term fads which are modeled by standard beauties. But no matter how attractive the word robe, it is what lies beneath that gives it shape. There is more to a body of meaning than the cut of sheer definition.

Metaphors are too soon worn and too late appreciated. Quickly taken for granted, they become the ritual realities of social meaning. It is the beginning of what is to end in a ceremonial use of the word, a kind of Word-Rite. Beneath this tribal ritual, however, every group of words retains a cabal of meaning; the sacred fire of metaphorical rejuvenation still is faintly evident in the embers of faded meaning. And the Gregorian-like chants to be herd around the elder's campfire resemble a repetitive musical rosary, where they mumble the dead doctrine of a meaningless catechism.

Language becomes a pale reflection, a reified process, mere fossil words of a now frozen experience that once grew from a primal existence where newly ripened metaphor retained a high degree of linguistic meaning, having still clinging to it the heat produced by its ancient compost.

What began as a meaningful journey along a natural path through a t(r)opical rain forest drenched with scenic images, ends as an escorted tour along a super-highway to the capital city of civilized definition, where the high priests of lan-

guage reside, pronouncing on meaning and legislating reality; it is a verbal tour de
force by the linguistic philosophers, the positivists of conversation.

All meaning is sent to the guillotine. Ordinary language philosophers are the
vigilantes of meaning who, upholding the letter of the law, hang on their every
word; they are so concerned with the order of words and phrases that they simply become Men of Letters, sentencing themselves to death.

Linguists have divided speech into a *la langue* and *parole*. The former is the
standard rule structure of language; the latter is each speaker's idiosyncratic usage.
La langue is the constitution, the structure of language, a "closed" system of rules
and meaning, whereas *parole* is a sort of private interpretation of what constitutes
meaning in its everyday functioning; it is freely created speech, a kind of First
Amendment of Language.

Parole seeks to change the established *la langue* through the lower metaphorical
Courts of Appeal. Occasionally, a ruling is judged in its favor, only, however, to
have the decision struck down by the philosophical Justices of the Supreme Court
of Linguistic Meaning. When this occurs, frequently enough, a popular revolution is in the making. But it is destined to essential failure, for the revolution
quickly establishes a new *la langue,* a new ruling class who mandate what constitutes meaningful order. The semantics seemingly change, but the social syntax
remains the same. As in political revolutions, rhetoric appears to change, but the
grammar of order remains eternally the same.

Revolutionary metaphors are now imprisoned, confined once again to *la
langue.* Since it was a popular revolution, the law breakers are treated leniently,
so that, in leaving their confinement, the polysemy do not mind. Metaphor is on
parole. And parole is sanctioned release from incarceration, from Sentence. Parole
dictates that a sentence is never completed.

Metaphor on parole creates custom meaning. And it must periodically justify
to an officer of the court its social relationship and merit. It must have socially re-
deeming qualities. Thus, all consensual metaphorical thoughts are jailor made;
they are formed around the mass produced mannequin of *la langue.*

We must all be students of language and syntax. Is that not why we have the
grammar school? But however good the education, it at best merely defines the
limits of a parochial universe, for the linguistic primer is the dictionary, a cultural
etiquette manual of correct verbal behavior. The teaching of metaphor is not in
the curriculum, even though it is by metaphor that pronouns "can be moved
about."[21]

Reality is born of the word, from the relationship of the word to language. It is
a child that never reaches full growth. Being a sickly child, its education goes
lacking. It learns reading, writing, and reality only from the thesaurus, that dictionary of mechanical cross-meanings. This is as close to metaphor as it will get,
for thesaurus meanings are but the mere calligraphy of thought, a sort of "brand
name" embellishment passing as metaphor.

The absence of metaphor creates other deficiencies as well. Metaphor is to thought what the telescope is to astronomy; it is our cognitive lens by which we bring the stars of meaning closer and which can be aimed at any universe of discourse no matter how many light years away. Without it, philosophers produce Ptolemaic thinkers in a Copernican world, entangling themselves in a maze of logical epicycles.

Indeed, the whole grammar of thought is infused with metaphor; common metaphor is related to language as body is to mind. Accordingly, metaphorical semantics and syntactics are to language what meanings and logic are to philosophical reasoning. In point of fact, syntactic metaphor is the score of the symphony of thought itself.[22] Both language and logic belong to metaphor; metaphor is the mother of thought. No one would deny, however, the autonomous rights of the children, only that they realize the influence of their heritage.

For all of logic's sharp-sightedness, it is neither clear nor obvious what is obvious or clear. The meaning it deflects is but a pale image of a once vital but now faded being, whereas mythic metaphor reflects and represents more closely what it signifies. Neither image, however, is a precise duplicate; the point being that we should not seek too sharp a definition, lest our very existence become empaled upon it.

Language in its encompassing universality stands in relation to itself. It is this fact that creates letters in search of a word, and words in search of sentences. The same is true of speech; it is always in search of a philosophy. Without the metaphorical connection, the brute fact remains: letters, words, and sentences merely bump into each other, merely stand in stark juxtaposition. Rhetoric is rendered tongue-tied, and philosophy is therefore left speechless.

The Word

Assuming that all meaning is social, dialogue is a reciprocal process of interpersonal translation via metaphor, where we do not know what we ourselves have said until the Other tells us. As Merleau-Ponty says, "We who speak do not necessarily know what we express better than those who hear us." Meaning is retrospective. (In a sense, then, only the Other can answer the question, "Who am I?".)[23] Conversation therefore serves to construct and reinforce metaphorical reality. But a silent vacuum is quite evident in the vast interstitial silent spaces between both individual thought and interpersonal conversation. As in the physical universe, there is more empty space than matter.

Meaning is separated by the various "strata" of language.[24] The flow of conversation is full of these ruptures, caused by metaphorically leaping from one strata to another to see what it has to offer as a tool of communication that other strata may lack. At best, the stream of conversation is plagued with a constant fractuation. These micro abysses are spanned by webs of metaphor. Even so, conversation is strained to the breaking point in trying to communicate these silent spaces. Across the cliffs of silence, we are essentially deaf mutes who gesture frantically in an attempt to reveal so that others might help us to define where and who we are. Conversation, then, serves the same function as the scream of bats.

All too often, however, strings of words function as a sentinal's lance; we hurl metaphors at each other as a defense maneuver somewhat like the vocalizations of Howler monkeys who scream to mark off the boundaries of their territory. In response, others howl back in ritual bluff. We are afraid of invasion, not realizing that the ground of meaning belongs to all, and that the advancement of Other merely makes visible an existential sharing which has been the state of affairs all along.

Words become hysterical symptoms destined to repetition; externally thwarted, they are condemned to only partially fulfill themselves. The metaphor is all we have that resembles what it tries to represent. This is the signature of the metaphor, and its significance; it is an insignia of what it signifies.

Words are metaphorical mirrors of "reality" and language, the structural abode of words acts as a house of mirrors where one's own reflection infinitely reverberates upon a series of cognitive harmonics. Thus the quest for ultimate meaning is illusionary.

METAPHOR, LOGIC, AND POSITIVISM

The Myopic Vision

In the beginning was not, as we have been told, the Word; in the beginning was *experience* giving birth to the image, which was transformed into the metaphor-word, which in turn faded and was frozen into the fossil-word, all of this culminating in formal logic and mathematics.[25] Such is the process of abstraction. And so it is that we have been given to believe the proposition that in the evolution of thought, from experience, to the monotonous and repetitive juxtaposition of the cypher and integer, we ascend from the simple to the complex. A sometimes-corollary of this lies in the notion that the direction of this evolution points toward epistemological Heaven, i.e., from the Land of Illusion to the Pearly Gates of Reality. Certainly experience is "mythic," only, in the sense, however, and by the same token, that logic and mathematics are but grim fairy tales. Epistemologically, the quest for certainty is the methodological and philosophical equivalent of the theologician's search for God.[26]

In fact, the evolution of this universe is from the complex to the simple, and logic and mathematics are the extreme of abstraction. The short of it is that those who maintain the sequence is from the simple to the complex have it all backwards (or upside down, depending on one's relational position in conceptual space).

Positivism: The Winter of Thought and Spirit

As the flow of living reason streams by, it is damned by logic. In the process of abstraction, fluid experience mixes with the shifting sands of consciousness and is thereby made concrete. Sedimented reason becomes the structure of thought, the architecture of informal logic. Eventually, it is transformed and reified into autonomous symbolic logic, the supreme bureaucrat of the institution of reason. Logic has been deified. Appropriately, it secedes from the union of earthly existence.

Logical positivists are prone to maintaining that all metaphor is just compressed poetry, and to say that metaphor has truth value is stretching things a bit, that metaphor is a sort of midget poet, telling a tall story. But it is not metaphorical reasoning that is far fetched; rather, it is linear logic that is strung-out. It is true, however, that metaphor is radical and logic conservative, for logic has little resiliancy, while metaphor is icon-elastic.

Moreover, formal logic is to psycho-logic what Euclid is to Lobachewsky: the latter *therefore* is nonlinear. And thus it is that *this* premise gives birth to its conclusion; it contains within it its incipient progeny. But since formal logic is the son of curved metaphor, it too is circular and turns incestuously in upon its own relations. The conclusion, therefore, is also the father of the premise.

Hence, all thought is talkological and speaks in tongues, and just before it swallows itself there is the aura of revelation. Logicians fail to realize that any verbal argument, in the end, entails metaphor. For example, to "argue by example" (for which they are notorious) is itself using metaphor. This should be too obvious to *mentation.*

Examples are to logical reasoning what experimental data is to scientific thinking; they are the limbs of ambulatory thought. Without them, we are unable to leave our minds; at best we are rendered beside ourselves.[27]

Empirical science, together with positivistic philosophy, has become a secular religion, where high priests of empirical data dictate by Papal decree what constitutes Knowledge and Sin. Advice from the positivistic Cardinals turns logic into a kind of pseudo-Platonic form capable of being translated into minor semantic variations on a syntactical theme in order to maintain a commonality among affiliated sects.

Ruling by philosophical fiat, empirical data substitutes for knowledge, and rules of inference for wisdom. The living church of reason is dead. Worship becomes a "Feast of Fools", devoid of sacred *experience.* The dream of science, to make all knowledge explicit and public, turns into a nightmare. It is a soulless religion where the Gregorian chants of high mass turn into a go-go dance, and communion into a brothel. And the positivist priests, instead of carrying on a dialogue with meaning, engage in a profane monologue with empirical data, a sort of silent prayer to the Anti-Christ.

The belief in scientific precision becomes a new root myth with its procedures transformed into high ritual and earthly ceremony which function to fixate belief to a concrete but false object. Experimental procedures and findings act as mere parables, handed down from one generation to another, documenting and keeping alive the ostensible word of God.

Thus a new form of "methodolatry" emerges. It is a new doctrine that teaches the faithful not to worship the graven image of metaphor. They are blind to the fact that their own catechism is but a body of dead doctrine, once very much alive, but which now serves at worst as a graven sign, and at best as a vacant symbol.

The positivist savior of meaning has come, sent from the Godhead of all living reason with the *Word*. But those who know the metaphorical origins of all things realize it is only a fossil sign and refuse to believe in His coming. So they are expelled from positivist meaning, to wonder forever in Sentence.

Increasingly is this religion secularized. Logicians, as a priestly class, as well as linguists, so to speak, become the "jet setters" of the ecclesiastical world, hurring to congress with their denuded habits. There is not a person, place, or thing that is as pure as once thought. And, while these jet setters arrive at their congress with penetrating speed, they miss a lot of the conceptual fields below. They are existential chauvinist high steppers due for a fall, when, in conclusion, they finally stumble upon their own premises.

It is a fundamentalist religion, for they "interpret" the empirical text literally. The weight of hermeneutics is considered unbearable. To them, description is clear; to interpret is not to understand the word of God. They read their Bible like a map, and believe they hold the key to its meaning. Indeed they do, but not as they think, for every description of this kind is based on a mere legend. The Vienna Circle was the Last Supper.

But the acid of positivism has eaten away at its own being until it has nearly consumed itself. Anemic logic needs infusions of metaphor. Now delirious, the positivists continually creates mirages in the desert, signs toward which they thirstily trudge. But as always, they evaporate and remain as distant as ever the nearer they approache them. In the end, if the positivists persist in their quest after these illusions, they will further dehydrate their very existence. On the other hand, the phenomenologists smugly sitting beside their eternal oasis, mediating on their internal navel, are bound never to travel very far (of course, it just may be that there is nowwhere to go, anyway).

But the positivists have had no movement either, for dehydration has rendered them constipated. In a frantic attempt at medication, the positivists brought in physics, supposedly to act as a kind of philosophical Ex-Lax with which to purge the bowels of meaning. But the order got confused, and positivism was given an acid enema that completely disemboweled it. And now all the positivists can do is break wind. In the end, physics is overtaken, so positivism now remains on the run. With its internal plumbing removed, its observed facts no longer hold water (all of this, of course, is hindsight).

Phenomenology turns exclusively in upon itself for its knowledge. Positivism looks simply at the "facts." The former is introverted to the point of being asocial; the latter is so extraverted that it leaves the social world. Lacking the etiquette of "correct" social intercourse, both are engaged in a sort of epistemological masturbation. and while it may be personally pleasurable, it is not genetically productive. With the exception of this one rather onerous behavior, both are in fact quite puritanical. But to produce "knowledge," as ancient Hebraic wisdom understood, is "to know" the desired body in question.

Without metaphorical phenomenology, logical empiricism duplicates itself, a sort of conceptual cloning. Similarly, without logical empiricism metaphorical phenomenology grasps its own being and replicates itself parthenogenically. An isolated datum-universe is a kind of linguistic gene pool that requires an external infusion to maintain its vitality. To "critique" a pool of knowledge, then, requires that we speak from another universe of discourse, a sort of existential Godel's theorem.[28]

Logicians borrow metaphor constantly, but, having little interest, refuse to give it credit. Pimp logic turns pristine metaphor into a whore. Logicians collect metaphors, for example, like so many harem girls. It is their way of proving their conceptual leisure time potency. No one would deny the ability of logic to conceive and construct an edifice of meaning. Indeed, it is not its powers of erection that are in question, but its futility.

It is the prowess of the ship of positivism that contains sterile seamen. And the lookout in the crowsnest observes nothing; its rudders flap aimlessly, like its flacid sails upon its empty sea of meaning. Caught in the safety harness of logic, the groins of metaphor are sorely heard from a constant chafing at the bit of its constrained existence.

Rhetoric, Polemics, and the Politics of Metaphor

Neither the density of metaphor nor the sheerness of logic convince or move anyone. Logical facts do not speak for themselves. If they do, it is in a whisper requiring metaphorical amplification. Logic alone is empty discourse; metaphor by itself is no discourse at all. Separately, there is speech but little meaning. Logic gives coherence; metaphor gives meaning and leads to discovery. Growing out of the motivational meaning base of the latter, polemics and rhetoric give forceful direction. A metaphor that is chosen to emphasize a point and/or to persuade a listener turns into rhetoric; one that is chosen to simply win an argument turns into polemic. Thus, from the point of view of the speaker, intention defines polemic from rhetoric. Pure discourse is a seller in search of a buyer. Polemics and rhetoric, therefore, are the P.R. men of meaning.

The selection of any particular metaphor is in part a political act. Granted, "political" is a relative term. As words are dead metaphor, so must politic and polemic also become faded and accepted as "literal," i.e., nonpolitical and non-polemical. Only those metaphors which deviate from the norm of meaning are viewed as rhetorically polemical. This, of course, includes those establishing different categorical connections.

To speak the "standard polemics" is not to be seen as political. To deviate is to be radical. A radical (new) metaphor brings an unorganized mass together. Metaphor, then, is a union organizer who breaks the contracts of established meaning. When this occurs, problems ensue, and the workings of reality require negotiation of a court injunction.

Despite the numerous volumes of critiques of metaphorical discourse, suffice it to say at this point that most critics seldom write a treatise justifying their own comments; they think only in the margins. Occasionally they add a footnote.[29]

In the court of logic, metaphor is considered a hearsay, as a statement of value, not as a statement of fact. It is not only held to be inadmissible evidence, but is reduced to the role of court jester, even though the very basis of legal reasoning rests on *comparing* cases to established precedent.[30] The whole affair becomes rather Kafkaesque, with the court ruling that metaphor is inadmissible while the very measure of the court's reasoning is gauged by it. It is at once the court's Magna Carta and its Maginot Line.

However they are used, logic and metaphor belong together. Metaphor is the very fabric of individual meaning; it is a sort of patchwork quilt stitched together by social logic.[31] Its function is to cover our naked reality. The syllogism puts sizing into a series of metaphors.

Logic and metaphor must learn to live in positive harmony; they must compose themselves. All too frequently and periodically, they dance to a different beat. But while the meter of a series of metaphors has its own rhythm which is not a linear swing, it is not entirely without the sway of logic. All too often, however, with measured steps logic composes its premises for the purpose of beating time to its own conclusions.

Still, logic and metaphor have similar movements. Both can be symphonic, but only metaphor is capable of a jam session. Essentially, however, it is metaphor that orchestrates the flow of living thought, while logic prestidigitates with relatively motionless signs (it merely notes the score).

Language, the musical off-spring melody of this relationship, has always been considered somewhat peculiar by chauvinist logic and therefore has had quite a time of it. Thus it was that she was noted, despite her punctuality, to have been carefully guarded lest she rest with any wandering ministrel who might come strumming along in search of a score, or an easy melody for a song. Thus is chauvinistic logic in constant refrain. In such a manner is retribution metered out on the scales of poetic justice.

Metaphor and logic dialectically condition each other. Together they syncopate thought; like the swing of Foucault's pendulum, they mark off the 360° of reason as the sphere of existence revolves beneath. It is madness for a civilization not to recognize this duet.

METAPHOR, MIND, AND MADNESS

Consciousness

The question remains: If metaphor is integral to thought itself, what is its relationship to the nature of awareness, and how is it that what is known as consciousness is constituted? As this study has attempted to demonstrate, the ground of thought lies in a vast network of concepts, themselves constituted by micrometaphorical relations. The process is what psychologists call concept formulation. Writ large, it evolves into thought. To better explain this evolution, however, it is necessary to briefly retrace the steps of classification that ultimately grow into the very footprints of consciousness itself.

The newborn child, excluding a priori structures, experiences, as William James has said, a "blooming, buzzing, confusion," the sound of its own spontaneously firing neurons, which slowly become structured by impinging external stimuli. Through (sheer contiguity and) metaphorical relations, objects are associated as belonging together. For example, not all objects that are labeled "chair" have the same shape, yet by their metaphorical relations these different objects are grouped under one heading by a rule of selectivity, the "rule" acting as a sort of primitive logic creating continuity and coherence.

As this basic process continues, lower order concepts are combined into higher order concepts, with each preceding one giving to, and integrally included as part of, the higher order concept. At this stage, consciousness is nascent, and as further interconnections develop, held together colloidally: embryonic thought is present. There are many such hierarchies along different levels of meaning and abstraction, but they are not absolute; they change relative to a given perspective – a higher order rule.

The stream of thought as manifested in a sentence or a series of sentences pulls these different levels into a continuous, single "plane" which, when reified, becomes a universe of discourse, sui genesis. To illustrate: imagine watching a porpoise darting playfully through the water, diving and resurfacing as it continues its journey along a certain course. What was observed was: the porpoise on the surface at T^1, at T^2 the porpoise dives under the water, at T^3 a porpoise surfaces, at T^4 the porpoise dives beneath again, etc. But now assume that what you thought to be a single porpoise was in fact a whole school of porpoise, all of which but one at any given time were submerged. As the school moved on, every time a porpoise submerged, a different porpoise surfaced, giving the impression that the observer was watching a single porpoise. So it is with a stream of thought.[32]

Just as, at the moment when the porpoise submerged, there is a visual void, so too do these fractures in the ostensible flow of thought, as they enlarge, become ruptures in the stream of consciousness (just as a "solid" pencil line, when viewed under a microscope, is really a shaggy series of dark blotches). As the eye must constantly scan its environs and engage in micro oscillations as its image fades and disappears, so too must thought constantly scan its network of concepts to maintain attention. It oscillates to scan the multitude of metaphorical relations (invariants) which hover around any complex thought process.

Thus, when we think we actually engage in a dynamic process of comparisons, if they occur fast enough, the dis-comparisons go unnoticed. Consciousness is a flickering process of blinking thought; occasionally, we catch it winking at itself.[33]

This is illustrated on a new level in the case of a new universe of discourse, where the lower and different levels appear not to fit. The process is occuring slowly enough to notice. Consciousness, then, is the result of metaphor collating multiple levels of invariants. And, in a coherent discourse, it is the "rule" of logic that staples them together.

The process continues to even higher levels of inclusion and integration. Theoretically, it is infinite. Perhaps at a certain level there exists an omega sphere which, when entered, creates the experience that Buddhists call nirvana. The feeling of oneness. The ultimate fusion of metaphors.

Be that as it may, what we ordinarily call conscious thought is a ramified integral of metaphorical relations, giving rise to an expansive hierarchy of metaphorical progression, manifested in a spiral of increasing ratios of proportionality. This structure is externally reflected in the logarithmic spiral and geometric progression, as well as the perceived order of the physical universe (though less precisely), i.e., subatomic particles are to the atom what the atom is to the molecule, and what the molecule is to the cell, what the cell is to the organ, what the organ is to the organism. Again, it is also reflected in the very structure of evolution, where species is to a genus what a genus is to a phyla, etc. Consciousness is a progressive harmonic of a basic neural theme of metaphorical organization.[34]

In conclusion then, consciousness is basically two-fold. In its general aspects, it is constituted by multiple levels of metaphorical imagery connected by various invariant relations; in its special aspects, it is devoid of imagery content and is simply metaphor of proportions, a progressive series of invariant ratios superimposed upon each other in harmonic fashion.

The Root Metaphor

Root metaphors in the works of writers extend to the reader multiple levels of meaning, leitmotifs pointing backward to their origins. At the same time, they conjure extant images and feelings giving rise to future perceptions. They signify, simultaneously, many levels of nuances.

Some of these root metaphors can be explicated, as they are constituted in fairly distinct words and phrases. Others, however, seem to be intangibly propertied in organization itself, to be a quality belonging to the silent relational spaces among otherwise segmented written symbols intimating consensual meaning, where, into the interval, the reader is mandated to project the depth of his or her own being and root metaphors. At other times, these root leitmotifs exert their brute presence through sheer juxtaposition. Root metaphor speaks rationally and irrationally; it at once expresses the connotative and dennotative that resonate the multiple nodes of meaning.

Michael Foucault's *Madness and Civilization*[36] will stand as an exemplification of the supreme use of such metaphors. Foucault has a penchant for extending his being through the written word. From the deepest layers he launches his natural language of inner space with powerful metaphors that pierce "rational" dialogue and begin to release and unravel the convolutions of existence which are not frequented in the cause of social conversation.

His is a writing that, if spoken, becomes at once religious and obscene. While his writing is rational, indeed almost hyper-rational, it bears the clear markings, the stigmata, of its deeper origins. His writings have a home.

Foucault is the phenomenological French connection of root meaning, the pusher of a strange kind of rational surrealism. *Madness and Civilization* turns Foucault into the E. A. Poe of the history of dementia. The reader is enticed into a network of metaphors that reflect the words composing the title of his book. The reader is drawn into a menagerie of historical data on the evolution of madness, a sort of living Rue Morgue of wondering madmen. But madness resides not in men, rather in a situation that sucks men into its meaning: madness exists only in relation to civilization, indeed it is only a mirror image of rational civilization where madness becomes a sort of left-handed sanity.

He demonstrates the historical swing of Western civilization's bout with madness from a time when it was *socially* nonexistent to a time when the (w)hole of Western culture becomes a snake pit. Foucault's pendulum marks off the historical dates of the evolution of insanity from a period when the madman was a sort of socially tolerated wandering minstrel to an era when the melody of madness turned socially cacaphonous. In the meantime, civilization continues its St. Vitas dance while Foucault beats out the tune of an irrational history to the rhythm of a swinging dialectic.

The semantic power of Foucault is immence. Like the black holes of the outer fringes of the universe that suck in all matter within their gravitational reach, one is irresistibly drawn into Foucault's linguistic space. As one is pulled into Foucault, one senses an organic, natural force surging through his paragraphs; there is a throbbing, pulsating, almost engulfing, tone about them, almost to the point of nausea, as he verbally vomits up the phelgm of historical congestion. It is a surrealistic documentary: Eyes bleed sweat and pores seep tears. Madness itself is poured into his words. One can feel the paranoid tensions produced by a description of a natural historical process evolving out of the control of Man; it is a process where a humane morality does not exist; there is only the unfolding force of a naturally ordered contingency. It is a Darwinian universe where wildness reigns. And, in the reading, one's cerebral convolutions drip with a nervous sweat and one feels drenched with a primal ooze recalling one's own evolutionary past; it is a universe where even wisdom trembles in the presence of understanding.

All this Foucault does with carefully placed metaphors which paint images that are painfully and indelibly etched upon the reader's mind. He is at once the Hieronymus Bosch of language and the Dali of semantics. He is a linguistic surrealist, painting the depths of reality. It is not just a hint that he gives, not just a thin or superficial Vermeer, but the naked starkness of existence itself punctuated appropriately with an occasional saving grace of an illusion. Through his reasonating metaphor, Foucault manages to transcend the mind/body schism. He is a poet creating the lyrics of a historical sensate sonata.

Unwrapping his tempered thought like finely sprung steel and with the tension produced thereby, the reader awaits its checked power to snap back to its original mythic bend, hoping that his imagery will be folded back into and forever entombed in its coils. In closing the soaking pages of his book, the reader sighs in relief to return to an everyday reality, and wonders if Foucault, himself, is not mad.

Metaphor and Madness

From the repetitive epochs of the evolution of Man's nervous system, metaphor undulates within him. Indeed, it ripples throughout the entire history of his nervous system. Man is "thrown" into a Sartreian world of meaning with metaphor "strapped" to his being.

The purile plea of the phenomenologist to return to the zero point of being may not reveal what he or she intends, for the natural leverage of this place is too great. Before reaching this (perhaps legendary) Archimedean point of existence, there are many levels of civilization and layers of a biological heritage to penetrate. At any step along the way, one is liable to get stuck or to misinterpret the signs. In any event, should this time traveler reach this source of being, he may merely find the pure hum of natural energy, which will be the sound of his own ten billion cell computer. At this asocial depth, the phenomenologist will not have to be concerned with listening for the "thing-in-itself," for the "he" or "she" will not be there to hear. Madness draws near.

Madmen merely operate from a different metaphorical system of categories; they have lost (or prefer not to adhere to) the consensual metaphorical categories of everyday reality. Their metaphors well up from different and older strata of existence. The study of madness should tell us a great deal about sanity.

To understand the relationship between madness and metaphor, then, we must reconstruct as best we are able the artifacts found in the ruins of ancient meanings, for metaphor is the curator of our living thought museum. We are therefore always partially linguistically entombed in the mausoleum of dead meaning images, with each of our concepts partly mummified, wrapped in the decaying cloth of ancient meaning, and partly newly bound in the sterile modern gauzes of antiseptic definition.

To descend into these archaeological digs, these dark catacombs of thought is not an amateur outing; one had better have a guide and a translator to transfer hieroglyphic experience into familiar meaning. Again, the phenomenologist's desire to plunge into the primal sea of self is at least as potentially dangerous and costly as it is prophetable. Even with proper equipment and expert training, diving for metaphorical treasures is hazardous.

At certain depths, especially if one stays for too long a time, one becomes light headed and giddy, and responds to the call of no return. For those who return from the depths of fluid metaphor, some may not return in the same condition as when they left. Some of them panic and surface too abruptly, developing psychic bends for which they must undergo long and painful decompression.

Thus, if one wishes to descend into these caverns of meaning to dig for phenomenological meaning, one should be of sufficient experience to check the structures on their way down, for, when reaching the gelatinous mass at the core there is liable to be a "shaking of the foundations." There comes a point when the shafts of phenomenological analysis, piercing deep into the ground of meaning, must, because of the gravity of that depth and the density of their own meaning, collapse of their own weight, leaving in shambles the delicate consensual structures of sanity.[37] For most phenomenologists however, there is little danger, for they are merely the strip miners of the meaning industry.

Indeed, if we brought our crouching inner selves to total visibility, would we be able to stand the sight of it? Recalling an ancient "myth," we must wear metaphorical lenses if we are to psychically survive staring at the Medusean head of metaphor.

The consensual world of sanity is composed of faded metaphorical structures and images at which we emptily gaze compulsively and transfixedly, afraid that, if we take our eyes off them, they will disappear. At heart, we are all trembling solipsists.

The crystallized categories of everyday existence fix us to a psychic place. But erosion is nature's instrument of change. And, as in the geologic universe, so too in the psychic world: uniformitarianism creates stability; cataclysmic upheavals produce trauma. But even in the best of eras, the ground of meaning is strained; at any moment, its gravity of meaning may weaken, releasing concepts to amoebically float amongst each other, becoming imperceptibly interchangeable, as in a dream where the metaphorical categories of everyday reality mingle unsegregated. Madness lurks on the fringes of rational concepts.[38]

In the phenomenological search for conceptual renewal, an almost religious care must be taken not to displace and render homeless the previous inhabitants of that area, leaving them to wonder aimlessly on a Laingean journey into the land of Knot,[39] a sort of weird schizophrenic safari into the deepest enclaves of Madagascan meaning where strange forms have evolved indigenously. It is here that madness and creativity dissolve into one.[40]

When leaving the mainland of meaning to land on a lawless frontier, wild creativity stalks the consensual metaphor. Existential paranoia lurks behind every thought and word. The world of deep metaphorical meaning structures is a primitive place where slithering insinuation lies coiled, ready to strike at any passing thought. If it is successful, it hits its mark and injects its venom, resulting in a feverish delerium, ending in either psychic death or revelation.

Out of the mouths of madmen spew primitive metaphors, a veritable schizophrenic "word salad" seemingly akin to speaking in tongues; strung together, metaphors ooze surplus meaning like so many surrealistic relational word images; meaning drips over edges of cognitive comprehension like a grotesque Dali mural; it is a world where categories melt their excess over the canvas of reality.

Such metaphor can become a revel-elation. And when the Brueghel blows, one either arises to the occasion or rests forever to the mournful sound of taps, sounded for the souls who have overshot the cannons of meaning. These madmen speak in strange parables belonging to another time, to another strata of discourse, for which there are few rules of transformation. As a consequence, their meaning reflects the curved space of their enclosed being; their words become the sine language of their souls seeking escape, their speech simply a cry in the night of meaning, a mere whimper reflecting a primal scream.

Encased in their linguistic sarcophagi, their musculature becomes frozen into strange, metaphorically expressive contortions in an attempt to communicate; thwarted meaning transforms their entire body into a living ideogram. And, in struggling to extricate themselves, they become further entangled in an epicyclic maze of metaphors. Theirs is an anti-universe where meaning revolves only around their own earthly being, a sort of Ptolemaic sanity.

The structure of madness is an anti-bureaucracy of private thought, where little of substance is communicated, where madmen send only memoranda which quickly get dispersed to the archives of a faded meaning. The insanity of this place is maddening amnesia where consensual metaphors cannot be remembered. They are in that interval of time, that plenum of nothingness, where there is only deafening quiet; it is a place where silent voices fall on deaf ears, where thought speaks only to itself; it a place where silent screams are amplified through muted gestural metaphors.

But gestural language only mimes meaning; it is a kind of anatomical onomatopoeia. Communciation becomes a charade. The madman waves his hand like a magic wand in an attempt to create familiarity. But he remains a Wizard of Awes.

When one descends into the phenomenological rabbit hole, into that metaphorical punderland, there is only the Mad Hatter spewing schizophrenic sentences, the Red Queen with her reverse causality, the Catapillar with his smokey meanings, and the disembodied Cheshire Cat with an ontological grin.

(Alice, too, was curious, and she ended up in the Magic Forest where nothing had a name. Alice, however, was lucky to have a guide: the Doormouse, who kept reminding her to keep her head. He was the only "sane" one in the lunch. But even he had his problems. As a defense against the dizziness of his surroundings, he kept falling asleep.[41]

Ostensibly, the phenomenological task is to disentangle the Gordian Knot of deep meaning structures, but to do so the phenomenologist will have to turn himself inside out and expose his raw nerves to the metalic touch of reality; to have the convolutions of his cerebral intestines tacked to his sides for the jackels of consensual meaning to tear and rip off. In the process, he will be denied social sustenance, and in the end will be forced to cannabalize himself. His very being will shrivel into a twisted mass from being exposed to the dryness of such a void.

Even a creative trip into the deep strata of language and meaning may not be all pleasure. When one descends into its womb, the stench of putrification brings one to the brink of vomiting up old verbal decay, for to give birth to creativity is not always successful: one must endure the pain of hard labor. The successful birth is natural and rhythmic; its embryonic meaning must slowly change position to ensure its transformational passage into the world of consensual beings. To skip a stage may mean choking on its own placental juices, and unless it skillfully executes its movement, it strangles itself on its own existence-giving umbilical cord, destined never to make it across the breach.

This is the way of growth. Primal decay fertilizes new linguistic forms, and from each new concept seeps a peculiar odor reflecting its origin.

One should therefore cautiously navigate phenomenological waters. Even at anchor, deep cross-currents of meaning may rip one's existential moorings from their hold and cast one adrift on a raging sea of insanity. Its logical ballast shifts, causing a dangerous list from its unbalanced load. The good ship rationality floats aimlessly on a fermented sea; it becomes a drunked "ship of fools." Without compass or sextant, not knowing which way to seek shelter, unable to make up its mind, it cannot get out of the whether. With ruptured hull, it lies derelict in the graveyard of ships—the Sargasso Sea of meaning. It will never dock at Portmanteau. Madness is isolated metaphorical monologue; and sanity is consensual confinement to a universe of dis-course.

The Architectonics of Body Metaphor

On the one hand, the body is an icon, a metaphor; it is a physical representation, a *sign* of historical structures external to it and of psychological structures existing within its internal space. On the other hand, and at the same time, the body replicates and extends itself upon a world that it constructs. The body therefore is both a reflection, a ramified metaphorical manifestation of the world, and a sort of Mercator projector throwing its own image upon the social terrain.[42]

Thus, from the coordinates of the external world one can map the inner and outer metaphorical structures of the body, just as from the coordinates of the body one can map its own inner structures, or the contours of its enveloping social space. Each space can be mapped from the other when superimposed into an extended series of matrices. While the coordinates of the Body shall be used here as the prime system from which to read the mythic structured meaning of a series of affective matrices, it is quite arbitrary, for any one of these can function as its "center." Hence no causal deductions should be made as to the interrelations of this analysis, even though the force of the analysis seems to flow from the coordinates of the Body.

It should be stated here at the start that contemporary bourgeois posture is hardly singular in its form, Historically, however, it can perhaps be said to merely imitate an earlier form of aristocratic poise. Whatever its genesis, it may be safe to say that any similar characteristics which it may appear to possess to any earlier forms stand in a mere homologous, not analogous, relationship.

By way of a general description, bourgeois body posture is similar to what is known as the "professional facade," the logical extension of which is to be seen in the frozen countenance of the bureaucrat which remains impervious to its impinging surround. Specifically, the body is held rigid, its steps are measured, and its speech, while seeming to flow, is static, the impression of movement being given by each new word merely bumping into the previous one on its way to stand in a verbal line, like a series of billard balls which, when struck in domino fashion, merely send the end ball flying while the others remain standing in place.

Bourgeois posture thereby gives the impression of a calmness: the face is neutral, as is its monotonic and deliberate speech, which eminates from somewhere within it; the eyes are still and staring, and the blink rate is well below normal, indicating extreme control. Only occasionally do the edges of the mouth turn upward. Even then, all that can be discerned is a thin, smirk-like grin. Accordingly, the clothes are worn like a suit of armor so the body may be kept in place. The necktie is worn as if to anchor the head to the rest of the torso, and girdles squeeze that feminine life-giving space into nonexistence.

The body, (like the mind) moreover, is cleaned of everything natural with soaps, deodorants, mouthwashes, and shampoos. The fingernails are cut and manicured, just as the hair is cut and neatly combed into place. No event can disturb this image – a nonresponsiveness is always present. Even the natural act of eating is similarly shaped. The cup and the fork, too, are held in calculated manner. All-in-all, bourgeois posture is mannequinesque.

Its message, like the economy to which it belongs, is: tame, constrain, control, conceal, and, most of all, conserve. These structures permeate all that the bourgeois touches. Just as the private savings account is metaphorical to the larger economic principle of the accumulation of capital, so too is the manicured look of the body isomoorphic to clipping and trimming of the bourgeois lawn; just as the body is stripped of its naturalness in an attempt to preserve it with cosmetics, so too is the bourgeois furniture varnished, painted, and waxed. Nature must be put into an order and preserved. Bourgeois World, like the bourgeois Body, is mummified. Brassiered breasts present only the shape of sustenance.

Its posture is anti-life. The body is a zombie, neither dead nor alive. The great calm and deliberations of the body posture are, in actuality, more of a paralysis; it is a catatonia of the soul projected onto the body; it is a hysterical symptom reflecting a profound and penetrating ambivalence regarding spontaneity and control, indeed of life and death itself. Consequently, the bourgeois remains petrified between two opposing forces. It cannot be spontaneous, for there is the "production line" that feeds it to which it must conform, as well as the increasing rationalization of the bureaucracy which sustains its relations to the Other and its very identity.

Paradoxically it is connected to a stasis by an umbilical cord originating in a social apparatus that is void of all life. Further it cannot live, for death is the logical consequence of living. This is why all must be sucked dry of its vitality and carefully preserved: the lawn, the furniture, the body: trimmed, encased, cadavered over, entombed.

Nothing must really exist in the sense of growth, for, as life implies death, growth implies decay. Movement must only be apparent movement, i.e., movement not in Time. Hence the static quality of the bourgeois house, body, and politics. All are of the same structure and indeed fold back in upon themselves in incestuous metaphorical replication, a sort of cloning process. Like a moving picture, all action is merely a series of still frames in a successive juxtaposition. Every instant and movement is an isolated datum. Every footstep in mere contiguous relation to the other. Continuity is annihilated, the movement of time simply means more of the same, just as bourgeois posture is a succession of frozen repetition, like a movie stopped dead in its tracks. Posture, countenance, lawn, possessions, life and a nationalized language – all entombed in Time.

NOTES

1. See Bruno Snell (1960), whose thesis is that mankind did not become conscious of self until historically recent times. His thesis is reminiscent of Jaynes's (1976) thesis of the bicameral mind, and of Vico (1948).

2. The term Phenomenology, like that of Structuralism and Existentialism, has become an umbrella term covering diverse and often contradictory notions. Its usage here will generally reflect (but not be limited to) the point of view of M.

Merleau-Ponty (1964): conscious perceptions (i.e., meta-structures) are considered to arise from deeper layers of "consciousness" (i.e., infra-structures).

3. See Giambattista Vico (1948) and Ernst Cassirer (1946). Both authors suggest that metaphor arises from sensory processes. Vico, like Snell and Jaynes, also suggests that consciousness is a late product of historical evolution. Jaynes in part bases his thesis upon recent split-brain data, where our right cerebral hemisphere is considered by some (Galin, 1974) to be a seat of "consciousness" of which we are not aware (see Sperry, 1968).

4. See the classic works of Allport (1955), Hebb (1961), Neisser (1967), and Vernon (1962).

5. The eye and body are in constant movement, rendering the visual world in constant flux which our visual and nervous system must hold constant by transformations of invariants. See Gregory (1966) and Platt (1958).

6. See Bergson (1923), Langer (1942), and Whitehead (1958, 1960).

7. I believe it was Henri Bergson (1923) who first introduced the idea of the mind as a reducing value (in modern terminology mind = nervous system). The idea is now almost commonplace in the psychology of perception. We constantly filter out stimuli at various levels of neurological processing. (See Dixon, 1981.)

8. See Quillian (1967) for an early formulation of this view.

9. See Vickery (1961).

10. Hayek (1952) describes a similar classification scheme to the one by Quillian presented, here only in terms of neurological pathways, under the heading "The Nervous System as an Instrument of Classification," p. 55. An almost identical scheme is given by D. O. Hebb (1961). Both have become "classic." Hayek says, "A wide range of mental phenomena, such as discrimination, equivalence of stimuli, generalization, transfer, abstraction and conceptual thought may all be interpreted as different forms of the same process of classification which is operative in creating the sensory order."

11. As Socrates says, "I am myself a great lover of these processes of division and generalization; they help me to speak and to think. And if I find any man who is able to see 'a One and Many' in nature, him I follow, and 'walk in his footsteps as if he were a god.'" (Plato, 1956).

12. As Cassirer (1946) suggests, "But what are concepts save formulations and creations of thought, which, instead of giving us the true forms of objects, show us rather the forms of thought itself? Consequently, all schemata which science evolves in order to classify, organize and summarize the phenomena of the real world turn out to be nothing but arbitrary schemes – airy fabrics of mind, which express not the nature of things, but the nature of mind." p. 73.

13. See Vickery (1961).

14. Moreover, since a category is put together by a rule, when the rule is removed it no longer coheres. It is here that we have the conceptual "analogue" of randomness: As Nagel (1961) points out, "The logically incoherent assumption

of an absolutely random distribution must therefore be replaced by the coherent hypothesis of *relative disorder* (or relative randomness), according to which a sequence of events is a random or disordered sequence, if the events occur in an order that cannot be deduced from any law belonging to some specified class of laws. On the other hand, though the occurrence of events of a certain type may be random relative to one class of laws, their occurrence may not be random relative to some other class of laws" (p. 334).

15. For philosophers' use of these concepts, see Goodman (1952), Mates (1952), and Burke (1954). Burke discusses Nietzsche's "eternal recurrence." The literature on induction is enormous and complex, but for a fundamental overview, see Kaplan (1964) and Oppenheimer (1956). For a "negative" view of analogy, see MacDonald (1960) and Ryle (1953). For an extensive analysis of models, see Hesse (1963). Indeed as Berggren (1962) maintains, a philosophical work has never been written which did not rely heavily upon the use of metaphor. Burke (1954) also suggests, "Indeed, as the documents of science pile up, are we not coming to see that whole works of scientific research, even entire schools, are hardly more than the patient repetition, in all its ramifications, of a fertile metaphor?" See also Honeck and Hoffman (1980), Ortony (1979).

16. See Agassi (1964); Anderson (1964); Bruner, Wallach, and Galanter (1959); Fisher (1916); Grose and Birney (1965); Jardine (1967); Mostofsky (1965); Osgood (1949); Pikas (1966); Wallach (1958); Wilner (1964).

17. The reader is referred to the following for the rudiments of several brief classifications: Black (1962), Edie (1975), Preus (1970), Sacksteder (1974), Shibles (1971), Turbayne (1963), Urban (1961), Vaihinger (1924).

18. The idea that metaphorical/analogical reasoning is an inherent property of the nervous system has occasionally been suggested. Little by way of direct hard data has been historically offered, however. The paucity of data linking metaphorical cognition with neurological research has been largely due to viewing metaphor as a simple figure-of-speech and not as a fundamental form of thought. Metaphorical function has not been considered an "instance" of stimulus generalization or transposition. The research of Gregory (1966), Hayek (1952), Pitts and McCulloch (1947), Platt (1958), and Thompson (1965) can be read as supporting neurological data. See also Haskell (1968, 1984) and Marks (1978). Recently, Sternberg (1977) has provided experimental work relating analogical reasoning to intelligence. As Aristotle suggested: "The greatest thing by far is to be a master of metaphor. It is the one thing that cannot be learned from others. It is the mark of genius" p. 101 (Cooper, 1960. It is interesting to note that the Miller Analogy Test, which is positively correlated to I.Q. tests and which predicts success in graduate study, has no theoretical foundation).

19. See Malinowsky (1923).

20. The Joycean scholar McLuhan (1964, p. 57) understands the pun. He says, "That it utilizes the manifold application of the same material, the accent, nevertheless falls upon the rediscovering of the familiar and upon the agreement be-

tween both words forming the pun" And in keeping with "metaphor" the information retrieval above, note: "Words are a kind of information retrieval that can range over the total environment and experience at high speed." Also, according to McLuhan, "We must understand that prose is no longer a useful technique for getting ideas across. It's too linear; it's too extended. You have to get things across by means of puns because puns condense ideas into single images" (p. 237).

21. Fernandez (1972) says in this regard, that the systematic study of metaphorical forms in human intercommunication involves the study of the movement they make in semantic space.

22. It has become cliche that, while metaphor has a semantics, it has no *syntactics*. See Watzlawick, Beavin, and Jackson (1967); also Edie (1975). To say "metaphor is too soon worn and too late appreciated" is to engage in syntactical metaphor. The syntax is "carried over" from the Dutch proverb, "We are too soon old and too late smart." The model is also a syntactic metaphor.

23. See Merleau-Ponty (1964). Also see Weick (1969), who makes the point that meaning is constructed restrospectively, which kind of puts a new slant on the rationality of planning and rhetoric.

24. See Waismann (1953).

25. What is being suggested here is that what we call logic is "dead metaphor." In the entire literature on metaphor/analogy that I am familiar with (of which the references quoted here are but a small portion), I have seen this notion explictly stated only recently. The reference follows: (Sacksteder, 1974) "It is rather the case that the utility of presupposed structural analogies is so prevalent and fertile that we might suspect that even the inferences of logic are instances of a rule derivative from our analogies. The more important sense in which a resemblance may be supposed to justify an inference arises from an inverse thesis, namely that any logic (that is, any structure of inferential rules) is based on an analogy. Were this the proper order of dependence, we should not seek through logic to justify an argument by analogy. *Rather we should justify a logic by the analogy on which it is itself based. Analogy is not a relatively poor use of logic: rather logic is a relatively good use of analogy"* (p. 242; emphasis added).

This notion is also implicit in Turbayne (1963). Turbayne's work is a good systematic explication relative to the reification of the metaphor of Euclidean geometry as it relates to logic. Here, then, we have the beginnings of an analysis of rhetorical movement on a very root level. (For the notion of "root metaphor" see Pepper, 1941).

In this regard, reference Frye (1966); ". . . whatever is constructive in any verbal structure seems to me to be invariably some kind of metaphor or hypothetical identification, whether it is established among different meanings of the same word or by the use of a diagram. The assumed metaphor in their turn become the units of the myth or constructive principles of the argument. While we read, we are aware of a sequence of metaphorical identifications; when we have finished, we are aware of an organizing structural pattern or conceptualized myth" (p. 73) (Also see Buchanan, 1962.)

26. Similarly, many phenomenologists are "psychological theologians." This study, however, is founded on the epistemology that social and psychological reality are constructivistic. See Ichheiser (1970), Scheff (1968), Schutz (1970), Butler (1969), and Neisser (1967).

27. Theoretically, the number of "metaphors" by which to describe reality is infinite. And theoretically they are arbitrary (i.e., no ultimate grounding). But in the pragmatics of everyday phenomena, this does not appear to be the case. Indeed, there seems to be "real" (non-metaphor-ical) realities. The explanation for this is two-fold. From the Kaleidoscopic flux of metaphorical configurations of reality, certain ones are "clicked" into frozen patterns by (a) contingent associational conditioning, and (b) experimental confirmation. The implications of these processes are of cardinal significance for a theory of metaphor. As to the first process, after constant association and other symbolic connections in time and space, and reinforcement, phenomena become fixed and accepted as "natural." Thanks to psychological learning theory, this process is well known, so more need not be said. As to the second process, experimental confirmation fixes a metaphor (hypothesis) to a "physical reality" by extending the metaphor to an experimental situation. The consequences of this process are not widely recognized, especially with reference to the epistemological problem of metaphor: According to empiricist doctrine, a hypothesis (metaphor) remains simply an "idea" until confirmed by experimental data. But logically this is merely "asserting the consequent," as some logicians put it. What this rather obtuse phrase means when unwrapped within the terms of this study is this: *experiments are the physical metaphorical expressions of an idea: they are as "examples" to the logician. From this perspective, experiments are physical metaphors expressing correspondence to the idea they are to confirm (or not to confirm).*

Moreover, in this view, the process of verification becomes the same process involved in any *comparison* or matching task. The rules of transformation regarding this "mapping" process are far from precise. Finally, what does the "metaphor" view of the experiment do to the problem of circularity (i.e., asserting the consequent) which "experimental" data is supposedly designed to break through? Presumably, this state of affairs simply moves circularity out one more orbit. Perhaps this is epistemological progress. In any event, it renders circularity a matter of degree, not kind.

The history of science is strewn with experimental analogues that ostensibly confirmed its corresponding hypothesis; i.e., for example, the Ptolemaic metaphor, the aether metaphor, the phlogistin metaphor, the germ-theory metaphor, etc.; see Kuhn (1962). See, also, Koestler (1959); the work of Rosenthal (1966), in experimenter bias and self-fulfilling prophecy of experimentation, leaves the force of the argument for the deification of experimental reification a little weakened.

28. One of the major criticisms of meatphor is, since it is a comparison, that it is therefore tautological; and to be tautological is to be excommunicated from the devine order of logical and rational beings, even though it has never been adequately explained why operational definitions and mathematics in general have been granted amnesty.

29. In terms of significant form, metaphor in rhetorical discourse has not been studied for its persuasive effect. A few early studies are: Bowers and Osborn (1966), Osborn (1967), Osborn and Ehninger (1962), and Reinsch (1971); once again, most such studies view metaphor in the traditional sense.

30. See Levi (1949) for a treatment of legal reasoning demonstrating its basis in reasoning by analogy.

31. As Gouldner (1965) suggests, "The truth reason seeks is sought, in part, because its possession is expected to have certain desired consequences. In particular, the use of reason is expected to provide a basis for social consensus.... Reason is a way of producing a consensus of beliefs on which the state can rest securely" (p. 167).

32. This metaphor I adopted from Hanson (1958), who used it in a different form and context.

33. From Western Rationalism (Whitehead, 1960) we find: "...it is our consciousness that flickers and not the facts themselves." From Eastern philosophy (Suzuki, 1956), we have: " 'The pennant is an inanimate object and it is the wind that makes if flap.' Against this it was remarked by another monk that 'Both wind and pennant are inanimate things, and the flapping is an impossibility.' A third one protested, 'The flapping is due to a certain combination of cause and condition'; while a fourth one proposed a theory, saying, 'After all there is no flapping pennant, but it is the wind that is moving by itself.' The discussion grew quite animated when Hui-neng interrupted with the remark, 'It is neither wind nor pennant but your own mind that flaps' " (p. 72).

34. According to Hayek (1952) we find, "In the higher centres there occur undoubtedly a great many impulses which do not uniquely correspond to particular stimulations of sensory receptors but which represent merely common qualities attributed to the primary impulses; these representatives of classes of primary impulses will in turn become the objects of further processes of classification; the classes for which they stand will be further grouped into classes of classes, and this process can be repeated on many successive levels. We need, of course, not assume that these 'levels' are clearly separated or that the same impulse may not form part of the following of several other impulses which belong to different 'levels' " (p. 70). And "This is probably the most important characteristic of the particular kind of classificatory mechanism which the nervous system represents" (p. 51). See also, Gerard (1956) for a hierarchic scheme of the various disciplines.

35. As Deutsch (1966) maintains, "*Consciousness* may be defined, as a first approximation and for the purposes of this discussion, as a collection of internal feedbacks of secondary messages *Secondary messages* are messages about changes in the state of parts of the system, that is, about primary messages. *Primary messages* are those that move through the system in consequence of its interaction with the outside world. any secondary message or combination of messages, however, may in turn serve as a primary message, in that a further secondary message may be attached to any combination of primary messages or to other secondary messages or their combinations, up to any level of regress" (p. 98). I have elsewhere suggested that consciousness (from a metaphorical point of view) is constituted in an expanding series of metaphorical levels, and suggested that this expansion be termed analogic (ratio, proportionality) progression. See Haskell (1968, 1968, 1969, 1978, 1984).

36. See Foucault (1965).

37. See Leary, Metzner, and Alpert (1964) on the hazards of descending into the depths of the self.

38. According to Maher (1968), the schizophrenic loses his or her ability to logically string together consensual metaphors. He says, "Single words have strong associational bonds with other words – as the classic technique of word association indicates. We know that the word 'black' will elicit the response 'white' almost instantaneously from the majority of people. The associational bond between black and white is clearly very strong. Strong as it is, it will not be allowed to dominate consciousness when one is uttering a sentence such as 'I am thinking about buying a black car.' Our successful sentences come from the successful, sequential inhibition of all interfering associations that individual words in the sentence might generate. Just as successful visual attention involves tuning out irrelevant visual material, so successful utterance may involve tuning out irrelevant verbal static" (p. 33). Further, "If one set of meanings intrudes into a sentence that is clearly built around another set of meanings, the effect is a pun, and an accompanying digression or cross-current in surface content" (p. 60).

"Uttering a sentence without disruption is an extremely skilled performance, but one that most of us acquire so early in life that we are unaware of its remarkable complexity. However, we become more aware of how difficult it is to 'make sense' when we are extremely tired, or ripped out of sleep by the telephone, or distraught, or drunk" (p. 33).

39. The psychiatrist R. D. Laing (1965, 1967) vividly describes the world of madness with its ideocyncratic metaphorical reality.

40. See Barron (1972). Also see Kubie (1961).

41. See Carroll (1962).

42. See Allport and Vernon (1933), Brown (1959), Eisenbert (1937), and Reich (1949). Each shows in its own way how the body is a metaphorical expression of inner states.

REFERENCES

Agassi, J. (1964). Discussion: analogies as generalizations. *Philosophy of Science, 31,* 4.

Allport, F. (1955). *Theories of perception and the concept of structure,* New York: Wiley.

Allport, G. W., & Vernon, P. E. (1933). *Studies in expressive movement.* New York: Macmillan.

Anderson, C. C. (1964). The psychology of metaphor. *Journal of Genetic Psychology,* 105, 53–73.

Barron, F. (1972). The creative personality akin to madness. *Psychology Today,* (July). p. 16.

Berggren, D. (1962). The use and abuse of metaphor. *Review of metaphysics, 16,* 237–258.

Bergson, H. (1923). Creative evolution. New York: Henry Holt & Co.

Black, M. (1962). *Models and metaphors.* Ithaca, New York: Cornell University Press.

Bowers, J. W., & Osborn, M. (1966). Attitudinal effects of selected types of concluding metaphors in persuasive speeches. *Speech Monographs, 33,* 147–155.

Brown, N. O. (1959). *Life against death: The psychoanalytical meaning of history.* New York: Vintage Books.

Bruner, J., Wallach, S., & Galanter, E. (1959). The identification of recurrent regularity. *The American Journal of Psychology,* 72(2), 200–209.

Buchanan, S. (1962). *Poetry and mathematics.* New York: John Day.

Burke, K. (1954). *Permanence and change.* Los Altos, Calif.: Hermes Pub.

Butler, J. D. (1969). Metaphoric logic and human integration. In D. Vanderberg (Ed.), *Theory of knowledge and problems of education.* Chicago: University of Illinois Press.

Carroll, L. (1962). *Alice's adventures in wonderland, And through the looking glass.* New York: Collier Books.

Cassirer, E. (1946). *Language and myth.* New York: Dover.

Cooper, L. (1960). *The rhetoric of Aristotle.* New York: Appleton-Century-Crofts.

Deutsch, K. (1966). *The nerves of government.* New York: Free Press.

Dixon, N. F. (1981). *Pre-conscious processing.* New York: Wiley.

Edie, J. M. (1975). Identity and metaphor: A phenomenological theory of polysemy. *Journal of the British Society of Phenomenology, 6*(1), 32–41.

Eisenbert, P. (1937). Expressive movements related to feelings of dominance. *Archives of Psychology, 211.* 241.

Fernandez, J. (1972). Persuasions and performances: of the beast in everybody...and the metaphors of everyman. *Daedalus,* (winter) 39–60.

Fisher, S. C. (1916). The process of generalizing abstraction and its product the general concept. *Psychological Monographs, 90,* 196.

Foucault, M (1965). *Madness and civilization.* New York: Mentor Books.

Frye, N. (1966). *Anatomy of criticism.* New York: Antheneum.

Galin, D. (1974). Implications of psychiatry of left and right cerebral specialization. *Archives of General Psychiatry, 31,* 572–582.

Gerard, R. W. (1956). Levels of organization. *Main Currents in Modern Thought, 12,* 5.

Goodman, N. (1952). On likeness of meaning. In Linsky, L. (Ed.), *Semantics and the philosophy of language.* Urbana, IL: University of Illinois Press.

Gouldner, A. (1965). *Enter Plato: Classical Greece and the origins of social theory, II.* New York: Harper Torchbooks.

Gregory, R. L. (1966). *Eye and brain: The psychology of seeing.* New York: McGraw-Hill.

Grose, R., & Birney, R. (1965). *Transfer of learning.* Princeton, NJ: Van Nostrand.

Hanson, N. (1958). *Patterns of discovery.* Cambridge, England: Cambridge University Press.

Haskell, R. E. (1968). Anatomy of analogy: A new look. *Journal of Humanistic Psychology, 8*(2), 161–169.

Haskell, R. E. (1968–69). The analogic and psychoanalytic theory. *The Psychoanalytic Review, 55,* 662–680.

Haskell, R. E. (1978). An analogic model of small group behavior. *International Journal of Group Psychotherapy, 27,* 27–54.

Haskell, R. E. (1983). Cognitive structure and transformation: An empirical model of the psycholinguistic function of numbers in discourse. *Small Group Behavior, 14,* 419–443.

Haskell, R. E. (1984). Empirical structures of mind: Cognition, linguistics, and transformation. *The Journal of Mind and Behavior, 5,* 29–48.

Haskell, R. E., & Hauser, G. A. (1978). Rhetorical structure: Truth and method in Weaver's epistemology. *The Quarterly Journal of Speech, 64*(3), 233–45.

Hayek, F. A. (1952). *The sensory order: An inquiry into the foundations of theoretical psychology.* Chicago: University of Chicago Press.

Hebb, D. O. (1961). *The organization of behavior: A neuropsychological theory.* New York: McGill University Press.

Hesse, M. (1963). *Models and analogies in science.* New York: Sheed and Ward.

Honeck, R. P., & Hoffman, R. R. (Eds.). (1980). *Cognition and figurative language.* Hillsdale, NJ: Erlbaum.

Ichheiser, G. (1970). *Appearances in realities.* San Francisco: Jossey-Bass.

Jardine, N. (1967). The concept homology in biology. *British Journal for the Philosophy of Science, 18,* 125–139.

Jaynes, J. (1976). *The origins of consciousness in the breakdown of the bicameral mind.* Boston: Houghton, Mifflin Co.

Kaplan, A. (1964). *The conduct of inquiry: Methodology for behavioral science.* San Francisco: Chandler Pub.

Koestler, A. (1959). *The sleepwalkers: A history of man's changing vision of the universe.* New York: Grosset and Dunlap.

Kubie, L. (1961). *Neurotic distortion of the creative process.* Toronto: The Noonday Press.

Kuhn, T. S. (1962). *The structure of scientific revolutions.* Chicago: Phoenix Books.

Laing, R. D. (1965). *The divided self.* Baltimore, MD: Pelican Books.

Laing, R. D. (1967). The politics of experience. New York: Pantheon Books.

Langer, S. (1942). *Philosophy in a new key.* New York: Mentor Books.

Leary, T., Metzner, R., & Alpert, R. (1964). *The psychedelic experience: A manual based on the Tibetan book of the dead.* New York: University Books.

Levi, E. (1949). *An introduction to legal reasoning.* Chicago: University of Chicago Press.

MacDonald, M. (1960). The philosopher's use of analogy. In A. Flew (Ed.), *Logic and Languages* (2 vols.) (pp. 80–100). Oxford: Basil Blackwell.

Maher, B. (1968). The shattered language of schizophrenia. *Psychology Today, 2,* 6.

Malinowsky, B. (1923). The problem of meaning in primitive societies. In C. K. Ogden & I. A. Richards (Eds.), *The meaning of meaning.* New York: Harcourt Brace and World.

Marks, L. E. (1978). *The unity of the senses: Interrelations among the modalities.* New York: Academic Press.

McLuhan, M. (1964). *Understanding media: The extensions of man.* New York: McGraw-Hill Co.

Merleau-Ponty, M. (1964). *Signs.* Northwestern University Press.

Mostofsky, D. (Ed.). (1965). *Stimulus generalization.* Palo Alto, CA: Stanford University Press.

Nagel, E. (1961). *The structure of science: Problems in the logic of scientific explanation.* New York: Harcourt Brace and World.

Neisser, U. (1967). *Cognitive psychology.* New York: Appleton-Century-Crofts.

Oppenheimer, R. (1956). Analogy in science. *The American Psychologist, 2,* 3.

Ortony, A. (Ed.). (1979). *Metaphor and thought.* Cambridge, England: Cambridge University Press.

Osborn, M. (1967). The evaluation of the theory of metaphor in rhetoric. *Western Speech, 31,* 126.

Osborn, M. & Ehninger, D. (1962). The metaphor in public address. *Speech Monographs, 29,* 223–234.

Osgood, C. (1949). Similarity paradox in human learning: A resolution. *Psychological Review, 56,* 132–143.

Pepper, S. (1941). *World hypotheses: Prolegomena to systematic philosophy and a complete survey of metaphysics.* Berkeley, CA: University of California Press.

Pikas, A. (1966). *Abstraction and concept formation.* Cambridge, MA: Harvard University Press.

Pitts, W. & McCulloch, W. S. (1947). How we know universals: the perception of visual and auditory forms. *Bulletin of Mathematical Biophysics, 9,* 127–147.

Plato, *Phaedrus* (1956). (W. E. Helmbold & W. G. Rabinowitz, trans.) New York: Bobbs-Merrill.

Platt, J. (1958). Functional geometry and the determination of pattern in moasic receptors. In *Year Book of the Society for General Systems Research.* (Ed.), Von Bertalanffy, L. (Reprinted from *Information Theory in Biology,* Yorkey, Platzman, & Quastler (Eds.), NY: Pergamon Press.

Preus, A. (1970). The continuous analogy: The uses of continuous proportions in Plato and Aristotle. *Agora, 1,* 20–41.

Quillian, M. (1967). Word concepts: A theory and simulation of some basic semantic capabilities. *Behavioral Science, 12,* 5.

Reich, W. (1949). *Character analysis.* New York: Noonday Press.

Reinsch, L. (1971). An investigation of the effects of the metaphor and simile in persuasive discourse. *Speech Monographs, 38,* 142–145.

Rosenthal, R. (1966). *Experimenter effects in behavior research.* New York: Appleton-Century-Crofts.

Ryle, G. (1953). Categories. In A. Flew (Ed.), *Language and Logic,* Series 2, London: Oxford Press.

Sacksteder, W. (1974). The logic of analogy. *Philosophy and Rhetoric, 7,* 234–252.

Scheff, T. J. (1968). Negotiating reality: Notes on power in the assessment of responsibility. *Social Problems, 16*(1), 3–17.

Schutz, A. (1970). *On phenomenology and social relations* (H. R. Wagner, Ed.). Chicago: The University of Chicago Press.

Shibles, W. (1971). *Analysis of metaphor in the light of W. M. Uban's theories.* Mouton: the Hague.

Snell, B. (1960). *The discovery of the mind: The Greek origins of European thought.* New York: Harper Books.

Sperry, R. W. (1968). Hemispheric disconnection and unity in conscious awareness. *American Psychologist, 23,* 723–733.

Sternberg, R. (1977). *Intelligence, information processing and analogical reasoning.* Hillsdale, NJ: Erlbaum.

Suzuki, D. T. (1956). *Zen Buddhism.* New York: Anchor Books.

Thompson, R. F. (1965). The neural basis of stimulus generalization. In D. Mostofsky (Ed.), *Stimulus generalization.* Palo Alto, CA: Stanford University Press.

Turbayne, C. (1963). *The myth of metaphor.* New Haven, CT: Yale University Press.

Urban, W. N. (1961). *Language and reality* (Chs. 9–10). London: Allen and Unwin; New York: Macmillan.

Vaihinger, H. (1924). *The philosophy of "as-if".* London: Routledge and Kegan Paul, Ltd.

Vernon, M. D. (1962). *The psychology of perception.* Baltimore, MD: Penquin Books.

Vickery, B. C. (1961). *On retrieval system theory.* London: Butterworth & Co.

Vico, G. (1948). *The new science.* (T. G. Bergin & M. H. Fisch, trans.) Ithaca, NY: Cornell University Press.

Waismann, F. (1953). Language strata. In A. Flew (Ed.), *Language and Logic,* (Series 2). London: Oxford Press.

Wallach, M. A. (1958). On psychological similarity. *Psychological Review, 65,* 103–116.

Watzlawick, P., Beavin, J. H., & Jackson, D. D. (1967). *Pragmatics of human communication: A study of interreactional patterns, pathologies and paradoxes.* New York: W. W. Norton & Co.

Weick, K. E. (1969). *The social psychology of organizing.* Reading, MA: Addison-Wesley.

Wheelright, P. (1962). *Metaphor and reality.* Bloomington, IN: Indiana University Press.

Whitehead, A. N. (1958). *Modes of thought.* New York: Capricorn Books.

Whitehead, A. N. (1960). *Adventures of ideas.* New York: MacMillian Co.

Wilner, A. (1964). An experimental analysis of analogical reasoning. *Psycho Reports, 15,* 136–158.

Author Index

Subject Index